EMINENT
CHURCHILLIANS

ALSO BY ANDREW ROBERTS

'The Holy Fox': A Biography of Lord Halifax (1991)

EMINENT CHURCHILLIANS

———◆———

Andrew Roberts

Simon & Schuster

New York   London   Toronto
Sydney   Tokyo   Singapore

Simon & Schuster
Rockefeller Center
1230 Avenue of the Americas
New York, New York 10020

Copyright © 1994 by Andrew Roberts

First published in Great Britain in 1994 by
Weidenfeld & Nicolson

1 3 5 7 9 10 8 6 4 2

Library of Congress Cataloging-in-Publication Data
is available.

ISBN 0-671-76940-5

Printed in Great Britain

To Dean Godson

Contents

Illustrations

Acknowledgments

I should like to acknowledge with thanks the gracious permission of Her Majesty the Queen to research in, and quote from, the Royal Archives at Windsor.

I should also like to thank the following for their kindness and hospitality to me, as well as their permission to quote from their family papers: Mr and Mrs John Birkbeck, Sir Edward Cazalet, Lord Clitheroe, Lord Crathorne, Mr Somerset de Chair, Sir John Lucas-Tooth, Mr and Mrs John Montagu, the Most Honourable the Marquess of Salisbury, Lord Sherfield, Lady Juliet Townsend and Mr Hugo Waterhouse. Lord Brabazon has kindly given me permission to reproduce the photographs his father took of the Norway debate. Lord and Lady Monckton have been extremely generous with their time and permission, and I should like to pay special tribute to them. I should also like to acknowledge the Trustees of the Liddell Hart Centre for Military Archives, King's College, London.

In the three years it has taken to write this book, I have had the benefit of many interviews and conversations both with contemporaries of my subjects and with scholars. For their unfailing courtesy and help I should like to thank: Lord Aldington, Lord Amery, Lord Armstrong, David Astor, Lady Avon, Lady Bangor, Lord Bauer, Mr Christopher Beaumont, Mr Michael Bloch, Mr Ion Calvocoressi, Professor Donald Cameron Watt, Mrs Doris Campbell, Mr Alan Campbell-Johnson, Mr John Charmley, the late General Sir Philip Christison, Sir Petre Crowder, Rt. Hon. Alan Clark, Mr David Clarke, Dr Richard Cockett, Lord Colyton, Mr Maurice Cowling, Captain Philip Chubb, Captain Graham de Chair, Lord Deedes, Captain Edward Dunsterville, Rear-Admiral Roy Foster-Brown, Lord Fraser of Kilmorack, Lord Gladwyn, Sir James Goldsmith, Rear-Admiral John Grant, Robin Harcourt-Williams, Sir Ronald Harris, Sir Conrad Heron, Lord and Lady Holderness, Mr Anyas Hopkinson, Mr Richard Hough, Sir David Hunt, the late Sir Ian Jacob, Mr Frank Johnson, Mr Paul Johnson, Dr Harriet Jones, Lord Keyes, Mr James Leasor, Mr Rhidian Llewellyn, Sir Ian MacGregor, Lady Alexandra Metcalfe, Christopher and Juliet Monckton,

Mr Anthony Montague Browne, Lady Mosley, Lord Norwich, Lord Orr-Ewing, Dr Nicholas Owen, Sir Charles Pickthorn, Sir David Pitblado, Sir Robert Rhodes James, Sir Frank Roberts, Mr Stephen Roberts at the Royal Commission on Historical Manuscripts, Dr A. L. Rowse, Mr Kenneth Rose, Sir John Ruggles-Brice, the late Sir Algernon Rumbold, Mr Rowland Ryder, Captain Iwan Sarell, Mrs Anne Seagrim, Dr Anthony Seldon, Mrs Barbara Sendall, Lord Shawcross, Mr Geoffrey Smith, Mr Anthony Sutherland, Lord Tebbit, the late Lord Thorneycroft, Mr Hugo Vickers, Mr Ian Weston-Smith, the late Captain Reginald Whinney, Mr Christopher York and Mr Philip Ziegler.

Linda Osband, my editor, and Ion Trewin, my publisher, have been if anything *too* forbearing and understanding. I only hope they are looking forward to working with me again as much as I am with them.

A number of friends have kindly read through various chapters for me and given me very useful advice. I should particularly like to thank Professors Katherine and Samuel Adshead, Mr Robin Birley, Mr Michael Bloch, Mr Claus von Bulow, Mr Jonathan Foreman, Mrs Leone Frieda, Mr Robert Hardman, Mr Simon Heffer, Mr Richard Hough, Lord Lambton and, especially, Mr Kenneth Rose. The delightful Miss Camilla Henderson has also helped in a myriad of ways.

I should also like to pay heartfelt thanks to the invaluable contribution made by Mr Piers Dixon, whose line-by-line appraisal of the entire manuscript was brilliant, elegant and often hilarious. Had he chosen academia, rather than politics, he would have made a splendid don. For so often putting my 'E.C.' before hers, Miss Laura Adshead has added yet another debt to the many I already owe her.

Finally, I should like to salute Dean Godson, for more than a decade of friendship and inspiration. *Eminent Churchillians* is dedicated to him.

ANDREW ROBERTS
June 1994

Introduction

In the two years after October 1938 the fortunes of Winston Churchill underwent the most dramatic reversal of any politician of modern times. At the time of Munich, Churchill was dismissed as a warmonger and a has-been, and many viewed his career to that date as a catalogue of the failures of an over-ambitious adventurer. Yet twenty-four months later he was the national saviour, personifying Britain's defiance of Hitlerism and enjoying almost unanimous public approval.

How did the British political and social elite, who had known and watched Churchill for half a century, adjust to this revolution? How did they react to the new reality of a man whom they had spent the last decade publicly discounting and privately reviling suddenly being accorded secular deification?

The subjects of this book are not Churchillians in the conventional sense of, say, Brendan Bracken or Lord Beaverbrook. They are instead meant to represent British public life during the Churchillian Era. When Lytton Strachey chose to write about General Gordon, Florence Nightingale and the others in *Eminent Victorians*, he did not do so for their personal connections with the Queen herself, but for the way they illustrated the Victorian Age. Similarly, my subjects are intended to throw light upon the period between 1940 and 1955, during which Churchill led the Conservative Party and, for nine years, the country.

The cleverer among them appreciated the changed circumstances early on, and came under the bough of his reputation, thus often escaping critical reappraisal. The royal family came round to Churchill – largely ungrudgingly – by Christmas 1940, and genuinely regretted his defeat in the 1945 general election. The 'patriotic' historian Arthur Bryant switched overnight from sustained hostility to slavering devotion. The Tory Party took far longer to appreciate what was happening than many of them cared later to admit. Lord Mountbatten paid lip-service to the man who had repeatedly and single-handedly saved his career, but was delighted when Churchill's 1945 election defeat opened the way for the liquidation of the Empire upon which Churchill doted.

'Charm', said Anthony Blanche in *Brideshead Revisited*, 'can be fatal to works of art.' It can be equally fatal in politics, harmful as much to the donor as to the beneficiary. British influence waned dramatically in the middle years of this century. Instead of the innovation, industry and raw energy that had characterized the country a century earlier, Britain had come increasingly to rely upon the charm of her diplomats and politicians to draw attention away from and shore up her declining strength. It is no coincidence that my subjects were all noted for their charm. Walter Monckton's was born of a genuine interest in others, but could be switched on like the light in a miner's head lamp; Bryant's was, in the words of his friend A.L. Rowse, 'something unaccountable, extreme, marvellous'; Mountbatten inserted his like a stiletto; Queen Elizabeth's was part of the job, but also came quite naturally. The Tory managers of post-war decline constituted probably the most congenial Cabinets of any this century. British power was slowly disappearing during the Churchillian Era, leaving, like the Cheshire Cat, only a wide smile behind.

Part of the problem lay in the tendency to believe myths created by wartime propaganda. The exigencies of war, and the necessity of keeping up domestic morale, meant that people were led to believe that Mountbatten was a successful destroyer commander, that the trade unions never damaged the wartime economy through strikes, that the peace could be won by the same collectivist methods as had supposedly won the war, and that 'Uncle Joe' Stalin was essentially benign. Even Churchill, who was in a position to know the truth, began to believe such Ministry of Information lines about all but the last.

The influence exerted by the idea of Commonwealth over the Eminent Churchillians is another central theme of this book. They each had their reasons for presenting it as more than merely a useful political fiction. To the House of Windsor it seemed to offer a wider *raison d'être* and post-imperial world role; Mountbatten leapt through every hoop Congress held up for him in order that India might join; the liberal Tories were more than willing to pay the price of immigration in order that it might serve as a fig-leaf to cover the loss of British prestige during decolonization; Bryant thought that it could provide the alternative to joining the Common Market. The psychological message it sent was that Britain was still a Great Power, long after she had ceased to be one. This in turn robbed Britain of the sense of loss, urgency and need for national regeneration which motivated the economies of Germany and Japan after 1945.

By the end of Churchill's post-war 'Indian Summer' Premiership, the liberal Tories in his ministry had managed to outmanoeuvre the inattentive and ailing Prime Minister over most issues. Such was his post-1940 status, however, that they eschewed direct confrontation and allowed him to remain in office long after they all knew he should have retired. When he reneged on one of the issues most important to them – closer European integration – they still trod warily and expressed their resentments only to one another.

When Churchill returned to Downing Street in October 1951, he brought with him the small, red, 'Action This Day' labels he had attached to important documents during the war. They were put in the Prime Minister's letter rack on the Cabinet table, but were never used. 'They had faded a bit since 1945, and had gone a little pink,' remembered his Private Secretary. They might serve as a metaphor for many of his ministers, who were tired, nostalgic and in headlong ideological retreat. A good number were wartime cronies of Churchill's; others were largely apolitical. Tories who believed in competition, deregulation and freer markets, such as Oliver Lyttelton and Ralph Assheton, were excluded from any influence over economic policy, which continued largely upon wartime corporatist models. Monckton, having flirted with Crippsian socialism during the war, converted to a Conservatism which in most essential features was indistinguishable from Labour collectivism, and few either noticed or much cared. R.A. Butler, commenting on Monckton's appeasement of the trade unions, said: 'If he'd gone on, it would have been disastrous, but during my period it was extremely convenient. It didn't do me any harm.'

Had the Conservative elite of the immediate post-war era shown half the energy and enterprise in peacetime as it had in war, it is hard to believe that Britain would have been reduced to her present stature of Italy with rockets. Physical courage on the battlefield did not translate into political courage in the debate over the post-war domestic settlement. The British ruling class – relieved, perhaps, that they had not suffered the same fate as their European counterparts – appeased the working-class movement, with ultimately disastrous consequences for Britain's competitiveness.

'Declinology' is, unsurprisingly, a major historiographical discipline in today's Britain. Some 'revisionist' historians blame Churchill himself for the disasters which have overtaken the nation since 1940. More mainstream ones explain British abdication and loss of will by reference to such factors as dwindling resources, gold reserves and adverse terms of trade. In this book I prefer to consider the role of those Eminent Churchillians who adapted themselves to the political reality of Churchill's supremacy, but never truly rose to the level of events, or shared his vision of the role which the British nation could play.

1

The House of Windsor and the Politics of Appeasement

In his book *The English Constitution*, Walter Bagehot made the famous distinction between the 'dignified' and the 'efficient' roles of the British Monarchy. The former was concerned with pageant, ritual and the image of royalty; the latter with the sovereign's tangible political contribution. In the reign of King George VI these roles could not have been more starkly differentiated, for while the House of Windsor excelled at carrying out the 'dignified' part of their duties, the forays they made into the 'efficient' sphere tended to display a serious dearth of political judgment. When they were launching ships, visiting bomb sites or holding investitures they were superlative; yet when they were involved in day-to-day politics, they tended to exhibit clumsiness and lack of foresight.

That is all the more extraordinary when contrasted with the deftness shown by the King's father, George V, when dealing with the great constitutional crises of his reign. Over the Parliament Bill, over Ramsay MacDonald's request for a dissolution in 1924 and over the formation of the National Government, the King was ably advised and displayed a sure political touch. It was only at the end of his reign, with the threat of the dictators looming, that the old King embraced an extreme pro-appeasement stance which was to percolate through his family.

Evidence for this period is necessarily elusive and piecemeal, because in the days before 'tell all' autobiographies – especially amongst people used to treating information on a 'need-to-know' basis – hard facts are difficult to come by. Royal papers are customarily subject to far longer periods of official secrecy than other documents, and are virtually the

5

only ones for which the Hundred Year Rule still applies. The King's diary is not open to historical research, and other papers, such as the correspondence between the royal family and the senior appeaser Samuel Hoare, have been closed to the public 'for an indefinite period'.[1]

Nevertheless, George v, who had been King during the First World War, clearly took an extreme stand over appeasement. In this he was dutifully reflecting the views of the vast majority of his subjects. In 1935, during the Abyssinian crisis, when British warships were dispatched to the Mediterranean for a possible clash with Mussolini's Italy, the King told the Foreign Secretary, Hoare: 'I am an old man. I have been through one world war. How can I go through another? If I am to go on, you must keep us out of this one.' Hoare recorded that the King's 'consuming desire [was] for some compromise that would avoid war'.[2]

To Lloyd George the King was more emphatic still: 'I will not have another war. *I will not.* The last one was none of my doing and if there is another one and we are threatened with being brought into it, I will go to Trafalgar Square and wave a red flag myself sooner than allow this country to be brought in.'[3] As for the Hoare–Laval Pact, which attempted to bring peace by rewarding Mussolini's adventures in Abyssinia, the King instructed his Private Secretary, Lord Wigram, to write the Foreign Secretary a generous letter of support; and when Hoare was forced to resign, he expressed heartfelt sympathy.

Such pacifist sentiments were of course common to a great many people in the inter-war period. There was no real appreciation that war was inevitable until Hitler seized Prague in March 1939, and no great popular desire for war before it actually broke out in September 1939. But the King's views, which were the same as Queen Mary's, coincided with those of all of their children, some of whom gave them an unappetising twist. According to a conversation between the journalist Robert Bruce Lockhart and the Kaiser's grandson, Prince Louis Ferdinand, in July 1933, the Prince of Wales 'was quite pro-Hitler, said it was no business of ours to interfere in Germany's internal affairs either re Jews or re anything else, and added that the Dictators were very popular these days and we might want one in England before long'.[4] Bruce Lockhart believed that the Prince had been influenced by his close friends Penelope and Angela Dudley Ward, 'both of whom are ardent Hitlerites'.[5] In June 1935 the Prince of Wales had to be rebuked by his father for the warmth of his public declaration of friendship for Nazi Germany in a speech to ex-servicemen.

Edward viii's short reign was pitted with expressions of sympathy for the dictators. When the exiled Emperor Haile Selassie of Abyssinia arrived in London in 1936, he was treated like a bacillus by the royal family. Buckingham Palace was closed to him on the King's instructions, and the most senior member of the royal family who would grant him an audience was the Duke of Gloucester, 'as a purely courtesy visit and as a recognition of the hospitality shown to himself ... at the time of the Emperor's coronation'.[6] After much negotiation between the Foreign Office and Buckingham Palace, the visit eventually took place on 11 June 1936 and was timed by an enterprising journalist to have lasted from 6.00 p.m. until 6.05 p.m. According to the report dictated to *The Times*, it was 'of a private and informal character'.

All this was done to placate fascist Italy, which had invaded and annexed Abyssinia. When Selassie expressed the wish to reciprocate the hospitality after he had returned from his health cure in Switzerland, 'the Duke warned this off by saying that he expected to be absent from London in the immediate future'. His aide-de-camp, Major Stamforth, agreed with the Foreign Office 'that we should continue to "hedge" on this subject'.[7] Edward VIII's abdication removed a King of markedly pro-dictator tendencies, and Lloyd George was right when he predicted that, unlike Edward VIII, the Duke of York would cause the Establishment no trouble.

Lord Crawford recorded how, when dining in York Cottage at Sandringham in 1923, 'after dinner, during the King's absence, the Duke of York amused himself by kicking footstools about the parlour'.[8] In May 1936 Crawford also noted how, at a Garden Society dinner, the Duke 'was gay and quite immensely tickled by somebody saying that some plant or other was "quite hardy in Cornwall" – he kept repeating "quite hardy in Cornwall" on all occasions, relevant or the reverse for the remainder of the evening'.[9] Although sporting, decent and conscientious, the Duke was 'just a snipe from the great Windsor marshes', according to Harold Nicolson. That, however, might have been because although the Duchess of York had enjoyed his latest book, her husband had read only one anecdote in it, and even then managed to get it wrong. Kenneth Clark's first impression of the couple was: 'She is not much better than the kind of person one meets at country houses, and the King somewhat worse.'

The key to the unfortunate forays George VI made into governmental affairs during his reign is not to be found in any latent political views he may have held, but merely in his lack of cunning. He himself never laid claim to outstanding academic talents. In his naval college exams at

Osborne he came sixty-eighth out of sixty-eight and at Dartmouth he was placed sixty-first out of sixty-seven. Margot Asquith's nephew John Tennant, who happily described himself as 'intellectually a non-starter', used to say that there had only been two people at naval college thicker than himself; the Prince of Wales and the Duke of York.[10]

'Bertie' did not want the job of King and, as his mother later told Harold Nicolson, 'he sobbed on my shoulder for a whole hour, there upon that sofa'.[11] Having bade goodbye to his brother, George VI confronted the daunting business of being King-Emperor. His naval background, language, sense of duty, love of regularity, tendency to worry and even his handwriting made the King reminiscent of his father. As second sons not expected to succeed, they both had to face world wars within a few years of accession. His decision to take George rather than Albert for his title emphasized this continuity, whilst playing down the German side of the family. But this shrewd move apart, the new King had none of that guile and ingenuity which might have sustained a man whose intellect corresponded to that of a 'moderate and politically uninterested London clubman'.[12]

Edward VIII had charisma in a way his younger brother never had. He may have been shallow, but he was a natural talker and crowd-pleaser. 'Bertie' by contrast was a stammerer who suffered from vertigo. As a child he had had to wear splints at night to prevent his getting knock-knees. Some considered him, as Nancy Mitford put it, 'a very dull man'.[13] His shyness was so acute that as a child he once sat in a darkened room rather than ask a servant to light a lamp. His various disadvantages, which were partly the result of an overbearing father, encouraged a certain obstinacy and sometimes brought on what his family called 'gnashes' – tantrums which could blow up in a moment, often over some obscure point of dress or procedure.

Unlike his father's rages, these left even his courtiers feeling sorry for him. After he had apologized for one such outburst, his equerry Peter Townsend commented: 'There was something so pathetic about the way he said it that I felt like putting my arm around the King-Emperor and saying, "Don't worry. It's OK. Forget it."'[14] The King's insecurity also explained his habit of keeping his Private Secretaries in the dark about political discussions he had had. As his official biographer, John Wheeler-Bennett, confided to a friend years later, 'The King never recorded what was the end of his discussions and was so secretive and conceited in a way that he might have kept things to himself to give himself power and assurance: "I know something that you don't."'[15]

In 1923 the Duke had married Lady Elizabeth Bowes-Lyon, who almost alone was to carry him through the early years of his reign. A genius at public relations, whilst possessing strong Christian convictions, this hardy daughter of a Scottish earl had, in Wheeler-Bennett's private opinion, 'a small drop of arsenic in the centre of that marshmallow'.[16] She has often protested that she is not as sweet a personality as is popularly supposed, but this has invariably been put down to modesty.

'It will be years,' predicted Harold Nicolson to his wife Vita Sackville-West on the day of the Abdication, 'for Albert the Good to build up a legend comparable to that of his brother.'[17] However, he had reckoned without both press goodwill and the influence of wartime propaganda. Royal journalists, who today would be looking for 'knocking copy', were in those days happy to present a picture of the royal family as touched up as the negatives of Cecil Beaton's photographs of the Queen, in which 'nips and tucks' were administered to her neck and bust. But this cannot have been the only, or even the primary, reason: half a century later the Queen Mother still stands serenely in the affections of the British nation.

No sooner was the Abdication over than the Tory MP, Henry ('Chips') Channon, reported: 'The Press is trying to work up popularity for the new regime and perhaps in time it will succeed.'[18] Proprietors and editors had exercised remarkable self-restraint in not publishing the news of Edward VIII's friendship with Mrs Simpson. It was the era of deferential, 'responsible' journalism and editors felt it as incumbent upon themselves to support the Yorks of the 1930s as their successors have found it necessary to denigrate the Yorks of the 1990s. They considered themselves part of the Establishment, and their attachment to the mores of the Respectable Tendency – for which the Abdication was a notable victory – was later applied to foreign affairs. There they coalesced behind Neville Chamberlain's appeasement policy with a near-unanimity and self-censorship which would today defy belief.

The new reign began with a decision which was to sour relations between the King and his brother. Instead of being treated with sympathy and generosity, the Duke of Windsor was dealt a series of humiliating blows by the Palace, which culminated in his family boycotting his wedding. 'What had happened,' wrote the ex-King's lawyer, Sir Walter Monckton, to the Tory MP, Victor Cazalet, late in 1937, 'was that all the chief Court officials ... had met together and decided it was best not to go.' When Lord Brownlow wrote to the King to ask whether he should attend the Windsors' wedding, his letter was ignored, on Monckton's advice, so he decided against.[19]

There were any number of sound legal, religious and political reasons which the royal family advanced for their treatment of the Duke and Duchess, but the fact remained that an abdication was a unique constitutional event and wounds could easily have been bound. Although the King and Queen's every action was approved – albeit sometimes retrospectively – by the Cabinet, the politicians generally deferred to the family's wishes. Once the Abdication was finalized, it was conveniently regarded by them as being largely a family matter.

When the news came that the Duchess of Windsor had been refused royal rank and the style 'Her Royal Highness', her husband expostulated: 'I know Bertie. I know he couldn't have written this letter on his own. Why in God's name would they do this to me at this time!' 'They' meant the Palace courtiers, and 'they' cloaked their vengefulness behind many different arguments. One of Edward VIII's biographers, Lady Donaldson, has stated how 'the best evidence suggests that the reason for withholding the title was because it was believed the Windsor marriage would not last' – which, on Wallis Simpson's past performance, was not impossible – 'would there be marriage and re-marriage? More than one HRH? ... Was there no limit to the possible damage to the Throne?'[20] As it was, at thirty-five years it turned out to be one of the family's longer-lasting marriages. But what also lasted was 'the Duke's sense of humiliation and shame at not being able to achieve a Royal title for the Duchess'.[21]

Stanley Baldwin, the Prime Minister during the Abdication crisis, was concerned about the King's decision over the Duchess's royal rank. But, as one historian has put it, 'George VI persisted in denying it to her and so created a wound that would never heal. He justified his decision with the argument that, since the people had not been prepared to accept her as Queen, they would resent her being given royal status of any kind.'[22] In fact, 'the people' had not been consulted, and the roles of Queen-Empress and Royal Duchess were hardly analogous. Although the Tory activists whom MPs consulted the weekend before the Abdication felt that the King ought to abdicate, the Mass-Observation movement found a good deal more support for him amongst the nation as a whole. Writing to Victor Cazalet in June 1937 the Duchess of Windsor suggested: 'Why not whisper to your Government to "ease up" a little on the anti-Windsor propaganda? We are really too harmless to be worth such efforts.'[23] But it was not primarily the Government which was to blame.

It is hard to escape the conclusion that it was the Queen's lively religious and moral sense, combined with the virulence of various courtiers against their former master – some of whom, such as Sir

Alexander Hardinge and Sir Alan Lascelles, despised him – which led to the breakdown in relations. None of this would concern a historian of politics for a moment were it not for the grave implications of what almost took place in the summer of 1940.

In public at least, the new reign began quietly. Channon believed that the cheers which greeted the King in February 1937 seemed 'prompted more by good nature than by any real enthusiasm'. Showing some early *savoir-faire*, when the new German Ambassador, Joachim von Ribbentrop, was presented at his first levee and gave the 'Heil Hitler' salute, the King 'did not seem in any way surprised but was very friendly'.[24] Hitler nevertheless ordered his envoy to bow when next he met the monarch.

In May 1937, the same month as King George VI was crowned, Neville Chamberlain succeeded to the Premiership. As Chancellor of the Exchequer he had handled the financial side of the Abdication, and although the papers are classified until 2037, it is clear he won the trust of the King and Queen.[25] In 1935 Chamberlain had described the Duchess of York as 'the only royalty I enjoy talking to, for though she may not be an intellectual she is always natural and moreover appears always to be thoroughly enjoying herself'.[26] The King had much in common with his new Prime Minister and a bond soon grew between them. Men of duty and family, they were both intensely private individuals. Furthermore, they both wanted to regard German claims in the best possible light, feeling as they did a deep dislike of Bolshevism. George VI probably recognized in Chamberlain his own best qualities.

Chamberlain inspired a personal devotion which we find difficult to credit today. His post-war reputation, as well as the umbrella, wing-collar and corvine appearance, all conspire to make it hard to understand the admiration he could command. At a luncheon for Dominion Prime Ministers in May 1937, the King was 'faltering' with his 'halting speech and resigned kindly smile, and everyone pretending that he had done it well'.[27] For such a man the advent that month of a tough, friendly and supportive Prime Minister was a godsend. It was not surprising that exactly three years later the King should have gone to great lengths to protect and support Chamberlain.

Chamberlain's appeasement policy commended itself to the royal family on a number of levels. Pessimism about their chances of survival is a characteristic of the British royal house. Edward VII introduced his son to Lord Haldane as 'the last King of England', and when after the war George VI learnt from Vita Sackville-West that Knole Park (her family home) was being sold to the National Trust, he flung up his hands in despair and exclaimed: 'Everything is going nowadays. Before long, I shall have to go.'[28] It was also correctly considered axiomatic that another war would spell doom for the British Empire. The royal family, which had watched the stock of monarchies diminishing after European wars, had acquired highly developed antennae for survival. The Franco-Prussian War of 1870 had led to the fall of the French imperial throne. By the end of the Great War the imperial crowns of Russia, Germany and Austria-Hungary lay in the dust.

The Second World War was to destroy the thrones of Italy, Albania, Bulgaria, Romania and Yugoslavia, so it was understandable that the British royal family should have embraced appeasement. Their sensitivities were nevertheless somewhat exaggerated. Even as tens of thousands were dying for King and Country in the trenches during the First World War, George v was fretting over the possible rise of republican sentiment. This persuaded him not to grant asylum in Britain to his cousin the Tsar when he had the opportunity in 1917. It was Mountbatten who, 'with all the authority of close kinship and apparent omniscience, gave currency to the legend' that Lloyd George had been responsible for letting the Tsar die in Russia when he could have been brought to safety in England on a destroyer. However, no historian can quote Mountbatten as an authority; it is now clear that it was George v who, out of fear of the industrial working classes' supposed antipathy for Tsarism, had refused the offer.[29]

Any lingering sympathy the royal family may have felt for their German cousins had been erased by the First World War, but King George vi had been present at the Battle of Jutland and, like his father, swore 'never again'. The King and Queen, the Gloucesters, Kents, Queen Mary and the Duke of Windsor – the last albeit from a more extreme position – were all convinced appeasers. They all failed to make the mental leap necessary to appreciate that feeding the Nazi beast whetted its appetite, and that only a firm stance early on could have averted war. The senior anti-appeasers all had fine war records – Duff Cooper, Anthony Eden, Harold Macmillan, Winston Churchill, Roger Keyes, Louis Spears and so on – whilst National Government ministers who advocated appeasement – Baldwin, MacDonald, Chamberlain, Hoare, Sir John Simon, Sir Kingsley Wood – had not themselves seen action.

Except for Edward viii, the royal family never expressed a word of sympathy for the Nazis and probably despised them. But neither were they noticeably concerned by the plight of the Nazis' victims, generally considering a country's internal political arrangements to be her own affair. (This view only ever seemed to apply to powerful countries; Czechoslovakia's handling of her Sudeten German minority was not treated as a purely internal matter.)

In February 1939, after the King learnt that 'a number of Jewish refugees from different countries were surreptitiously getting into Palestine', he had his Private Secretary write to the then Foreign Secretary, Lord Halifax, to say that 'he is glad to think that steps are being taken to prevent these people leaving their country of origin', which was often Germany or Austria.[30] Two days after the King's message, the Foreign Office telegraphed the British Ambassador in Berlin to ask him to urge the German Government 'to check the unauthorised emigration' of Jews from the Third Reich. He was of course not to know that those who did not manage to leave their country of origin were doomed, but his letter was written some four months after the *Kristallnacht* outrages, when the Nazi treatment of Jews was well known.

If it was felt so necessary to prevent Jews entering Palestine, there were a number of alternative arrangements that were being actively considered that would have been better than merely asking the Nazis to tighten their security arrangements. The King's views on Palestine were predictable: commenting on the Balfour Declaration, which in 1917 had announced British support for a Jewish national homeland, he told the diplomat, Sir Miles Lampson: 'Old Balfour was a silly old man; and had given (or promised to others) something already belonging to someone else!'[31]

Posing little threat to the Empire, but a supposed one to Bolshevik Russia, Nazi Germany was not believed to be so dangerous an enemy that the royal family felt inclined to risk what they feared might be everything in directly opposing it. Certainly the Nazi maltreatment of minorities did not strike appeasers as a valid reason for taking up an aggressive stance. In the spectrum of German appeasement, with Chamberlain and the junior Foreign Office minister, 'Rab' Butler, very much in favour, Halifax and Eden increasingly sceptical and Churchill completely against, the House of Windsor was politically to be found staunchly behind Chamberlain.

This was further reinforced by their personal loyalties and friendships, as well as their antipathies. After becoming Home Secretary in June 1937, Samuel Hoare attended the Coronation Review, where 'both the new King and Queen were kind enough to say that they were glad enough to have an old friend as the Minister who was most closely in touch with the court'.[32] Hoare's book on the Russian Revolution was, according to the King, 'one of the most interesting books I have ever read'; not in itself too much of an encomium, but it shows the respect in which Hoare was held.

Another senior Chamberlainite was the Tory MP, James Stuart. Handsome and gallant, he had won the MC in the Great War. Like the Queen, he had a father who was a Scottish earl. They had known each other since childhood, and, when they grew up, their names were linked. Stuart had been equerry to the Duke of York in 1920 and has been credited with introducing the couple. A senior figure in the Whips' Office from 1935, Stuart was involved in a violent row with Churchill over his support for the anti-appeasement Duchess of Atholl in 1938. The finishing piece in the jigsaw that makes up the royal family's enthusiastic stance over appeasement was Winston Churchill.

Lord Randolph Churchill had fallen out with the Prince of Wales over the Lady Aylesford scandal of 1876, and relations between the royal family and his son Winston had never been close. Churchill, though a 'vehement' supporter of the institution of Monarchy, did not always enjoy good relations with its current incumbents.[33] With his heavy Hanoverian humour, Edward VII had remarked how 'Churchill's initials – W.C. – are well-named'. Of his son George V, Churchill once wrote: 'The King talked more stupidly about the Navy than I had ever heard him before. Really it is disheartening to hear this cheap and silly drivel with which he lets himself be filled up.'[34] Even in this exasperated state Churchill observed the constitutional proprieties: the King had not filled himself up with the 'drivel'; instead, his advisers are blamed. The sentiments were more than reciprocated. George V was furious when he thought that Churchill had tried to involve him in the constitutional crisis of 1911, and considered one of the happiest by-products of the formation of the National Government four years later was that Churchill was removed from the Admiralty.[35]

When Wheeler-Bennett was writing his biography of George VI in the mid-1950s, he told Bruce Lockhart that

> his task would be lightened if and when Churchill and the Duke of Windsor were dead ... first, as regards Churchill, George VI did not like [him]. He was an admirer of Chamberlain and was one hundred per cent pro-Munich. He disliked Churchill's attitude at Munich, and doubtless Churchill's championing of the Duke of Windsor at the time of the Abdication did not commend itself to George VI and his Queen ... it is on record that he told

Roosevelt that only in very exceptional circumstances could he consent to Churchill's being made Prime Minister.[36]

Churchill was also unpopular with the courtiers, most of whom had known him for decades. During the First World War, after Churchill had attacked the Government's war policy, Alan Lascelles told Lady Guendolen Osborne: 'The Arch-Mountebank has shown himself a supreme cad in his methods many times before.' Three days later he described him as 'the harlequin/politician who can lay aside the King's uniform the moment it becomes unpleasantly stiff with trench mud'.[37] In their attitude both to Churchill and to appeasement in the 1930s, the royal family swam firmly in the mainstream of British opinion at the time; what is interesting is how long and how strongly they continued to paddle even after the current had changed direction. There were no rebels in the family over the appeasement policy, unless it was the Duke of Kent, whom Bruce Lockhart described in October 1937 as 'strong in the German camp'.

When Hitler's Foreign Minister, Baron von Neurath, a former ambassador in London, considered coming to Britain in June 1937, the King let the Foreign Office know that he was

> greatly interested to hear of the forthcoming visit ... it must in itself have a good effect on our relations with Germany. His Majesty says he would certainly be pleased to receive Freiherr von Neurath, whom he happens to know already, and could do so at 11.30 a.m. on Friday 25th ... no doubt the actual hour could be altered.[38]

Late 1937 saw the Foreign Secretary, Anthony Eden, make determined efforts to bring America into more active opposition against Japan in the Far East and closer involvement in the darkening European scene. He hoped this could become a crucial factor in slowing both Japanese and German *revanchism*. The failure of this attempt is considered to be one of the great missed opportunities of the pre-war period. The King, however, sided with Chamberlain in his scepticism about American involvement. He wrote to Eden saying that he only welcomed American co-operation 'provided that it does not lead to any measure which will drive Japan to desperation'. The King rather assumed that it would fail and 'bring inevitable recriminations as to who has left who [*sic*] in the lurch'.[39]

Eden resigned from Chamberlain's Government in February 1938. The King was understandably angry to hear about it first from the *Sunday Express*. The occasion provided the first example of the King's practice of implying to ministers that he secretly sympathized with them, when in reality he did not. He had found the departing Foreign Secretary 'difficult to talk to' and, as he told one Dominion Prime Minister, 'he had not been able to establish personal relations with Mr Eden'. Although he fully supported Chamberlain's policy over Italian *rapprochement* and American involvement, he still contrived to send a radically different message to Eden himself.[40]

When he arrived to surrender his seals of office, Eden had what proved to be 'the friendliest audience I had with [the King]. His Majesty said that he had sympathy with my point of view and that he did not think it would be long before he saw me again.'[41] The King's Private Secretary, Sir Alexander Hardinge, told Eden that he had read the relevant telegrams and 'in my judgment you were right on all points', but Hardinge's growing opposition to appeasement was to set him at loggerheads with his master, and more especially the Queen. She 'never liked Anthony Eden ... he was too charming and weak and film-starry'.[42]

The King's great-uncle, Prince Arthur, Duke of Connaught, was actually pleased when Eden resigned, regarding him as 'a very dangerous and conceited man'.[43] They all far preferred his replacement, Lord Halifax. High priest of the Respectable Tendency, Halifax was credited with 'a safe pair of hands'. His family had long served the Crown in a personal capacity, his father having been Groom of the Bedchamber to Edward VII and his grandfather a confidant of Queen Victoria's. George V had been helpful in securing Halifax the Viceroyalty of India in 1925 and Lady Halifax was one of the Queen's friends and Ladies-in-Waiting. The King and Queen used to dine *à quatre* with the Halifaxes at their home in Eaton Square.

One of Halifax's first actions on becoming Foreign Secretary was to dampen speculation that Hermann Goering might be invited to England. There had been talk of his being asked to shoot at Sandringham, and Lord Derby had let it be known that he was prepared to have him to stay at Knowsley Hall should the Reichsmarschal wish to attend the Grand National.[44] Discussion about such visits occurred regularly over the next eighteen months. But at no time was it suggested that the King might not wish to shake the hand of Goering, the man responsible for the Night of the Long Knives, the Nazi massacre of June 1934. The duty of the British sovereign is to act as instrument and mouthpiece of current foreign policy, and this perforce sometimes involves them in awarding honours to men such as Romania's Nicolae Ceauşescu or making pro-European speeches in Brussels. According to a report by Hitler's adjutant, Fritz Wiedemann, Halifax had said in July 1939 that he 'would like to see as the culmination of his work the Führer entering London at the side of the English King amid the acclamation of the English people'.[45] It is always possible that the statement was exaggerated, but when the conversation was made public after the war, Halifax made no attempt to deny it.

In February 1938 Ribbentrop was ordered to sound out opinion as to the likely British reaction to the enforced ingestion of Austria into the Reich. After meeting the King, as well as some senior politicians and the Archbishop of Canterbury, Ribbentrop concluded correctly 'that England will not do anything in regard to Austria'.[46] Soon after the *Anschluss* took place, the Permanent Under-Secretary at the Foreign Office, Sir Alexander Cadogan, was asked to dine at Buckingham Palace. He recorded in his diary how the King was 'rather fussed about Austria but sensible. Gloomy about French Government – against going to the League [of Nations].'[47]

On 16 April the Government signed an agreement with Italy, which was to come into effect in November, designed to limit Italian participation in the Spanish Civil War. In return Britain recognized Italian sovereignty over Abyssinia and made a number of other concessions to Mussolini. The agreement was bitterly criticized by the Opposition in Parliament and subjected to a vote there. But such considerations did not deter the King from sending a telegram *en clair* from Windsor to Halifax's home in Hickleton, near Doncaster, which read: 'The Queen and I wish you many happy returns on your birthday. You must be pleased that it coincides with the conclusion of the negotiations which you have conducted with such energy and skill.'[48] Halifax, delighted at this support for his policy of appeasing Mussolini, replied, also using the open telegraph system, thanking them for 'speaking so generously of my part in working for Italian agreement'.

Dining at Windsor Castle later that month, the National Liberal MP for Bristol, Robert Bernays, sat on the King's right after the ladies had withdrawn:

> There was an awful pause and I with difficulty resisted the temptation to treat the Monarch as a constituent and attempt to put him at his ease [he wrote to his sister], but all that was happening was he was struggling for the first word. When that was over there was no more trace of stammer ... he talked mainly about Germany and the difficulty of making friendly contacts. He told me that when Ribbentrop came to say goodbye to him on the morning of the invasion of Austria Ribbentrop denied all knowledge of it, to which, said the King, 'I replied that I understood that he was Foreign Minister of Germany. I thought after that it was not wise to press the matter further'.[49]

Despite the King's expressed desire for 'friendly contacts' with the Nazi Government, Bernays came away from Windsor believing that, contrary to recent gossip, 'the King was not a member of the Cliveden Front'. Queen Mary had been a visitor to Cliveden since 1935 and she, the King and Queen and the two Princesses visited Lady Astor's Buckinghamshire home again in April 1939, long after well-publicized but unfounded allegations about the pro-appeasement 'Cliveden Set'.

The royal visit to Paris in July 1938 was a public relations success and shows how expertly the King and Queen carried out Bagehot's 'dignified' side of their constitutional duties. However, privately it left the French Prime Minister, Edouard Daladier, thinking that the King was 'a moron' and the Queen 'an excessively ambitious young woman who would be ready to sacrifice every other country in the world so that she might remain Queen'.[50] This observation may, however, say more about Daladier than it does about the Queen.

The question of 'friendly contacts' with Germany arose again in May 1938, after a crisis in the Sudetenland which had almost led to open hostilities. In a party which included Oliver Stanley's wife, Lady Maureen, Lady Birkenhead and the anti-appeasement MP Ronald Cartland, Harold Nicolson discussed 'the question of conciliating Goering' with the Foreign Secretary. 'Halifax says that he would be pleased with an invitation to Sandringham. Ronnie and I say that we should resent any such thing.... It would lower our dignity. Halifax is rather startled by our vehemence.'

The Duke of Windsor was meanwhile writing to 'Dear Sam' Hoare, to say that he continued 'to hold the same firm conviction that Neville Chamberlain stands out pre-eminently among the world statesmen of today and that the Foreign Policy which he and his Cabinet are pursuing is the only one that has any chance of preserving Peace'.[51] Over this issue it would be impossible to differentiate between the Duke of Windsor's views and those of his younger brother, and as Munich approached the King was determined to do everything in his power to help Chamberlain – which unfortunately was to include going beyond the bounds of constitutional propriety.

The King's offers to write to Hitler as 'one ex-serviceman to another' were twice turned down by the Government. They represented the first of a large number of attempts he made to write to fellow heads of state, which were either considered by the Government as unlikely to do much good or were spurned by the recipients. Chamberlain recognized the importance of keeping the King content, however, and during the Sudeten crisis he insisted that Hoare should not break his engagement to spend the weekend of 5–9 September 1938 at Balmoral. The only other guest there was the equally enthusiastic appeaser, the Archbishop of Canterbury, Cosmo Lang. Hoare recorded that 'there were many opportunities for intimate talks that helped me to understand the reactions of the crisis on the King and Queen'. In the event of London being bombed, the royal family were to be moved to Madresfield Court in Worcestershire, Lady Maud Hoare's family home.

Chamberlain's 'Plan X' personally to visit Hitler to resolve the Czech impasse was given 'cordial concurrence' by the King.[52] When Chamberlain returned from Berchtesgaden on 16 September, he was greeted by a letter from the King, which read:

> My dear Prime Minister, I am sending this letter to meet you on your return, as I had no opportunity of telling you before you left how much I admired your courage and wisdom in going to see Hitler in person. You must have been pleased by the universal approval with which your action was received.

In fact, the Labour and Liberal Parties were undecided about the negotiations over Czechoslovakia, and a small but vocal section of the Conservative Party and of Society were aghast at the way Nazi aggression was being rewarded yet again. Sacrificing Czechoslovakia may have been necessary to save peace, but it could only be regarded as a defeat for the West. Yet the King, like so many others, allowed his relief to cloud his judgment enough to treat it like a victory. As the national figurehead it turned out to be more serious in his case than in theirs.

As it became clear that Hitler intended to increase the demands he had made at Berchtesgaden, a mood of resignation descended on London. On 28 September the King was, according to Duff Cooper, 'envisaging the War with great equanimity'.[53] But later that day the news arrived that Hitler had invited Chamberlain to Munich. Queen Mary and the Duke of Kent were watching from the Gallery of the House of Commons as the Prime Minister made the announcement, and in an extended diary entry she recorded:

> It was a most dramatic and wonderful ending to the speech and the relief felt all round the House was remarkable and all the members of the Conservative and National Govt cheered wildly – I was so much moved I could not speak to any of the ladies in the Gallery, several of them, even those unknown to me, seized my hand, it was very touching.... I went to see Bertie – A most wonderful day – God be praised.[54]

When Chamberlain returned to Heston Aerodrome two days later the King almost went there to welcome him in person. Lieutenant-Colonel

Arthur Grenfell, a cousin of Halifax's by marriage and a neighbour, had left a note with the Foreign Secretary that morning 'suggesting the King should go to Heston'. Cadogan talked to the Halifaxes about it, but 'expressed doubt'. Instead, he 'thought it better PM should go straight to Palace'. The Chancellor of the Exchequer, Sir John Simon, coincidentally arrived at the Foreign Office at 11.00 a.m. There they agreed to settle for the lesser option of the King inviting Chamberlain to Buckingham Palace. Simon was due for an audience with the King at noon, and it was agreed with Halifax and Cadogan that he should 'put this to his Majesty'. The King therefore sent his Lord Chamberlain to Heston with a message inviting the Prime Minister to the Palace, 'so that I can express to you personally my most heartfelt congratulations on the success of your visit to Munich'. Meanwhile, Mrs Chamberlain was picked up and taken there too.

When six decades earlier Disraeli and Lord Salisbury had returned from the Congress of Berlin bringing real Peace with Honour (and Cyprus as well), they formally reported to Queen Victoria and then went on to Downing Street for the political side of the celebrations. On Lloyd George's return from the Versailles Conference in 1919, King George V had gone to meet him at Victoria Station, but he had added many millions to the population of the Empire, whereas Chamberlain had merely sacrificed a small country for a set of promises from a proven liar. Nevertheless, King George VI and his Queen actually invited Mr and Mrs Chamberlain on to the balcony of Buckingham Palace, where they stood together in the rain waving to the crowds.

As a breathless journalist reported in a special two shilling Munich souvenir issue of the *Illustrated London News*:

> London's ovation to Mr Chamberlain ... reached its climax when he drove straight from Heston Aerodrome to Buckingham Palace.... He was shown to Their Majesties' private apartments, where his wife was already present, and received the Royal congratulations.... Presently the King and Queen with the Premier and his wife, appeared on the balcony. Mrs Chamberlain tried to remain in the background, but the King led her forward to stand beside him. The Queen was on the left next to the Premier. They stood there under the beam of the searchlight ... then the King motioned Mr Chamberlain forward, and he stood alone in the front, acknowledging the acclamation.

It was the first time that a monarch had invited a commoner, let alone a politician, on to the balcony of Buckingham Palace. It was a gesture of royal approval of his policy which was as unmistakable as it was unconstitutional. Had Chamberlain called a snap general election to solidify his political success and further isolate his critics, as some of his advisers such as Sir Horace Wilson and Sir Joseph Ball were counselling, this complete public identification of the Monarch with the Prime Minister's policy would have been a huge electoral factor in his favour.

Appeasement of the dictators had been controversial enough to have prevented Goering being invited to the Coronation. None the less, in direct contravention of the tenets of political impartiality central to a constitutional monarchy, the King, by inviting Chamberlain to wave from the balcony at Buckingham Palace, committed what one distinguished political commentator has called 'the most unconstitutional act by a British Sovereign in the present century. Whatever the rights or wrongs of the Munich Agreement, the relevant point is that it was denounced by the official Opposition and was to be the subject of a vote in Parliament.'[55]

Labour did indeed divide the House over Munich, believing that Chamberlain had not obtained good enough terms for the Czechs. Churchill called the Agreement 'the first foretaste of a bitter cup which will be proffered to us year by year', and, finding himself unable to look in the mirror unless he did, First Lord of the Admiralty Duff Cooper resigned from the Government. So criticism of the King's conduct is not mere pedantry. Instead of performing his Bagehotian duty of warning the Government at a crucial moment in his country's history, King George VI completely suspended any critical judgment he may have had.

The next day the King wrote to his mother: 'Yesterday was a great day ... the PM was delighted with the result of his mission, as we all are, and he had a great ovation when he came here.' As Christmas approached, *The Times* offered its readers the opportunity to buy a special Christmas card bearing the 'exclusive souvenir photo' of the King and Queen together with Mr and Mrs Chamberlain, waving from the balcony. Halifax also received a handwritten note on Buckingham Palace writing paper letting him

> know how gratefully I recognise the untiring support which you have given the PM in his search for a peaceful solution of the recent European crisis. The responsibility resting on the Foreign Secretary at a time like this is indeed overwhelming, and the wisdom and courage with which you have borne it have earned for you the admiration and gratitude of the whole Empire.

Before returning to Balmoral on 2 October, the King issued a remarkably complacent message to the public, of the sort for which

Chamberlain was later so severely criticized. 'The time of anxiety is past,' he told the people. 'After the magnificent efforts of the Prime Minister in the cause of peace it is my fervent hope that a new era of friendship and prosperity may be dawning among the peoples of the world.' For Queen Mary the opportunity of taking a crack at Churchill was too good to miss. She passed on to her son a letter she had received from the Kaiser, in which the old warlord wrote: 'I have not the slightest doubt that Mr Chamberlain was inspired by heaven and guided by God.' She added a postscript: 'I am sure you feel angry as I do at people croaking as they do at the PM's action.' She went on to say that for once she agreed with Margot Asquith: ' "He brought home Peace, why can't they be grateful?" ' The King believed that 'some day the Czechs will see that what we did was to save them for a happier fate'.[56]

Not all those around him were so sure. Hardinge had been sceptical about Munich and, according to the diplomat, Oliver Harvey, 'he had a mind of his own and didn't hesitate to state it'. When Hardinge finally resigned in July 1943 – and the debate about whether he jumped or was pushed still continues – Harvey noted in his diary that 'he is a belated victim of Munich'. He then crossed the words out and wrote instead: 'There has been friction for some time (beginning from Munich and NC) largely caused by the Queen who was determined to get him out ... the King is fundamentally a weak character and certainly a rather stupid one. The Queen is a strong one out of a rather reactionary stable.'[57] This opinion did, however, come from a man who admitted that he stood left of centre.

When Duff Cooper went to return his seals of office a few days after Munich, he was told frankly that His Majesty 'could not agree with me, but he respected those who had the courage of their convictions'. It was a more honest statement than Eden had got, or that the War Secretary, Leslie Hore-Belisha, was to receive. A fortnight later the King was recording the notes of his meeting with Chamberlain: 'The PM agreed with the King that the future policy must be the cultivation of friendly relations combined with intensified rearmament.... As regards reconstruction of the Cabinet on a broader basis, the Opposition might help in producing armaments, but would criticize the PM's foreign policy as being a paradox to the rearmament programme.'[58] So the King supported Chamberlain's decision, taken in the face of advice from moderates such as Halifax, not to place the Government on a truly national basis and thus send a signal to Hitler that Britain was prepared to fight.

November 1938 saw the rejection of the King's suggestion that he write to King Victor Emanuel III of Italy to express satisfaction that the Anglo-Italian treaty was at last in force. Considering that the Italians were flagrantly contravening its major provisions, this was clearly right. One head of state to whom he did send congratulations was Hitler on his fiftieth birthday on 20 April 1939, the exact wording of which was worked out by the Foreign Office. In June he also replied kindly to Hitler's condolences on the loss of the submarine HMS *Thetis*. However, these were no more than the conventional courtesies which traditionally took place between all heads of state.

The royal visit to Canada and America in June 1939 was another public relations triumph. 'That tour made us,' the Queen told the Canadian Prime Minister. Mackenzie King interpreted the remark as meaning that it helped to sustain the Empire, 'but pointing to herself, she said, "I mean us, the King and myself." She spoke of it coming just at the right time.'[59] It is an interesting insight on how insecure the royal couple still felt themselves even two years after their Coronation. The American popular magazine *Scribner's* expressed what a number of Britons were privately thinking when it told its readers that 'King George VI is a colourless, weak personality largely on probation in the public mind of Great Britain, as well of the United States.' In a leading article which the editor of *The Times*, Geoffrey Dawson, felt important enough to cut out and keep in his files, *Scribner's* went on to say what many Britons only confided to their diaries about the King: 'He is of poorer royal timber than has occupied Britain's throne in many decades. Regardless of what you think of this situation, it must be faced realistically.'

Roosevelt certainly felt no awe for the King, and at the end of the dinner at his country house in New York State on 12 June 1939, he even tapped the King-Emperor on the knee and said, 'Time for bed young man.' The King responded well to this avuncular treatment, asking: 'Why don't my Ministers talk to me as the President did tonight? I feel exactly as though a father were giving me his most careful and wise advice.' It was misleading advice, however; for instance, when the President assured him, 'if he saw a U-boat he would sink her at once and wait for the consequences', or 'if London were bombed the USA would come in'. In fact, it took a German declaration of war after Pearl Harbor in December 1941 to force America into the European conflict, some sixteen months after the start of the Blitz on London.

Despite the importance of the subjects raised in the two long conversations, the King's language was astonishingly naive. His report reads:

I told him how difficult it was for us to help the Balkans as there was the

Mediterranean to convoy things through and they would want all they had got in a war. I explained to him Roumania's position as to frontiers, having four to cope with. Because of the air we were only just becoming frontier conscious ourselves. In the whole of America he has none.

At the culmination of this fourth-form geography essay – Romania in fact had five frontiers and America two – Roosevelt showed why he was taking the trouble to give all this 'wise and careful' fatherly advice. He brought up the outlines of a plan which was later to become the highly advantageous Destroyers-for-Bases deal of September 1940.

The King was certainly taken in by the various Presidential assurances. According to one of the three correspondents travelling on the royal train, when asked whether he thought the trip would produce American support for England in the event of war, the King replied, in a charmingly breezy, Woosterish way: 'It's in the bag.' This amazingly indiscreet and mistaken remark had to be censored for a decade so as not to inflame isolationism and anti-British sentiment.[60]

Using the traditional combination of charm and accessibility, the King and Queen captured American hearts. *Time* magazine noticed how 'his standard device was to exclaim about the youth of the people he met'. Thus, when introduced to the Under-Secretary of the US Treasury, he said: 'You look very young for such an important post!' The Queen told New York's Mayor, Fiorello La Guardia: 'There is nothing nicer in the world than friendship. Friendliness is about the nicest thing in the world, isn't it?'[61] This sort of effusiveness – supported by a good deal of American media 'hype' about the visit – did the trick.

Once back in England the royal couple lost no time in again opposing the widening of the Government's political base. In July 1939 a newspaper campaign began which advocated the enlistment of their *bête noire*, Winston Churchill, and a huge advertisement asking 'What Price Churchill?' appeared in the Strand. His inclusion in Chamberlain's ministry at such a time would have sent precisely that defiant message to Germany which Britain so desperately needed to give. But Chamberlain rode out the demands, and by late July was able to crow to his sisters:

> As for the Churchill episode, it has in [US Ambassador] Joe Kennedy's picturesque phrase 'fallen out of bed' ... even [Lord] Camrose has now dropped it in 'The Telegraph'. I hear that Winston himself is very depressed and he certainly looked it at the dinner at Buckingham Palace on Monday. In particular he is distressed by a couple of witty articles making fun of the suggestion that he would help matters in the Cabinet.

At that dinner Chamberlain sat between the Queen and the Duchess

of Kent and 'neither of them left me in any doubt about their sentiments'.[62] So, whilst sitting at the same table but presumably out of
Churchillian earshot, the Queen and the Duchess encouraged Chamberlain not to take the anti-appeaser back into the Government. The 'witty
articles' the Prime Minister referred to were in fact merely a pedestrian
series of allegations vilifying Churchill in the magazine *Truth*, which was
secretly controlled by Chamberlain's friend and fishing partner, Sir
Joseph Ball, of the Conservative Research Department.

In mid-August 1939 the Duke of Connaught was lunching with
Wheeler-Bennett. When he learnt that the writer was about to visit the
Kaiser, he leapt up. It was less than a month away from the outbreak of
war, but nevertheless the King's cousin

> went without hesitation for a certain drawer and began to burrow in it like a
> terrier at a rabbit hole. Masonic orders, foreign orders and other relics of his
> past were thrown over his shoulder and then at last he found what he had
> sought ... a blue velvet gold-enamelled baton which he shook ... triumphantly
> saying ... 'I may be an old man, but you tell my nephew William that I am
> still proud of being a Prussian Field Marshal.'

In the prevailing political circumstances Wheeler-Bennett diplomatically forgot to pass on the message.[63]

In late August the King offered to write 'a friendly message direct to
the Emperor of Japan'. This was ruled out for fear of the near-inevitable
rebuttal. What he felt such messages could really achieve in the face of
the terrible logic of Japan's Tripartite Alliance with Germany and Italy,
let alone the inevitable antagonism between British and Japanese interests
in the Far East, is hard to fathom. But the King was ever the optimist.
Sir Miles Lampson recorded in his diary that, after the Nazi–Soviet Pact
later that month, which made war inevitable by securing Hitler's eastern
flank, 'His Majesty thought that there would almost certainly be peace
and that this time Hitler's bluff had been called'.[64] When it was clear
that the exact opposite was the case, the King said: 'It was utterly
damnable that that villain Hitler had upset everything.' In his endearing
P.G. Wodehouse style, he did not have World Peace in mind, but that
week's grouse shooting.

The outbreak of war on 3 September 1939 was not about to change
the Palace's attitude towards the Windsors. When the Duke returned to
England from France, there was no state or family representative to
welcome him at Portsmouth; and when he was cheered in the streets,
the news caused consternation at the Palace. In mid-September 1939 the
War Secretary, Leslie Hore-Belisha, recorded in his diary that

the King sent for me at 11 a.m. He was in a distressed state. He thought that if the Duchess went to [visit military headquarters around the country] she might be given a hostile reception. He did not want the Duke to go to the [headquarters] in England. He seemed very disturbed and walked up and down the room. He said the Duke had never had any discipline in his life.

The King was probably not worried that lack of hospitality would be shown to the Windsors, but the problem was smoothed over by Hore-Belisha's suggestion that the Duke should go to France as a liaison officer. Once there, however, the vendetta continued, with the Duke of Gloucester changing his mind about which units his brother could inspect. He eventually informed the Chief of the Imperial General Staff (CIGS), Sir Edmund Ironside, that he should not be allowed to visit any lesser formation than General Headquarters. This decision came directly from the King, who 'presumes ... that he ... not be allowed to go drifting about at his pleasure among the Units of the Expeditionary force'.[65]

When Cadogan visited Buckingham Palace on 9 September 1939, it was just after the American Ambassador, Joseph Kennedy, had been talking to the King about the 'loss of prestige of the British Empire in the changed circumstances in which we live since the last war'. We do not know whether or not the Ambassador advanced his private opinion that the Allies would lose the war. 'Buck House to see the King', recorded Cadogan that evening; 'called in about 6.10 and stayed till 6.50. He rather depressed – and a little *defaitiste* – result, I think, of a talk with Joe K who sees everything from the angle of his own investments.'[66] Putting the word into French makes it no less extraordinary that within a week of the outbreak of war, the senior official at the Foreign Office could find the King-Emperor to be defeatist about British war prospects.

Perhaps on Cadogan's advice the King wrote a letter to Kennedy the next day, to set the record straight about what was said. It would have been highly embarrassing, even dangerous, if anything '*defaitiste*' had been reported back to Washington. But even in that letter he effectively admitted that 'England would be broke at the end of this war'. It asked whether, if the Ambassador thought America would be broke too, 'is it not possible for you to put this fact before the American press?' How he thought this might have increased the likelihood of closer American involvement is hard to imagine.

The King went on: 'England, my country, owing to its geographical position in the world is part of Europe.' He added that 'Japan has been very rude to both our nations in the last few months but with her preponderance of naval, military and air armaments in that sphere even she has not dared to molest either of us, as she realizes the prestige we both hold in the world.' He concluded: 'We stand on the threshold of we know not what. Misery and suffering of war we know. But what of the future? The British Empire's mind is made up. I leave it at that.'[67] Wheeler-Bennett called this opinion 'simple and courageous', commending the King's 'capacity for honest and simple reasoning'. A further display of the King's simplicity came on 24 September, when he confided to his diary: 'After three weeks of war many strange things have taken place. It is an amazing puzzle.' A couple of days previously he had written one of his 'friendship' letters to King Boris of Bulgaria, which, unlike earlier ones, actually did get sent. It did nothing to affect Bulgarian policy, which was to stay as neutral as possible before finally joining the Axis.

In October 1939 the King suggested to Chamberlain that he should have an audience with the Opposition and trades union leaders to try to persuade them to be less critical of the Government. Chamberlain readily agreed to the idea and on 24 October, on the eve of a debate on policy towards India, the King spoke to Attlee. Chamberlain told His Majesty that the Leader of the Opposition had emerged in 'a chastened mood'.

In mid-November 1939 the Queen sent Lord Halifax a copy of Hitler's *Mein Kampf,* advising him not to read it, 'or you might go mad and that would be a great pity. Even a skip through gives one a good idea of his mentality, ignorance and obvious sincerity.'[68]

January 1940 saw the King again showing his readiness to take his prerogative to the limit when he actively conspired to bring down the War Secretary, Leslie Hore-Belisha. Tactless, ambitious and insensitive though he might have been, Hore-Belisha, as Neville Chamberlain put it after his fall, also 'did more for the Army than anyone since [the great reforming War Secretary Lord] Haldane'.[69] Senior army officers unanimously disliked the dynamic Jewish War Secretary, whose restless energy and reforming zeal threatened their domination of the War Office. Furthermore, as Hore-Belisha was later to complain, they resented his appointment because he was 'a Jew and an ordinary person not of their own caste'.[70] One army marching song, before Hore-Belisha had it banned in October 1939, went as follows:

> Onward Christian Soldiers,
> You have nought to fear,
> Israel Hore-Belisha
> Will lead you from the rear.
> Clothed by Monty Burton,

Fed on Lyons pies,
Die for Jewish freedom
As a Briton always dies.[71]

George v had involved himself closely in army politics during the First World War, both by defending Field Marshal Sir Douglas Haig and by colluding with Haig to bring down Sir John French as Commander-in-Chief. The royal family had long tended to interpret their constitutional duties broadly when it came to the armed forces; Queen Victoria insisted that every military appointment over the rank of colonel was submitted to her before it was made. But, as well as their traditionally close relations with the armed forces, the royal family may have had a personal reason for antipathy towards Hore-Belisha. This had nothing to do with anti-Semitism – since the reign of Queen Victoria, and certainly that of Edward viii, the royal family had been refreshingly free of that virus – but with the fact that Hore-Belisha had been one of the few Cabinet ministers to support Edward viii during the Abdication crisis. He was certainly the first to visit the Duke of Windsor afterwards. Telling the military historian, Basil Liddell Hart, 'I don't believe in deserting friends', and without consulting his Cabinet colleagues, Hore-Belisha had called on the Duke and Duchess of Windsor at the Hotel Meurice in Paris in September 1937. According to the Duke's official biography, 'the contact with official London was immensely important to the Duke'.[72]

A key figure in the Generals' Plot to remove Hore-Belisha was 'Boy' Munster. The fifth Earl of Munster had been Chamberlain's Paymaster-General and, from January until September 1939, was Hore-Belisha's Under-Secretary at the War Office. It was felt that a Tory grandee was needed in the post to 'balance' the pushy Liberal Nationalist, and Munster had succeeded Lord Strathcona, who had found that he could not get on with his boss. By June 1939 the Chief of Staff to the British Expeditionary Force (BEF), General Henry Pownall, was recording in his diary: 'Trouble is boiling up in the W.O. [War Office] between H-B and Munster; the latter reckons he is not properly treated and gets no work – in fact is generally ignored. If Munster cuts up on top of Strathcona ... H-B will have the greatest difficulty laughing it off.'[73]

General Ironside, the CIGS from the outbreak of war, was a former aide-de-camp general to George vi from 1937 until his appointment as Governor and Commander-in-Chief in Gibraltar the next year. He retained close contacts with the Monarch. In late June 1939, after a meeting with Hore-Belisha, Ironside wrote in his diary: 'How have we got into this state of affairs? I have to go to see the King tomorrow.

What shall I tell him?'[74] One may be certain that he was not complimentary about his Secretary of State. The campaign to remove the War Secretary had been rumbling on since the summer of 1938, but shifted into top gear in October 1939 after a row between Ironside and Hore-Belisha over the issuing of orders. The next month it came to a head over a dispute over pill-boxes. On 19 November, after returning from a tour of the Front, Hore-Belisha had told Ironside that he was 'disappointed' that there was no model pill-box and alleged that Lord Gort, the Commander-in-Chief of the BEF in France, 'hadn't used all the sappers we had sent him'.

John Standish Surtees Prendergast Vereker, sixth Viscount Gort, was not considered very intelligent, but neither was he a man Hore-Belisha ought to have crossed unless he felt himself on strong political ground. He had won the Victoria Cross serving with the Grenadier Guards in 1918 and enjoyed enormous prestige in the country. Ironside warned Hore-Belisha 'that he must be careful how he dealt with his Commander-in-Chief. He was put in by the King and must not be monkeyed about.' Earlier that month the King had, in an audience with Samuel Hoare, been 'critical about Army' – which, as the discussion had been about policies rather than administration, may be taken as implied criticism of Hore-Belisha rather than of the soldiers.[75]

Three days after Ironside's warning, Hore-Belisha wrote to Gort saying, 'I really think that the pill-boxes should spring up everywhere', and told him that Eden and the Dominion representatives who had recently toured the Front had 'commented on their absence'. The French Commander-in-Chief, General Gamelin, had told Hore-Belisha that one could be built in three days if working to a pattern.[76] The army was already on the counter-attack. The same day Pownall recorded how he 'went to see Hardinge at B.P. ... I discussed with him pretty frankly the virtues and failings of Hore-Belisha at the WO [War Office], on CIGS and various other generals. It's awkward to be asked questions of this kind but if one is I reckon one has to tell the truth, the King at least must not be deceived.' The implication was clearly that the King had instructed Hardinge to speak to Pownall about Hore-Belisha. Hardinge, who had also served alongside Gort in the Grenadiers during the First World War and had been a major before entering royal service, could be relied upon to take the army's side against the politicians.

Hore-Belisha then told the army's Engineer-in Chief, Major-General Ridley Pakenham-Walsh, that at a recent War Cabinet the Prime Minister had 'expressed himself ... as very perturbed at the reported weakness of the British section of the line'.[77] This roundabout verbal communication, which Hore-Belisha wished Pakenham-Walsh to pass on to Gort – who had been arguing that it took three weeks rather than three days to construct a pill-box – was a serious error, especially in an institution which sets store by correct lines of communication. Passing on messages through a third party in this way was considered sharp practice by the Army High Command. Despite his public school and Oxford background, First World War mention in despatches and membership of White's, Hore-Belisha was never one of them.

Flying to France to inspect the pill-box situation, Ironside 'found all GHQ in a devil of a rage' over Pakenham-Walsh's message. The CIGS sided with Gort and the next day Pownall recorded of Hore-Belisha: 'I pray to heaven this may be the last of him. I am doing my best to make it so.' Back from France, Ironside had a row with Hore-Belisha: 'We both got a bit heated about it,' he wrote in his diary.[78] The King then asked Chamberlain to see Ironside and, according to the Prime Minister's diary, 'although he said no more, something in his manner indicated that he had a reason for this suggestion'.

Chamberlain told Hore-Belisha of the King's remark and when he saw Ironside he was surprised that 'his report turned out to be entirely about pill-boxes . . . he was definitely critical of the Secretary of State'.[79] The King had thus been instrumental in ensuring that army discontent with Hore-Belisha got to the ears of the Prime Minister. This was nothing out of his constitutional duty to be consulted, to encourage and to warn – which in themselves of course had no statutory authority in law – but the King had enthusiastically fallen in with the Army's need to put independent pressure on the Prime Minister. Ironically, one of the criticisms the Army Command were making was that Hore-Belisha sent messages to the Commander-in-Chief outside proper channels of communication, when that was precisely what they were doing themselves.

On 4 December the King arrived in France to visit the BEF and was swiftly made privy to the High Command's complaints. From Hoare's earlier comments it is likely that he was a willing listener. The Duke of Gloucester was the Chief Liaison Officer at GHQ. He 'bitterly resented Mr Hore-Belisha's strictures' and it was he who was showing his brother around the Front.[80] At a lunch party at the Restaurant Galbert in Amiens there were present, as well as the King and his brother: Gort, Ironside, Hardinge, Munster (who had become ADC to Gort on leaving the Government), the Adjutant-General and the Quartermaster-General. The next day Pownall confided to his diary:

... both the King and Hardinge are under no illusions about Hore-Belisha and realised that he must go. We did not fail to keep them fully informed of all the details of H-B's recent disgraceful behaviour and there's no doubt we have the Palace on our side against him. The King, when I sat next to him at dinner, went so far as to ask me who, in my view, should replace H-B at the War Office. I told him [the Colonial Secretary] Malcolm MacDonald and he seemed rather to like the idea.[81]

The political decision, not only to dismiss the War Secretary but also who should replace him, was therefore being bandied about by a cabal of soldiers and courtiers, encouraged by the Monarch.

As soon as he got back to London the King saw Chamberlain. According to the Prime Minister's diary: 'He told me, and Alec Hardinge also more clearly told me, that things between [Belisha] and Gort were very unhappy.' Under Palace pressure, Chamberlain agreed to visit the BEF himself. On 14 December the King wrote a private letter to Gort, a copy of which exists in Munster's papers. It told the Commander-in-Chief how much he had enjoyed his visit, and 'from what I did see I was able to tell the Prime Minister on Tuesday that there was no reason for him to be worried about the work you were doing. I am so glad that he is going to visit you on Friday, and I hope very much that you will be frank with him about what has happened.'[82] The King was thus encouraging the Commander-in-Chief to criticise Hore-Belisha to the Prime Minister.

The King then directly contradicted his War Secretary's assertion by saying, 'I know that the War Cabinet has never criticised either yourself as Commander-in-Chief or the BEF and that Ironside came to see you on his own initiative.' He thought 'that my visit came just at the right moment'.[83] Cadogan was mystified the next day when, whilst having a cigarette with the King after presenting a Venezuelan diplomat, His Majesty 'indulged in some rather disparaging reflections on Hore-Belisha, but I can't quite make out why'.

When Chamberlain arrived in France soon afterwards, he found criticism of Hore-Belisha rampant. Yet on his return he told the King that he would not be replacing him, and saw the War Secretary himself soon afterwards to express confidence in him. The King wrote regretfully to the Duke of Gloucester on 3 January to say: 'I don't think he means to make a change at the W.O.' As a letter from Field Marshal Sir Archibald Montgomery-Massingberd put it to Munster ten days later, 'I think it would be better not to put my views on the late happenings at the W.O. on paper! They are rather violent. Poor old Army, why should it be given an S of S like that?'

Something happened between 20 December and the New Year to make Chamberlain change his mind about Hore-Belisha. On 1 January 1940 Halifax told Cadogan, after a conversation with the Prime Minister, that 'H-B must be got out of W.O. and will be offered the Ministry of Information'. Cadogan thought that this was 'blinding – and exquisitely funny', but on reflection he 'came to the conclusion that Jew control of our propaganda would be major disaster'. Chamberlain rated Hore-Belisha, for all his personal defects, very highly indeed as a War Secretary, but nevertheless told him that 'incompatibility of temper' made his resignation necessary.[84] Hoare's contemporary notes of the affair contain the line 'Rumours Palace', which may give an indication as to what helped change Chamberlain's mind.

When Hore-Belisha resigned on 5 January, his post was taken by Oliver Stanley, the son of the seventeenth Earl of Derby and grandson of the seventh Duke of Manchester. Despite his father's unpopularity at the War Office during the First World War, Stanley was far more congenial to the Army High Command and the Palace than Hore-Belisha. Ironside noted his 'feeling of intense relief on the whole.... It will be much better to get on with him.' Congratulating Munster on his victory over Hore-Belisha, Hardinge wrote from Windsor Castle: 'I understand that they like [Stanley] very much at the WO, he is no doubt helped by the character of his predecessor!'[85]

George VI's official biographer claims that 'the King was as much surprised as anyone' when he heard of Hore-Belisha's departure.[86] This seems highly unlikely, considering the efforts to which he had gone to secure his removal. Suspicions about his involvement were widespread. Leo Amery noted on the day of Hore-Belisha's departure: 'rumours of intervention even by the Duke of Gloucester and the King'. The Queen seems to have had little direct involvement in the affair beyond telling her brother, who repeated it to the Tory MP, Harry Crookshank, an amusing story about Hore-Belisha's architectural solecisms. After being shown around Windsor Castle, Hore-Belisha had said to the Queen that 'he now realised how much we owed to Queen Victoria for building it'.[87]

Chamberlain wrote to the King on 8 January to say that Hore-Belisha had gone because 'there existed a strong prejudice against him for which I do not hold him altogether blameless'. There had been no policy difference between Hore-Belisha and the Cabinet, but press speculation and Society gossip were intense. As usual Chips Channon had his ear closest to the ground and noted on the same day:

London is agog with Belisha tales ... as it has now leaked out that the King himself insisted on Leslie's resignation.... Ever since the Abdication, the Court minions have been intriguing his downfall ... all this will do the Monarchy harm, as they should not interfere or dabble in politics.... George VI is not George V, and Alec Hardinge is certainly not [George V's Private Secretary] Lord Stamfordham.

(The King's father had been more robust in accepting personal responsibility for his actions. When Stafford Cripps had attacked 'Buckingham Palace influence' in a speech, and later denied that he meant George V himself, the King asked Eden: 'What does he mean by saying that Buckingham Palace is not me? Who else is there I should like to know? Does he mean the footmen?')

When Hore-Belisha arrived to return his seals of office, the King attempted to distance himself from any hint of personal involvement in the affair. 'This is a sad moment', he said as he was handed the red box. 'Not at all, Sir,' answered Hore-Belisha politely. 'It has been a privilege to serve you and I have tried to do what I could for the Army.' 'You have indeed, and how quickly you have done it. No man could have done more.' In the rest of the thirty-minute interview Hore-Belisha recorded how: 'H.M. expressed his regret at my departure and his last words were: "I hope very much, and I have no doubt that I shall be handing you back seals again." '[88] When Hore-Belisha asked him about his trip to France, the King 'pulled himself up and said: "My goodness, I meant to see you immediately on my return." ' This would have been sound constitutional practice, but of course he had actually been intriguing against Hore-Belisha at the time.

'I sent you a message,' claimed the King, 'but was told that you could not come, as you had a meeting.' This most transparent of excuses was duly noted by Hore-Belisha, along with its follow-up: 'He said he had been meaning to see me since, but he had had so many engagements and it had gone out of his head.' Hore-Belisha, who had heard the rumours and had been told by Chamberlain that the King had asked him to see Ironside over the pill-box controversy, could hardly question His Majesty's veracity and merely answered: 'I was very surprised at this. I told him that I had received no message from him after his return from France but did not know how it could have happened but I did not receive it.'[89] The King was relieved after the interview was over and wrote in his diary: 'Luckily he was pleasant and there was no need to open up the question of his resignation.'

After Hore-Belisha's resignation speech, Channon thought that he 'must now know who are the architects of his downfall, and he made two clever digs which could be taken by the uninitiated to be slurs on the Prime Minister, but which now seem to be sad, sly allusions to the Sovereign'. Hore-Belisha had said: 'I am reluctant to believe that any of the high officers with whom I have been associated would have been so unfaithful to the code, which imbues the whole Army, as to make any representations irregularly, or that, if he had done so, it would have been countenanced' – which might have been one of the 'sad, sly allusions' to the King's involvement.

Beaverbrook felt no such reticence; at a dinner with the Tory MPs Samuel Hoare, Alan Lennox-Boyd and Sir Terence O'Connor, the press magnate quoted the line from *Hamlet*: 'There's such divinity doth hedge a King', leaving Channon to reiterate that 'the Monarchy by interfering has cheapened itself though it has certainly won the round'.[90] As a result of the plot against him, Hore-Belisha is not today remembered as the tough-minded War Secretary who attempted to modernize the army and get it ready for combat in 1940, but instead as the man who installed yellow beacons next to pedestrian crossings.

February 1940 found the King agreeing with the Information Minister, Sir John Reith, that 'we ought to have some sort of the efficiency of dictatorship states', probably without surmising whom the egotistical tyrant doubtless had in mind as dictator. In his first interview with the new head of MI6, Stewart Menzies, instead of discussing the worrying 'Venlo' incident, in which the Germans had kidnapped two top Intelligence agents, 'the King showed interest only in the health of the old Kaiser'. In March he managed to mystify Halifax when 'describing the Maundy ceremonies in Westminster Abbey, quite seriously he asked me if I knew what they were, and I, thinking there was some more subtle answer than the obvious, let him continue, which he did by saying, "of course they were the pensioners". I have been wondering ever since what he meant.'

Concerned that Chamberlain's Government was still too narrowly based, Hardinge wrote to 'Boy' Munster: 'I do wish that we had a really national Government.... I think it a great weakness, even though the Trade Unions and Labour leaders are on the whole being very helpful.'[91] Meanwhile, the Queen was concerned with the religious side of the war and its effect upon morals. Sitting on her left at dinner at Buckingham Palace on 4 March, Reith was delighted by the way she 'agreed emphatically with me that the Christian ethic should be the basis of postwar policy'. She thought the King might make a pronouncement about it: 'He believes it, you know.'[92] Less happy was her reaction to her children's enthusiasm for the RAF's bombing of military targets in Germany. She told Halifax, 'as a strange commentary upon the demoralising effect of modern warfare and modern science', that her daughters had even said to her, 'Isn't it grand about Sylt?', the German naval base which had been successfully attacked the night before. 'Very good, of course, for them to be pleased,' was the grown-ups' reaction, 'but it seemed somehow odd when children welcomed bomb-dropping.'[93]

The Queen's moral sensibilities re-emerged a fortnight later when she refused a request from Halifax to send a message to the Young Womens' Christian Association in the United States. She had ascertained that the Admiralty had plans to violate Norwegian neutrality in order to forestall a German invasion. 'I would like to assure myself, before deciding to do it,' she wrote to Halifax on 1 April, 'that anything we intended to do in a warlike manner in the near future, is absolutely honourable and right. Because I do not feel that I can talk of high ideals and the right ways of life if at the same time the neutrals are accusing us of not keeping our word.' She concluded: 'We *must* beat the Germans, but the neutrals won't like it whilst it's going on! If they *do* mind very much, a broadcast from me might do more harm than good.'[94] Eight days after her difficult moral dilemma, Norway was invaded and quickly subjugated by Germany. By the time the Queen did agree to a broadcast, this time to the women of France on 14 June, it was sadly too late to do any good, as that country capitulated three days later.

In April 1940 the King had got as far as signing one of his many inter-head of state letters, which were all written on ministerial advice. This one was to the King of Italy, but in the event the Cabinet recalled it just before it was sent. Since King Victor Emanuel was powerless to influence Mussolini in the direction of Italian foreign policy, it seems to have been a largely pointless exercise. During a lull in the fighting in Norway, Churchill made an attempt to ingratiate himself with the Monarch, who, he knew, had reservations about him. After receiving a somewhat premature letter from the King congratulating him on 'meeting the German move against Scandinavia', the First Lord of the Admiralty – he had been appointed on the outbreak of war – replied on 15 April: 'I hope Your Majesty will command me [to visit] whenever there is a lull or indeed at any time.'[95] It was a letter he may have soon come to regret, leading the King to expect personal attention from Churchill, 'lull' in the fighting or not. Two days after the King wrote to Churchill British forces failed to take Trondheim, and after a fortnight they were forced to evacuate Namsos on the Norwegian coast.

The Palace did what it could to offset the May crisis, which brought Chamberlain down and Churchill to power. When Crookshank met Hardinge in St James's Park after lunch at the Guards Club on the day Chamberlain resigned, he was told that 'much advice had been given for some time past on desirability of changes, but Neville was always stubborn'.[96] This might have been a reference to Hardinge's own oft-stated belief that the Government needed widening; but it could also possibly be a reference to the King's offer, after the Government had on 7 May 1940 suffered damaging blows on the first day of the House of Commons debate on the Norway campaign, to intervene with Attlee and ask Labour to join a coalition government which Chamberlain would lead.

The Prime Minister asked the King, during an audience that evening, to postpone any such move until after the Labour Party Conference had ended.[97] The King asked, 'would it help if I spoke to Attlee about the national standpoint of the Labour Party and say that I hoped they would realise that they must pull their weight and join the National Government'. Had that happened, and the King had appealed to him to serve under Chamberlain in the national interest, Attlee might have found it hard to refuse. Indeed, had the Labour Party Conference not coincidentally been taking place, it is likely that the King would have acted to keep Chamberlain in power in this way.

At that audience the King 'told the Prime Minister that I did not like the way in which, with all the worries and responsibilities he had to bear in the conduct of the War, he was always subject to a stab in the back from both the House of Commons and the Press'.[98] Since the depoliticization of the Monarchy after the death of Queen Victoria, British monarchs have tended to consider their Prime Ministers, irrespective of their talents or politics, as 'good men trying to do a difficult job under very trying circumstances', and have given them their support on that basis. It was essentially a managerial rather than an ideological attitude towards politics: government as administration carried on with general goodwill. The business of carrying on government was seen as far more important than doctrinal or personal differences between the various politicians.

Those who opposed the Prime Minister were liable to be seen as 'the awkward squad', who were written off as 'unhelpful'. In Queen Mary's post-Munich letter to her son, the anti-appeasers were people who found it 'always so easy . . . to criticise when they do not know the ins and outs of the question'. The advantage of this view, which the House of Windsor adopted towards politicians, is that after a Prime Minister's fall his successor automatically becomes the next 'good man trying to do a difficult job in trying circumstances'. Although this phenomenon worked against Churchill in the first four years of George VI's reign, by December 1940 it began operating in his favour. 'It was most unfair on Chamberlain to be treated like this after all his good work,' thought the King on the 'unprofitable' Thursday, 9 May 1940. He believed that 'the Conservative rebels like Duff Cooper ought to be ashamed of themselves for deserting him at this moment'.[99] Considering that Duff Cooper had resigned from the Government over Munich, and had consistently opposed Chamberlain's policies since then, it seems hard that the King should have expected him to have stood by the Prime Minister during the May crisis.

When Chamberlain arrived at Buckingham Palace to resign on 10 May, the King 'told him how grossly unfairly I thought he had been treated and that I was terribly sorry that all this controversy had happened. We then had an informal talk over his successor. I, of course, suggested Halifax.'[100] The 'of course' is telling. The King liked Halifax personally and had bestowed upon him a unique mark of favour by giving him the key to Buckingham Palace's gardens. He could therefore take a scenic route between his Eaton Square home and Whitehall. The Queen had also offered him the use of the garden house, which had chairs and a telephone. Diffident, moral, family men, the King and Halifax both had speech impediments, which caused them to dislike microphones and distrust Churchill's ebullient grandiloquence. They had many good qualities in common, and their views on appeasement and politics in general largely coincided, but they were the wrong type of men to lead Britain in a world war. Fortunately, Halifax appreciated this fact about himself.

Halifax had a reputation for sound judgment, and never did he exercise it better than when he refused the Premiership on 9 May 1940. Halifax's new role was to work with Chamberlain in the War Cabinet to restrain Churchill, and it must have been a relief for him to know that, if the new Prime Minister did turn out to justify their worst fears, the ultimate prerogative to dismiss him lay with a monarch whom the 'Respectable Tendency' could trust to act in their best interests. In the event it was never to come anywhere near that, but the psychology of politics is often about knowing what could happen in the last resort, and

Churchill knew that throughout 1940 the Palace was Halifax's ally rather than his.

At his resignation audience at tea-time on 10 May, when Chamberlain observed that Halifax, as a peer, could 'only act as a shadow or ghost in the Commons, where all the real work took place', the King was not convinced. He confessed that he 'was disappointed over this statement, as I thought H was the obvious man, and that his peerage could be placed in abeyance for the time being'. But Chamberlain seems to have dismissed this notion.

At forty-two, Eden was considered too inexperienced and, as Dominions Secretary – even though he was effectively Foreign Secretary emeritus – too junior for the top job. Leo Amery had no political following and had not held office for a decade. The Home Secretary, Sir John Anderson, was new to Parliament and was considered more administrator than politician. Sir John Simon and Hoare had been part of the reason for Chamberlain's downfall. All the other *Munichois* barring Halifax himself were ruled out, yet the Prime Minister had to be a Conservative because of the Party's overwhelming Parliamentary majority, which the electoral truce preserved in aspic for the duration of the war. Ideally it also had to be someone with a good understanding of modern warfare, and such people were surprisingly thin on the Tory ground. In 1941 and 1942 even such outsiders as Jan Smuts, Robert Menzies and Lord Beaverbrook were considered for the post, 'should something happen to Winston', before Eden established his position as heir apparent during 1943.

Therefore, Churchill was the only possibility once Halifax had ruled himself out. The King had no choice, as he himself put it: 'there was only one person I could send for'. Whenever that phrase appears, emphasis has been put on 'one person', as though Churchill were the obvious choice; in fact, the emphasis ought to be placed on 'only', because there was no viable alternative. In one of the very few moments this century when the royal prerogative came decisively into play, with the political establishment split and the decision really resting with the Crown, the King would have preferred any halfway suitable compromise candidate to Churchill to lead Britain in the Second World War, had one been available.

Within the Palace, doubts about the new appointment were rife. The King's Assistant Private Secretary, Lascelles – universally known as 'Tommy', except to Churchill who called him 'Alan' – 'shared the King's misgivings about Churchill'.[101] Even after one of the new Prime Minister's great speeches in the summer of 1940, Lascelles remarked: 'It is too early to judge whether he will be a great Prime Minister. What I am certain is that he will go down in history as a great poet.' Lascelles, who once said that 'the only three books in any language that I really know are "Kim", "Puck of Pook's Hill" and "The First Jungle Book" ', had much the same academic achievements as the King. He had twice failed his Foreign Office entry examination, getting zero in his Political Science paper and only 81 out of 600 for Logic. 'My brain just lay down,' he explained.

More serious opposition to Churchill came from another quarter. As Lascelles told Lord Birkenhead when he was interviewed for the official biography of Lord Halifax: 'When Chamberlain fell the King felt that he ought to send for Halifax. Alec Hardinge knew that Winston was the man, but had a hard job selling him to the King as the Queen was very anti-Winston.'[102] Evidence for so sensitive a subject as the royal family's private views on the man who, as Isaiah Berlin put it, was 'the saviour of his country', is hard to come by. But, when Wheeler-Bennett told Harold Nicolson in 1955 that, according to his research, the King 'was bitterly opposed to Winston succeeding Chamberlain', the adverb employed is instructive.[103]

It was felt that Churchill's support for King Edward VIII during the Abdication crisis had alienated the new King and Queen. Certainly, when Churchill was appointed on 10 May 1940, Chamberlain's Private Secretary, John ('Jock') Colville, hoped and believed that the King '(remembering perhaps the Abdication) is understood not to wish to send for Winston'. Colville believed nothing could stop Churchill, 'because of his powers of blackmail – unless the King makes full use of his prerogative and sends for another man'.[104] Queen Mary sent a message to Colville, through his mother Lady Cynthia, who was one of her Ladies-in-Waiting, to say that he should refuse to serve under Churchill. On the evening of 11 May, the Halifaxes were walking through Buckingham Palace gardens, where they 'ran into the King and Queen'. The Queen 'spoke very strongly about the House of Commons' behaviour'. Halifax came away with the understanding that the King 'was clearly apprehensive of Winston's administrative methods', which mirrored his own views entirely. Writing in her own hand on 17 May, the Queen expressed at length her family's sorrow at losing Chamberlain as their Prime Minister. She clearly felt little need to maintain even the fiction of royal impartiality in politics:

> Dear Mr Chamberlain [she began], I must write to you one line to say how deeply I regretted your ceasing to be our Prime Minister. I can never tell you

in words how much we owe you. During these last desperate and unhappy years ... we felt so safe with the knowledge that your wisdom and high purpose were there at our hand. I do want you to know how grateful we are, and I know that these feelings are shared by a great part of our people. Your [resignation] broadcast was superb. My eldest daughter told me that she and Margaret Rose had listened to it with real emotion. In fact she said 'I cried, Mummy'.

The Queen concluded by saying of the struggle then taking place in Holland and Belgium: 'You did all in your power to stave off such agony and you were right. With again my heartfelt thanks for all you have done for this dear country of ours, I am, yours very sincerely, Elizabeth R.'[105]

With Labour and the Liberals joining Churchill's new Government, a radical reorganization took place. On the surrender of his seals as Home Secretary, Hoare noted on 12 May: 'talk with the King (evidently anti-Max [Beaverbrook])'. Unfortunately in Hoare's private papers it states baldly that 'this material has had to be extensively weeded and re-shuffled', so little more can be assessed from this source. But it is known that the King had the gravest misgivings about Beaverbrook becoming Minister of Aircraft Production.[106] Historians still debate the extent of the Canadian's actual achievement at the Ministry – the truth about aircraft production seems in retrospect to be more prosaic than Beaverbrook's myth-making machine implied – but at the time it was taken for granted that the dynamic press baron had entered the Ministry, terrorized officials using colourful journalist's language, and hugely increased production at the crucial period of the Battle of Britain and the Blitz. He came, he swore, he conquered. The King, however, seemed more concerned with the 'respectable Canadian opinion', which had always deprecated Beaverbrook's methods.

The first letter the King sent Churchill after he had formed his Government, far from sounding a note of encouragement and support, warned him 'of the repercussions, which I am sure will occur, especially in Canada, at the inclusion of the name of Lord Beaverbrook for air production in the Air Ministry. You are no doubt aware that the Canadians do not appreciate him.' 'To warn' was one of the sovereign's constitutional duties, according to Bagehot, and George VI asked his new Prime Minister to 'reconsider ... as I fear that this appointment may be misconstrued'. The titular head of the 'Respectable Tendency' was beginning to act like its commissar, but Churchill shrugged off the suggestion that the best man for this vital job should not be chosen for it because, as the King pointed out, 'The Air Training Scheme for pilots and aircraft is in Canada' and 'respectable Canadian opinion' was running against its most famous, if least favourite, son.

The King was equally sceptical about Churchill's other friend and confidant, his Parliamentary Private Secretary Brendan Bracken. The New Prime Minister had put his 'faithful chela' forward for a Privy Counsellorship. Halifax recorded how the King was 'much surprised and not a little disturbed' by this. He had Hardinge write to Churchill to remonstrate that Bracken had not 'attained high office' and was thus not qualified for the honour. Churchill replied vigorously, not forbearing to mention his period in the Wilderness: 'He has sometimes been my sole supporter in the years I have been striving to get this country properly defended.... He has suffered as I have done every form of official hostility. Had he joined the ranks of the time-servers and careerists ... I have no doubt he would have attained high office.'[107] The King backed down within twenty-four hours. Nevertheless, contrary to the normal practice where there was some badinage between the King and his ministers after Privy Council meetings, the occasion of Bracken's installation was 'Very formal – no chat'.[108] As Colville, who had ignored Queen Mary's advice and become Churchill's Private Secretary, commented, 'Winston will get his way, but it is clear that the King has a mind of his own.'[109]

The King's broadcast to the nation on 24 May had, according to the Government's Home Intelligence reports on moral and public opinion, 'a steadying but not a deep effect. It was generally liked but most frequent comments were on the improvement in H.M.'s delivery and on the slightly impersonal note of the broadcast.'[110] One listener, the Tory MP Cuthbert Headlam, wrote in his diary, 'Poor little man – one is very sorry for him', hardly the desired reaction to a King-Emperor's broadcast to his people at their most perilous hour.'[111] Feeling sorry for the King, and commenting on how he spoke rather than on what he said, was becoming a national pastime and explains why in 1940, as Philip Ziegler has put it, Churchill began to 'usurp the King's place as the focal point of the nation's fervour'.[112]

The royal family quickly understood and adapted to their diminished role, although there is evidence to suggest that they may have sometimes resented it. When, for example, soon after D-Day, Eden, the Foreign Secretary, was told that he could not join the royal visit to the troops in France, his Private Secretary, Pierson Dixon, put it down to 'the fear that as well-known a figure as A.E. might steal some of HM's thunder.

Lascelles, I thought, was a bit deceptive about it and might have told me the real feelings of the Palace sooner.'[13]

Late May 1940 saw military collapse on the Continent and the capitulation of the Belgian army. It is indicative of the changing nature of the King's relationship with Churchill that he did not protest against what he knew to be an undeserved slur on King Leopold III of the Belgians by the Prime Minister. Leopold had written to George VI on 25 May warning him of his country's imminent surrender, a fact proven by the King's answering telegram to Brussels the next day urging him not to become a prisoner. The King therefore knew that Churchill was guilty of a particularly gross 'terminological inexactitude' for his depiction of the Belgian capitulation three days later as a treacherous surprise. On the day of his return from the Continent, Britain's special envoy to Leopold, Admiral Roger Keyes, was visited by an Intelligence officer, who demanded all the documents from his mission. Keyes successfully concealed them and showed them to the King to disprove Churchill's calumnies.'[14]

Thus the King knew the truth, as did Churchill. Seven months later, sitting in an air raid shelter with Roosevelt's adviser, Harry Hopkins, he 'expressed a good deal of sympathy with King Leopold', and although he refused to allow his brother monarch to be stripped of his colonelcy in the British army, or have his Garter banner removed from St George's Chapel, George VI did not, as Leopold had hoped, 'insist that his Prime Minister should uphold, rather than pervert, the truth concerning these circumstances'. Admiral Keyes's son has since stated: 'Had the existence of Leopold's warning letter to George VI, or even a paraphrase of its contents been made public ... the French, Belgian and British Prime Ministers' false allegations would have been completely demolished.'[15] Whilst it might be understandable for *raisons d'état* for the King to have kept silent in the summer of 1940 when Britain desperately needed a scapegoat to explain the Allied defeat, the King permitted this unwarranted slur to continue after the war, even to the extent of Leopold not being invited to Princess Elizabeth's wedding in 1947.

To Harry Hopkins the King had confided the view that the Belgian Monarch 'should have left the country and established his government elsewhere'. Yet this was precisely the course that the British royal family has constantly been given credit for having refused to contemplate in their own case. Much has been made of the fact that, as A.J.P. Taylor claimed, 'the King practised revolver shooting in the grounds of Buckingham Palace and intended to die there fighting'. The King told a visitor that, in the event of a successful German invasion, he would have offered his services 'at once, in whatever capacity', to the leader of the British resistance movement.[116] The personal courage of the man who raised himself from his sick-bed to fight at the Battle of Jutland is unquestioned. But, despite his robust intentions in 1940, in practice had the Germans invaded he would quite rightly have been taken to one of the four large country houses earmarked as refuges, and eventually been evacuated to Canada. The Queen's famous line that the children would be staying with her, she with the King and the King was not leaving, as well as the courageous statement: 'I'm not going down like the others', were sublime. Churchill also played on this line, at one point telling the House of Commons that the King would stay to fight. But it must be doubted that this is what would have happened in reality.

During the Blitz the King and Queen left London every evening to join the Princesses at Windsor Castle, and had bombing become too intense there was an armoured car on standby to evacuate them to relative safety. This was mere common sense for, had the British Isles fallen, the Empire's continued resistance would have been conducted from Canada even if, somewhat unhelpfully, Roosevelt had warned in May 1940 that some of the Latin American states might not take too kindly to the restoration of monarchy on the American continent. Doubtless Churchill, despite his brave talk of 'going down fighting amid the ruins of Whitehall', would also have seen the logic of continuing the war in exile. As Charles de Gaulle recorded in his *War Memoirs*: 'Certainly the King and Government would have left for Canada in time.'[117]

After Buckingham Palace was bombed in September 1940, Home Intelligence reported that for as many people who were pleased that the royal family were sharing the nation's dangers, there were as many who were angry that these national figureheads had been put in such danger in the first place. In fact, the King's family were, quite rightly, exposed to far less danger than the average Londoner. After some discussion about whether Queen Mary should be evacuated to Canada, it was finally agreed that she should live as the guest of the Duke and Duchess of Beaufort, where she spent the war pursuing a personal vendetta against the ivy at Badminton. When the Queen's brother, David Bowes-Lyon, sent his children to safety in America, it almost cost him his propaganda job in the British Embassy in Washington.

In the field of wartime rationing, also, the royal family's experience was significantly different from that of the average Briton. This would hardly be worthy of comment had not the propaganda services made so much play in trying to suggest otherwise. Far from sharing precisely the same privations as the rest of the nation, it has recently emerged that the Queen and other members of her family each received on average over twenty times the number of clothing coupons above their normal ration. As game, fish, fruit and vegetables were never rationed, the royal family – which had eighty rabbits sent to Windsor each week – also ate considerably better than ordinary urban families.[118] Considering how much the family needed to be seen in public, inspiring morale and carrying out the 'dignified' part of their duties, it was important that they should be well-dressed and healthy.

Senior decision-makers were expected to devote a large amount of time to the royal family. Private Secretaries were not considered good enough for keeping them informed of developments, 'lull' in the fighting or not. On 16 May, after the Dutch surrender and the piercing of the French line near Sedan, as Guderian's panzers were racing towards Amiens and Arras and the fate of Europe hung in the balance, Halifax spent his afternoon as follows: 'Tea with Princess Paul, the Queen and the Duchess of Kent.... I had to leave at about ten to six, as I had to go and see the King ... after half an hour with him I had to see Queen Wilhelmina, so I could hardly have had a more Royal afternoon.' It turned out more royal than he had bargained for, because after leaving the King a footman mistakenly took him back to Queen Elizabeth, 'of whom I had taken my leave half an hour before. I had to explain to her it was the other Queen I wanted.'

On 5 June Halifax recorded how the King 'was funny about Winston, and told me that he did not find him very easy to talk to. Nor was Winston willing to give him as much time, or information, as he would like.'[119] This is an extraordinary statement considering what Churchill had to deal with the day after Dunkirk. When Gort had returned from the Continent, and the Cabinet was desperate to know what had gone wrong in the campaign, he could only go to Downing Street after first seeing the King. Such constitutional niceties were rigorously observed, and when, during the Battle of France, Churchill was too indisposed for his regular audience with the King, he was criticized for it.

Speaking to Halifax on 18 June, the King 'complained a good deal of the difficulty of making contact with Winston'.[120] During the previous eight days Italy had declared war, Churchill had visited the French Prime Minister at Tours, the Wehrmacht had entered Paris, Roosevelt had declined a French appeal for help, France was offered Perpetual Union with Britain, the Russians had occupied the Baltic states, and Marshal

Pétain had replaced Paul Reynaud and declared his intention to seek an armistice with Hitler. Yet still the King was demanding the Prime Minister's time and 'complained a good deal' when he did not get it.

Italy's declaration of war baffled the King, who noted in his diary: 'Mussolini gave no reason.' This shows how naïve he still was about the dictators' methods. The only advice which history records the King giving Churchill in those days of the French collapse comes from Hugh Dalton on 31 May: 'The King says that he has to remind Winston that he is only PM in England and not in France as well!'[121] Perhaps because of receiving advice like this, Churchill kept his audiences at the Palace as short as possible. Royal complaints about this continued into August; one of the Queen's Ladies-in-Waiting, Lady Hyde, told Colville

> that although the King and Queen appreciate Winston's qualities and see that he is the man for the occasion, they are a little miffed by the off-hand way in which he treats them. They much preferred Chamberlain's habit of going to the Palace regularly, once a week, and explaining the situation in a careful and unhurried way. Winston says he will come at 6.00 p.m., puts this off by telephone to 6.30 and is inclined to turn up for ten hectic minutes at 7.00.

Colville instead commented to his diary about the way the King 'has chosen to oppose Winston on a number of questions' – the offer of a peerage to General Ironside being one – but concluded that 'Winston, however cavalierly he may treat his sovereign, is at heart a most vehement royalist'. Working flat out to save the King's dominions, he simply did not have time to do what Halifax complained about the day after the Destroyers-for-Bases deal was announced: 'Had to go and see the King at six o'clock who kept me for an hour and a quarter talking about nothing in particular.' In mid-September the Health Secretary, Malcolm MacDonald, told a friend how, due to the King and Queen's demand for personal briefings, he was 'not able to start serious work until about 3.00 p.m.'.[122] The King was not the only member of his family to take up the time of otherwise busy people in this way. As Nancy Astor, the Tory MP and Lady Mayoress of much-bombed Plymouth, was to complain to a friend in mid-August 1940, she 'had the Duke and Duchess of Kent at Cliveden for many more hours than she liked'.[123]

None of this, however, had such potential for disaster as the royal intervention into the arrangements for the future employment of the Duke and Duchess of Windsor. After the fall of France the Windsors had moved south, first to the Riviera and then to the Iberian peninsula. Both Spain and Portugal had neutral but dictatorial regimes, and were dangerous places for a man who some thought had as good a right to the British throne as the present incumbent. Sure enough, a German plot was hatched in Berlin to lure the couple back to Spain and intern them. Both Hitler and Franco were privy to the plan, which was co-ordinated between Ribbentrop and the German Ambassador in Madrid, Eberhard von Stohrer.

The royal family's continuing disapproval of the Duchess, and their refusal to make any gesture whatever of hospitality or friendship, effectively kept the Windsors in the Iberian peninsula. However, questions of protocol can be no excuse for their selfish behaviour in staying in this position of danger. As the Duke was later to write to his brother, 'Ever since I returned to England in 1939 to offer my services and you began to persecute [me] and then frustrate my modest efforts to serve you and my country in war, I must frankly admit that I have become very bitter indeed.'[124] The couple had attempted, foolishly, to establish conditions, 'financial and otherwise', before they returned to Britain, as they wanted to avoid the embarrassments they had confronted on their arrival in September 1939.

This gave the King the opportunity nine months later to pronounce that 'he will hear of no conditions about the Duchess or otherwise'.[125] The Windsors did not think that he was the driving force behind this tough stance. When the son of the leading Spanish fascist, Primo de Rivera, had two conversations with the Windsors in Lisbon, they told him that they had 'less fear of the King, who was a complete nincompoop, than of the shrewd Queen who was intriguing skilfully against the Duke and particularly against the Duchess'.[126] This has long been dismissed as the paranoiac fears of the semi-royal couple, but a letter exists that proves it was substantially accurate.

It was clearly in Britain's interests to get the Duke out of danger, especially considering, as the Ambassador in Madrid, Sir Samuel Hoare, warned Churchill on 27 June 1940, that the Duke 'had always disapproved of the war and considered it even a greater mistake to go on with it'. Hoare believed that

> you will never have peace unless you can find something for him ... anything in G.B. might be troublesome to the Palace and you. I do feel strongly that this is the moment to get them both back to England and clear up the situation. If the chance is lost, there will be a Prince over the water who will be a nuisance and possibly an embarrassment.[127]

If he fell into German hands, as Ribbentrop was plotting, it could have been far worse. But instead of bringing them out of potential danger as soon as possible, the feud between the Queen and the Duchess (their husbands seemed more tractable) kept the couple in uneasy exile in the Iberian peninsula.

By 29 June the Duke's demands were pathetically trifling. He had altogether dropped his request for a job in England and even equal status for his wife. As Hoare reported to Churchill, it had 'boiled down to both of them being received only once for a short meeting by the King and Queen and notice of this fact appearing in the Court Circular'.[128] But even a 'once only' meeting for 'a quarter of an hour' to show that the couple were not in social disgrace was too much for the Palace, which demanded the couple's complete unconditional surrender.

Churchill's idea of sending the Duke to the Bahamas as Governor, which would, in the words of the Colonial Secretary, Lord Lloyd, 'keep him at all costs out of England' and in a backwater for the rest of the war, was inspired. Yet a letter to Lloyd from the Queen, handwritten on Windsor Castle paper and dated 6 July 1940 – the original of which has either disappeared or been destroyed – makes it clear how far the Queen was willing to go in insisting on a decision which she believed to be right. It proves that the suspicions the Windsors had about the 'shrewd' Queen were largely justified.

> I feel certain, [the Queen's letter began] that if the Duke of Windsor is made Governor of the Bahamas then a very difficult situation will arise over his wife. To the average Briton the home and marriage ties are considered sacred, and the fact that the Duchess of Windsor has three husbands alive will not be pleasing to the good people of the Islands. The Church takes the view that the divorce is against that vital and fundamental truth – that family life is the basis of all stability and true happiness in the community, and this fact again will create great difficulties with the Governor's wife.

Having disposed of the moral argument the Queen got down to the personal side of the question:

> The people in our own lands are used to *looking up* to their King's representative – the Duchess of Windsor is looked upon as the lowest of the low – it will be first lowering of the standard hitherto set, and may lead to unimaginable troubles, if a Governor's wife such as she is to lead and set an example to the Bahamas. These objections are on moral grounds, but in this world of broken promises and lowered standards who is to keep a high standard of honour, but the British Empire?[129]

Quite what 'unimaginable troubles' might have beset the Empire if a divorcee became a Governor's wife she left to Lloyd's imagination. But he was ready to be convinced, as two days later he told Bruce Lockhart that he was 'very worried because Winston had told him to make Edward VIII Governor of Bahamas – George VI does not want him there – Lloyd thinks more dangerous in Bahamas.'[130]

'These few words are written from the point of view of general policy,' the Queen claimed, 'they are not personal.' But the only genuine statement of policy she mentioned was that 'the Americans will not approve. It may be dangerous.' There was little evidence to support this analysis; in fact, it turned out so false that the Palace demanded that the Windsors went direct to the Bahamas and not via New York, out of fear of demonstrations of support for them.[131]

Fortunately for all concerned, the Windsors were able to leave Lisbon on 1 August 1940. As a postscript to this absurd but potentially disastrous tale, it is worth recording that two days after landing in the Bahamas the Duke discovered a telegram sent weeks earlier from Buckingham Palace instructing Government House officials that the Duchess should not receive curtseys or be addressed as 'Your Royal Highness'. This puts into perspective the Queen's plea to Lloyd that 'it might ease matters if the Duke and Duchess of Windsor went to the Bahamas as visitors *first*. Then it would be helpful to feel the reaction of the people to her, and give time for thought on the future.'[132]

The Queen's reference to American opinion was significant in the light of the royal family's distinctly sceptical tone towards the American alliance. Over the deal in which Britain received fifty destroyers in return for allowing America ninety-nine year leases on military installations in the Caribbean and Newfoundland, the King wrote to Halifax: 'I do not feel happy about the lease of the bases as the Americans wanted too much written and laid down. Everything was done in their interests, no give and take in certain circumstances.' He added suspiciously: 'I do hope that the Americans will not try to bleed us white over the dollar asset question. As it is they are collecting the remaining gold in the world, which is of no use to them, and they cannot wish to make us bankrupt. At least I hope they do not want to.'[133]

Royal suspicions could only have been heightened by the way they felt they were being treated by the American President. Speaking to Victor Cazalet in July 1941, the King confided: 'It is about five weeks since I wrote [to Roosevelt] and I have never had an acknowledgment yet!' The Queen chipped in and said: 'I also wrote to Mrs Roosevelt and I have never had an answer.' Cazalet told Halifax: 'Naturally I did not go into the discussion but I felt so sorry for them sitting down and writing long letters to the President and Mrs Roosevelt and never even getting them acknowledged. I do think it is quite funny.'[34] Roosevelt's successor was no less underwhelmed by the King. 'George VI sent me a personal letter today,' wrote Harry S. Truman to his wife Bess about 'the limey king' before embarking on a tour of Europe; 'not much impressed ... save it for [their daughter] Maggie's scrap book'.[35] When Truman was invited to stay at Buckingham Palace, he later altered the arrangement in order to lunch on a British battleship instead.[36]

In general, as he told Hugh Dalton later in the war, the King thought that 'the Americans are inclined to be troublesome and take things too much into their own hands e.g. in North Africa'. His brother-in-law David Bowes-Lyon went further, complaining how 'we crawl too much to the Americans. Recent telegrams of the PM to FDR have been almost nauseating in their sentimental and subservient flattery.' When the King met Truman for the first time, he asked the President for his autograph, 'for my wife and daughters'.

One of the major gripes against America by the royal family was over its scepticism about the British Empire. A conversation which the Queen had with the Secretary of State for India in July 1941 shows how she felt about it. 'Dined with King and Queen,' noted Leo Amery. 'Talked with the Queen after dinner mainly about the Empire. She is anxious that we should really be more imperial minded after the war.... On the other hand a bit worried by the unpopularity of the word Empire which we discussed at length.'[37]

September 1940 saw what Churchill called the King's 'narrow escape', when two bombs burst in the quadrangle of Buckingham Palace thirty yards away from him. This stroke of luck for the royal family could hardly have come at a more opportune moment. The very day before the Information Minister, Harold Nicolson, had recorded how 'everyone is worried about the feeling in the East End where there is much bitterness; it is said that even the King and Queen were booed the other day when they visited the destroyed area'.[38] Although this was blamed on communists, it sounds more like the griping of the East End housewife, who was recorded as saying: 'It's all very well for them traipsing around saying how their hearts bleed for us and they share our suffering, and then going home to a roaring fire in one of their six houses.'[39]

Any chippy criticism of that sort was completely silenced by the bombing of Buckingham Palace. 'Almost before the wreckage cooled off,' noted one member of the Household, 'here they were the two of them. Calmly making their way about like people crossing a river on

stones.'[140] The Luftwaffe may have caused little relative damage to the
Palace, but the propaganda value to the royal family was inestimable.
The bombing gave rise to one of the most memorable lines of the war,
when the Queen, with her unerring sense for public relations, said that
it meant that she 'can now look the East End in the face'. Their visits
to the bombed-out streets of the East End, in which Cockneys went into
ecstasies of devotion ('Oh, ain't she lovely, ain't she just *bloody* lovely!')[141]
were the ultimate examples of their success in the 'dignified' part of royal
constitutional duties.

The Mass-Observation organization monitored cinema audiences'
responses to the appearance of national figures on the newsreels shown
before movies. They reported: 'Since the bombing of Buckingham Palace
the King's popularity has risen, as instanced by one out of seven
appearances applauded at the outbreak of war, to over one in three
appearances applauded since the Blitz.'[142] Less comforting to the royal
family was the fact that 'the Duke of Windsor, who is not often seen,
has the highest score of all, maintained throughout the war'. Interestingly,
although Hitler was invariably booed, Goering was only hissed.

The royal family's concern at the popularity of their charismatic
predecessor may have been justified, as a report on newsreel content
compiled in January 1940 showed how out of thirty-eight wartime
newsreels, the King and Queen appeared eleven times and were
applauded only twice and thrice respectively, the same as Churchill and
Hore-Belisha with only half the appearances. The Duke of Windsor,
however, received applause for six out of eight appearances – a three-
quarters success rate compared to the King's one-fifth.[143]

By June 1940 Mass-Observation was reporting: 'There has been very
prolonged applause for Churchill every time ... the Royal Family,
however, receive less applause than before.' Whereas Reynaud and
Generals Weygand and Gort were 'clapped every time they appeared',
this investigation into public figures' relative popularity discovered that
'at the first showing of this the King was applauded for two seconds –
Reynaud had received five seconds applause a minute before – at the
second showing there was no clapping at all. On each occasion the shots
of the Queen were greeted with dead silence.'

Yet after the bombing of Buckingham Palace Mass-Observation's
monitor, Mr England, found, as his report of 6 October 1940 concluded:
'Now the King is clapped, not so much as a man, but as a symbol of
the country.' One speech of his was clapped for seventeen seconds. 'The
Queen, however, though more popular than at the beginning of the war,

is not as well received as she was in 1939.' The Duke of Windsor had not appeared at all except for the newsreel of his installation as Governor of the Bahamas. Then, however, of his four appearances, three were applauded – another 75 per cent hit rate, against the Queen's 7 per cent. 'Once the reel was seen in a half empty West End cinema where responses are usually very low; here he was applauded for seven seconds, a very long period.' The impression that the King's wartime broadcasts were listened to by a large proportion of the population is also false. Mass-Observation estimated that 22.7 per cent of the country listened in 1939, and only 9.3 per cent by 1941.

For all the caricatures of deference which took place when the royal family toured the East End ('Oh, don't you worry about us, Mum. You look after yourself. You're important, but we don't matter much. We'll always be alright as long as we can 'ave a cup o' tea'), there were those such as Chips Channon for whom the royal family 'do not impress me or thrill me at all ... they do their job well, but "the divinity which doth hedge a King" is completely lacking'.[144]

The popularity of their public appearance is also noteworthy, considering how tongue-tied the King could get. After having presented Polish airmen to him with the courtier, Sir Louis Greig, in August 1940, Victor Cazalet recorded that the King 'is hard to talk to and there were long periods of silence. Louis Greig and I did our best.'[145] Leo Amery discovered the same problem. 'HM would not start any subject himself and I had to take up one after another,' he complained. The supreme example of this phenomenon came during an inspection of an ATS unit in Italy in 1944, when 'of each girl in turn he asked, with a slight stammer, "And how long have you been in Italy?" They had all come out on the same day and this date was monotonously repeated down the file, but it never occurred to the King to ask the next girl a different question.'[146]

Halfway through November the King told Halifax that he did not relish the prospect of William Temple, the Archbishop of York, succeeding to Canterbury 'on the ground that he is "a socialist" '.[147] This political partiality, which was noted by other socialists such as Hugh Dalton, did not alter the attitude of such staunch Labour monarchists as the Supply Minister, Herbert Morrison. After a Cabinet Civil Defence Committee meeting that month, Harold Nicolson was amused by 'Morrison's almost sobbing reference to the King's visit. He spoke about the King as Goebbels might have spoken about Hitler. I admit the King does his job well but why should Morrison speak as if he were a phenomenon?"[148]

Chamberlain died in November 1940 and on his deathbed explained to Halifax the nature of his relationship with the King and Queen: 'He felt that he had been in a sense their godfather – or something like it. He said "S.B. [Stanley Baldwin] left a good deal of all that to me" with a chuckle.' Chamberlain had good reason to chuckle; for in the two major crises of his career, Munich and May 1940, the royal family had been his greatest champions, more loyal at the end than his own Cabinet. Even as late as November 1940, after the Battle of Britain and during the Blitz, they still had some doubts about his successor. A line in Amery's diary the day after Chamberlain died tells of Mrs Ronnie Greville's 'great secret that Queen Elizabeth, voicing royal apprehension about [Churchill], had remarked that he was alright as a *war* Prime Minister', implying that she would not like him to be a peacetime one.

Mrs Greville also told Victor Cazalet that 'the King and Queen feel Winston puts them in the shade. He is always sending messages for the nation that the King ought to send.'[49] It was not until Christmas 1940 that the King noted in his diary that he was entirely happy with Churchill, whom he by then thought the best man for the job. During the rest of the war their relationship blossomed, until by 1945 the King greatly regretted his defeat in the general election.

In April 1937 the Select Committee on the Civil List had reported that 'the current usages, ceremonies and traditions centring upon the Crown have become ... a bulwark against dictatorship'. It was an argument presented to help explain the expense of the Coronation, but was it true? In Italy it certainly was not, and the accommodation King Victor Emanuel reached with Mussolini was to cost him his throne. The Hohenzollerns for the most part welcomed Hitler enthusiastically and the royal families in of Yugoslavia, Bulgaria, Romania, Sweden and Belgium all came to arrangements of differing sorts with the Nazis. In Britain constitutional precedent was clear, and it would have been George VI's explicit duty to read a King's speech which had been written by a Mosley government, had one been elected in the 1930s.

Considering that King George VI's sixteen-year reign spanned *Anschluss*, Munich, the Second World War, the communist domination of Eastern Europe, the loss of India and the twilight of Empire, post-war Austerity and Britain's eclipse as a global superpower, one might sympathize with Evelyn Waugh's valediction: 'George VI's reign will go down in history as the most disastrous my country has known since Matilda and Stephen.' Of course, the King was in no way personally to blame for any of this. When writing the official life, Wheeler-Bennett privately told a friend that he was 'depressed about it. He cannot find any evidence that the King exercised any influence or ever thought about anything.'[50]

Whereas in King George VI and Queen Elizabeth Britain found a conscientious and hard-working couple for the 'dignified' part of their duties – indeed, except possibly for their daughter there has been none better – on the 'efficient', political side they represented the most unprepossessing aspects of conventional wisdom, at precisely the time when it was proving dangerously mistaken.

Lord Mountbatten and the Perils of Adrenalin

Louis Mountbatten adored speed. From his earliest years he thrilled to tales of his father's naval exploits, which had usually been executed at 'Full Speed Ahead'. When he was older, he drove sports cars as fast as possible – claiming once to have made the journey from his home in Park Lane to Portsmouth Barracks in ninety-two minutes. That was in 1924, in the days before by-passes, motorways and four-wheel brakes. Servants at his country home in Hampshire used to point proudly at the skidmarks which his lordship left outside the front gates. He was twice blackballed from the Royal Yacht Squadron, as much for his habit of racing his forty-knot speedboat in quiet waters as for his thrusting personality. He led, as Enoch Powell once wrote, 'a jet-propelled life'.

There was an infectiousness to Mountbatten's energy, drive and boyish enthusiasm which tended to close people's eyes to other, less attractive features. For he was also a mendacious, intellectually limited hustler, whose negligence and incompetence resulted in many unnecessary deaths – the numbers of which increased exponentially as his meteoric career progressed. The eager, even impetuous 'Boys' Own' image was never more popular than in the closing days of Empire – and when the hero was good-looking, charming, brave and royal, the combination was irresistible. For all too many people, Mountbatten seemed like the swashbuckling hero of one of his friend Douglas Fairbanks Jr's films. As a result, he was promoted wildly above his abilities, with consistently disastrous consequences.

When the distinguished biographer, Philip Ziegler, wrote his authorized life of Mountbatten in 1985, he brought out what one reviewer called

Mountbatten's 'combination of gargantuan vanity with cockily unlimited self-assurance and conceit'. He also revealed the lengths to which Mountbatten went to exaggerate his achievements and exonerate himself from blame. In the end the author resignedly put a sign on his desk which read: 'Remember. In Spite of Everything, He Was A Great Man.'

Over the great issues of his life, however, and above all over the decolonization of India, Mountbatten was acquitted of error, manipulation and double-dealing. It is a verdict that is no longer 'safe'. Much new evidence has emerged since Ziegler's book was published, and the view of a new generation of historians of Indian independence is radically different from those who fell under the spell of Mountbatten's undeniable charm and *chutzpah*. Mountbatten's reputation must ultimately stand on his record as the last Viceroy of India, and that is now ripe for revision.

Prince Louis Francis Battenberg was born on 25 June 1900. His mother was Princess Victoria of Hesse, a granddaughter of Queen Victoria. His royal connections are important, not least because of the way he exploited them ruthlessly, whilst contriving to make them seem a handicap. What is generally advanced as a defining moment in his life came when he was fourteen, when his father, the First Sea Lord, was hounded from office because of his German lineage. This humiliation is considered to be the primary motivation for Mountbatten's all-consuming ambition. It might also explain Winston Churchill's eagerness to help the son. As the First Lord of the Admiralty at the outbreak of the Great War, Churchill had left the politically sensitive decision to mobilize the Fleet to Battenberg and had also, albeit regretfully, had to accept his resignation soon afterwards. It was the end of a brilliant career, and Churchill reputedly felt guilty for not having done more to combat the xenophobia which brought it about. He was to repay this debt of honour to the son often and heavily, until he came bitterly to regret it.

During the Great War, Lord Louis Mountbatten – his name was de-Teutonized by royal decree in 1917 – served in the North Sea in Admiral Beatty's flagship. Afterwards he went up to Cambridge for five months, where he befriended his cousin, Edward, the Prince of Wales. He read little there; indeed, throughout his life 'his thinking consisted of doing'.[1] His favourite authors were Agatha Christie and Barbara Cartland. Otherwise he 'rarely took up a book unless it was one of genealogy, most especially relating to his own forebears'.[2] His friend Solly Zuckerman noticed that 'sometimes as he read his lips moved, as if he were reading the words aloud'.[3]

On coming down from university, he pulled the necessary family strings to get himself invited on to the Prince's tour of the Empire. This cemented his friendship with the heir to the throne; however, his bumptiousness irritated everyone else on board the ship. His diaries of the tour show that apart from a number of jolly adolescent japes – leap-frogging, ducking, defenestration and so forth – his principal source of amusement arose from the social solecisms committed by colonials failing to address the Prince correctly. In Barbados in March 1920, Mountbatten poked special fun at 'one old fat woman' in a 'crowd of niggers', which at least has the distinction of offending against every canon of political correctness. 'With his characteristic unselfishness,' reads a typically coy sentence, 'the Honourable Piers divulged this priceless information to Lord Claud, who dutifully woke up H.R.H. and told him.'

One looks in vain in the diaries for affection, kindness, generosity or feelings of any sort for anyone – except the Prince of Wales. As well as being boisterous, Mountbatten could also be cruel. In India in February 1922, he encouraged Sir Godfrey Thomas, the Prince's kind, long-suffering Personal Secretary, to 'come and touch this bullock and something very funny will happen to you'. In Mountbatten's words: 'So Godfrey, very trustingly, put his finger on the spot indicated, whereupon the old bullock let fly with his hind leg and caught him on the upper part of his leg. The look of pained surprise that crossed Godfrey's face as he staggered back kept me in fits of laughter the whole afternoon.'

His royal connections saved him from the Geddes Axe in 1922, when defence cuts forced many naval officers of independent means to resign their commissions. As a memorandum by the Duke of Windsor later explained, 'Being related to my father, the Admiralty referred Dickie's case to King George V. Sensing that he had the potentialities of a sailor, I and others recommended his retention in the Service.'[4]

Whilst in India with the Prince, Mountbatten proposed to Edwina Ashley, the granddaughter of Edward VII's phenomenally rich friend, Sir Ernest Cassel. As one historian has put it, 'Sociologically the match was perfect: she had wealth; he had status; they both had ambition.'[5] They were betrothed on St Valentine's Day 1922, having only met one another a couple of times, and married by 18 July, with the Prince of Wales as best man. The marriage soon settled down to a mutually convenient arrangement, rather than a love-match. Cassel had recently left his granddaughter £2 million, at a time when Mountbatten was earning £610 per annum. Her money came in very useful on such occasions as when, in Malta in 1937, Mountbatten collided his destroyer with that of a brother officer during an unauthorized race; it was used to repair both vessels privately without the incident needing to be reported to the Admiralty.[6]

Until the outbreak of war, Edwina Mountbatten was a spoilt playgirl, a woman so self-absorbed that she could forget where she had sent her two daughters and their governess on holiday. Mountbatten, on the other hand, was a doting father. Lady Mountbatten was consistently unfaithful, to the extent that at their Park Lane home, 'the butler at Brook House would be hard put to it to keep "Hugh", "Laddie" and "Bunny" unaware of each other's presence when the three happened to call simultaneously'.[7] He also had Mike, Larry and Ted to consider. She saw no great causes to engage her considerable intelligence in the 1920s and 1930s, and took refuge in nymphomania and bisexuality. One of her lovers alleged that she found sex tedious, but, as one reviewer of her biography has recently put it, that 'must have meant that she spent a large proportion of her life bored stiff'. Despite much gossip to the contrary, it appears that Mountbatten himself was not bisexual. He half-heartedly took mistresses, possibly to avoid being ridiculed or pitied as a cuckold.

Mountbatten opposed the appeasement of Germany. Remembering, perhaps, what happened to his father, he knew that he could not afford to be suspected of being soft on his German cousins. After the war he claimed that: 'Most of my German relations did their best to oppose Hitler.' He also held some foggy but fashionable beliefs in 'progress', telling people as early as October 1936 how he 'would prefer a Left victory in Spain – even Communist'.[8] After the war he greatly exaggerated his anti-appeasement credentials, claiming that Anthony Eden and Lord Cranborne had visited his country home, Broadlands, in 1938 to ask advice on their forthcoming resignations, until it was pointed out that the weekend in question had taken place in September and they had resigned the previous February.

For all his much-vaunted friendship with the Prince of Wales, Mountbatten found that discretion was the better part of valour during the Abdication crisis. The speed with which he transferred his allegiance from Fort Belvedere to the new residents of Buckingham Palace almost left burn marks on the red carpets. He knew that his career would require the active support of the Monarch, be it cousin David or cousin Bertie, and that he could not afford to be caught in the losing camp. Mountbatten visited the Duke of Windsor at Enzesfeld in Austria in March 1937 to assure him that the royal family would be attending his wedding, but in the event he did not even go himself, claiming later that he had not been invited. In fact he had been, and had even written to thank the Windsors for their 'kind invitation' on 5 May 1937. In that letter he said that he had not 'given up all hope' of attending, but thought the chances did not 'look too good', as 'other people have stepped in and have produced a situation that has made your friends very unhappy'.[9]

When he was ordered to pick up the Duke and Duchess from Cherbourg in September 1939, Mountbatten told the officers of his destroyer 'not to be impressed by their charm'.[10] After the war he became something of a figure of fun to the Windsors. One of their companions in Parisian exile remembers how whenever it was announced that Mountbatten had been appointed to an official body – such as the Commonwealth Immigration Commission – the couple would exclaim: 'There's no need to worry; Dicky's on the case!'[11] Despite having seen so little of the Windsors after the war, at the occasion of the Duke's lying-in-state in June 1972, Mountbatten made a BBC Radio broadcast in which he hypocritically claimed: 'he was more than my best man, he was my best friend all my life.... We shall all miss him. But nobody more than myself.'[12]

On the outbreak of war, Lady Mountbatten underwent a total conversion. She abandoned her sybaritic Bright Young Thing existence and became a frenetic organizer of good causes, whilst also working for left-wing, fellow-travelling political ends. It is debatable in which incarnation she was the more insufferable. She became pro-Soviet, anti-colonialist and increasingly caustic about the capitalist system which had given her everything. 'How easy it is for a semi-royal millionairess,' noted Chips Channon in September 1944, after hearing her views on abolishing all forms of monarchy, 'who has almost exhausted all the pleasures of money and position, to turn almost Communist!'[13]

Pursuing his naval career, Mountbatten eschewed the glamorous areas, such as gunnery, and concentrated instead on the more technical side, especially telegraphy and wireless. This proved a shrewd move as neither his intelligence nor his seamanship would necessarily have marked him out for special advancement in the more popular areas of the Service, and with his flashy cars and rich wife he needed to acquire a reputation for solid, hard-working dependability. He proved competent at his job, learning, with Teutonic thoroughness, the name of every telegraphist in the Mediterranean Fleet.

He also made a name as an inventor of naval gadgets and gained great credit in the process. Former shipmates point out that his famous station-keeping device was, in fact, in regular use in the French navy when he patented it. As one who served with him, and who readily admits to 'great affection, almost worship' of Mountbatten, has put it, 'He never invented anything, he just sponsored and helped those who did invent them. In fact he knew nothing about the sea at all, he went into the navy because it was in his family rather than in his blood.'[14] Nevertheless, he was an outstanding Fleet wireless and telegraph officer; it was only when he was given more important posts that his failings came to light.

Once he received his own command, Mountbatten proved a singularly ill-starred destroyer captain and flotilla commander, who allowed his excess of adrenalin and thirst for glory to get the better of him. 'Whenever we went anywhere,' remembers one of his crewmen in his destroyer HMS *Kelly*, 'it was always at top speed.'[15] This impetuosity, combined with a lack of natural seamanship and some bad luck, led to a series of incidents, which meant that, as another who served on the *Kelly* recalls, 'out of the first eight months of war we only spent fifty-seven days out of the dockyard!' The various tales of Mountbatten's incompetence and the chapter of accidents in which the *Kelly* was involved have been well told elsewhere, not least by the *Kelly*'s biographer, Richard Hough, and Ziegler himself.[16] The comedy of Mountbatten's errors would be funny had not sailors died as a result of them.

Yet despite his repeated mistakes, Mountbatten was constantly promoted. It is one of the recurring features of a career seemingly touched by a magic wand that his failures and absurdities were rewarded each time with ever more important jobs. It is not unknown in the Services, any more than in business or politics, that under-qualified, problem people are promoted partly in order to get them out of the way. There was an almost audible sigh of relief in the Admiralty, where an inquiry had recently criticized one of his engagements as not having 'been up to the required standard', when Mountbatten was moved to take charge of Combined Operations in November 1941.

'Among the officers', remembered a destroyer captain who served with Mountbatten, 'there were those of us who ... knew that as a captain in command he was consistently unfortunate, with one glorious defeat after another.'[17] Another admitted that 'no officer I knew had any respect for him as a seaman', yet the ratings under his command adored him. Glamorous, rich, with film-star looks and, above all, royal connections, Mountbatten was a constant favourite below decks. It is a feature of his career that approval of him seems to have varied in inverse proportion to social class. People from similar backgrounds to his, less impressed by who he was and keener to judge him on his merits, often felt scepticism about Dickie's abilities. To them he sometimes appeared a ludicrous figure. His ambition was palpable. One contemporary recalls how, 'when he shook hands with you, you could see his eyes looking around the room for more important people'.[18]

If many of his colleagues and contemporaries saw through Mountbatten relatively easily, his naval ratings – and, later, the general public – worshipped him. This is all the more noteworthy as it was they who usually had to bear the brunt of his mistakes. When suddenly without warning and for no particular reason Mountbatten swung HMS *Kelly* sharply to starboard while going at full speed ahead in the North Sea, it was a stoker who fell to his death rather than a brother officer. His crewmen seemed to have had a far greater capacity to take such losses in their stride than the Admiralty. Social deference was a stronger phenomenon in the 1930s and 1940s than today, and while Wellington once observed that 'soldiers dearly love a lord', in the Senior Service – which boasted King William IV, George V and George VI as alumni – they preferred royals.

For all his errors and ill-fortune at sea, Mountbatten did, however, have spectacularly good luck in the timing of the near-sinking of HMS *Kelly*, which took place when he should have been escorting a British cruiser but had dashed off to chase a submarine and tarried too long.[19] To compound his error, Mountbatten began flashing messages with powerful Aldiss signalling lights. One read: 'How are the muskets? Let battle commence.' This vaingloriousness served to advertise his presence to the Germans, and at 11.05 p.m. on 9 May 1940 battle did commence when the *Kelly* was torpedoed 100 miles west of Denmark. Mountbatten saw the torpedo approach and only had the chance to exclaim, 'Thank God, it's a dud!', before it exploded and ripped a forty-foot tear in the port side, killing twenty-seven men. 'This ship is not going to sink,' he remarked, and for the first time since the outbreak of war he got something right.

Four hours later Hitler unleashed his invasion of the Low Countries, and within days the BEF was on the retreat towards Dunkirk. Mountbatten's courageous action in bringing the *Kelly* home over the next four days made superb copy for British propaganda, in contrast to the depressing news from the continental land operations. Partly due to the need for morale-boosting news in May and June 1940, Mountbatten became one of the first heroes of the shooting war, and, in the best traditions of British military defeats, the Ministry of Information managed to make him seem almost the victor in all his various engagements. Desperate for any good news during the army's retreat, the press ignored the fact that he had been highly inept and had largely brought the sinking upon himself through pointless, gung-ho signalling. The story of Dunkirk has been described as 'the necessary myth'; so, too, was the contemporaneous cult of Mountbatten's personality.

When he got back to the Admiralty after the *Kelly*'s near-sinking, Mountbatten pressed for himself to be awarded the Distinguished Service Order (DSO). His cousin, the Duke of Kent, wrote in to propose him, possibly not without encouragement. Mountbatten asked his wife, as she went out to canvass influential people on his behalf, 'to learn up the arguments by heart and make out you got them from my officers direct'. However, he failed to convince the Admiralty that he had sunk a single U-boat, despite his having claimed two, and the fact of the crippling of the *Kelly* 'once again caused by Mountbatten's own misjudgment and carelessness, not to say disregard of orders,' also tended to count against him.[20]

He was soon back at sea, on HMS *Javelin*, as commander of a flotilla. On the night of 24/5 November 1940, in an action against three German destroyers, Mountbatten turned his five destroyers ninety degrees to port, in contravention of all naval experience since Nelson. One of the officers on board remembered how, 'Not only did it throw the gun-director off his dimly-seen target as the ship, careening wildly over, swung round at high speed, but it offered to the enemy a perfect target for his torpedoes.'[21] Two torpedoes hit the ship and, as Mountbatten recorded, they were 'lucky to escape with fifty killed and the bow and stern blown off'. He was later to claim that there had been five German destroyers ranged against him.

This action was reported in the press as a victory – although none of the German destroyers had been touched – and Churchill invited Mountbatten to Chequers on his return to offer him the post of Vice-Chief of Naval Staff. The initiative for this may have come from the King, who took an active interest in naval appointments. On 29 October 1940 he had written to Churchill with a list of eight captains he thought suitable for the post, adding, 'I have not put Dickie Mountbatten's name down on purpose, but he can be borne in mind.'[22] Mountbatten was flattered by the offer, but turned it down, saying that he 'preferred to remain at sea and finish off their destroyers'. As Hough, in a book generally favourable to Mountbatten, has commented, 'It seemed at the time, to some at least, that he was more likely to finish off his own destroyers.' The next month he received the DSO.

When the *Kelly* was finally sunk altogether, on 23 May 1941, during the Battle of Crete, it was through no fault of her captain. Ever the diligent curator of his own legend, Mountbatten began to tell people, as soon as he had landed, that 'he and his men were machine-gunned in the water by the German planes'.[23] Standing next to him on the bridge when it capsized, and close to him in the water afterwards, was Captain Edward (Dusty) Dunsterville. When asked about the machine-gunning, he answers: 'Please don't ask me. I don't believe it.' Lieutenant Peter Ashmore, who was on the bridge of the rescuing destroyer *Kipling*, also denied any further Stuka action took place after the initial sinking. One of those who pulled the *Kelly* survivors out of the water, Captain Philip Chubb, saw 'no signs that they had been machine-gunned. Often in action people think all sorts of things happen which don't happen.'[24] Of no one was this more true than Mountbatten.

In November 1941, having been promoted again and given command of the aircraft carrier *Illustrious*, then under repair in America, Mountbatten was chosen by Churchill to take over as Adviser on Combined Operations. When he made the standard protest about wishing to stay in the navy, Churchill merely growled: 'What could you hope to achieve except to be sunk in a bigger and more expensive ship this time?' The diary entry of the American military attaché in London epitomizes the illogical stance many took towards Mountbatten's naval career: 'He is in possession of a really fine record as a fighter, having had two ships shot from under him in the war.' As Jock Colville wrote, 'nothing influenced Churchill more in a man's favour than an act of gallantry on the field of battle. It was at least partly to this that Lord Louis Mountbatten owed his promotion, though he subsequently lost favour because Churchill doubted his judgment and disliked his overt support for the Labour Party.' But sheer personal bravery, unaccompanied by mature judgment or operational competence, does not necessarily make a successful commander.

Mountbatten's task at Combined Operations was to singe the Führer's moustache, with a series of operations to harry North-Western Europe and thus keep the maximum possible number of German troops away from the Eastern Front. 'Winston adored funny operations,' recalled Major Desmond Morton, his intelligence liaison officer. 'Unfortunately he seemed unable to connect up funny operations with the great strategic plans, or to see the effect of one upon the other. He addressed his mind to them as the Managing Director of a vast railway might have, as a hobby, a miniature railway in his garden.'[25]

Mountbatten later put about the story that Churchill had chosen him for Combined Operations because of the prescience he had shown over Hitler's June 1941 invasion of Russia. He had predicted that Operation Barbarossa would result in another 1812. In this he was right, but for the wrong reasons. He believed that Stalin had liquidated a Nazi fifth column in the Red Army, and that the Russians would fight stubbornly because 'the Communist ideology was strong'. In his obsessive attempt to rewrite history, always with a view to giving himself a more prominent role, Mountbatten regularly claimed to remember conversations verbatim which had taken place twenty years before and of which he had made no contemporary notes. When, after the war, he wrote for verification of his theory about his appointment, neither Churchill nor Lord Ismay, the Military Secretary to the War Cabinet, had any recollection of it being a factor. Considering that Operation Barbarossa had taken place six months before his appointment, and the war in the East was still going Germany's way throughout 1941, this was hardly surprising.

Although it was the fiasco of the raid on Dieppe in August 1942 which dominated Mountbatten's period as Director of Combined Operations, he was also responsible for planning a number of other raids which could have been equally disastrous. One such was the proposed attack on Alderney in May 1942. The island's population had been evacuated before the Germans arrived, and it was then converted into a fortress. Slave-labourers modernized the heavy Victorian fortifications by adding gun emplacements, pill-boxes and concrete casements. As one of the men trained to capture it said, 'when they had finished it was more like a grounded battleship than an island'.[26]

Nigel Nicolson, one of the Grenadier officers in charge of a raiding party, recalls that, 'in order to cross the wide moat surrounding the strongest of the forts, the Guards were expected to fire grappling hooks at the battlements and swing across, then climb up long ropes and overwhelm the garrison at the top'. Furthermore, 'you would not swing free in an unimpeded arc but smash against the fortress wall, crippling yourself while a torrent of fire descended on your head from a parapet forty feet above'. It was not even intended that the island be held once captured, but that it be evacuated after twelve hours. 'Only in retrospect,' writes Nicolson, 'do I question the absurdity – in fact the suicidal wickedness – of the scheme.' Solly Zuckerman, then serving in Combined Operations, worked out that 'barely a handful of bombs could hit the island itself, let alone the guns that had to be silenced'.[27] Yet the plan was not cancelled because of its unfeasibility, but aborted at the last moment because the navy and air force found their plans irreconcilable, one wishing to operate at night and the other by day. When the cancellation was announced to the guardsmen, they cheered.

In a field a couple of miles outside the seaside town of Dieppe in Normandy, there are the graves of those who fell in the Combined Operations raid mounted on 19 August 1942. 'In the mosaic of victory we gave a precious jewel – our son', reads the gravestone of a nineteen-year-old flight engineer buried there. But his parents were tragically mistaken, for, in truth, contrary to Mountbatten's later assertions, Dieppe contributed nothing to 'the mosaic of victory' and taught military planners hardly anything that common sense and normal research and development would not anyhow have dictated.

Of the 4,963 men of the Canadian Second Division who crossed the Channel in Operation Jubilee, 3,369 were killed, wounded or captured in nine hours. Tanks were landed on the wrong side of a sea wall, on loose shingle on which their tracks could not get a grip. Only eleven of twenty-seven managed to make the esplanade, where they were each knocked out in turn. It was the largest operation on the French coast between Dunkirk and D-Day, and one of the most expensive in lives of the war. The raid was a politically inspired move to encourage the hard-pressed Russians. As so often with military operations stemming primarily from political objectives – such as Gallipoli, or the attempt to protect Greece in 1941 – it turned out badly.

Whatever the strategic imperatives behind it, the planning of the Dieppe raid was Mountbatten's personal responsibility. One may be sure that if it had succeeded, he would have claimed all the credit. It was a combined operation, planned and organized by his department and carried out under his auspices. If he, as Director of Combined Operations, had at any stage – even once the operation was launched – thought it would fail, it was his duty to abort it. For all his and his confederates' attempts to shift the blame elsewhere – on to Lieutenant-General Bernard Montgomery, on to the Canadian Major-General Ham Roberts and many others – it was Mountbatten's operation and his alone.

'I could never see what was hoped to be achieved,' recalls one of Mountbatten's former shipmates, Captain Iwan Sarell. 'Here was a narrow beach and a high sea wall at the end of it, with a tourist esplanade. Once the tanks had landed on the beach there was no way out. The whole thing was demented. No wonder the Chiefs of Staff never agreed to it.' There is still some controversy over whether the Chiefs of Staff Committee ever finally approved Mountbatten's plan or not. Sir Ian Jacob, the Assistant Military Secretary to the War Cabinet, remembered that 'it was a terribly bad plan. The Canadian on the ground was ... made a scapegoat for the whole thing. It was a most ridiculous plan. Mountbatten wanted to have something done and use the knowledge and equipment he had built up.'[28]

Whatever the truth about the intricacies of the planning stages of the operation – at which Mountbatten was not always present – the waters have since been muddied so successfully that today hardly anything about the raid is undisputed. Lord Lovat, who led the commandos' attack, believed that Mountbatten was 'over-bold and prepared to take unjustified risks'. In his autobiography he asked why the attack took place in daylight, what military objective justified the use of a whole division, and why heavy bombers had not been used to destroy the German batteries, harbour facilities, shipping, radio stations and air fields. Lovat was outraged by the way General Roberts had been 'made a convenient scapegoat to carry the can'. When, later in the war, an 'ugly moment' came when Lovat feared that he would have to serve under Mountbatten again, he used 'strong argument' to resist.[29]

Mountbatten liked recruiting friends on to his staff, some of whom were more congenial company than they were competent soldiers. Ten days after the raid, General Loyd, the Army Commander of Southern Command, told a friend that Mountbatten's staff was 'the laughing stock of London'.[30] Mountbatten adored being surrounded by admirers and cronies, acolytes who were nicknamed 'Dickie Birds'. The intelligence operation which failed so spectacularly at Dieppe was directed by the Marquess de Casa Maury, a Cuban playboy and an unsuccessful racing-driving friend of the Mountbattens from before the war, who was months afterwards forced to resign. A special forces operation carried out by Phantom Force prior to the raid, in which German radar equipment had been captured and the area reconnoitred, had concluded that Dieppe was the wrong target, but this advice was ignored.

Mountbatten began his disinformation campaign about the raid as soon as it was over. As with the *Kelly*, he was adept at snatching small victories from the jaws of large defeats. At the Cabinet meeting held the next day, as Leo Amery recorded in his diary, 'Mountbatten told us the whole story of the Dieppe Raid, which while essentially unsuccessful in itself, has certainly led to the immediate destruction of something like one-third of the German air force in the West and will force the Germans to keep not only more aircraft but more troops in France'. Both the figures and prognosis were absurdly exaggerated. When asked by Amery whether it would not have been better to land 'at some undefended point and career around the country doing the maximum amount of damage', Mountbatten was swift to assert 'that he had a scheme of that sort but it had been vetoed'. The truth was almost exactly the opposite; in fact, Montgomery had called off the Dieppe raid 'for all time', and Mountbatten had personally resurrected it.[31]

The next day, 21 August, found Mountbatten speaking to General Eisenhower. According to the diary of the latter's naval aide, Captain Henry Butcher, Eisenhower, who had thought 'the raid was a fiasco', felt a little better about it after talking to Mountbatten, who blamed the defeat on the bad luck of the raiding party having met a German convoy sailing along the French coast just prior to the operation. 'E-boats and flak ships turned loose and raised hell. Couldn't happen once in a hundred times, but it did this time,' recorded Butcher.

It is true that the operation had been hopelessly compromised in a sea battle with a heavily armed German patrol at 3.30 a.m., which had alerted Dieppe's military garrison to the attack, but new evidence uncovered by the Canadian historian, Hugh Henry, shows that the officer in charge of the raid, Captain (later Vice-Admiral) John Hughes-Hallett, received two or more Enigma warnings of the patrol via Bletchley Park, where its presence had been detected thanks to the cracking of the German naval codes. It is inconceivable that Hughes-Hallett, who was with Mountbatten at the time, did not consult his superior over calling off the raid. Writing to a friend, the homosexual Labour MP Tom Driberg, years later, Mountbatten said that 'the incompetence was displayed, I am sorry to say, by the Canadian General who wouldn't follow my plan and insisted on a frontal assault without preliminary bombing'.[32] As overall commander it was Mountbatten's job, not General Roberts's, to decide on matters as important as that.

Few things got past Sir Alan Brooke, the CIGS, and at a dinner at Chequers the weekend after the raid he 'made very outspoken criticism of the manner in which the Dieppe Raid was planned'. Mountbatten, his career on the line, professed himself 'dumbfounded' at this, especially after Churchill asked him on to the terrace after dinner and demanded an explanation about 'how the military side of the Dieppe Raid was planned'. The report Mountbatten submitted to Churchill managed to implicate General Paget for choosing Canadian troops; Major-General Roberts's training of them; Montgomery, who 'attended all the principal planning meetings and personally supervised the military plan, and General Crerar, who later took his place.[33] The only person seemingly not culpable in the entire enterprise was Mountbatten himself.

After he retired, Hughes-Hallett wrote a memoir, entitled *Before I Forget*. Much of it was an explanation of his and Mountbatten's actions during the raid. It catalogues the errors made by everyone involved, except them. In the light of what is now known about Hughes-Hallett's decision to disregard the Enigma warnings, it makes chilling reading. He wrote of 'the spirit of exaltation – almost a joy of battle' which he felt once the raid was launched. 'Perhaps the most remarkable thing about the operation was that it had actually been launched despite so much obstruction and so much frustration that had dogged Combined Operations since early 1942,' he wrote, describing how 'the experience of watching literally hundreds of ships and craft as far as the eye could see wherever we looked, and knowing that all were under our command and committed to the greatest amphibious operations since Gallipoli, had a certain dream-like quality'. It had a nightmare quality for the Canadians, most of whom were in their late teens or early twenties, and who were cut down by the fully alerted German defenders as soon as they emerged from the landing-crafts. In his memoir, Hughes-Hallett wrote off these young men as 'almost entirely devoid of anything that could be called conversation'.

The whole impression given by Hughes-Hallett's memoir is of an operation which he and Mountbatten had set their hearts on, and which was not about to be aborted at the last minute because of some Bletchley decrypts about German naval activity. It is hard not to agree with Nigel Hamilton, Montgomery's biographer, who has written that, as Chief of Combined Operations, Mountbatten was 'a master of intrigue, jealousy and ineptitude. Like a spoilt child he toyed with men's lives with an indifference to casualties that can only be explained by his insatiable, even psychopathic, ambition.'[34] The first rehearsal for the operation, held on 20 June at Bridport, had had to be called off because 'none of the Battalion Commanders had apparently been briefed concerning the Raid'.

Montgomery and Mountbatten watched the second rehearsal, in which everything that could have gone wrong did. Hughes-Hallett recalls how at the inquest held on 8 July he demanded that there should be a formal enquiry into why so many things went awry. However, 'our attention was deflected by a strong rumour that General Marshall was about to be appointed as Supreme Commander in the United Kingdom and Channel area, with Mountbatten becoming his Chief of Staff'. So, rather than embarrass Mountbatten, the inquest was shelved. Three days later, in consultation with Hughes-Hallett, General Roberts and Air Marshal

Leigh-Mallory, he decided to remount the raid without any more rehearsals. Years afterwards, Mountbatten claimed that the raid had been 'elaborately rehearsed'.

Later on in his memoir – a masterly exercise in blame-shifting – Hughes-Hallett asked why the Canadian troops 'failed to exploit their success and got pinned down and massacred'. His only answer was that 'it is not for me – a professional sailor – to adjudicate'. But then he goes on to do just that, blaming in turn Montgomery, Leigh-Mallory, General Roberts, 'too many observers', and even the Canadian troops themselves – to whom he ascribed a degree of cowardice without a shred of evidence to support it. Trying out an argument Mountbatten was enthusiastically to take up later, Hughes-Hallett claimed that 'it would be wrong to exaggerate the losses', which were 'cheap in comparison with the lessons that were learned'.[35] After the war Hughes-Hallett became a Tory MP.

Mountbatten subsequently explained that 'Dieppe taught us lessons which had to be learnt.... But above all it helped *me* evolve what I call my philosophy of invasion.' He further argued that, 'for every one man who died at Dieppe in 1942, at least twelve or more must have been spared in Normandy in 1944'.[36] This was arrant nonsense. A lance-corporal could have told Mountbatten not to attack a well-defended town without proper air and naval cover. As Jacob has said, 'I don't believe for a minute that Dieppe taught us anything about D-Day.' Captain Sarell is even more dismissive: 'There was no lesson to be learned, it was all crazy. Anybody should have known that landing on a beach like that would lead to catastrophe. You didn't need Dieppe to teach you that. Mountbatten was just living up to his Admiralty nickname "Master of Disaster".' In the twelve hours of autobiographical film Mountbatten made for the BBC in the 1960s, the Dieppe raid was allotted a total of three-and-a-half minutes.

When in 1954 Tom Driberg wrote a coruscating biography of his former employer and protector, Lord Beaverbrook, he sent Mountbatten the section about Dieppe for his comments. The raid, in which so many young Canadians had been cavalierly sent to their deaths, had understandably produced in Beaverbrook 'an absolute paroxysm of rage which even those accustomed to his moods found alarming'. Had he known about the overlooked Enigma signals, his anger might have been greater. As it was, at a dinner in Mayfair shortly after the raid he called Mountbatten a 'murderer' to his face. Mountbatten sent the proposed passages on Dieppe from Driberg's book to his friend Peter Murphy for his comments.

Murphy had been a fellow undergraduate at Cambridge. An active homosexual and extreme left-winger, he fitted in well with the Mountbattens' bohemian milieu. In January 1942 Mountbatten recommended his best friend 'very strongly' for a job with the Foreign Office with the commendation that the was 'very pink and almost Communist, but "the sixth best brain in England" '. Some have seen him as a sinister, Svengali-like fixer, to whom Mountbatten turned for advice and support. Sadly we cannot tell exactly the influence Murphy had on Mountbatten, as his papers are kept – along with those of the royal family and the Mountbattens' various lovers – in the secret 'S' file at Broadlands, closed to researchers. His answer to the Driberg enquiry, however, is in the Mountbatten papers at Southampton University, and was written in a vernacular which shows how Mountbatten's circle viewed Dieppe after the war.

'I have always imagined that Max [Beaverbrook] was sniffing up the wrong lamp-post when he called you the murderer of Canadians,' wrote Murphy, 'since it was they who (for exhibitionist and other reasons) had insisted on being murdered!!'[37] Mountbatten stuck closely to the alterations Murphy suggested to Driberg's script, incorporating every one. In his letter back to Driberg, Mountbatten claimed that Montgomery had only called off the raid 'for all time' for reasons of security, whereas it was really, as Jacob has attested, because 'Monty thought the plan absurd'.

Mountbatten need not have been concerned about his reputation with the public after Dieppe. Only a month afterwards, in September 1942, a film appeared which depicted him as one of the great British naval heroes. For all its campness, Noël Coward's *In Which We Serve* is one of the great films to come out of the war. It added immeasurably to the cult of Mountbatten's personality. It is the story of HMS *Kelly*, with Coward playing Mountbatten (Captain Kinross), and even wearing his cap. *Kelly* survivors appeared in the film, which was about a D-class destroyer sunk by dive-bombing during the Battle of Crete, after which the survivors are machine-gunned in the water. 'HMS *Kelly* became the most renowned rather than the most needlessly battered ship of the war.'[38] At one point Mrs Kinross (played by Celia Johnson) asks why her husband was 'making such a rush job' of commissioning the ship. 'I like things done quickly,' answers Kinross/Coward/Mountbatten.

Mountbatten was understandably 'wildly enthusiastic' when Coward told him of the projected film and promised that the Admiralty would give him all the support he needed. He wrote to the Hollywood film mogul, Darryl Zanuck, asking him to help Coward 'for the sake of the

Allied Cause'.[39] He took the script to the King and Queen before trying to persuade Brendan Bracken, the Minister of Information, to lend his support for the film. Coward remembered how at one point, 'when everything was going wrong ... I rang Mountbatten to ask for his help. He told me to come straight round to his house. When I got there he was in the bath, so I sat on the lavatory seat and told him all my problems. He then sorted them out.' In a recent book by the Canadian historian, Brian Loring Villa, Mountbatten has been criticized for spending time visiting the set of *In Which We Serve* which might have been better devoted to planning the Dieppe raid. Certainly, his exertions for the film would doubtless not have been so forceful had it not been so transparently adulatory.

Mountbatten's promotion to Supreme Commander of Allied Forces in South-East Asia was, once again, Churchill's decision. In June 1943 the Prime Minister had told Leo Amery that Mountbatten was 'not big enough' for the task, but because the campaign to recapture Burma was (wrongly) believed to be largely an amphibious operation, he was preferred over the far more experienced Admiral Sir Andrew Cunningham. The logic behind the decision was summed up by Jacob: 'He could talk to the chaps everywhere. The Americans loved the royal connections and he got on well with them. He had [General Sir Henry] Pownall − [Field Marshal] Gort's old Chief of Staff − and a very good one. So it did not matter that he wasn't a very good strategist.'[40]

Montgomery was under no illusions about the appointment: 'Dickie Mountbatten is, of course, quite unfit to be a Supreme Commander. He is a delightful person, has a quick and alert brain and has many good ideas. But his knowledge of how to make war is really NIL.'[41] He contented himself with the fact that, as Brooke told him, with Pownall as Mountbatten's Chief of Staff, 'we have secured Dickie down on to a bit of concrete.... I hope this may ensure that the output of this dynamo is directed in proper channels and does not swing in new directions with every breeze it meets!'

'I came out to do a very hard job indeed. To defeat a very tough enemy,' said Mountbatten with customary egotism. 'My enemy was Japan at the peak of her power.' Montgomery had a slightly less exalted view of Mountbatten's role, noting in his diary in April 1944 that, in South-East Asia, 'the situation is very poor indeed, but again I do not think it matters overmuch; all we want to do there for the moment is to have no disasters'. This was the case for the early period of Mountbatten's time as Supreme Commander, until General Sir Oliver Leese arrived as

Commander-in-Chief of Allied Land Forces in South-East Asia in November 1944 and began planning for the reconquest of Burma, which began on New Year's Day 1945. With Leese directing the strategy, and General William Slim, the Commander of the Fourteenth Army, in charge of tactics, Mountbatten was left to concern himself with diplomacy, administration, morale, long-term planning and public relations.

This set-up suited London well, for as the CIGS's biographer writes, 'Brooke thought Mountbatten an overpromoted nuisance as Chief of Combined Operations ... and a totally inadequate – and professionally unsuitable – Supreme Commander South-East Asia.'[42] Apart from a timely intervention in the Battle of Arakan, when he flew the Fifth Indian Division to Imphal on his own initiative, Mountbatten played a surprisingly small part in the reconquest of the country from which he took his title. Indeed, in the opinion of the distinguished military historian John Keegan, Mountbatten 'took no part in any of the campaigns that contributed decisively to victory'.[43]

As another historian has recently put it, 'there was about almost everything Mountbatten did an element of the makeshift, the insubstantial, the incomplete and the disingenuous'.[44] Yet there was nothing insubstantial about the headquarters Mountbatten set up in Kandy in Ceylon – nearly two thousand miles from the front line. When asked to justify his Combined Operations set-up in 1943, Mountbatten had boasted that 'the Command had grown from about eight thousand to roughly eighty thousand, and headquarters from 23 to 540 people!' A skilled departmental in-fighter, Mountbatten knew the advantages in Whitehall of building up large personal empires, and he soon set about the process in Ceylon, until his staff numbered nearly eight thousand. The King's Pavilion had a band of thirty musicians and nine-hole golf course, but when the American General, 'Vinegar Joe' Stilwell, attended Mountbatten's planning conferences there, his diary records them as 'terrible', 'dumb', 'sad' and 'zero'. For most of the period Kandy was little more than a talking shop. 'I never felt at ease in such make-believe acts,' he recalled. When General Christison of the Fifteenth Army visited Kandy, he 'had the use of Dickie's fabulous Cadillac, though after the first day I dispensed with the motorcycle outriders and the screaming sirens'. General Carton de Wiart, who was Churchill's liaison to the Chinese Nationalist leader, General Chiang Kai-shek, believed that Kandy 'was miles away from the front because Mountbatten had nothing to do'.[45] He nicknamed Mountbatten 'The Archduke Charles', after the elegant but militarily inadequate Hapsburg general.

'In these days when manpower is the vital thing it does make one wonder if it is right', wrote Admiral Sir Charles Layton, Commander-in-Chief in Ceylon, to Admiral Cunningham in February 1944, 'that one Commander should collect together seven thousand able-bodied men and women to plan and supervise operations the scale of which ... is likely to be distinctly less than was contemplated when the staff was estimated at four thousand.'[46] Ziegler excused Kandy by saying 'Mountbattens do not come on the cheap' – which is fine as far as it goes, but it is hard to see what good Mountbatten did by coming at all.

When at last the day dawned on which Slim could take the offensive against the Japanese in Burma, it was he – along with his immediate superior Sir Oliver Leese – who took all the major military decisions and masterminded the campaign. Yet when in the 1960s Mountbatten made an hour-long documentary about the Burma campaign, he claimed most of the credit, relegating Slim's contribution to three minutes and hardly mentioning Leese at all. In the course of the film he also castigated General Stilwell as 'rude' and 'prejudiced', and said that Chiang Kai-shek was 'always a problem' and had 'no conception of our logistical problems'. He called Orde Wingate, the Chindit leader, 'a sick man in a hurry', whose ideas were 'unrealistic'.

Mountbatten may have been no great strategist, as Pownall's despairing diaries show, but he was a genius when it came to public relations. He was a far better handler of men than of ships or armies, and when dealing with press, propagandists and cameramen he showed an ability amounting to brilliance. His troops, too, responded well to the plucky, spontaneous vitality. He had not watched *In Which We Serve* twelve times for nothing. When visiting units in the jungle, he would drive up in his jeep, jump out, 'notice' a nearby packing case (which had been carefully positioned there in advance), leap on to it and ask the troops to break ranks and gather round.

He would then deliver an 'impromptu' speech: 'They tell me you call yourselves the Forgotten Army [pause]. Well, you're not [pause]. No one's ever hear of you [longer pause]. But they will!' It was splendid music-hall stuff and worked every time. Allied to the good looks and famous name was a flesh-pressing ability that any American congressman would envy. Mountbatten had a great ability to remember – or, having been well briefed beforehand, to appear to remember – names. He concerned himself minutely with the business of obtaining honours for people and distributed photographs of himself, in the royal tradition.

These were public relations skills which the British officer class had traditionally avoided, but they worked spectacularly.

One method Mountbatten employed in order to look active, and make Churchill and the Chiefs of Staff think that he was getting things done, was periodically to sack his senior commanders. During his time as Supremo he got rid of no fewer than four Commanders-in-Chief, at least three of whom were, upon almost any criteria except political ability, superior strategists to himself. A general, admiral and air marshal were all removed, in one of Mountbatten's few successful combined operations.

He also got rid of Sir Oliver Leese. Leading Leese to believe that he approved of his plan to give Slim a rest after the fall of Rangoon, Mountbatten promptly dropped the former desert commander when it looked as if the move might rebound against him. Slim had prostate troubles and had asked for home leave, and Mountbatten told Leese to discuss leaving the next stage of the South-East Asia campaign, the attack on Malaya and Sumatra, to General Christison, who had greater experience of the amphibious warfare which it involved. When Slim objected and took steps to protect his position, Mountbatten performed a swift *volte face* and arranged to have Leese sacked. Leese, who had never lost a battle in his life, had been completely outmanoeuvred by Mountbatten, who, except for some Whitehall forays, had never won one.

'I gather I'm carrying the can for Dickie over this,' was all Leese told Christison. 'Oliver's attitude towards Mountbatten,' explains Ian Weston-Smith, Leese's aide-de-camp, 'can only be explained by Army upbringing – you don't ever publicly disavow your Commander-in-Chief. You debased yourself if you did.' After the war Leese never mentioned the affair which effectively ended his brilliant military career, even in his unpublished autobiography. Throughout his life, Mountbatten benefited from the reticence of those he had betrayed, who conformed to a code totally lacking in him.

Brooke interviewed Leese on his return, and years later remembered that 'at the bottom of my heart I had a feeling, and still have a feeling, that, although he may have been at fault, he had a raw deal at the hands of Mountbatten'.[47] Just before Japan surrendered, Brooke's diary entry of 7 August 1945 reads baldly: 'Seldom has a Supreme Commander been more deficient of the main attributes of a Supreme Commander than Dickie Mountbatten.' Leese was a 'a fighting soldier, an old-fashioned Guardsman, straight as a die, he was not prepared for the more devious world of Kandy and Calcutta'.[48]

In the script of a BBC television series on his career, Mountbatten – with Slim, Brooke and Leese all safely dead – gave his own version of events. His attack on Leese was venomous. 'He tried to do a Monty and he wasn't a Monty,' he declared. 'He became very unpopular.... I became more and more dissatisfied with him and when finally he made a complete botch up of the reappointments after the campaign in Burma was over, when he tried to remove Slim from the Fourteenth Army and so forth, it was a bit too much.... So I sent him back. He was a broken man.'

When Montgomery took over the Eighth Army, his new ideas at first made him unpopular, but they led directly to the defeat of the enemy. Similarly, when Leese had first arrived at South-East Asia Command [SEAC] in November 1944, he was amazed to find Mountbatten's strategic plan for 1945 was merely to establish the Fourteenth Army in central Burma. Having been personally urged by Churchill to recapture Rangoon swiftly, he put plans into operation to take the city before the June monsoon.

It was largely his energy and drive which helped to achieve victory in Burma before the monsoon, in five months against the eighteen Mountbatten had envisaged. As Christison has commented, 'It was quite wrong for Mountbatten to take "Burma" as his title ... it should have been "Leese of Burma".[49] It is unlikely that Leese, a modest man with a sense of proportion, would have taken the name of a country over twice the size of Britain.

In the course of achieving this feat, Leese certainly did upset some staff officers in a few of the various SEAC headquarters who resented his distinctive Eighth Army ways. That is sometimes the price of leadership. Mountbatten gave instructions that the television series should only be broadcast six months after his death. He was posthumously attempting to obscure – if not obliterate – Leese's immense contribution to the recapture of Burma. The young age at which Mountbatten was appointed to senior posts meant that he could outlive, and then slander, most of his contemporaries. Not content with falsifying his own record, he attempted to falsify theirs too.

Before Mountbatten's plans to attack Malaya and Sumatra, code-named 'Zipper' and 'Mailfist', could be put into full effect, Japan surrendered. This was fortunate, as they were fatally flawed. When the 25th Indian division put 'Zipper' into operation on 9 September 1945, without an enemy to oppose them, the troops sank up to their waists in the wet sand. Had it not been for Hiroshima, Mountbatten might have been responsible for an attack which would have made the Dieppe raid look like a textbook example of military planning. In typical fashion, Mountbatten later claimed that he had heard the news of Japan's surrender at the Admiralty, dashed across Horse Guards Parade and been the first to tell the Prime Minister, Clement Attlee. Before his story gained currency, however, Jock Colville pointed out that in fact it had been he who had 'brought the news into the Cabinet room, where Attlee was closeted with Lord Louis Mountbatten, who was professing Labour sympathies'.

Whether or not Mountbatten had been professing socialism in London, he certainly promoted it, as well as anti-colonialism, in the territories liberated from Japan which he administered in 1945. These covered over one and a half million square miles and comprised 128 million people. 'We had to do many things all at once and *very* fast,' he said. In November 1944 he had somewhat naïvely written to an American general to say that he thought that Chiang Kai-shek should stop 'trying to keep the Communists outside his organisation'.[50] As soon as the war ended, Mountbatten exhibited his sympathies with anti-Western nationalist movements all over South-East Asia, despite the fact that most had been ranged beside Japan and against Britain. In 1967, during the Vietnam War, he justified his refusal to crack down on the nascent post-war communist movements in South-East Asia: 'I was trying to promote good-will, not ill-will, and I'd do the same thing again.'

In Indonesia, 'Nobody gave me an idea of the strength of the nationalist movements. Edwina was the first person to give me an inkling of what was going on.'[51] He could hardly have had a less objective informant. 'Edwina's left-wing prejudices, American anti-colonialism and the practical problems of administering the liberated territories led Mountbatten to sympathise with the local resistance leaders,' concluded Julian Amery. Mountbatten urged the French to appease the Viet-Minh in Indo-China, the Dutch to deal with Sukarno in Indonesia, and he himself took the view that 'any young Burmese of spirit could have been expected to accept the Japanese offer of independence'. This apologia for treachery – Japan was hardly offering Burma genuine independence – stretched as far as support for nationalists who still wore Japanese uniform, against those who had suffered for their loyalty to the British Crown.

Mountbatten, the 'imperial undertaker who never wore black', was greatly influenced in this by his wife, who Tom Driberg said 'showed an instant strong sympathy with any Asian nationalist'.[52] Sir Reginald Dorman-Smith, the Governor of Burma who had been forced to leave for India when Japan invaded, was given little support by Mountbatten, who preferred the claims of U Aung San, the good-looking, thirty-one-year-old Burmese nationalist leader. This was despite the fact that until March 1945 Aung San had been fighting for the Japanese. As one British intelligence officer, Brigadier Lindop, graphically reported about the Burmese nationalists:

Only on their eleventh hour discovery that they were on the wrong side, and it needed the eruption of our armour into the Schwebo Plain to convince them, have they changed the heading of their notepaper from the 'Greater East Asia Youths' League' to the 'Anti-Fascist League', but without any change of heart or intention.

Lindop found that loyal Burmese villagers

expressed the opinion that we are consorting with our enemies and cannot understand how we accept them. They report the Burmese National Army, acting under cover of being 'allies', demand free food and women from villages they visit and also collect funds for 'the Allied Cause'. In the villagers' eyes the B.N.A. are worse than the Japanese.[53]

Dorman-Smith and Lindop considered early free elections a vital pre-condition for Burmese independence, but Mountbatten seems to have had more than a sneaking sympathy for the nationalist guerrillas' anti-British stance. He certainly took the line of least resistance with Aung San, whose demands increased the more he appreciated the fact.

A good deal of the Mountbatten myth depends upon depicting the British colonial administrators as hide-bound and desk-bound fools, which they very rarely were. For all Mountbatten's later attempts to portray Dorman-Smith as a Blimp, the Governor, as he had explained in a wide-ranging letter to Mountbatten on 10 March 1944, wanted to bring Burma carefully towards self-government after the victory over Japan. His was a policy which, had it become the norm of the withdrawal from Empire, might have left many former British colonies as functioning democracies – especially in Africa – rather than the one-party-dominated states they so often became after the Mountbatten model of a short time-limit and a pre-emptive scuttle was followed.

Mountbatten made the rare error for him of libelling a living former opponent. In 1955 Dorman-Smith was paid damages by *Reynolds News*, which, in a series of articles entitled 'Lord Mountbatten's Brilliant Career', alleged that Burma would have stayed in the Commonwealth had not Mountbatten handed over control to him in October 1945. The source for the newspaper's opinion became very obvious fourteen years later, when, in an interview in *The Times*, Mountbatten made the almost identical allegation that 'Burma would still be in the Commonwealth but I turned it over to people who mucked it up'.[54]

After returning from the Far East, Mountbatten went back into the navy. He was, as he never tired of pointing out, the youngest Vice-Admiral since Nelson, although he rarely mentioned that where Nelson's rank had been substantive, his was merely Acting. In the summer of 1946 he met Zuckerman in Oxford and told him 'the one job he felt he could have done was that of Prime Minister, but that office had been closed to him because of his royal connections.... He and Edwina would have known how to handle the settling of servicemen, and so on.' It was not long, however, before an almost equally difficult task beckoned.

Once again, Mountbatten was to be the beneficiary of a 'necessary myth'. There was little real doubt after the Second World War that India had to be evacuated by the British; the questions were when and how, and whether it would be left entire or partitioned, with a separate Muslim state in the north. The loss of India was necessitated by financial, administrative, strategic and political imperatives, but it became government policy to hail the British retreat as a great achievement in itself.[55]

In Cabinet on the last day of 1946, Aneurin Bevan, the conscience of the Labour left, pointed out that

> withdrawal from India need not appear to be forced upon us by our weakness, nor to be the first stage in the dissolution of the Empire. On the contrary, this action must be shown to be the logical conclusion, which we welcomed, of a policy followed by successive governments for many years. There was ... no occasion to excuse our withdrawal. We should rather claim credit for taking these initiatives.

For reasons of both national prestige and party political advantage, therefore, the Labour Government was determined to present the surrender of India as a triumph for British statesmanship, although it was by any yardstick of *realpolitik* a national humiliation.

Attlee's forthcoming statement on the subject was thus re-drafted to include a long historical preamble. As he put it on 20 February 1947, the policy was made to look like 'the fulfilment of Britain's mission in India'. It was as though Britain's weak position in the years of post-war austerity was in no way to blame for this loss of power and prestige. Far from personifying steady and stately progress towards self-government, Mountbatten chose instead to vacate India with haste, leaving a security situation so fraught with danger that it led directly to the deaths of hundreds of thousands of innocent people and the displacement of millions.

For Attlee the choice was an obvious one. Mountbatten had shown his sympathy for Asian nationalism when ruling over 120 million after the Japanese surrender. He had a plausibility and charisma that was lacking in the incumbent Viceroy, Field Marshal Lord Wavell. It was believed that his royal connections might help blunt the hostility of the imperialist right of the Conservative Party, for whom the whole process of withdrawal was highly distasteful, even if they failed to produce any alternative plan. As at SEAC, it was felt that Mountbatten's impulsiveness could be kept in check by a 'concrete' Chief of Staff, and General Sir Hastings 'Pug' Ismay was deputed to the task. The choice was doubly fortuitous as it was thought that he might also be able to retain the political support of Churchill.

By contrast, Wavell had a plan for withdrawal which, considered naïve and defeatist at the time, in retrospect might well have resulted in far less loss of life than did Mountbatten's. It envisaged an immediate transfer of military forces to the disputed Muslim areas in the northern provinces of the country with a simultaneous transfer of power to the Congress Party in the predominantly Hindu provinces. Attlee feared this might be seen as 'evidence of decline in British power and resolution', or even worse, 'the beginning of the liquidation of the British Empire', as though either could be in any further doubt. On 17 December 1946 the King had recorded in his diary that the Prime Minister felt the Wavell Plan 'savours too much of a military defeat and does not realise that it is a political problem and not a military one. Attlee doubts whether he has the finesse to negotiate the next step.'

When military and security problems inevitably arose from Mountbatten's political 'finessing', the British soon found that they had been so concerned about saving face that they could no longer save lives. The myth that Britain wound up her Indian Empire in an orderly and honourable way, fulfilling her mission of trusteeship to the letter, has largely endured to this day. The deaths which occurred – far greater in number than was ever officially admitted – are routinely presented as being both unavoidable and fewer than might have been expected. The truth is tragically different.

At the end of a speech Mountbatten was delivering to the Joint Services Staff College on 20 February 1947, Rear-Admiral Sir Cyril Douglas-Pennant, the Commandant, looked at his watch and announced that at that very moment the Prime Minister was telling Parliament that

Mountbatten was to be the next Viceroy. When the audience of 200 began to clap, Mountbatten acknowledged it with the remark: 'It is not a matter for applause, I assure you.' In the course of attempting modesty, he hit upon the cold truth.

In the 20th of February 1947 statement, Attlee said that Britain would hand over to a government 'capable of maintaining peace' not later than the end of June 1948. Mountbatten later claimed that he had had the idea of the time limit and had had great difficulty in 'bringing Attlee up to it'. It was intended to concentrate Indian minds wonderfully on co-operating over the details of the transfer of power. Instead, it 'destroyed any hope of preserving Indian unity. [The Muslim League leader, Mohammed Ali] Jinnah had only to say no for any proposal short of an independent Pakistan to have his way. The Congress leaders could hardly beg Britain to stay. From the moment Mountbatten landed in Delhi, partition became inevitable.'[56] It was perhaps inevitable anyway, but the announcement of a time limit, especially such a short one, exacerbated precisely those pressures on the Government of India that it was designed to allay. Telling the two sides where the finishing line would be encouraged both to transform what should have been an orderly march towards self-government into a sordid scramble for power.

The allocation of a mere sixteen months to wind up three and a half centuries of British presence imposed fearful strains on an already seriously over-stretched civil administration. It also gave Britain no room to manoeuvre, and made communal violence more, rather than less, likely, because of the ever-present reminder that on 1 July 1948 there would be either a Congress-dominated India or a partitioned sub-continent. This proved a spur rather than a disincentive to disorder. Muslims, Sikhs, Princes, Untouchables and all the other natural opponents of a Hindu-ruled India were given a date by which they had to establish their positions, by violence if necessary, in order to forestall the dictatorship of the majority. The story of the transfer of power has until recently been written from an almost entirely pro-Congress, almost triumphalist, point of view. Scholars are only just starting to challenge this historical orthodoxy.

Attlee later called his choice of Mountbatten 'an inspiration', explaining that he was 'an extremely lively, exciting personality. He had an extraordinary faculty for getting on with all kinds of people, which he had shown when he was Supremo. He was also blessed with a very unusual wife.'[57] The general reaction to his appointment was one of acclaim, although Sir John Reith bemoaned the fact that 'more can be done by the Viceroy in the next year than in the last hundred, and they choose that fraud and counterfeit'. Brendan Bracken thought Mountbatten 'a miserable creature, power-mad, publicity-mad', who had fallen under Nehru's spell at Singapore at the end of the war.

Churchill, to his lasting regret, approved the appointment. When Larry Collins and Dominique Lapierre were writing a hagiographical account of his Viceroyalty for their book *Freedom at Midnight*, Mountbatten was at pains to emphasize this, telling them: 'I showed you that cutting from *The Times* when he had paid a tribute, don't forget. The particular thing is – in his congratulations ... Winston Churchill said he wished to congratulate the Government on their perspicacity in appointing someone of my intelligence. He made some remark, you remember, I do want that quoted.'[58] Speaking into a tape-recorder, Mountbatten was encouraged by the sycophancy of their questioning ('Did you have an enormous sense of relief and achievement?', 'Could your personal conviction explain your huge success in India with the Indians?') to indulge his fondness for rewriting history.

Mountbatten flew to Delhi on 22 March 1947 and was sworn in as Viceroy two days later. As he told Collins and Lapierre:

> What a ceremony! Everyone who mattered was there. All the Princes. All the leaders. All the diplomats. I put on everything. My white full dress uniform. Orders, decorations, medals, the whole lot.... Obviously I wore the Garter. Then I wore the Star of India, I was the Grand Master of the Order. I wore the Star of the Indian Empire and then I wore the Royal Victorian Order and that made the four; that's all you're allowed to wear. And I wore the *aiguillettes* as personal aide-de-camp to the King-Emperor.

It was claimed that the justification for the pomp at which the British Raj excelled was designed to impress the credulous natives. From Mountbatten's schoolboy glee at the pleasures of dressing up, that patronizing explanation was not perhaps the whole story. 'What a popinjay,' said Harold Macmillan of Mountbatten, 'all those uniforms!'[59]

Not content with the splendour of the ceremony, Mountbatten characteristically also felt the need to denigrate someone else, in a way few true gentlemen, let alone a former Viceroy, would have done. He told Lapierre and Collins that 'Lady Wavell looked exactly like my wife's maid. She was very, sort of, mundane. And people out there were enormously struck by the difference.... we went in with a *panache* which was entirely lacking before.' He forbore to mention that amongst the less 'mundane' differences between Lady Wavell and Lady Mountbatten was the fact that the former was in love with, and faithful to, her husband. The

Mountbattens had only been in India a week before the Private Secretary to Field Marshal Sir Claude Auchinleck, the Commander-in-Chief of the Indian army, was noting in his diary that 'Nehru's relationship with Lady Mountbatten is sufficiently close to have raised many eyebrows'.[60]

Mountbatten plunged himself into negotiations with the principal Indian leaders as soon as he landed. 'The sense of urgency took hold of me at once and never left me,' he said. He had known the Congress leader, Jawaharlal Nehru, since their time together in Singapore at the end of the war. A man who used his own charm as a weapon, Mountbatten could also fall prey to that of others, and he was soon bewitched by Nehru's personality. He saw Nehru as an aristocratic radical leader in his own mould. 'When Nehru began to call Edwina and me his "dear friends",' Mountbatten was later to gush, 'I began to get the feeling that we were halfway home.' Nehru professed to believe Mountbatten to be 'a straightforward English socialist'.

From the moment of their first meeting on 5 April, Mountbatten and Jinnah, the Muslim League leader, failed to establish a personal rapport. The Viceroy found Jinnah 'most frigid, haughty and disdainful'. They discussed all the possible outcomes, and Jinnah asked for the Indian army to be divided fairly between India and Pakistan after a slow and orderly British withdrawal. He found the June 1948 deadline too early, and melo-dramatically asked whether it was Mountbatten's 'intention to turn this country over to chaos and bloodshed and civil war?'[61] Jinnah might be criticized for not making more of an effort with Mountbatten, but he had seen through the Viceroy, and both knew it. 'Jinnah was a lunatic,' Mountbatten told Lapierre and Collins. 'He was absolutely completely impossible. I don't think we could have waited for him to die because I don't think ... we could have afforded the time, nor could we have felt certain of it.'[62] Other words the ex-Viceroy used to describe the founder of Pakistan include 'evil genius', 'clot', 'psychopathic case' and 'bastard', whilst all the time he claimed in public that he had been totally impartial.

A conference of all India's provincial governors took place on 15/16 April 1947, the main purpose of which, according to one historian, was 'to prepare the ground for the new line rather than listen to the advice of the old Indian hands'.[63] Mountbatten's later claims that no one expected that the massacres in the Punjab would take the form they did are exploded by the warnings given before and during that conference by Sir Evan Jenkins, the Governor of the Punjab, and others. Jenkins warned that partition of his province would cause 'an immediate blow-up', and on the day before the conference he met the three senior members of the Viceregal staff – Ismay, the Chief of Staff, Sir Eric Mieville, the Principal Secretary, and George Abell, the Private Secretary – to 'warn that partition would mean a huge military problem'.

Mountbatten, however, was 'little impressed by the opinions of the Governors of the Punjab and Bengal about the horrific consequences of partitioning their provinces'.[64] His instinctive belief that he knew the Indian situation better than men who had spent their entire working lives there was a recurring feature of the Viceroyalty. Since his visit with the Prince of Wales a quarter of a century before, he had only spent a few months in India in the winter of 1943, before moving to Kandy in Ceylon. Nevertheless, he was quick to denigrate the views of those professional administrators who had devoted their careers to the subcontinent, often portraying them as blinkered, bigoted Blimps. He later observed: 'I thought I had a great advantage in not having devoted my life to India ... they were too steeped in the old British Raj thing and they would always try to find a solution which would do the least possible violence to the system as it then existed.' It is true that they did not, like him, believe that 'Mahatma Gandhi will go down in history on a par with Jesus Christ.'[65]

Amongst those on Mountbatten's staff was Alan Campbell-Johnson, his Press Adviser, who became the first and only Press Attaché to a Viceroy. Campbell-Johnson had joined Mountbatten as War Diarist at Combined Operations, aged twenty-nine, and had performed an invaluable function as public relations officer to the Supremo at SEAC. There he had received memoranda from Mountbatten asking him to emphasize 'my personal intervention' in various engagements, and to play down the roles of commanders such as Somerville, Giffard and Peirse, who were about to be sacked.[66] One of the founders of the modern PR industry, Campbell-Johnson was a talented and tireless aide. He attended almost all staff meetings and travelled constantly with the Viceroy. His diaries of the period, entitled 'Mission with Mountbatten', constitute an invaluable record.

The propaganda Campbell-Johnson put out at SEAC was considered some of the best in any theatre of the war, and helped ensure that the Fourteenth was never really the 'Forgotten Army' and that Mountbatten was certainly never the forgotten Supremo. Writing in the PR industry's house journal, *Persuasion*, in 1949, Campbell-Johnson recorded how he gave 'press guidance' to the 100 correspondents resident in Delhi. Sitting in on staff meetings also meant 'the field was clear for me to ensure that the PR implications of any proposed action were considered promptly and at the highest level'. As such, he can lay claim to have been the first political 'spin-doctor'.

Mountbatten started off in India as he meant to go on. At the second staff meeting he declared himself 'very much in favour of Honours on a considerable scale being granted to members of Princely families'. He instructed Campbell-Johnson 'to ensure that all issues of the Court Circular were in future rendered to him, through the Personal Secretary, for approval'. He also wanted it stated that he 'received' people at audiences. Top of the agenda for the fifth staff meeting on 29 March 1947 was a directive to Campbell-Johnson 'to find out and inform him whether the complete lack of publicity given by *The Statesman* that morning to the party he had given the previous day ... was deliberate, and whether an account of this event had been sent to London'. By the seventh item, the Viceroy was directing his Military Secretary 'to arrange that the actions of only himself, Her Excellency and the Hon. Pamela Mountbatten [their younger daughter] were reported in the Court Circular', as it had come to his attention that news about Ismay had somehow crept in. An inordinate amount of time was later spent by Mountbatten on the ceremonies for the transfer of power. Discussion of them, and 'Flags for the New Dominions', often came far higher on the meetings' agenda than, say, 'Situation in the Punjab', which was usually relegated to the end.

On 7 July 1947, for example, when the province was in uproar over the resignation of the Nawab of Mamdot from the Punjab Security Committee, Mountbatten was in his element, telling his staff that 'it would be a good plan for him to have a special Governor-General's flag. This would probably be blue with a gold crown and the name of the Dominion.' Discussions about flags, titles, salutes, honours, cars, uniforms, medals and toasts were a constant feature of these meetings, and had to be settled at the very highest level. On 5 August Mountbatten was considering whether his Buick limousine should be flown to Karachi.[67] In matters relating to his own prestige, Mountbatten never delegated.

Also evident from the minutes of these meetings is the clear and unrelenting bias – so long and vehemently denied – which Mountbatten felt against Jinnah, Muslims and Pakistan. The examples are legion. At his fourth staff meeting, after Mieville had observed that 'Pakistan would definitely be unworkable without Calcutta', Mountbatten said that 'Chittagong might suffice as part of Eastern Pakistan instead', as though these Hill Tracts, comprising roughly half a million people, might in any way compensate Pakistan for the loss of the greatest entrepôt and largest city of India.

The question of a referendum in Calcutta arose on 25 April. Jinnah told Mountbatten that he thought the Muslim League could win there. The prospect of Calcutta, with its vast Muslim population, cleaving to Pakistan rather than to India worried Mountbatten. He had a mere fortnight earlier 'intended to make it clear to Mr Jinnah' that areas within provinces would have to be given the right to decide which country to join, but suddenly he came up with objections. It was 'not time for a plebiscite anywhere'; surrounding areas would have to be included in the vote; it might 'lead to bloodshed and excessive delay'; Calcutta might become an open city; and any referendum might have to 'be held at a later date'. As Mountbatten revealingly told his staff, 'it would be most undesirable to lay down a procedure for self-determination which would give the wrong answer'. This statement alone shows how much of a democrat he really was. The staff's true feelings were articulated by Abell, who said that 'Calcutta was a creation of the British and Hindus as far as capital investment was concerned'.

At staff meetings, items such as the 'Plan of Action in the Event of Possible Clashes or Disturbances in the Neighbourhood of the Borders Between the Two Dominions' were discussed openly in front of the Hindu, V.P. Menon, who was invited to attend more and more as time progressed. No Muslim was allowed to be present.[68] India was thus made privy to British contingency plans in the event of open warfare breaking out between India and Pakistan. It was little short of a scandal that Menon, officially Mountbatten's Constitutional Adviser but also clearly a senior office-holder in any future Congress Government, should attend such sensitive staff meetings. As a future Prime Minister of Pakistan was later to complain:

> It was known to Mountbatten, and indeed to all, that V.P. Menon was, to use Alan Campbell-Johnson's phrase 'the trusted confidant of [Congress politician] Vallabhbhai Patel', who was thereby not only kept informed of the inner councils of the Viceroy, but was also able to influence the Viceroy's policies through his mouthpiece. If a Muslim officer had been in V.P. Menon's position and was known to maintain a liaison with Jinnah, no Viceroy would have tolerated it without laying himself open to charges of partisanship.[69]

On 25 April Mountbatten was musing to his staff about 'whether there were likely to be sufficiently intelligent Muslim officials to administer Pakistan'. On the next day, 'His Excellency said that the last thing which he wanted to see, and it would indeed be most disastrous, would be that

Hindustan [India] left the Empire irretrievably and Pakistan remained within irretrievably.'[70] By early May, when Nehru complained about the Governor of the North-West Frontier, Mountbatten said that although 'he was personally convinced that Sir Olaf Caroe was completely honest', nevertheless 'circumstances might lead to his having to call for his resignation'.

When, on 10 May, Mountbatten returned from a crucial meeting with the Congress leaders, Nehru and Krishna Menon, where they had suggested 'the early transfer of power to India on a Dominion status basis', Mountbatten said that he intended to discuss it with the Congress Party boss, Sardar Patel, but 'he did not intend to raise the matter with Mr Jinnah until after the announcement of the Plan'. Six days later he told his staff 'that he had already cautiously tried out threatening Mr Jinnah'. He warned that he might pass on power to an all-India interim Government with Dominion status. Jinnah had taken this threat 'calmly' and said that he could not in any event prevent such a step. This had Mountbatten telling his staff 'that this abnormal reaction, which was typical of Mr Jinnah, was rather disturbing'. Mountbatten suspected that Jinnah 'would derive great satisfaction by going down to history as a martyr for his cause, butchered by the British on the Congress altar'. This is not language he ever used against any Congress leader, despite the fact that Jinnah was merely demanding a constitutional outcome in which the sub-continent's 92 million Muslims would not be forced into a single state inevitably dominated by 255 million Hindus.

On 10 June Mountbatten, who four days earlier had said that he hoped Pakistan 'would not set up diplomatic missions in too many foreign countries', told his staff that, 'to his mind, Pakistan was breaking away from India', rather than starting afresh as a new Dominion simultaneously. It took Ismay to point out to him that the idea that Pakistan was somehow seceding from an established authority 'was highly derogatory'. But Mountbatten was unconvinced; he said that he could not see the difference 'whether it was to be stated that the Provinces which were going to make up Pakistan were seceding from India, or whether India was going to be divided into two'. The reason he gave for this myopic stance was that 'Pandit Nehru had always stressed the continuity of India as such'. The Viceroy then said that he 'had tried to impress on Mr Jinnah the point that, if the latter obtained his sovereign independent state and extracted the assets to which he was entitled, he should be satisfied'.

Mountbatten's bias seems to have stemmed from the way in which his modish leftist views coincided well with the Congress hierarchy's plan for the sub-continent to be run as a secular, centrally controlled, socialist republic. It was bound to be the stronger and richer Dominion, run by people he and his wife liked. Time and again carrots were dangled for Nehru, whereas Jinnah only ever experienced the stick. Mountbatten could hardly have been surprised when his plan to become Governor-General of both Dominions after independence came to nothing. Equally futile were his attempts to persuade Jinnah to adopt a flag for Pakistan which had a Union Jack in the top corner. These seem to have been largely cynical and designed solely for the independence ceremonies, however, for as Mountbatten wrote to Jinnah on 24 June: 'I need hardly tell you that if you adopted this flag to begin with, there would be nothing to prevent your changing it after your new constitution had been adopted.'[71]

The fear that Calcutta and large parts of the Punjab and Bengal might wind up in a 'big' Pakistan after referenda spurred Mountbatten to sudden action. It would be impossible to hold such votes if he drastically shortened the time of transfer and kept the drawing of the frontiers in British hands. As early as 9 May 1947 he had begun thinking in terms of withdrawing that year, rather than in 1948, telling his staff that the administrative problems 'could be overcome, in the same way that apparently insurmountable difficulties had been overcome during the War'. An earlier than expected transfer of power would, he said, have six main advantages. Firstly, it would gain the United Kingdom 'tremendous credit'; secondly, it would lead to a quicker 'termination of the present responsibilities'; 'a request by India to remain in the Commonwealth would enhance British prestige in the eyes of the world, this factor alone was of overriding importance'; fourthly, it would be 'of the greatest advantage to the prestige of the present British Government in the eyes of the country'; it would also make India more likely to stay pro-British; and lastly, he felt that 'even after three years the Indian Army would still need British officers'.

So amongst his closest advisers Mountbatten did not spell out the reason that he was later to present for quitting India in August 1947 rather than on the original date of June 1948: namely that the level of communal violence meant that it was vital to transfer power before catastrophe overtook British India altogether. This is hardly surprising, as it would not have convinced the experienced public servants, who knew that an over-hasty withdrawal would inevitably lead to more rather than fewer deaths.

The true reasons for Mountbatten's 3rd of June Plan, which stated that power would be transferred to a partitioned India and Pakistan at midnight on 14 August, were to do with the prestige of the Attlee Government, with keeping India – but not necessarily Pakistan – in the Commonwealth, and with the future employment of British officers after independence. After 250 years of responsibility there, Mountbatten gave Britain a mere seventy-three days to get out. He had special calendars printed which counted down the number of days left. It fitted in perfectly with his love of action. Mountbatten and Ismay presented the Plan to the British Cabinet and flew back to India on 31 May. As Ismay remembered about the flight, 'The idea of a reasonable degree of comfort never entered his head. Speed was all that mattered.'[72]

As the historian of the Muslims of British India records, the 3rd of June Plan 'was a bitter pill for Jinnah to swallow. It represented the disappointments of all those hopes for a "big" Pakistan.... Jinnah would not record his acceptance in writing but only by a silent nod.'[73] At that meeting, held at 10.00 a.m. on 2 June, Mountbatten brusquely told the leaders of the communities that, in view of the 'terrific sense of urgency', power was to be transferred as soon as Parliament passed the India Bill.[74] Jinnah then asked for a week to get the opinion of his movement, but 'Mountbatten said he could not wait for a day'.

Mountbatten later told Lapierre and Collins that 'the reason for speed was not to go and muck up Pakistan', even though they had not suggested that it was. He might have been protesting too much. 'It was because the thing was breaking up in my hands.... I could feel the damn thing simmering. It's like standing on the edge of a volcano and feeling the moment of explosion.' He never explained why India and Pakistan should have been more likely than Britain to cope with such a situation. Historians and commentators, who are usually highly critical of hypothetical or counter-factual history, have in this case been the first to state categorically that had Mountbatten stuck to the original 1948 deadline, the massacres would have been worse.

Many who had served there, such as Sir George Cunningham, a former Governor of the North-West Frontier and Private Secretary to the Viceroy, believed the Punjab disturbances were the direct result 'of Mountbatten's unwisdom in accelerating the date of partition so suddenly. I am sure that if the Punjab had been given time (say eight or nine months) to sort out their services properly the terrible massacres of August–September–October would never have happened on anything approaching the scale that they did assume.'[75] An extra nine months was precisely the period the Government of India originally had under the terms of Attlee's 20th of February statement, before Mountbatten's excess of adrenalin got the better of him. Sir Ronald Harris, the Private Secretary to Lord Listowel, the Secretary of State for India, recalls: 'All our instincts said, surely it could have been done without it leading to these terrible events. It is arguable that the time limit was too tight. All the senior officials in the Indian Office were most unhappy.'

Mountbatten had never had any experience of the administration of India, and Ismay had also been out of touch with it for over a decade. As one historian of Partition has pointed out:

> To both Mountbatten and Ismay Hindu–Muslim conflict looked extremely dangerous and ugly. They probably did not think, as a Deputy Commissioner or a [Provincial] Home Secretary would have done, that law and order could be brought about by using extremely ruthless and drastic methods. Instead of taking the view that power should be transferred only after law and order had been brought about, they thought that the situation might deteriorate into anarchy for which the British would be blamed.[76]

Whenever he had to exhibit toughness, Mountbatten took the most invertebrate line possible. Staff meetings minutes are full of instances in which he decided against cracking down on anarchy and communal violence, actions which would have been second nature to earlier Viceroys. Even Lord Irwin – the most liberal Viceroy of all – said that fewer things had given him more pleasure than issuing a press law which muzzled the more extreme section of the Indian press. But such a course repulsed Mountbatten, who prided himself upon his progressive credentials. He had shrunk from it in Burma in 1946, and at his second staff meeting he 'decided to take no action over the provocative articles on communal issues which were appearing in the Congress and Muslim League papers. All he would do was ask them "to exercise restraint".'

Desperate for the approval of Nehru, liberal Indian opinion and the approbation of the British and American publics, Mountbatten deliberately adopted a soft approach to security issues. In his judgment, speed of transfer might avoid the troubles. In practice his decision precipitated them. It was a situation entirely of his own making. On 26 July, when an Emergency Committee was desperately required and disturbances in the Punjab had become extremely serious, Mountbatten was discussing the designs for his new flag as Governor-General at the morning staff meeting. Nothing had been done to facilitate the transfer of populations in less than three weeks' time, as he had promised at the press conference which launched the 3rd of June Plan, and the refugee camps were insufficiently supplied. But Mountbatten did express concern that 'the lion's whiskers on the specimen brassards and flags handed round at the meeting were too big'.

The timing of the transfer of power – midnight on 14/15 August 1947 – was chosen by Mountbatten because it was the second anniversary of the Japanese surrender. There was no greater planning or reasoning to it than that. Mountbatten later boasted: 'The date I chose came out of the blue. I chose it in reply to a question [at the press conference to announce the 3rd of June Plan]. I was determined to show I was master of the whole event. ... This ludicrously early date really put the cat amongst the canaries, really frightened them all.' When asked if it was a surprise to London, he answered, 'news to everybody. I heard myself saying it!' Yet in his 'Report on the Last Viceroyalty' he wrote that 'the decision to transfer power on 15th August was not made hurriedly'. Both Campbell-Johnson and H.V. Hodson, the man Mountbatten chose to write the official history of Partition, have repeated the line that it was almost off-the-cuff, but in fact the new date had been cleared by the Viceroy with Lord Listowel, the Secretary of State, in a letter sent the day before.[77] Mountbatten chose that day despite the fact that it coincided with a Muslim religious festival.

Often hailed as a triumph for Mountbatten, in fact the press conference which launched the Plan was full of such remarks as: 'I am the mechanic who keeps the car running, but I do not actually sit in the driver's seat.' With uncharacteristic modesty, Mountbatten severely underestimated the strength of his position as Viceroy if he had persuaded himself that he was merely the mechanic. To Lapierre and Collins his view was different. He told them: 'One had an immense feeling that was it, this was being endowed with an almost heavenly power. I realised that I had been made into the most powerful man on earth.' As the historian of the end of empire, R.J. Moore, has pointed out, 'Not only some Conservatives but also the Chiefs of Staff favoured striking separate arrangements of Dominionhood with non-Congress areas (i.e. Princely States, Sikhs, Muslims, etc.), if Congress eschewed the Commonwealth.'[78]

Mountbatten resisted all attempts to reinforce British India militarily prior to the transfer of power. As he told his staff meeting on 9 May, 'If India was granted Dominion Status [i.e. independence within the Commonwealth] in 1947, it would clearly be desirable for all British forces to leave the country as soon as possible.' This policy was to have horrific consequences when the Punjab divided. He was soon to fall out with Field Marshal Auchinleck, the Commander-in-Chief, both over this and because of his consistently pro-Congress policy. In order to offset this criticism, Mountbatten cleverly attacked 'The Auk' for being 'branded pro-Pakistani'.[79]

It is argued that Mountbatten had little power to suppress the communal disturbances – which constituted his public justification for quitting India early. Against that, however, there is the evidence of two staff meetings which took place on 31 May, just before the 3rd of June Plan was announced. The attention of an earlier meeting the same day had been drawn to a letter from the Governor of Bengal, which warned that Partition was 'very likely to lead to very serious trouble', and Mountbatten said that 'the present laws provided for the use of minimum force to suppress disturbances and that he had no intention of attempting to change these laws'. In fact, all that was required was a tough interpretation of the powers he already possessed, but drastic action – such as internment of potential terrorists – he considered illiberal, and so the disturbances continued. These in turn created exactly the 'very serious situation' that he needed to justify his 3rd of June Plan, and thereby to keep India in the British Commonwealth, as well as to 'muck up Pakistan'.

Persuading India to join the Commonwealth consumed more of Mountbatten's time and energy than did security questions. 'The Commonwealth meant so much to me,' he was later to explain, 'and with this emotional background I began to grasp at every straw in the right direction.' It now seems that the reason for his obsession with the issue did not, as might have been expected, arise from any strategic notion of keeping India out of the Soviet bloc, but instead from the desire for international prestige – his own and Britain's. The threat not to join the Commonwealth gave the Congress leaders a lever over Mountbatten which they used to the full.

One of the most serious defects of the 3rd of June Plan was the absurdly short length of time it gave the eminent London barrister, Sir Cyril Radcliffe, to draw the frontier between India and Pakistan. He had never set foot in India before, and later said that he could have done the job properly had he been given two years.[80] Mountbatten gave him forty days. His Boundary Commission was ordered to finish its work by 14 August. It was an impossible task, further compromised by the early discovery that the four Hindu and four Muslim senior judges assigned to help Radcliffe could not work together and had to be dismissed, leaving him to continue on his own.

Mountbatten knew from the start how explosive Radcliffe's decisions (known as the Awards) were likely to be. At the very staff meeting in which he emphasized to Radcliffe that his report had to be finished by 14 August, Mountbatten 'considered a telephone message from the Governor of the Punjab concerning certain difficulties which had arisen' after the Commission's first meeting. Put very simply, Hindus in the western part of the Punjab were terrified of being caught in Pakistan after Partition, whilst Muslims in the eastern parts of the province felt identically about remaining in India. They feared attack, confiscation of property, religious discrimination and persecution, whatever guarantees were given. The moment the Award was announced, and they discovered to which country their towns and villages had been allocated, people left in the wrong state would migrate to that of their co-religionists.

The situation was further endangered by Sikh threats to attempt to carve out a separate Sikh state by the use of terror, particularly directed against their Muslim neighbours. As early as March 1947 the senior Superintendent of Police in Delhi was predicting that 'once a line of division is drawn in the Punjab all the Sikhs to the west of it and all the Muslims to the east will have their penises chopped off'.[81] It has been estimated that as many as twelve million people emigrated from one side of the border to the other during the four months after Partition. Once the refugees began pouring over the frontiers, in vast straggling columns of tens of thousands each, they fell prey to gangs of the opposing side, armed with Second World War weapons and bent on communal revenge, rape and murder.

The Radcliffe Commission was instructed 'to demarcate the boundaries of the two parts of the Punjab on the basis of ascertaining the contiguous majority areas of Muslims and non-Muslims. In doing so, it will also take into account other factors.' Exactly what these 'other factors' were was not spelt out, but if a letter from Listowel to Mountbatten about the Commission having 'terms of reference such as will keep the Sikhs quiet until the transfer of power' is indicative, they can be assumed to have had security, as well as geographic, religious and economic aspects.[82]

Radcliffe did his best. Ten days of public hearings were held in Lahore, but he did not attend these in person as he had to be in Bengal. In his Final Report he announced that it was 'impossible to arrive at any agreed line'. So he had to impose one. He was the first to admit that 'the drawing of a boundary line cannot avoid disrupting such unitary services as canals, irrigation, railways and electric power transmission', but could only recommend co-operation between the two Dominions over these.

The Commission was created in order to distance Mountbatten and the British Government from direct responsibility for the boundary line, because of the anticipated controversy. It has long been assumed that Mountbatten himself took no personal interest whatever in which parts of the sub-continent ended up in which Dominion. His claims of disinterest have generally been taken at face value. Recently, however, evidence has emerged to challenge that assumption. It casts yet more doubt on his protestations of impartiality towards Nehru's India, of which he was to become the first Governor-General, and the rump Pakistan, which he privately derided and whose leader he personally detested.

In February 1992 Christopher Beaumont, a retired circuit judge, made a series of revelations, after having obtained the Foreign Office's permission to do so, about Mountbatten's gerrymandering of the Awards in India's favour in the last few days before Partition. Beaumont had been Secretary to the Radcliffe Commission and was moved to reveal his knowledge when he saw his grandson had chosen *The Transfer of Power in India* as his special subject for Part II of the Cambridge History tripos.

When it became clear that the Boundary Commission's Awards would be available around 9 August, Sir Evan Jenkins asked Delhi for information as to the Commission's intentions for the Punjab. 'This was a matter of ordinary prudence,' he wrote the next year. 'The troops and police were already extended and I was entitled to some indication of what in the British Army used to be called "The Worst Possible Situation".'[83] According to Beaumont, this was 'so that troops could be sent to those areas which were most under threat of violence from the inevitable dislocation which Partition involved'.[84]

Beaumont therefore told George Abell, the Viceroy's Private Secretary, where the line had been drawn by Radcliffe, and Abell sent Jenkins a sketch map and an accompanying letter. The map showed that the Punjabi *tehsils* (sub-districts) of Ferozepur and Zira had been allotted to Pakistan. These were Muslim-majority areas, contiguous with the western Punjab lying in a salient east of the Sutlej River. Together they comprised over half a million people; in Zira 65 per cent were Muslim and in Ferozepur 55 per cent. According to the terms of reference of the Radcliffe Commission, these *tehsils* should automatically have been awarded to Pakistan, unless 'other factors' intervened. That 'other factor' turned out to be Mountbatten's support for a strong, post-independence India against a weakened Pakistan.

Abell's map and letter arrived at Government House in Lahore on 8 August. On 11 August Jenkins received a telegram from Abell which simply read: 'ELIMINATE SALIENT'. This meant that the Sutlej salient, where Ferozepur and Zira were located, had in the intervening period been awarded to India rather than to Pakistan. As Jenkins was to put it the next year, 'I recall this clearly: Mudie and I were sitting together at the time and I understood simply that the whole of the Ferozepur district was to be in India.'

Sir Francis Mudie, a former Governor at Sind, had spent twenty-five years in the Indian Civil Service and was Jenkins's successor as Governor of Pakistan's West Punjab after independence. He remembered the occasion too. Ferozepur housed an important Indian army arsenal, and, as he put it in his unpublished memoirs, when the telegram arrived,

> this meant that Ferozepur was to go to India, thus depriving the Pakistan Army of most of its weapons. No explanation of why this sudden change was made at the last moment was given, or has ever been given, but I find it difficult to believe that it was not the result of pressure put on Radcliffe by Mountbatten and his Government.[85]

The loss of the Ferozepur arsenal was a crippling blow to Pakistan, which suffered badly in the subsequent division of stores and military equipment when the Indian army was divided.

When Jenkins's own Private Secretary, Stuart Abbott, asked whether the sketch map, accompanying letter and amending telegram should be destroyed, the Governor replied that as he had already shown it to his successor Governors of East and West Punjab, 'it would be pointless and perhaps discourteous to do so'. Therefore, this *prima facie* evidence that the boundary had been retrospectively altered stayed amongst his papers, until it was discovered by the Pakistan Government after independence. How these important areas were moved from Pakistan to India at the last minute has remained something of a mystery, until several crucial clues were provided by Beaumont forty-five years later. He has alleged that Mountbatten, under pressure from Nehru and the Maharajah of Bikaner – whose State bordered on Ferozepur – persuaded Radcliffe, the deliberations of whom were meant to be impartial and free from all political considerations, to alter the Award to place Ferozepur and Zira in India. The canal headworks which controlled the irrigation of Bikaner were located at Ferozepur and the Maharajah – an old friend of Mountbatten's – feared that should they be allocated to Pakistan, his State's agriculture would in effect be controlled by Jinnah. But how had Nehru, Mountbatten and the Maharajah discovered what was in Radcliffe's supposedly secret Awards?

Beaumont had been appointed Secretary to the Boundary Commission on 7 July 1947, the day after Radcliffe's own appointment as Chairman. On the next day Rao Sahib V.D. Ayer was appointed as Assistant Secretary, a post involving purely clerical duties. 'Ayer had doubtless been a loyal servant of the Raj,' says Beaumont, 'but the Raj was disappearing.' It was a mistake to have an Indian as one of only three people who knew how the Commission's frontier-drawing was progressing. Ayer was a Hindu and Beaumont thinks it highly probable that he was keeping V.P. Menon and Nehru informed of the way the frontier line was being formed. All over India at that time, hitherto impeccably sound public servants were looking to the future of their countries, beyond the 15th of August deadline, and Ayer was probably no exception.

Admittedly, the evidence that Ayer was the source of the leaks is largely circumstantial. On 12 August Nehru voiced great alarm at the prospect of the overwhelmingly Hindu and Buddhist Chittagong Hill Tracts being awarded to Pakistan, and this was the day *before* Beaumont actually presented the Commission's Report to the Viceroy. As Beaumont points out, 'it seems that the only way in which Nehru could have known of the projected allotment of the Chittagong Hill Tracts to Pakistan was that Ayer had told him'. The diary entry of Shahid Hamid, Auchinleck's Private Secretary, for 9 August reads: 'Everyone is talking about the impending Boundary Awards. ... Many of its salient points have already leaked out through the staff of the Boundary Commission and [Mountbatten's] own staff.... It is common talk that Mountbatten is busy changing it, giving India ... the Ferozepur headworks. The Muslims are very jittery.'[86] Hamid's diary only emerged after the publication of Ziegler's biography of Mountbatten in 1985.

The Muslim League was right to feel jittery. The influence Nehru had over Mountbatten was evident to certain members of the Viceregal staff. On 9 August John Christie, one of the Assistant Private Secretaries to the Viceroy, wrote in his diary that he had been told by Abell that Mountbatten 'is in a tired flap and is having to be strenuously dissuaded from asking Radcliffe to alter his awards'.[87] This was written at a time when even Mountbatten himself should not have known where the line had been drawn. Indeed, on 12 August he asked Christie and Campbell-Johnson to 'call on Radcliffe and find out when we might expect the Awards to be in the Viceroy's hands'.[88] If Beaumont is correct, Mountbatten already knew what they contained. Campbell-Johnson cannot believe that he was being misled by Mountbatten, but if he was he would have been neither the first, nor the last.

The Congress hierarchy made their own attempt to persuade Radcliffe to alter the Award, either with or without Mountbatten's connivance. V.P. Menon visited Radcliffe's bungalow at midnight on 11 August to see him. Beaumont, who also lived there, 'told him politely that he could not. [Menon] said that Mountbatten had sent him. I told him, less politely, that it made no difference. He departed with good grace. I think he anticipated the rebuff.' In the maelstrom of the final week of the Raj, it would have been surprising if, having been leaked the demarcation line, the Congress leadership had not tried everything in their power to alter the final frontier. This would have been all the more understandable if, as Mudie pointed out, much of the military equipment needed for a possible future war between the two Dominions was located in Ferozepur.

It was Mountbatten's duty to rebuff all these Congress advances – which Ziegler believes he did. 'The most likely explanation', he wrote in the official biography, 'seems to be that at one point, Mountbatten, under pressure from Nehru, did contemplate asking Radcliffe to amend the Awards.' When writing the book, Ziegler believed that sanity had prevailed and Mountbatten 'may have been guilty of indiscretion, but not of the arrant folly as well as dishonesty of which his enemies accused him'. Those words were written seven years before Beaumont's revelations. Today, Ziegler thinks that 'the nugget of doubt that remained about Mountbatten's impartiality' had, after he had seen Mr Beaumont's statement, 'now become a boulder'.[89]

At breakfast the morning after Menon's midnight visit, Beaumont told Radcliffe what had happened. Later that same morning, Radcliffe told Beaumont that he had been invited to lunch by Ismay, but had been asked not to bring along Beaumont on the pretext that 'there would not be enough room at the table for the extra guest'. Having lived for months in the house Ismay occupied, Beaumont knew this to be untrue, 'but my suspicions were not aroused as they should have been', despite it being 'the first time when Radcliffe and I had been separated at any sort of function'. That same evening the Punjab line was changed, with Ferozepur and Zira going to India.[90]

Beaumont believes, and the evidence certainly seems to support him, that Radcliffe came under pressure from Mountbatten and Ismay to change the line to run along the Sutlej River. Radcliffe had only been in India for six weeks and was thus not *au fait* with the political situation in the Punjab. For all the true statements about Radcliffe's having 'monumental integrity and independence of mind' (Ziegler), and being 'a highly experienced legal luminary' (Campbell-Johnson), it is likely that if it was stated that it was his patriotic duty to draw the frontier so as to place the arsenal in India, Radcliffe would naturally have responded to the patriotic call.

As one historian, Alistair Lamb, has put it, 'It was always improbable that the highly professional government of British India, even in its dying days, would leave matters of prime importance to amateurs like Radcliffe, who, although a distinguished jurist, had never been to India before he came to draw the partition line across Punjab and Bengal.' Lamb believes that the Radcliffe Commission was 'a device to load the onus of the details of partition on to the shoulders of a non-"Indian", so as to leave Mountbatten blameless of responsibility for unpopular decisions.... Mountbatten hoped to be Governor-General of both India and Pakistan and this device would have made his task infinitely easier.'[91]

Whether that is true, or, as Campbell-Johnson put it in a letter to the *Daily Telegraph*, the Commission was 'a crucial and organic part of the inevitably improvised partition process', the fact remains that the boundary was secretly altered to the detriment of Pakistan. Campbell-Johnson blames 'the Punjab mafia', in which he includes Jenkins, Abell and Abbott, for the way the news of the alteration got out. Had Jenkins taken Abbott's advice and destroyed the map, it would not have fallen into the hands of the Pakistan Government. It did, however, and the Foreign Minister, Zafrullah Khan, later denounced the alteration to the Security Council of the United Nations. Beaumont, back in England by then, visited Radcliffe in his chambers to ask him directly what had happened. 'He was very sheepish and never denied it. He didn't welcome my visit, said he was busy and shuffled me off.'[92] However, he could not do the same to Philip Noel-Baker, the Secretary of State for Commonwealth Relations, who was asked by Attlee to look into the subject after Zafrullah Khan's denunciation.

According to Noel-Baker's report to the Prime Minister, Radcliffe had admitted that 'he showed the first draft of the proposed Award to the authorities in Delhi and that, on further consideration, he made the Award in terms which departed from the first draft'.[93] By then Radcliffe had destroyed all his papers and notes relating to his work with the Boundary Commission. Mountbatten later criticized his work, informing Lapierre and Collins: 'I'll tell you something ghastly. The reasons behind his Awards weren't very deep-seated at all.'

Beaumont believes Radcliffe yielded 'to what he thought was overwhelming political expediency' and 'allowed himself to be overborne' by Mountbatten. When the affair came to light, Mountbatten made strenuous attempts to deny it and to shift the blame. He wrote to Ismay in London in February 1948: 'I am fairly satisfied that there can be no evidence in Jenkins' file to support any accusation that the Award was tampered with', hardly a ringing denunciation of the slander. He went on to ask his former Chief of Staff to get Abell to 'explain the situation to Jenkins, Radcliffe, Abbott and Beaumont in case this subject is ever raised again'. Abell and Beaumont, supported by Abell's junior, the Viceroy's Assistant Private Secretary, Ian Scott, considered that it would be best not to discuss what Mountbatten had done. 'We all agreed it was better for relations between the two countries for us not to spill the beans,' says Beaumont. Although Sir Penderel Moon was informed of what had taken place, he agreed to 'skirt around it' in his history of British India.[94]

When, still in India, Mountbatten learned that the Pakistan Government was considering publishing Abell's map, letter and telegram, he contacted Ismay again in an attempt to distance himself from the controversy altogether: 'A reply will have to be published. The question is who should issue it. I am sure you will agree that it should not come from me.' Mountbatten was keen that either Attlee or Radcliffe should answer Zafrullah Khan's accusations. He went on to ask that Ismay, in further talks with Abell and Jenkins, should emphasize that 'the point that arises here was that Abell sent the letter concerned without *my* knowledge'. He admitted that 'it may be hard to convince people that that was so. It will look to have been an odd procedure.' Considering that Abell had been his Principal Private Secretary, and specifically authorized by Mountbatten to keep Jenkins fully informed of developments, this was no more than the truth. Mountbatten's attempt to distance himself, and in effect to blame Abell, has drawn the private ire of those in the know, including Ian Scott. True to their 1948 commitment, however, they are still reluctant to discuss exactly what happened. Fortunately, a piece of *prima facie* evidence has survived, much against Mountbatten's wishes, which makes it quite clear what really took place.

Amongst Ismay's papers there is a copy of the letter Mountbatten sent him on 2 April 1948, once he realized that he was on the verge of being unmasked over Ferozepur and was attempting to co-ordinate the British response in such a way as to absolve him from any blame. The letter was ostensibly to 'remind' Ismay what they had both said to Radcliffe. Mountbatten asked him to burn the letter after reading it, but Ismay knew better than that, and instead added some highly instructive marginalia on Mountbatten's script. 'We felt that both sides would be equally dissatisfied [with the Award] and that instead of 15th August being celebrated as a day of national rejoicing they might well turn it into a day of mourning for the portions of territory they had lost,' Mountbatten 'reminded' his former Chief of Staff of the events of eight months earlier. Mountbatten then claimed that Abell had not informed him of the map sent to Jenkins 'because he said it was done on "staff level" '. He added: 'If memory serves me right George [Abell] stressed that this was not the final award since Radcliffe had yet to balance the East and West Pakistan Awards.' There was certainly no mention of any such 'balancing' operation in the original letter Abell sent Jenkins; indeed, it seems to be the first occasion at which such a concept was introduced.

'About this time I met Radcliffe with you at your house,' continued Mountbatten. 'The main object of this meeting was to discuss the date of the announcement of the Award. You will remember that I asked Radcliffe whether he could delay his final decision until after 15th August and you will also remember that he was quite firm and said that he could not delay it beyond the 13th at the very latest.' All this is well documented, but Mountbatten then wrote:

> So far as I remember I said to him that the Sikh attitude had become rather worse than we had anticipated, and that when he was balancing up the boundaries of East and West Pakistan I sincerely hoped that he would bear the Sikh problem in mind.... I think I went so far as to say that ... I trusted that any generosity to Pakistan should be given more in Bengal than the Punjab since there was no Sikh problem in Bengal.

Beside this statement Ismay pencilled 'I do NOT remember this!' in the margin of Mountbatten's letter.[95] Had Mountbatten's first worry really been the Sikhs – rather than the arsenal or Bikaner's concerns – he might have been expected to have taken more vigorous action himself. His real preoccupations are made clear in the next paragraph of his letter to Ismay.

In Mountbatten's own words:

> the conversation then turned to the irrigation canals and headworks and so far as I remember [Radcliffe] made some comment about having tried and failed to obtain agreement for joint inter-dominion working of the headworks and I think he remarked that the boundary was particularly difficult to adjust round about Ferozepur from this aspect, and I remarked that provided the overall east–west boundaries were scrupulously fair between the two dominions, it seemed to me that he could make any adjustments necessary for balancing out the boundaries in Bengal and the Punjab.

Mountbatten then added: 'I must confess that I did not dictate a record' of the conversation, because it was 'of such a very "off the record" nature.'[96]

Ismay replied on 11 April, making it clear that he could not agree with such a sanitized version of what had been said. 'My recollection of events is very different from yours,' he wrote. Had Ismay destroyed the 2nd of April letter, as requested, it would not be known that Mountbatten and Ismay ever did have an 'off the record' meeting with Radcliffe, during which, under the guise of 'balancing' the east and west Awards – which had nothing to do with Mountbatten anyhow – Radcliffe was asked to 'make any adjustments necessary' in the specific case of Ferozepur. Here is *prima facie* evidence both that Mountbatten brought pressure to bear on Radcliffe to alter the Awards in India's favour, and that he attempted to construct a 'line' for Ismay to take in order to conceal the fact.

In another letter, also sent on 11 April, Mountbatten quoted to Ismay what Jenkins had recalled, namely that 'Abell says that the question of giving me advanced information was raised several times at your morning meetings and that you approved the information being given'. Mountbatten proposed that the best way out of it – and he personally intended, in his own words, to 'keep right out of it' – was to say that he 'had at staff meetings *generally* given permission to Abell to keep Jenkins informed; but he had not *specifically* told me of what he intended to send or when he sent it'. It thus all becomes a question of who knew what and when he knew it. Much depends on whether one still believes Mountbatten's protestations of innocence. As even Sir Penderel Moon, the pre-eminent historian of the British in India who was generally sympathetic to Mountbatten, was privately prepared to admit, 'I wouldn't personally have trusted him very far.'[97]

Further corroboration is to be found in a little-known book published in Delhi entitled *Reminiscences of an Engineer*, the memoirs of Kanwar Sain, the Chief Engineer of Bikaner. He served in the Punjab Irrigation Department between 1922 and 1947, and in his memoirs he claims to have been ordered by the Maharajah of Bikaner to go with Sardar Panikkar, the State's Prime Minister, to visit Mountbatten on 11 August 1947. The Maharajah, whose State neighboured Ferozepur, believed that Bikaner's irrigation might have been very adversely affected if the canal headworks there had been allotted to Pakistan. He threatened to accede to Pakistan rather than to India, in the event of the two sub-districts of Ferozepur and Zira being awarded to Pakistan. In the diary of Shahid Hamid there is a passage which reads: 'The canal headworks at Ferozepur have been awarded to India on the instigation of [Mountbatten's] great friend, the Maharaja of Bikaner, who, on the 11th, sent his P.M., Sardar Panikkar, and Chief Engineer to see him and were given a long interview.'[98]

It has been pointed out by Mountbatten's apologists that there is no record in Mountbatten's papers or diary of any meeting between the Viceroy and Sardar Panikkar and Kanwar Sain. As has already been seen, however, in matters concerning the Boundary Awards he purposefully did not keep records of conversations which he considered 'off the record'. According to Kanwar Sain's account, when the Maharajah's threat was communicated to Mountbatten, his face changed colour.[99] Bikaner was a relatively large State of nearly a million inhabitants, its ruler an old and close friend both of Mountbatten and the British Raj.

Moon admitted in 1982 that certain documents – some of them quoted in full by Kanwar Sain – were 'missing from the records'. This is hardly surprising if Mountbatten was intending to bring pressure to bear on Radcliffe to alter his Award. Mountbatten was Governor-General of India for many months afterwards, and thus in a position to cover his tracks regarding incriminating documents. It is unlikely that Mountbatten could have refused to have seen the Maharajah's emissaries, and hear their message that 'if the Ferozepur headworks and the Gang Canal were allocated to Pakistan, Bikaner would have no option but to join Pakistan'.[100]

If, added to the pressure from Nehru on the same subject the day before, this message had sunk in on 11 August, Christie's diary entry about Mountbatten's desire to pressurize Radcliffe begins to fit into the general picture. So, too, does V.P. Menon's midnight visit and the meeting Mountbatten and Ismay held with Radcliffe, from which Beaumont was excluded. Other members of Mountbatten's staff have also recalled that Mountbatten had to be prevailed upon not to alter the Awards. Seen in the wider context of his visceral bias against Jinnah and Pakistan, and in favour of the stronger, larger and more powerful Commonwealth country of which he was about to become Governor-General, Mountbatten's actions over Ferozepur fall into place. They were, however, a dereliction of duty. Inherent in his orders from Attlee, his Viceregal oath and his 3rd of June Plan was a duty of strict impartiality as representative of the British Raj. Mountbatten betrayed that trust.

The hereditary principle, and lack of democratic accountability inherent in the whole concept of a Princely State, offended against Mountbatten's progressive principles. Nevertheless, such States covered more than one-third of the sub-continent in 1947 and comprised 100 million Indians. The Princes therefore constituted a serious threat to Congress's plans for a unified, socialist, secular republic. Despite Mountbatten's assurances in his speech to the Chamber of Princes on 25 July, most realized that the Congress Party would not allow the Princes to retain their autonomy as before. 'I am not asking any State to make any intolerable sacrifice of either its internal autonomy or independence,' he told them with tongue wedged firmly in cheek. 'In no other matters [than defence, foreign policy and communications] has the Central Government any authority to encroach on the internal authority or sovereignty of the States.' Those assurances were soon shown to be totally worthless, as Mountbatten knew them to be when he made them.

Despite being declared 'inviolate and inviolable' when they were signed, these ancient treaties with the Princes were reneged on by the British. 'I am afraid that the Viceroy', wrote Lord Salisbury to Harold Macmillan, 'has not played a very distinguished part over the Princes. Whatever the Government may have said about our not bringing pressure on them, we have in fact never ceased to bully and badger them to come in, and I suspect that this will leave a legacy of bitterness among our best friends.'[101] Mountbatten's treatment of the Princes, harrying them into acceding to one or other Dominion by 15 August, was all the more reprehensible in view of the pride he took in having been personally friendly with many of them since his visit with the Prince of Wales in 1921–2.

'The Princes of India were in a pathetic situation,' he later told Lapierre and Collins. 'They belonged to the past – the remote past – and most of them had no idea how to conduct themselves with the people who were going to be India's new rulers. They were disunited, proud, frightened, some of them angry and all of them uncertain.... Wandering around like a letter without a stamp.' That he himself might have been responsible for a situation which they could hardly have foreseen – of a British Viceroy completely in the pocket of people they despised as a gaggle of lawyers – can hardly be blamed on the Princes.

The Maharawal of Dungarpur later explained to the Political Agent, Charles Chenevix-Trench, how close some of the Princely States came to banding together to form a bloc of thirty million people covering 300,000 square miles, an area as large as Pakistan:

> But it was not to be. It was an end brought about by one man and his wife. By making them sign the Instrument of Accession, the Viceroy perpetrated the rape of the States. Had the Princes been left alone, Congress could never have got them to sign away their powers and heritage within a fortnight. No,

never. Being a member of the Royal Family, many Princes took Mountbatten as a friend. Nothing could be further from the truth ... the Princes expected justice and fair play, not lies and half-truths to beguile them into a snare.[102]

Mountbatten accorded them one last right, which was personally to choose, without democratic reference to their people, whether to join India or Pakistan. This became particularly contentious when, as in the case of Kashmir, the ruler was not of the same religion as the majority of his subjects. Mountbatten ought either to have followed the logic of his plan to deprive the Princes of their paramountcy, and institute plebiscites in the States to decide which Dominion to join; or to have left them with a significant degree of autonomy, inside a federal structure. Many – such as Mysore – were run with an efficiency and fairness far in advance of the rest of India. The bureaucratic structure of Congress rule actually held many States back after independence. For all the Mountbattens' opposition to nepotism, their friends, the Nehru family, have governed India for three-quarters of the post-independence period.

Sir Conrad Corfield, the Political Adviser responsible for the States, believed that certain regional merger schemes might have given the Princes a stronger voice when bargaining with Congress over their future. He believed that 'the values of personal indigenous rule were ... not negligible and should not, I think, have been obliterated'. After his South-East Asian experience, Mountbatten was immune to the paradox of working against the interests of those who had fought loyally for the Empire in two world wars, but in support of those who had advocated non-cooperation even when the Japanese were poised at the gates of India.

Mountbatten felt differently from Corfield about the loyal, conservative and stable States, and used guile, persuasion and, in the end, bullying to encourage the Princes 'to ensure adherence before the lapse of paramountcy'.[103] Corfield presented an alternative policy, which gave them a measure of autonomy over economic questions, whilst the central Government in New Delhi decided defence and foreign policy matters. The Viceroy, however, kept Corfield 'at arm's length and dealt more and more with the embryo Indian States Ministry in the persons of Vallabhbhai Patel and V.P. Menon'. From then on, 'the policy of dissuading the Princes from any pursuit of independence or separate Dominion Status and of persuading them to make terms with the new regimes was essentially Mountbatten's'.[104]

Mountbatten had lunch on 2 June 1947 with the Maharajah of Bikaner and the Nawab of Bhopal. Until then, the latter thought that the Princes could constitute an important 'third force' in Indian politics. After lunch he declared: 'Once more His Majesty's Government have left us in the lurch. Whatever Dominion we join, it will utterly destroy us.' As the then equerry to the King-Emperor has put it, 'This royal son of the Prophet had accurately forecast the dire truth.' Hyderabad, the largest and most powerful State, which believed itself capable of becoming a nation state in its own right, attempted to hold out for independence, which it was legally entitled to do. On the orders of Nehru and V.P. Menon, India invaded Hyderabad on 17 September 1948. A year earlier Mountbatten had told the Prime Minister of Hyderabad that, 'the present leaders of the Congress Party were the conservative right-wing elements and really in the circumstances of today were the natural allies of the Princes'.

The key to understanding Mountbatten's stance over Kashmir – which like Hyderabad had not acceded to either Dominion before Independence Day – was his anti-Pakistan bias. Ian Stevens, editor of the English-language Indian paper *The Statesman*, dined with the Mountbattens on 26 October 1947. A few days earlier Pathan tribesmen, believed to be supported by Pakistan, had attacked western Kashmir. At dinner with the Mountbattens, Stevens was 'startled by their one-sided verdict on affairs' and thought that they had both 'become wholly pro-Hindu'. Mountbatten claimed that Jinnah was waiting outside Kashmir at Abbottabad, eager to drive to the capital Srinagar in triumph. In fact, Jinnah spent all late October either in Lahore or Karachi.

Mountbatten claimed that India's policy towards Kashmir was 'impeccable'. In fact, it is now known that Indian troops had moved into Kashmir *before* the tribesmen had crossed the border. A full-scale airborne Indian invasion was under way the morning after the dinner with Stevens, and three million Muslims in a vital region were forced to become Indian citizens against their will. Four out of five Kashmiris were Muslim, and in permitting India to invade and subsequently annex Kashmir – albeit whilst promising plebiscites there at a later stage – Mountbatten went back on the whole concept of his 3rd of June Plan of partitioning the sub-continent into areas according to religion. The plebiscites were never held. As a precedent for India's action, Mountbatten used the fact that the small principality of Junagadh had acceded to Pakistan after independence, despite being mainly Hindu. When the Indian leadership showed Ismay their plans to invade Junagadh, Ismay wrote to his wife to say that he had reminded Nehru 'of Hitler's behaviour and told them that the world would think they were copying it'.[105]

That Mountbatten did not even allow the invasion of Kashmir to take place at arm's length is confirmed by Stevens, who described Mountbatten as 'persuasive, confident, charming, a successful commander on the eve of an important operation'. By 7 November Sir George Cunningham's diary reported Lieutenant-General Sir Frank Messervy, the Commander-in-Chief in Pakistan, as 'surprised to find Mountbatten directing the military operations in Kashmir'. When Wavell met his successor a fortnight later, on the day of the royal wedding of Princess Elizabeth to Prince Philip of Greece, he also noted that he 'has very much gone over to the Congress side ... says Jinnah has become an impossible megalomaniac and that Nehru has shown himself a really great man'. It is impossible accurately to quantify the personal responsibility for the tragedy of Kashmir as the Mountbatten papers relating to the issue at the India Office Library and Records are closed to scholars for an indefinite period.

Just as Ferozepur and Zira had gone to India despite their Muslim majority, so three out of the four *tehsils* of the Gurdaspur district north of Amritsar were also awarded to India, despite the fact that two of them had significant Muslim majorities. Ferozepur had an arsenal, but Gurdaspur had something just as valuable: the road from India to Kashmir. In this case the 'other factor' was that only with Gurdaspur in India would there be a direct road between India and the land of Nehru's ancestors.

Mountbatten's letter of 2 April 1948 in which he 'reminded' Ismay of their meeting with Radcliffe to 'balance' his Awards is sufficient indication that he considered he had the right to pressurize Radcliffe over just such 'other factors' as these. Hamid saw the Indian corridor to Kashmir via Muslim Gurdaspur as Mountbatten's 'parting kick' to Pakistan. Mountbatten well-understood the strategic implications, and told the Nawab of Bhopal on 4 August that Kashmir was 'so placed geographically that it could join either Dominion, provided part of Gurdaspur were put into East Punjab by the Boundary Commission'.[106] If gerrymandering took place in the case of Ferozepur, it is not too hard to believe that Mountbatten also pressurized Radcliffe to ensure that Gurdaspur wound up in India. The circumstantial evidence is once again overwhelming. As Lamb has stated, 'The essential access for India along the road was made possible by the Award of the three *tehsils* to India despite the Muslim majorities.'[107]

Nehru had warned Mountbatten ever since late April that 'the future of Kashmir might produce a difficult problem'. Just before he flew off to

Srinagar on 17 June, Mountbatten asked Nehru to draw up a note on Kashmir for him to use with the Kashmiri leadership. In it, Nehru argued that despite 77 per cent of the Kashmiri population being Muslim, 'the normal and obvious course appears to be for Kashmir to join the Constituent Assembly for India ... it is absurd to think that Pakistan would create trouble if this happens'.[108] Half a century later, Pakistan is still fighting an undeclared war over Kashmir. Corfield, whom Mountbatten had deliberately not taken on the visit to Srinagar, believed that 'quiet negotiations' might have produced a partition of Kashmir acceptable to both sides. Corfield eventually resigned after Mountbatten broke faith with the guarantees given to the Princes by the British Government in May 1946, undertakings which Mountbatten had specifically reiterated in the 3rd of June Plan.[109]

When Mountbatten returned to London to attend the royal wedding on 20 November 1947, Indian troops were busy fighting the Pathans and establishing control over the province. On the day Mountbatten flew off, 16 November, Mr Kripalani, the President of Congress, resigned, fearing 'the ghastly tragedy of war between India and Pakistan'. On page three of *The Times* of 21 November, there was a description of the Indian relief of the town of Khotli after a twenty-six-day siege, during which 'the town was being heavily shelled, food stocks were nearly exhausted and the garrison was dangerously reduced by casualties and sickness'. On the very next page it was recorded that at Westminster Abbey, 'at eleven o'clock the Precentor and two minor canons escorted to their places in the Sanctuary the first procession of royal guests, including Lord and Lady Mountbatten'. His genealogical ambitions had achieved their ultimate connection, between his nephew and the future Queen of England.

He had worked for the match ever since introducing the couple in 1939, when she was thirteen and he nineteen, and was determined not to miss his moment of apotheosis through a mere fratricidal war, even if he was Governor-General of one of the potential combatants. Mountbatten later claimed that if he had not attended the wedding, 'it would make the atmosphere of crisis even worse'. On his return to India he found 'the atmosphere of crisis was still intense'. After King George VI's funeral in 1952, Mountbatten made the assertion to an assembled house party of royal guests at Broadlands that 'the House of Mountbatten now reigned' in Britain. The thought kept Queen Mary awake all night, and Churchill and the Cabinet soon asserted formally that the royal house's name of Windsor would remain unchanged.[110] Mountbatten's next attempt in 1960 to change the surname of certain of Prince Philip's descendants to Mountbatten-Windsor met with more success.[111] Princess Anne signed herself 'Mountbatten-Windsor' on her wedding certificate, and some of the Queen's great-grandchildren will take that surname.

Mountbatten's bias in favour of India seems all the more extraordinary in view of his wife's love affair with Nehru. Self-absorbed as he was, it was something he could hardly have missed, yet there is no evidence that he minded. Perhaps after twenty-five years of marriage he had lost interest in that side of his life. Considering that the affair was the gossip of New Delhi's insiders, his behaviour is in no way more understandable if, as some commentators have claimed, relations between the Congress leader and the Vicereine were platonic. To the end of his life he was not certain. Edwina once told her husband that the relationship was 'most of it spiritual'. Her official biographer, Janet Morgan, denies that Nehru ever cuckolded Mountbatten, explaining at one point that there were 'servants ever-present'.

'Nehru respected Dickie,' the biography continues. 'He would have considered it disloyal, ill-mannered and wrong to deceive his friend.' For her part, she 'had entrusted herself to Nehru in a way that was more profound than a mere physical embrace. Nothing could be allowed to degrade this precious relationship.' From the love letters and diary entries quoted elsewhere in the book, which was authorized by the Mountbatten family, less trusting conclusions might also be drawn. When Edwina wrote that 'nothing we did or felt would ever be allowed to come between you and your work or me and mine', she was presumably not merely referring to the long talks they had together in Delhi, after the servants had been dismissed for the night. Philip Ziegler tacitly admits the relationship was probably not so platonic, commenting that, 'if there was any physical element, it can only have been of minor importance to either party'.[112]

Such sexual gossip would not detain the serious historian for a moment were it not for the fact that this affair had wider, political implications. It understandably aroused great suspicion amongst some Muslims. Hamid's recently published diary alleges that 'to achieve his end, [Nehru] has cultivated Edwina Mountbatten and is on very intimate terms with her. There are all sorts of conjectures about their relationship.... Mountbatten seems quite happy about it. This friendship suits him very well. Her relationship with Nehru has been of immense help to Congress.' After a small dinner at Viceregal Lodge on 12 June, where he watched the couple closely, Hamid could only remark that 'frankly I do not know what Nehru sees in her'.[113]

The answer, as well as real affection for a committed political supporter and friend, probably also lay in her potential as a conduit of information and influence, one which was completely closed to the Muslim League. Nehru and the Vicereine would stay up talking until the early hours, and it is impossible to know what the clever politician managed to extract from the besotted middle-aged woman. 'The thought of any reservations ... between us', she once wrote to him, 'frightens me.'[114] In the words of the Labour MP, Woodrow Wyatt, who knew all the people involved, she 'became bewitched by Nehru'.[115] As one commentator has put it, 'Whether it was carnal or merely gooey, this affair hopelessly prejudiced the atmosphere of the talks that led up to Partition', by further convincing Jinnah that no equity could be expected from the Mountbattens.[116]

Edwina certainly suspended her critical judgment when it came to politics. 'Of course we think that Gandhi and his friends are absolutely right,' she told a friend, 'we must try to fit in with what they want us to do.'[117] In 1950 she found Hewlett Johnson, the pro-Soviet 'Red Dean of Canterbury', 'riveting ... and extremely balanced ... very progressive in his views'; whereas she felt the distinguished soldier, Major-General Sir Gerald Templer, had a 'completely mad approach' to the Malaya which he was successfully to pacify. Just prior to independence, Campbell-Johnson was deputed to ensure that in their coverage of the event, the BBC avoided the 'dangers' of broadcasting reports which 'emphasise the British record of achievement' in the sub-continent. Pride in what the British Raj had achieved was deliberately to be kept to the minimum, on Lady Mountbatten's instructions. Writing to Delhi from London, Campbell-Johnson said that 'Her Excellency's advice on the subject' had been 'stressed' to the BBC's Director-General and, as a result, 'any apologia for the old order' would be kept off the airwaves.[118]

Ismay was feeling increasingly disillusioned with the direction of events. Even before Mountbatten arrived in India, he had felt that 'there was a danger of an issue being made of Mountbatten's selection as a pro-Hindu and anti-Muslim League appointment'. His letters home to his wife show how increasingly critical he was becoming: 'I was horrified at Dickie's speech,' he told her of the address Mountbatten had given at India House in November 1947, in which he had said that 'only' 100,000 people had died. Ismay was disgusted by the way the Governor-General was

making light of the situation out here. It seems to me immaterial whether one hundred thousand or a million have actually died.... The essential facts

are that there is human misery on a colossal scale all around one and millions
are bereaved, destitute, homeless ... and worst of all desperately anxious and
almost hopeless about their future.'[119]

A decent man, who had loved India since his days as a subaltern on
the North-West Frontier, Ismay told his wife that he was 'furious with
Dickie ... the dead are really the lucky ones; and in any case they are
at the moment a fraction of the vast sum of human misery. Does he
really forget the millions that are destitute, homeless and without hope?
Or does he fail to understand it!' When Mountbatten returned after the
royal wedding, he was 'full of the wonderful reception that he got from
all in England and from the overwhelming congratulations he got on his
work here', but Ismay merely noted that he was 'such a confirmed
optimist, and so prone to believe what he wants to believe, that I take it
with a pinch of salt'.

When Radcliffe got back to London in August 1947, he lunched with
Robert Bruce Lockhart at the Ivy Restaurant and 'wondered how long
Ismay, to whom much credit is due, will stand him.... Ismay is obviously
a little tired of Mountbatten's exuberant personality and thirst for
publicity.'[120] Unlike Mountbatten, Ismay never attempted to play down
what was happening, telling his wife on 10 August that he thought it
likely the British would 'have to return home with all our work destroyed
and leaving behind anarchy, and misery and measureless slaughter'.[121]
When speaking privately to friends, such as Lieutenant-General Sir
Reginald Savory, the Adjutant-General of the Indian army, Ismay was
willing to be 'outspoken about things'. Savory's diary was not made
available to historians until recently. It casts further light on the way
Ismay's mind was moving concerning the Viceroy.

On 7 October Ismay had vouchsafed the view that

Mountbatten is no longer impartial. ... Ismay said that his own role was to
be impartial and that he told Mountbatten that in certain circumstances he
(Ismay) would go. [Auchinleck] has however persuaded him to stay on until
25th November when Mountbatten returns from the [royal] wedding. All
does not appear to be particularly plain sailing between Mountbatten and
Ismay.

After another meeting the next day, Savory thought that Ismay was
'beginning to realise the strong anti-Mountbatten feeling (in which he
himself must be involved)'.[122] By February 1948 Ismay was telling Bruce
Lockhart that he 'thinks Dicky has stayed too long'.

It was not just for his physiognomy that Ismay was nicknamed 'Pug';

his loyalty was a by-word. As one who had served at high level through all the vicissitudes of the Second World War, Ismay stood by Mountbatten publicly and accorded him carefully worded praise in his memoirs. Rab Butler privately informed a friend in 1950, however, that 'Ismay (a great friend of mine) resigned in India because Mountbatten took sides'. Butler's other remarks on that occasion are worth recording, both because he was a senior figure in the Conservative Party at the time and someone for whom India had been a major preoccupation for much of his life: '[Mountbatten's] conduct in India not good. Took sides. Anti-Muslim/pro-Hindu. Ten million displaced and one million killed: his fault. Didn't foresee and take precautions, but in history books his winding-up of India looks O.K.'[123]

In the division of the weapons, stores and assets between the two Dominions, the Indians were loath to part with anything more than the bare minimum to Pakistan. It would have taken a very fair-minded Governor-General to see fair play between the two countries, and Mountbatten was anything but that. His covert bias was obvious to many of the British serving in India. Auchinleck told Savory in September 1947 'that Mountbatten is no longer impartial: and that therefore the sooner we go the better, even though reconstitution may not be complete so far as States, etc. are concerned'.[124] Sir George Cunningham's diary for 7 November related how he had been told by Messervy, the new Commander-in-Chief of the Pakistan army, that 'Mountbatten is daily becoming more and more anathema to the Muslims, and it certainly seems as if he could see nothing except through Hindu eyes.'

As well as the content of the Radcliffe Awards, Mountbatten's actions over their timing implies he was guilty of the 'arrant folly as well as dishonesty' of which Ziegler had thought him innocent. At first Mountbatten had been pressing upon Radcliffe to hurry up with his report, but after 9 August, in the words of the Viceroy's Deputy Private Secretary, 'he back-pedalled furiously to put it off until after August 15th'.[125] It had dawned on Mountbatten that the Awards would inevitably be followed by large-scale violence. As H.V. Hodson has said, 'It could have been announced two or three days before, but why have the hangover before the celebration? ... The day of independence had to be one of triumph.'[126] Hamid accurately summed up the situation on 9 August:

> [Mountbatten] is terrified to announce before the Independence celebrations as disturbances may ensue on a large scale which would be his responsibility and that of H.M.G. to handle and control.... He is afraid the injured party may boycott the celebrations.

Therefore, Mountbatten deliberately ensured that the Awards were made public on the second day after independence, the 17th, so that the killings which inevitably followed were technically the responsibility of the incoming Dominion Governments, rather than his. On 9 August 1947, at the Viceroy's staff meeting, 'it was stated that Sir Cyril Radcliffe would be ready that evening to announce the Award of the Punjab Boundary Commission'. With exceptional frankness, the Viceroy had then said, 'It was now for consideration whether it would in fact be desirable to publish it straight away. Without question the earlier it was published, the more the British would have to bear the responsibility for the disturbances which would undoubtedly result.' He then 'emphasised the necessity for maintaining secrecy, not only on the terms of the Award, but also of the fact that it would be ready that day'. He did not want his Viceroyalty to end in a tidal wave of blood, preferring instead that his Governor-Generalship should open with his being called upon to deal with a problem apparently not of his making. Using the excuse that 'the printers were going on holiday, and we were leaving for Karachi', the Awards were not circulated as soon as they were received from Radcliffe, but put in the safe at Viceroy House until power had safely been transferred out of Mountbatten's hands.[127] 'It couldn't be on the day itself,' Mountbatten told Lapierre and Collins, 'it might have been a day or two earlier. If it had been five days or a week earlier it might have helped. A day or two couldn't make any difference.' Yet, as Mountbatten well knew, the Punjab part of the Awards *was* ready exactly five days earlier.

Mountbatten delayed the Award in the face of advice from the men on the spot, such as Jenkins, who believed that there would be administrative advantages from publication whilst the British still ruled India. He did this entirely for reasons of prestige. Had the Punjab boundary been announced as soon as Radcliffe had it ready, on 9 August, the movement of populations there could have been undertaken under British authority, with British troops and officials enjoying full power to act. Punjabi inhabitants, who after independence were terrified of being caught in the wrong country, might have been far calmer. It was the atmosphere of anarchy and terror which led to so much bloodshed, and this might well have been avoided.

Above all, law and order should have been established *before* the transfer of power and the resulting exodus. The Muslim fear that the new Government in Delhi was covertly sanctioning their persecution would not have troubled the refugees had it been the British Raj which arranged, supervised and protected them. Instead, pushed up against an absurdly early and arbitrary deadline for independence, the ideal conditions were created for mass panic. Even before Partition, on 11 August, Messervy, who four days later was to become Commander-in-Chief of the Pakistan army, was 'of the opinion that the postponement of the Boundary Commission Award is causing uncertainty and immense bloodshed'. Hamid agreed that the delay 'is having a most disturbing and harmful effect ... the wildest rumours are current and being spread by mischief-makers, of whom there is no lack'.

Logic should have told Mountbatten, even if Jenkins and other Governors had not, that Partition would be followed by Sikh terror tactics against the Muslims of West Punjab, which in turn would create a Muslim exodus to Pakistan. The path to have followed in order to avoid such a cataclysm should have been the early division of the Indian and Pakistani armies, their deployment in the disputed areas, with law and order established by martial law if necessary, followed only then by the announcement of the Boundary Awards. Any population transfers that were then demanded could have been properly supervised and protected. Then – and only then – the country could be partitioned and the two States declared independent. In not following this commonsense sequence – indeed, in taking the steps in almost the reverse order, with such horrific consequences – Mountbatten deserved to be court-martialled on his return to London.

At the end of his last staff meeting, held at 5.00 p.m. on 12 August, after directing Abell to inform the Governors of Punjab and Bengal of the delay in publishing the Awards 'as early as had been hoped', Mountbatten got down to discussing 'Royal style and titles'.[128] Out in the country, people's minds were on other things. As one historian of the Sheikhupura district of the Punjab relates:

> The fears of the non-Muslims were somewhat allayed by the hope that the Boundary Commission would allot the district to India and they would be permitted to keep their homes and lands. For this reason no large-scale exodus took place before 17th August, on which day the Radcliffe Award was announced and a stampede for safety began. The minorities were taken at a disadvantage, arrangements for evacuation could not be made immediately ... and for several days no escape was possible.[129]

Those who have swallowed Mountbatten's line that the British had no idea such serious unrest would result from Partition, cannot have seen the twenty-three predictions, reports and warnings sent to him over a three-month period by Jenkins.[130] Mountbatten's claim in his 'Report of

the Last Viceroyalty' that 'not one of us ... anticipated the exact form
or magnitude of what was to follow' was true only of the word 'exact'.
Campbell-Johnson's published diary reports some of the warnings Jenkins
had been giving. From the Governors' Conference of 15 April, when
Jenkins 'felt bound to draw attention to the seriousness of the situation
in the Punjab', to his statement twelve days later that 'there was a real
peril we would be handing over to chaos ... there is grave danger of
civil war', he had been busy pointing out what would shortly happen.
Serious, informed warnings from responsible officials had been received
by Delhi for months. Even before Mountbatten arrived in India, the
Chief Secretary to the Punjab Government had reported that 'large-scale
rioting ... is everywhere taken for granted in the near future', and in
May 1946 there was 'a growing tendency for all three communities to
organise and equip for what is openly and challengingly called civil
war'.[131]

For two months running, the Commandant of the Viceroy's Body-
guard, Major Patrick Massey, had reported that his senior Sikhs had told
him that their co-religionists in Patiala, Faridkot and Nabha States
were planning to dispossess Muslims of their farms immediately after
independence. He was ordered by Colonel Currie of the Viceroy's staff
'to desist, as [his] reports were causing offence'.[132] Radcliffe, talking to
Bruce Lockhart, 'says it is far worse than anyone here realises and
predicts that there will be further divisions and further civil wars.... The
whole of the Viceregal establishment lived in another world apart.'

That world was brought savagely home to them when Mountbatten
flew back from the independence celebrations in Karachi on 14 August.
Whilst there, Mountbatten had bravely accompanied Jinnah to the
ceremony in an open car, despite a bomb threat against the founder of
Pakistan – a fact he later asked Campbell-Johnson to emphasize in a
book he was writing. At the dinner to celebrate Pakistan's independence,
Mountbatten gave his own explanation for why he had brought the date
forward so drastically. 'The best way to teach a youngster to cycle', he
said, 'was to take him to the top of a hill, put him on the seat and push
him down the hill. By the time he arrived on the flat ground he will
have learnt how to cycle.'

'At the stroke of the midnight hour, when the world sleeps, India will
wake to life and freedom,' said Nehru in his oration at the birth of
independent India. (In fact, Britain and the Western world were wide
awake at Delhi's 'midnight hour'.) Even before that hour, however,
Punjabis were waking to death and anarchy, whilst the world looked

elsewhere. 'What a marvellous, dramatic idea, having that midnight meeting while the rest of the world sleeps,' Mountbatten said later. 'This was not done because we wanted a dramatic moment, but because I'd chosen the wrong day! Because the astrologers said the day wasn't propitious!'[133]

For the first time in history a great empire was voluntarily being given away, with nothing being asked in return. Yet the donors allowed themselves to be hamstrung by all sorts of terms and conditions attached by the joint beneficiaries. Mountbatten's overriding assumption was that it was best always to do things their way, as they were the eventual inheritors. His other responsibilities – to the Princes, Muslims, Sikhs, Untouchables and the Indian masses – always took second place. The result was that power was transferred largely according to the dictates of Congress's agenda.

In his address to the Indian Constituent Assembly in New Delhi on 15 August, Mountbatten said that the acceptance of his 3rd of June Plan had been 'hailed as an example of fine statesmanship throughout the world', as if there were anything particularly statesmanlike about their accepting the offer of a sub-continent. As he told Lapierre and Collins, he got 'this marvellous feeling that you get at the end of a war, when both sides have won!' Ismay had dysentery on Independence Day and so could not attend the celebrations. He did not mind, as 'I was in no mood for unrestrained rejoicing.... I had deep forebodings about the immediate future.... Many of my Indian friends were likely to lose their lives, and many more were certain to lose their homes.'

According to the unpublished memoirs of A.A. Williams, the District Magistrate in Lahore, 'the precipitate departure of August 1947 made communal civil war almost inevitable'. Mountbatten's decision 'to hand over power in August 1947 was a plain invitation to politicians in power to stay there by whatever means they could, and to those who were not in power to get there by destroying what was in their way'.[134] As early as June, the Sikh capital Amritsar was under forty-eight-hour curfew.

The most serious oversight was the lack of boundary, which on Independence Day was still not known. At the airfield on the 15th, Williams said goodbye to Jenkins, whose 'last view of Lahore was of billowing clouds of smoke from a burning city'. The next day the few British officers who were left had 'to dash through a sort of no-man's land, now the battlefield of warring communities'. The situation angered Williams, a conscientious servant of the Punjab for fifteen years. He thought it 'an act of betrayal and even cowardice; one does not leave in the lurch and to bloody slaughter people who trusted in one's will and ability to protect them'. He believed that:

the responsibilities become a trust not to be discarded unless there is a successor at least as well able to maintain it. In India there was a gross abdication of trust and duties; a wholly arbitrary date had been set for the transfer of power – an act in itself inviting violence for its seizure; much deference was paid to the wishes and interests of the Hindu Congress, and the Muslims were left to feel that they were regarded as at best a nuisance.

Savory had little doubt that it was the Sikhs who had initiated the terror. Far from establishing a separate Sikhistan, the 3rd of June Plan and the Radcliffe Awards split the Sikh people in half. They responded with a martial fervour and savagery which a glance at their history should have told Mountbatten was inevitable. On several occasions he was advised to have the more extreme of the Sikh leaders interned before Partition, but his liberal instincts balked at imprisoning people without trial for crimes they had planned but had not yet actually carried out. By 17 August Savory was writing from Government House in Bombay that 'the Punjab is in a very bad state with the Sikhs playing up and turning the country from Lahore to Jullundur into a battlefield'. A week later he wrote that 'things in the Punjab are very bad, with the Sikhs going quite mad over the Boundary question. Lahore is in ruins and the countryside in anarchy.'

Writing from the headquarters of the Supreme Commander in New Delhi on 28 August, Savory explained to his wife how the Sikhs were

going around in organised groups of about five hundred strong, burning, massacring and looting. Practically no trains are running into Pakistan from Delhi, as too many of them have been held up and looted and the Muslim passengers hacked to pieces. The Muslims are doing the same to the Sikhs and Hindus further west in Pakistan. Refugees are pouring into Delhi starving and diseased.

All this came within a fortnight of what Nehru called India's 'tryst with destiny'. Mountbatten admitted in his Final Report that 'my threats to the Sikh Rulers and Leaders may now appear to be empty', and explained that 'the provincial Muslim and provincial Sikh political leadership was in the hands of unbalanced and seemingly unintelligent men'.

As early as 19 May 1947, Mountbatten had been told by Jenkins – whom Campbell-Johnson considers 'probably the ablest administrator in India' – that the Sikh leader, Master Tara Singh, was warning that, after Independence Day, 'in Pakistan the Muslims would massacre all the

Sikhs and Hindus and that in the other part of the Punjab the Sikhs and Hindus would massacre all the Muslims ... the only possible remedy was for Government to take really strong action'.[135] Even after the 3rd of June Plan was announced, Mountbatten had ten weeks to take precautions. Tara Singh had made it clear that, to avenge a massacre of 2,000 Sikhs in Rawalpindi in March, he would wait 'and, after the British went, he would, if necessary, see that the Muslims were dealt with'. Yet Tara Singh's proposals for a population exchange prior to independence were rejected out of hand by Mountbatten.

When evidence appeared in the first week of August of Tara Singh's association with plans to disrupt railways, destroy canal headworks, make bombs and even to assassinate Jinnah during the independence celebrations, Mountbatten, 'in secret consultation with Nehru, Sardar Patel and Mr Jinnah, decided to round up the ring-leaders, including Tara Singh, on the eve of transfer of power'. This decision was subsequently cancelled on the advice of Nehru, but against that of Jinnah.'[136] By the time the 'communal war of succession', as Jenkins called it, broke out two weeks later, the Sikhs were ready and organized. 'The massacres in the Punjab,' as one recently-published doctoral thesis has pointed out, 'in all their gruesome efficiency, bore all the imprint of military training and organisation.'[137]

The Sikhs had mobile headquarters, military uniforms, messenger and signalling systems, and no shortage of weaponry. Two million Indians had served in the armed forces during the war, and many had kept their weapons. The Sikh *jathas* (armed bands) were armed with light machine-guns, hand-grenades, tommy guns and mortars. Sometimes, for an assault on a large refugee column – which could be twenty-five miles long – several *jathas* would combine into forces around six thousand strong. Against these the authorities would often only be able to pit a couple of armoured cars. The Indian writer, Nirad Chaudhuri, is astounded that Mountbatten 'has been represented as a great statesman. If generalship were judged by the same criteria, Napoleon's greatest achievement should be his ordering the Retreat from Moscow.'

As early as 28 July, after discussing the possibility of open war between the two Dominions, the Viceroy's staff meeting considered a report by the Director of Intelligence to the effect that the Sikhs intended to start trouble 'on a big scale', if the territory of Nankana Sahib was not included in eastern Punjab. Mountbatten's response was merely to criticize Jenkins for having banned a Sikh demonstration over the issue. To make matters worse, Mountbatten had been making extravagant promises about law and order, which he later busily ensured that he was not in a position to fulfil. In an interview with the former President of the Indian National Congress, Maulana Abul Kalam Azad, he gave his

> complete assurance. I shall see to it that there is no bloodshed or riot. ... Once Partition is accepted in principle, I shall issue orders to see that there are no communal disturbances anywhere in the country. If there should be the slightest agitation, I shall adopt the sternest measures to nip the trouble in the bud. I shall not use even the armed police. I will order the Army to act and I will use tanks and aeroplanes to suppress anybody who wants to make trouble.[138]

He made an identical promise to the British Cabinet.

When the Maharajah of Patiala warned that his Sikhs would fight, Mountbatten responded: 'If they do start a war, Maharajah Sahib, it will be against the entire might of India and will be ruthlessly put down.'[139] Mountbatten spoke loudly, but was all the time discarding the big stick. When, a few weeks later, the Maharajah's private army, the Patiala State Forces, were supervising and taking active part in the slaughter of thousands of Muslims in Narnaul, firing 'their machine-guns on unarmed and desperate refugees', the authorities in Delhi did nothing and the Maharajah was soon afterwards appointed Chairman of the All-India Refugee Committee.[140]

The organization intended to keep law and order, the Punjab Boundary Force (PBF), was set up under Major-General Thomas Rees, who had commanded the 19th Indian Division in Burma during the war. Announced on 22 July, it was to be a neutral force under the control of neither India nor Pakistan. It became operational nine days later, on 1 August, but existed for only thirty-two days. It was a classic case of too little, too late, for which Mountbatten must bear the major share of the blame. In order to protect a region of 37,500 square miles – an area larger than Ireland – with a population of fifteen million, 90 per cent of whom lived in 18,000 villages, Mountbatten earmarked a force of only 15,000 men. Even when reinforced, by 23 August it amounted to only 23,000. Despite Mountbatten's later claim that the PBF was at the strength Jenkins had desired, in fact the Governor believed that nothing less than 60,000 men could police the region effectively. Historians have regularly overestimated the size of the PBF; Sir Penderel Moon put it at 'less than a hundred thousand', when detailed study has shown that it was always less than a quarter that size.[141]

'At its greatest strength', writes Robin Jeffrey, the Force's historian, 'the PBF was in a position to allot four men to every three villages, or fewer than two men per square mile; to the population it stood in a ratio of one to six hundred and thirty'. In his Final Report, Mountbatten boasted that the PBF 'was about the largest that has been concentrated in one place in time of peace'. This was true, but irrelevant, because by the time the PBF became operational, the Punjab was not at peace. Very soon it was all that stood between the Punjab and genocide.

Mountbatten recommended that the British army 'should have no operational functions whatsoever; they should not be available to be called on for internal security purposes, nor for use on the North-West Frontier, nor in the [Princely] States ... though they might in an emergency be used to save British lives.' The second battalion of the Black Watch stationed in Lahore, for example, remained in Pakistan for another six and a half months, but were, in the words of its Commanding Officer, Neville Blair, 'expressly forbidden to take part in operations "in aid of the civil power" ... nor was the battalion to intervene in any outbreak that might occur between Muslims and Hindus'. On 24 July Hamid, Auchinleck's ubiquitous Private Secretary, noted in his diary that 'the Sikhs have decided to ignore [the PBF] and put their plan of vengeance into operation. British troops have not been included in the Force despite the Auk's recommendations.... He maintains that British troops would have been most effective and, at the same time, impartial.'[42]

Mountbatten could not accept that, once 'the midnight hour' had struck, Britain had a continuing responsibility for her former subjects, even though all the planning and timing and arrangements for Partition had been his. He took refuge in the formula that if British troops had been used to combat communal disturbances, 'they would doubtless have incurred the odium of both sides'. The imperatives of trusteeship and imperial responsibility were lacking in him, in a way that they were not in Auchinleck, Ismay, Savory, Messervy, Jenkins, Williams, Cunningham, Abell and others. Mountbatten later claimed that using British troops might have been worthwhile if thousands of innocent lives could have been saved, but, with a sense of historical determinism, he convinced himself that massive loss of life was inevitable.

Campbell-Johnson agrees: 'The troops were there only to pick up the bodies, not in a position to stop the killing. It didn't matter if they were there or not. They had no relation to the nature of the catastrophe. The decision to disband the Force didn't affect the nature of it ... the only thing the troops were thinking about was going home.'[43] He also argues that Indian leaders would never have accepted the use of British troops after independence, although Pakistan had no qualms requesting them. Had independence taken place *after* Partition had been safely policed by the divided armies, rather than a tiny *ad hoc* force, the question would never have arisen.

It is shameful that an Empire which had three years earlier landed fourteen divisions on the beaches of Normandy could not put more than a handful of volunteer officers into the task of peacefully winding up two centuries of British rule. Britain had over a million men under arms at the time, of whom half were in occupation forces in Germany and Palestine. None the less, it was felt that none could be spared for this historic duty and that all British troops in India should be withdrawn as soon as possible. At a Cabinet meeting held eleven days before Partition, it was pointed out that some thirty-four thousand Indian troops were stationed in the Middle East and South-East Asia and were not due for repatriation until the end of the year. These at least could have been moved to the Punjab and their place taken by some of the thousands of British national servicemen available. When Major-General Walter Lentaigne, the Director of Military Operations at GHQ, came up with the idea of a twenty-five-mile strip of territory on either side of the boundary being evacuated and policed by Gurkha troops, Savory remarked that 'no one has taken any notice of the suggestion, though Mountbatten is furious'. The Viceroy knew of Nehru's dislike of the 'imperial' Gurkha troops and always reacted badly to any plans which assumed that there would be large-scale disturbances after Partition.

Churchill had no difficulty in putting his finger on the absurdity of the situation. 'Can the House believe', he asked in the Commons, 'there are three or four times as many British troops in little petty Palestine as in mighty India at the present time? ... What is the point or sense of this distribution of our forces? ... Two bottles of powerful medicine have been prepared, but they are sent to the wrong patients.' Churchill ended his peroration with the plea: 'Let us not add – by shameful flight, by a premature hurried scuttle – to the pangs of sorrow so many of us feel, the taint and smear of shame.'[44]

Years later Mountbatten told Lapierre and Collins that Attlee had said to him: 'Churchill's attitude towards the whole thing was so bitter and difficult that "neither I nor any of my Government could possibly persuade him. He's fond of you, he trusts you. You're the only person who has a chance to persuade him at all", and, of course, I did.' This was untrue. Far from reconciling Churchill to his Indian policy, the massacres which followed it put a severe strain on their hitherto friendly relationship. When he returned from India, Mountbatten found that Churchill would not speak to him.[145]

The PBF was three-quarters Muslim. So demoralized did they become, through witnessing the massacres of their co-religionists and countrymen, that they gave way to communalism themselves and eventually had to be disbanded. Martial law, which was never declared – Mountbatten only agreeing that it 'should be examined' – might have made a difference. As it was, the Force was created solely to assist the civil power and, therefore, had merely to hand over terrorists when they were caught, although often prosecutions did not result. Morale could not be sustained under such circumstances.

In his Final Report, Mountbatten said 'that one step which could have been taken in the Punjab ... was a properly organised wholesale transfer of population from each half of the province', but declared this impossible because 'Nehru and Jinnah turned down the suggestion'. Campbell-Johnson also maintains that 'neither side was prepared to consider a plan to transfer populations. If you'd insisted on one you'd have had no settlement. It would have implied you could not run your own country. We're talking about the art of the impossible.'[146] In fact, on 12 December 1946, Jinnah had written in *The Statesman* that population exchanges could take place on a voluntary basis. He had hoped, as he wrote three days later in the *Hindustan Times*, that the border might resemble that between American and Canada.

Even assuming Jinnah's mind had changed irretrievably by the announcement of the 3rd of June Plan, this ignores the fact that administrative Partition should have taken place *before* independence, when anyone wishing to move from one country to the next could do so under supervision by British troops. Such a promise had been mentioned by Mountbatten at the press conference which launched the 3rd of June Plan. The Congress and Muslim leadership might well have complained, but statesmanship involves facing down special interest groups. They would hardly have jeopardized the Plan, which gave them so much without their having to fight for it, just because it included provisions for a voluntary and peaceful exchange of populations prior to Partition. Mountbatten was simply not willing to attempt to bully or bluff Congress in the way that he was with the Muslims and the Princes. So, as Sir Penderel Moon has stated, 'In furtherance of the advice to people not to leave their homes, assurances of protection to minority communities were freely given', in the full knowledge that they could not be honoured.

Congress soon came round. On 16 August, the day after independence but before the Awards were announced, the Congress leader Sardar Patel told Mountbatten that 'the only solution to the Punjab award was a transfer of population on a large scale'.[147] India completely rejected the idea of using British troops, although that did not stop Nehru himself asking for a British guard to be detailed to protect his own home.[148] Explaining why more troops were not stationed in the Punjab, Mountbatten said that it would have 'involved weakening the garrisons in the rest of the sub-continent'. However, in the very next sentence of his Final Report he admitted that 'it was apparent that communal warfare was much more likely to start in the Punjab than anywhere else'. He also explained that 'the reconstitution of the Armed Forces ... would have been seriously delayed if more units had been sent to the Punjab'.

That a very few British officers in the PBF could achieve miracles during the unrest was proved again and again by Major-General Rees and his tiny band. On the first afternoon after independence he arrived at Amritsar. The night before in Lahore, during 'the midnight hour' when India 'woke to life and freedom', twenty Sikhs had been burned to death. In Amritsar Rees and a handful of British officers managed in the nick of time to stop the Sikhs taking their ritual revenge of stripping naked and parading Muslim women, raping them, killing them and burning their bodies in the street. Once the Sikhs had cut the telegraph wires, information about attacks often arrived too late for effective action to be taken. From 10 August, when the incoming Superintendent of Police in Amritsar had disarmed the predominantly Muslim police, panic had taken hold. The policemen fled with their families and the subsequent massacres had a profoundingly demoralizing effect on the Force.

The best way to have kept the combatants separate, as the long refugee columns traversed the Punjabi plains in opposite directions, was by use of air power. It had proved singularly effective in pacifying the hill tribes of the North-West Frontier; and in the Aden Protectorate, where the mere threat of action was usually sufficient to keep order.[149] The British Cabinet had been told in May 1947 that it was Mountbatten's 'considered view that the only hope of checking widespread communal warfare was to suppress the first signs of it promptly and ruthlessly, using for this purpose all the force required, including tanks and aircraft'.[150] When it came to the crunch, however, even in an area of operation where virtually no British loss of life could be expected, Mountbatten shrank from the task, fearing the public relations consequences of British pilots being seen to bomb Indians, whatever the circumstances.

In his diary for 26 July 1947, three weeks before independence, Savory wrote that 'the Pakistan authorities are getting anxious about the situation on the North-West Frontier and have asked us to place RAF squadrons at their disposal for bombing the tribes'. This would not necessarily have resulted in much loss of life; for instance, on 25 August 1947 *The Times* reported gangs dispersing very quickly at the sight of a single plane. Pathan tribesmen had been periodically raiding the North-West Frontier and Kashmir for decades, but were always kept back by their knowledge of the British determination to use air power against them. Now, for the first time in living memory, they realized that the Raj would no longer afford protection.

The decision was taken during July, 'at the highest political and military levels', that planes would not be used offensively after independence. So Sikh marauders working in *jathas*, which were easily identifiable from the air, were able to attack without fear. The Pakistan authorities were informed that the RAF would not help as 'it is not in accordance with India's and Pakistan's demand for us to quit and leave them independent', and 'the squadrons have begun to quit in any case and are therefore not available'.[51] This was not wholly true; when the division of forces was announced on 12 August, seven squadrons of Tempest fighters went to Indian and one to Pakistan. This was an indication both that planes were available and that the division of resources was disproportionate. Refused permission to fire bullets at the *jathas*, the brave pilots were forced to let off Verey flares and try to unhorse them by flying very low. On 10 August the commander of the PBF's fifth brigade was begging Rees to allow aircraft to 'fly continuously over the area and work to a programme proposed by us', but Rees could not disobey Delhi's instructions. The Force's morale dropped yet further.

Robin Jeffrey thinks that it could have worked had other units of the Indian army been concentrated in the Punjab in May or June 1947. This, however, 'would have highlighted the Punjab problem at a time when it was in Mountbatten's interest to play down the dangers of Partition'. Despite the fact that reports had been coming in regularly since May of 'very serious disturbances indeed', the use of aircraft 'would have been a confession of the gravity of the situation in the Punjab'. Lieutenant-General Sir Francis Tuker, the Commander-in-Chief of Eastern Command, stationed in Bengal, had advocated an all-Gurkha force, but instead ten of the PBF's seventeen battalions were raised from the Punjab, with all the dangers for communalism which that implied.

'To have imposed peace by military means on the Punjab', Jeffrey believes, 'would have required a larger force than the maximum of about twenty-three thousand men which Rees had under his command.... The decision not to use aircraft offensively was, from a military point of view, inexplicable.' The PBF was disbanded from midnight on 1 September. Its task was far beyond what it had been created to perform, and the Force was a casualty of Mountbatten's wishful thinking, lack of foresight and determination that Partition should not take place before independence or under British supervision.

The number of people who died in the communal violence which occurred during the partition of India continues to be disputed, but that they died in the most horrifying circumstances is not in doubt. 'Women and children were mutilated and innocent people butchered mercilessly,' wrote a future President of Pakistan, about both sides. 'All human qualities seemed to have been snuffed out and the whole edifice of culture and civilisation crumbled during those terrible weeks.'[152] Arson, torture, looting, mass rape, desecration of temples and indiscriminate murder were commonplace across north-west India for the three months after 15 August. This was the reality behind what Mountbatten was to call India's 'unbelievably happy beginning'.

Typical is the report Sir Francis Tuker received from the Commanding Officer of the Second Battalion of the First Gurkhas, which had left Peshawar for Allahabad on 31 August. They had discovered a train at Lulamsu in the Punjab, filled with 200 dead Muslims, ambushed by Patiala Sikhs. 'The majority of wounds had been caused by sword and spear thrusts,' the report said; the victims included 'a small girl aged four or five with both legs hacked off above the knees but still alive; a pregnant woman with her baby ripped out of her womb – she died; an old man, who had served in the Hong Kong and Singapore Artillery, with six spear wounds and still alive'.[153]

The anarchy which reigned across huge swathes of northern India after Independence Day reached a scale where the authorities were able to do no more than note down reports of massacres, especially after the disbandment of the PBF. A single attack, such as that on a Muslim train at Attari on 22 September, could claim over a thousand lives. 'It was communal war at its vilest depths,' wrote Tuker. This process began when the Sikhs attempted to force the Muslims out of East Punjab by terror tactics, inviting Sikhs from the western Punjab to take their homes and farms. Jenkins had warned Mountbatten in July that this was likely to happen, but no steps had been taken by the central government to prevent it. The Muslims, faced with mass liquidation, soon retaliated and full-scale civil war developed.

When, on 20 September, Pakistan's Prime Minister called for an emergency Commonwealth Conference to be held on the massacres, 'Mountbatten's reading of the situation was that Liaqat Ali wanted to establish the culpability of the Sikhs before the world'. On his advice, the British Cabinet turned down the Pakistani request, Attlee having said it was futile. It was virtually the only indication from the British Cabinet's minutes that any disturbances were taking place in India at all. In their discussion of the 3rd of June Plan, the Prime Minister had told his colleagues of Mountbatten's fears that 'unless a very early announcement was made of the method by which H.M.G. intended to transfer power, widespread communal disturbances would be inevitable. In the Punjab, in particular, the proposed announcement was likely ... to provoke serious disorder and bloodshed.' Yet Mountbatten still managed to propagate the myth that he could have had no idea of what was likely to occur.[54]

Ismay remembered how at this period Mountbatten was 'in his element. He was Captain of a Destroyer flotilla, Chief of Combined Operations, Supreme Commander and Governor-General, all rolled into one.' As if that wasn't bad enough:

> The worse the situation got [Mountbatten recalled], the more excited I got at the challenge. And I *was* excited, it was the most exciting period of my life. I mention this because if people wonder why I was able to do it, it was because I never, never worried. I felt I was doing my best. There was nothing more I could do. The riots and migrations and troubles – what I did was immediately to set up a proper war room, maps, take charge, run the thing; but I wasn't worried about it. Nobody, absolutely nobody, had given me any warning.[55]

He said this despite the fact that ever since March, Jenkins and many others had been warning Delhi that 'only by use of force' could catastrophe be averted in the Punjab.

One officer serving in the North-West Frontier at the time recalled that 'army officers all over the sub-continent begged Mountbatten to defer Independence until both the Indian and Pakistani armies and police forces had been reorganized and were functioning as new, separate Indian and Pakistani entities'.[56] Auchinleck's opinion was that 'if the original timetable had been adhered to, which was that the division take place in 1948, it might have been possible to reconstitute the forces without bloodshed'.

Mountbatten's complete peace of mind and lack of doubt is confirmed by observers. Only once did he display a scintilla of doubt about any of his actions. At a Joint Defence Council meeting on 16 August, he 'tried to humour everyone and admitted that he hoped that he had not made too big a mistake by not announcing the Award on 9th August. He said that the storm had not been unexpected but the extent could not have been anticipated.'[157] This seems to have been the agreed line to take. When Ismay addressed the Chiefs of Staff in London two months later, he used almost identical language: 'it was a mistake to imagine that the storm which broke out in August, and which was still raging, was unexpected ... although no one had predicted quite the extent of it'. On 16 August Mountbatten also 'said he now realised that if he had rounded up the Sikh trouble-makers, including Tara Singh, he would never have had to face this day'.[158] This single flash of frankness aside, there is no other indication that Mountbatten ever questioned his own actions.

Very soon afterwards he constructed a lifelong doctrine of his own infallibility. As he told one of his biographers, 'It is a curious thing, but a fact, that I have been right in everything I have done and said in my life.'[159] As time went on, this inability to admit that he had ever been wrong about anything amounted almost to a psychological disorder. Talking to a *Times* journalist in 1969 he said: 'I am glad to tell you that I think I was right from the point of view of history. I have always looked ahead, ten, twenty years ahead in history. ... In another twenty years people won't be able to understand the point of view of those who criticised me.'[160]

Tom Driberg may also have inadvertently stumbled on another reason why his friend evinced so little concern about the massacres. Mountbatten saw human beings in the mass 'as supremely complex machines rather than as persons'. Having no great spiritual depth himself, he was only interested 'in man as technician or social engineer, or raw material of social engineering. ... I do not know if he is capable of compassion.'[161] As Stalin once said, 'One death is a tragedy, one million a statistic.'

For evening relaxation, Mountbatten devoted himself to drawing up relationship tables, which plotted the family connections of all the European royal families, going back to the Middle Ages. Thus on page 121 it states that Alexandra Victoria, Princess of Schleswig-Holstein-Sonderburg-Glucksburg, was born in 1887 and in 1908 married August William of Prussia, who comes complete with nickname ('Auwi', pronounced 'Ouvee'). With every person properly labelled – Mountbatten's elder daughter, Lady Brabourne, is H 4B4A/V3A4A, for example – it is possible to discover exactly how they are related to one another. One can therefore work out exactly what relation the Princess was to, say,

Marquat, the Hereditary Count of Solms-Rodelheim-Assenheim, who appears on a different page. The system was not Mountbatten's invention; it is also used for pedigree cattle. The section on the Battenbergs omits to mention that Mountbatten's own grandfather, Prince Alexander of Hesse, was actually the offspring of his mother's lover, Baron von Grancy, a Court chamberlain with whom she lived openly after separating from her husband, the Grand Duke, in 1820, and thus had no right to the title of Prince at all.[162] It is inconceivable that so dedicated a student of family history as Mountbatten should not have known this fact about himself, as it was recounted in a number of books, including Prince von Bülow's memoirs, Maurice Paleologue's biography of Tsar Alexander II and Count Corti's history of the Hesse family.

Meanwhile, conditions in the refugee camps, which were suddenly expected to accommodate millions, grew foul beyond belief. Medicine, food and water ran out and sanitary arrangements collapsed, leading to epidemics of cholera and smallpox. Many camps were soon faced with starvation. To make matters worse, security had not been properly considered and communal massacres even took place inside the camps themselves. Chairing the second meeting of the new Emergency Committee, on 7 September, Mountbatten made the stupendously banal observation that, 'In his opinion the trouble had grown up through refugees arriving in such large numbers before any refugee organisations were ready to receive them.' At this point Edwina Mountbatten came into her own, organizing relief work in the camps with tremendous energy.

In mid-September 1947 Ismay spoke to Jinnah of the situation in Delhi: 'Fighting between large bodies in some districts; arson, looting and individual murder in others; crowds of destitute refugees; food supplies disrupted, telephone system dislocated; the hospital choked with wounded and dying and the dead lying where they had fallen because there was no one to collect and bury them.'[163] Of primary concern to Mountbatten was the public relations aspect and 'the world-wide effect that continued disturbances in Delhi, the capital city, would have'. He ordered that no troops or lorries should leave Delhi to relieve the West Punjab, which was in an even worse state, and particularly stressed 'how embarrassing it would be' if anything untoward happened to the American Ambassador or Commonwealth High Commissioners in the capital.

The refugees crossed the frontier on foot, in bullock carts, crammed into lorries and clinging to the sides and roofs of trains, ever prey to attack. Meanwhile, Mountbatten was addressing the first contingent of

British soldiers leaving India. Quoted in *Time Only to Look Forward*, the appropriately titled collection of his Viceregal speeches, he said that, 'with the departure of British Forces, the outward and visible sign of British rule in India disappears. And its place is taken by something very much more valuable – a really great friendship between the British and the Indians.' He told the troops that Nehru sadly could not be present as he was at a conference 'to settle the difficulties of the Punjab'.

Before the 'difficulties' were settled, months later, houses were burned and looted in the presence of policemen; women and children were flung off moving trains; the District Engineer of Lahore was attacked in his office, tied to a post and sawn into pieces; shrines were routinely desecrated; patients were murdered in their hospital beds; babies were cut in half and returned to their mothers; villages were mortar-bombed; there were mass suicides; Sikhs were forcibly circumcized; mobs stamped people to death; corpses were thrown into wells and cisterns to defile water supplies; people were ordered to stand or sit in long rows to wait to be shot one by one; and children were burnt alive in pits.[164] And so it went on, for week after genocidal week.

It is instructive that although he completely denied any responsibility for the massacres, Mountbatten consistently attempted to play down the numbers killed. It is impossible, especially at this distance in time, to do more than estimate how many lost their lives in the North Indian holocaust of autumn 1947. Again and again the annotation 'EFNA', standing for 'Exact Figures Not Available', would be found at the end of reports which came in to the authorities. There were often no eyewitnesses and people were killed all across the provinces in many different ways and in different circumstances, at a time when the administrators were inevitably more concerned with protecting themselves and their families than in collating statistics. When 800 Hindus died in a single incident in Hariawan, Mudie noted that 'the most interesting thing, however, about the whole matter was that it had never been reported to anyone in Lahore. Even if it had been, there was nothing anyone could have done about it.' For the first two months after he took over as Governor of West Punjab on 15 August, he had to 'ignore any report of a riot unless it alleged that there were at least a thousand dead. If there were, I asked for a further report, but I cannot remember any case in which I was able to do anything.'

When Mountbatten visited London for the royal wedding in November 1947, he gave a speech in which he put the number of deaths at 'only' 100,000, and contrasted that number with the numbers who died in the

Bengal famine during the war, estimated by historians at over a million. Ignoring the essential difference between natural and artificial disasters, Mountbatten later explained to Lapierre and Collins that, 'the famine of 1943–44 killed two or three million. ... And, in fact, I let the Indians have five per cent of my military shipping to bring food to them. We saved many more lives by doing that than were lost in 1947.'[165] Of the 4,000 files in Mountbatten's personal papers at Southampton University, only one – and a thin one at that – concerns the atrocities. Anything which clashed with Mountbatten's doctrine of infallibility was rigorously weeded out. One professor who has worked on the papers believes there is even 'evidence to suggest that a certain number of Mountbatten's papers were added to at a later date. He was an awful crook.'[166]

When in 1961 Sir Penderel Moon came up with the figure of 200,000 dead, he did not stop there, adding that 'it must really be accorded a mercy that Lord Mountbatten did not foresee more clearly the magnitude of the calamity that threatened the Punjab. Had he done so, he might have fumbled and faltered.' As it was, 'the Punjab had to pay in blood the price of freedom'.[167] Mountbatten, the 'Dickie Birds' and the Labour leadership concurred with this sophistry and collected around the 200,000 figure with a suspicious unanimity. 'The feeling we had was not that it was horrific but that it could have been much worse,' explains Campbell-Johnson. 'The figures are grossly exaggerated. By the end of September it was all over. I was running a war room so I know. The casualties were about two hundred and twenty thousand. Not all dead, that includes the wounded.'

In fact, as the sole file on the massacres in Mountbatten's papers shows, it was not all over by late September. A document prepared by the Indian Government for the Governor-General showing incidents reported in the nine days between 12 and 21 October includes:

> train derailed and fired on by Sikhs, two bombs thrown at military police, three Muslims thrown off train, Muslim orphanage attacked, village bombed, non-Muslim mob abduct twenty-four Muslim girls, refugee camp attacked, troops fired on refugees across border, crowd killed two police, two hundred Muslims killed by Sikhs, attempt to derail refugee train.[168]

In the middle of that period, on 17 October, Mountbatten wrote to Ismay to say that he had that morning returned 'from a pleasant holiday in Mashobra, and found ... there were hardly any incidents worth recording'.[169] By mid-November Savory was noting that 'cocktail parties have started now that the massacres are over for the time being, but I avoid them'.

'Broadly speaking the thing went off well, I think,' said Attlee in 1961. He admitted that there had been 'terrible massacres', but that they 'were not just the result of handing over, or of any feebleness by the Government. They'd been brewing up for a long time.' The Sikhs were 'very undependable and rather a rough people: they were the biggest cause of the trouble. Whether we could have stopped it then if we'd still been in control I don't know – it's very doubtful but there it was.'[170] We now know that at the time Attlee doubted Mountbatten's judgment in bringing forward the date of independence. Talking to Savory in Downing Street in late October, one of his questions concerned 'the speed of the hand-over ("was it too quick?")'; he also asked Ismay on his return whether he 'felt that we had taken the wrong course or had rushed things too much'.

There is evidence to suggest that Attlee considered having Mountbatten superseded. His Private Secretary, Leslie Rowan, wrote him a memorandum on 14 May 1947, which referred to 'the plan ... for a Minister to go out to India to settle matters there with full powers and the minimum of reference home'. Listowel was discounted as 'too new', A.V. Alexander was tied up with the Conscription Bill, Herbert Morrison had thrombosis, Ernest Bevin had just returned from a long trip behind the Iron Curtain, and Attlee did not want Sir Stafford Cripps to go, or risk going himself. So nothing was done, despite Rowan telling the Prime Minister that, 'if you pulled it off, it would be a master stroke'.[171]

Citing Moon as his source, Ziegler also puts the numbers killed at around 200,000, and argues that had Mountbatten not transferred power so quickly, 'two hundred thousand dead could have become two million, even twenty million'.[172] Plenty of people in a good position to know, however, profoundly disagree. Sir Algernon Rumbold, who was Political Secretary in the India Office until 15 August and head of the Indian desk in the Southern Asia Department at the Commonwealth Relations Office afterwards, had the job of collating the figures in London. He recalls that 'it was my unhappy duty to receive the daily telegraphs regarding the massacres attendant on the break-down on law and order in Northern India. Based on the reports I got in during the autumn of 1947 I formed the personal impression at the time that the death toll might have been six hundred thousand.'

Additional information came from Rumbold's conversations with the British High Commissioner in Pakistan and Deputy High Commissioners in Peshawar and Lahore. Rumbold felt that:

The great mistake was to divide the provinces simultaneously with transferring power at the centre. It was most desirable for the Central Government to continue to be as strong as possible and in position at that point to superintend the partition of the provinces for a few months *before* power was transferred at the centre. To do it all on the same day created the ideal conditions for mistrust and massacre. Unacceptable demands were placed on police and army loyalty.[173]

Two of the most distinguished soldiers of the day agreed. Montgomery saw Savory at the War Office for an hour in early October and 'was scathing about Mountbatten: "He's made a mess of things, I'll write and tell him so."' Later Savory heard from Field Marshal Auchinleck that he 'would accept a KG [the Garter] if offered it: but not on recommendation of MountB., who he considers has made a mess of things'.[174] Ismay, too, declined an honour from Mountbatten. He told a friend how one day in Delhi, 'on going into Mountbatten's study to talk with him, I noticed on his table in front of him a typed list of what were certainly recommendations for honours on the Declaration of Independence and I could see my name among the GSCI's'. Ismay, who was already a GCB, told him: 'You should have asked if I was willing to be recommended to a lower order. But that is not the point. Nothing on earth would induce me to accept an honour for the most painful and distasteful episode of my career. I must ask you to delete my name at once.'[175] Mountbatten's own Viscountcy was elevated to an Earldom on Independence Day.

One officer at the time, Louis Heren, formed the impression, after talking to many of the senior military officers involved, including Major-General Rees, the commander of the PBF, the Governors of East and West Punjab and various District Commissioners, that around half a million died. 'There was no real way of knowing. The dead of the refugee trains could be counted ... but there were more than seventeen thousand towns and villages in the Punjab and tens of thousands must have been buried, or cremated or left to rot in ditches unnoticed.'[176] Rees told Heren that he believed a million people were killed outright or died later of wounds.

Sir Lawrence Graffey-Smith, the High Commissioner in Karachi, put the death toll at 800,000. Lieutenant-Colonel Philip Mitchison of the PBF stated that, 'there is reason to believe something of the order of a million men, women and children, civilians, was by no means unlikely for the total killed. It has always been my own view and one which I have not departed from.'[177] Wynford Vaughan-Thomas, the BBC war correspondent, has said, 'I know a figure of a quarter of a million has been suggested and almost officially accepted ... but I think I would go on record, stick my neck out and say nearly a million died.' He also pointed out that 'you couldn't possibly make an accurate account because these massacres were taking place in lonely places, in all sorts of villages, little towns and all through the Punjab and Sikhistan'.[178] And the *Daily Telegraph* correspondent, Douglas Brown, noted in late August 1947: 'The number of killings is difficult to estimate as each band takes with it a burial party.'

This testimony from those who were working in India at the time sharply contradicts the received opinion Mountbatten hoped to have accepted. Sir Francis Mudie, Governor of West Punjab whilst the massacres were taking place, believed that 'according to the best estimate I could make in all about half a million were killed in trying to get to the West Punjab. There were of course also Hindus escaping from the West Punjab.'[179] Ismay himself told Churchill's Private Secretary, Anthony Montague Browne, that over a million people lost their lives during Partition. Montague Browne believes that 'the reason Churchill saw through Mountbatten was because Pug – whom he always respected and listened to – told him all about the massacres'.[180]

In late October 1947 Churchill said in the House of Commons that 'At least half a million Indians have already perished at each other's hands by violent means and now some seven or eight millions are homeless fugitives.'[181] No one disputed his figures. When in 1951, during a dinner on the *Queen Mary*, Churchill said that 'more than a million people had died' as a result of Mountbatten's policies, the ex-Viceroy merely commented that 'this grand old man ... really is past his prime'. One Conservative politician, Rab Butler, believed a million lost their lives, and another, Julian Amery, thinks 'one million dead would be a conservative figure'.[182] Christoper Beaumont thinks that 'more than half a million died. No one knows – it could have been anything up to seven hundred thousand.'[183] Sir Ronald Harris, the Private Secretary to the Secretary of State for India, puts the figure at 'around a million', but Mountbatten 'created this mystique through his extraordinary magnetic qualities that you felt anything he did must be unavoidable'.

Another historian of India wrote that 'approximately one million [refugees] never reached their promised nation alive'.[184] Gopal Khosla, whose book *Stern Reckoning* includes a meticulous, 180-page analysis of the massacres almost village by village, put the death toll at half a million, and Leonard Mosley in *The Last Days of the British Raj* estimated it at 600,000.

Even when checked, corroborated and scaled down to take exaggeration into account, the numbers are likely to have been considerably in excess of 200,000. They certainly constitute one of the greatest man-made tragedies ever to have overtaken humanity in time of peace. The nearest Mountbatten himself came to discussing it at the time was to write in his Conclusions to his 'Report on the Last Viceroyalty' that the population transfers 'were carried out in appalling circumstances ... some were murdered on the way'. In his nineteen-point explanation of his actions, Mountbatten criticized the Joint Defence Council, the Provincial Sikh and Muslim leadership in the Punjab, the British Intelligence Organization and the Muslim League, but did not accept that he himself had made a single error. 'Speed seemed essential,' he wrote.

A historian today, confronted by the overwhelming evidence now available, must challenge the 200,000 deaths postulated by Moon, Campbell-Johnson and Ziegler. Even so, we must still accept their broad strategic concept, stated in the last paragraph of Moon's mammoth *The British Conquest and Dominion of India*, that British rule had largely come to the end of its utility after the First World War. Mountbatten should have given Radcliffe at least six months to make his Award (from, say, April to October 1947). During the next six months he should have deployed a massively enlarged PBF in the general area of Radcliffe's proposed frontier – and particularly in Sikh territory. The Indian army could have been split between the two Dominions in that time, and also deployed. The first signs of trouble should have been met with the full force of modern weaponry, as Mountbatten had originally threatened. Then, in April 1948, he could have announced the Award, sustained by an undertaking that Britain would provide safe conduct for any Hindu, Muslim or Sikh family which wished to migrate across the frontier. The original deadline of June 1948 could then have been adhered to, and the new states not born during a bloody haemorrhage.

Mountbatten had gone out to India with five specific instructions from the British Government. The first was 'to obtain a unitary Government for British India and the Indian States'. The second was concerned with handling over power 'on the due date' in June 1948. The third was to persuade the Princes to enter into 'fair and just arrangements' for their future. The fourth proclaimed that 'the keynote was to be the closest co-operation with the Indians', which then included Muslims as well as Hindus. The last was 'to avoid a break in the continuity of the Indian Army'. In each and every one of these objectives, which he himself had helped to draft, Mountbatten failed.

On coming back from India, Mountbatten returned to the navy. He confided in Zuckerman in 1951 that, 'with all his political experiences, he might have made a better job of leading the country than had Attlee'. In October 1952 he narrowly escaped killing himself and his sister, the Queen of Sweden, when he turned his Riley sports car upside down on a stone wall in Malta. In 1955 he realized his childhood ambition of becoming First Sea Lord. His behaviour during the Suez crisis was predictable. He more than earned Eden's description of him as 'a congenital liar' when he claimed in 1976 that he had advocated using the Marines to capture twenty-five miles of the Canal in three days. In fact, the records show that at the time he had recommended 'that unilateral action by the Royal Navy and Royal Marines should *not* be taken'.[185]

After combining the three Services into a single Ministry of Defence, he became Chief of the Defence Staff in 1959. It was during this period that Sir Gerald Templer made the celebrated remark: 'You're so crooked, Dickie, if you swallowed a nail you'd shit a corkscrew.' According to the Permanent Secretary at the War Office, Mountbatten was 'probably the most distrusted of all senior officers in the three services', partly because of his practice of deliberately misreporting decisions that had been taken at the various committees on which he sat.[186] He left the Services in 1965, after only one of the forty senior people there thought that he should be reappointed.[187]

The prospect of retirement to a man of action was distasteful, and he did everything possible to keep himself busy. He never refused an invitation, especially if it gave him the opportunity to wear his decorations or to make a speech. The sound of his own voice proved a constant solace to him in old age. He showed an awesome stamina for touring and public engagements. In the late 1960s he spoke to the Hampshire Fire Brigade, Hovershow '66, the Isle of Wight Sea Scouts, the 'Batti-Wallahs' Society Luncheon, Poplar Boys' Club, the Borough of Ryde Garden Show, the Veterinary Association Conference in Brighton, the opening of the Portman Building Society's administrative centre, the Charter Presentation dinner dance of the Romsey Lions club, the opening of Lymington Marina, the Mothers' Union Rally, the opening of a new sun lounge in Romsey Hospital, the inauguration of a cookery centre in Andover, and so on and so on. When the Variety Club gave a dinner in tribute to Sir Billy Butlin in 1973, Mountbatten went along. He also toured the world. When visiting Puerto Rico in 1970, he was greeted by a larger-than-life-size bust of himself modelled in lard.

In retirement he starred in a twelve-part television series about his life and times, with each part given titles such as 'The Azure Main', 'The Stormy Winds' and 'United We Conquer'. It presented a totally distorted view of his career and induced equal mixtures of anger and hilarity amongst those who knew the truth. Parts defy satire, such as when he remarks that 'You must never let ambition interfere with the job in hand, which must be done for its own sake.' At the end of the concluding programme he asks:

> All I want to know is was I right, were they wrong? Will they eventually come round and see it? Or are they so dumb that it will have to be their children or grandchildren who will perhaps see this series of films in fifty years' time and see that I was fairly reasonable and the people who thought I was wrong were the ones who were unreasonable.

Then there was the farcical occasion in May 1968 when Cecil King, the Chairman of Mirror Group Newspapers, offered Mountbatten the post of titular head of Government after a coup had overthrown the Prime Minister, Harold Wilson. Such was Mountbatten's vanity that he listened to the proposal even after his friend and adviser, Lord Zuckerman, had walked out of Mountbatten's flat in Kinnerton Street declaring that the plans amounted to 'treasonable nonsense'. In 1975 Zuckerman wrote to the fourth person present in the room, Hugh Cudlipp, recalling that 'Dickie at first wanted to hold me back, but I insisted on leaving'.[188] Mountbatten did not, as he later claimed, wind up the meeting immediately after Zuckerman's departure, but continued for a short period to listen to King's proposals. As Zuckerman put it about Mountbatten, 'he was impulsively interested in almost any suggestion that looked as if it might lead him back to the national stage'.[189]

In May 1979 he returned to the international stage with a speech to the Stockholm International Peace Research Institute about nuclear weapons. He attacked the American delay in ratifying the Salt II Treaty, and spoke emotionally about 'the terrifying experience of the two atomic bombs that effaced the cities of Hiroshima and Nagasaki off the map'. He might have recalled his own diary entry for 6 August 1945, when he was dining at Windsor Castle, which read: 'Everybody was in good form as the atomic bomb has just fallen.'[190] In 1979 NATO adopted its 'Twin-Track' decision to deploy Cruise and Pershing II missiles in Europe, while continuing to negotiate with the Russians about the elimination of such systems. As the *Observer* put it in September 1987, 'despite public agitation and the parading of conscience through the streets, NATO was not deterred and the policy obtained its objectives spectacularly'.

Mountbatten's demand for a ban on tactical nuclear weapons that year was a call for appeasement at precisely the time when the NATO policy most needed support. His speech was later widely distributed in leaflet form by the Campaign for Nuclear Disarmament. It was yet another example of his lack of judgment.

The entry he wrote for himself in *Who's Who* omitted nothing. He was 'KG, PC, GCB, OM, GSCI, GCIE, GCVO, DSO, FRS, Hon. DCL, Hon. LLD, Hon. DSc., AMIEE, AMRINI'. The list shows his lack of a sense of the ridiculous, or appreciation of the absurdity of putting his Associated Membership of the Institution of Electrical Engineers in the same list as the Order of the Garter and the Order of Merit. People usually mention their parents only, but Mountbatten managed to list five ancestors, including Queen Victoria. Lady Mountbatten did not just die in 1960, but 'in North Borneo on tour as Superintendent-in-Chief, St John Ambulance Brigade'. In the same list as Viceroy of India, one learns that he was 'qualified as an interpreter' and is a member of the Inner Magic Circle. The entry covers an entire page, while another Earl in the same edition, Lord Home, a former Prime Minister and Foreign Secretary, summed himself up in a few lines.

This need to boast all his achievements in such an encyclopaedic way might have been because, as John Keegan has written, Mountbatten was essentially 'an insecure and ultimately lonely man, who craved an affection his wife would not give him'. He was someone who 'had countless friends and a dozen "best friends", but no real intimate of his own class and age'.[191] One exact contemporary of his, the Queen Mother, reportedly viewed her husband's cousin with semi-amused mistrust, not least because of his swift change of coat during the Abdication crisis.[192]

Mountbatten died in an act of communal outrage on 27 August 1979. He was killed when an IRA bomb exploded on his small fishing boat off Mullaghmore Harbour in County Sligo. Despite the clear security risk, he holidayed in southern Ireland every August. He was told not to go there by the Irish police, the Garda, a week before his last visit, although the British authorities annually gave him clearance.[193] Perhaps at seventy-nine he thought himself no longer an IRA target. He certainly thought of himself as popular in Ireland, ignoring the huge 'Brits Out' sign painted on a Mullaghmore hillside. It is not inconceivable, given his vanity, that he felt himself to be too big a target or, as an emancipator of peoples from British rule, an illogical one. He listed his Irish address and telephone number in *Who's Who*, and a television film he made of his life and times had shown him on his boat. It was announced that 'in the month of August the whole Mountbatten family assembles at Classiebawn' and that 'prawning in the harbour of Mullaghmore is just one of the rituals of the Mountbatten holiday'.[194]

As one who saw a good deal of him in old age has said, 'he always wanted to die a violent death, preferably at sea. He got both. He was getting frail and didn't like it.' Ziegler put it far better:

> To die with no time for fear or regrets, doing what he enjoyed most with the people who were above all precious to him, escaping the horrors of increasing decrepitude or senility, to end not with a whimper but with a bang that reverberated around the world – that truly was the fate Mountbatten would have chosen for himself.[195]

If there was an element of a Nelsonian death-wish in the decision of Mountbatten to have a holiday at the same time, in the same place, doing the same things in Republican Ireland every year, it was profoundly irresponsible, not just because of the risk to himself, but to those members of his family who were killed and maimed in the same explosion. Right to the end, then, Mountbatten was careless with other people's lives.

3

The Tories versus Churchill during the 'Finest Hour'

'Seldom can a Prime Minister have taken office with the Establishment ... so dubious of the choice and so prepared to find its doubts justified,' wrote Jock Colville of Winston Churchill, adding 'within a fortnight all was changed'.

This has since become the accepted version of history, convenient both to Churchill and the Establishment. It has been presented as the story of the Conservative Party swiftly recognizing him as a national saviour and, as the Battle of Britain and the Blitz raged, quickly falling in behind him in a spirit of defiant solidarity. The truth could not have been more different.

Old men forget, but old politicians forget selectively. Many are the self-serving memoirs of Conservative MPs who prefer not to remember both the depth of the mistrust they felt for Churchill and the length of time that they continued to feel it. Such was the post-war deification of Churchill for his sublime leadership in 1940–1 that it would have been a brave Tory who told the truth about the undeclared guerrilla warfare which was fought between the new Prime Minister and the Conservative hierarchy over those fateful months. For Churchill had to employ every weapon in a Prime Minister's armoury, including one which involved changing the constitution, to establish and then press home his political advantage before he was safe.

Far from reflecting the national mood, many Conservatives in the Commons maintained a position of scepticism towards Churchill and his coalition which lasted until the summer of 1941. Criticisms, mutterings, disloyal asides and a general feeling of mistrust continued to make

Churchill's leadership insecure, at least in Parliamentary terms, for far longer than is generally recognized today.

Not surprisingly, the evidence for this is somewhat patchy. People's views were changing quickly and often drastically in the highly volatile and stressful period of national peril. Because of the way Churchill's reputation stood after the war, personal reminiscences are unreliable, and only directly contemporaneous evidence is of much use. Those patrician Tory MPs who looked upon politics as a public duty rather than a career very often did not keep political diaries, especially during the period of emergency and nightly bombing. Sometimes – like the dog which did not bark in the night in the Sherlock Holmes story – it is a silence which gives the clue. The tale has therefore to be pieced together from scraps amongst hundreds of public and private sources. When it is, the picture which emerges is radically different from the accepted Tory version. The history of the period has tended to be written by the Churchillians, or at least by those sympathetic to his victorious vantage-point. It is instructive to look at it instead from the defeated Chamberlainites' point of view.

In November 1917 Churchill watched Clemenceau from the diplomatic box in the French Chamber and saw 'all around him was an assembly which would have done anything to avoid having him there, but having put him there felt they must obey'. The same may be said of Churchill and the Conservative Party in May 1940. As one of his Private Secretaries was later diplomatically to put it, 'Churchill's position in the Conservative Party was never wholly free from ambiguity, and he was conscious of it."

After crossing the floor of the House in 1904, Churchill had soon afterwards described the Tories as the 'Party of great vested interests ... corruption at home, aggression abroad to cover it up ... sentiment by the bucketful, patriotism by the imperial pint; the open hand at the public exchequer, the open door at the public house; dear food for the millions, cheap labour for the millionaire'. They reciprocated this hostility and in 1915 their leader, Andrew Bonar Law, agreed to take the Tories into Lloyd George's coalition on the condition that Churchill was not in the Cabinet. Having, in his words, 'ratted' on the Party once, Churchill only returned to the Tory fold after Bonar Law's death. In 1931 he 're-ratted', going into the Wilderness in protest over the Party's policy on India. There he accused the Tory stalwarts, Samuel Hoare and Lord Derby, of altering evidence to a Select Committee.

In 1935 Churchill's son Randolph stood against the official Conservative candidate in the Wavertree by-election with his support. He split the vote and allowed Labour to win the seat. Hoare correctly surmised: 'The fact that [Randolph] kept our man out will do ... Winston a good deal of harm in the party'.[2] Over the Abdication crisis the next year Churchill further angered the Tory grandees. As Balfour's niece, Blanche (Baffy) Dugdale, put it in her diary: 'the possibility, amongst others, of the country being split into a King's Party versus the Government is one which fills responsible minds with anxiety'.

These 'responsible people' – the Respectable Tendency of British politics – were confirmed in their view of Churchill as a maverick, but took solace from the fact that, as one Cabinet minister, Walter Elliot, put it, 'he has no support in the country, so I was in no way afraid of him'.[3] Whilst staying at Belvoir Castle during the crisis, Churchill 'felt the *atmosphere* of our [house] party was against him', which, as the Duchess of Rutland remembered, 'was alas true'. Rutland's son, Lord Granby, did not even bother to take up Churchill's offer to sign his books, as he 'really thought Winston was "finished" '.[4]

By the time of the Norway debate of 7 and 8 May 1940, the sense of distrust which existed on the Tory benches towards the First Lord of the Admiralty had hardly been diminished by his eight months in the War Cabinet. Despite Churchill's vigorous defence of the Chamberlain ministry in the debate, in a winding up speech which the Liberal MP, Dingle Foot, thought 'the least impressive of his career', many Tories suspected – not least because a number of Churchill's friends had gone into the 'no' lobby – that Churchill secretly wanted their leader to lose. Lord Curzon's daughter, Lady Alexandra Metcalfe, watched the debate from the Gallery and recorded seeing 'Winston, like a fat baby swinging his legs on the front bench, trying not to laugh when told by Lloyd George that the Government were using him as their air raid shelter. Stony faces on each side of him.'[5]

It was only with difficulty that Eden and Churchill's Parliamentary Private Secretaries were persuaded to vote for the Government. As one of them, Jim Thomas, put it in a letter to his fellow anti-appeaser, Lord Cranborne:

> It was pointed out as a PPS to Winston and Anthony, so close to the War Cabinet, a hostile vote by [Brendan] Bracken and myself would be taken as the private view of our Chiefs.... It was a sad ending to a day for which I had waited since 20 February 1938 [when Eden, Cranborne and Thomas resigned from the Chamberlain Government together]! And I am still not sure we were right.[6]

Since 1931 the National Government had been a coalition of Conservatives, National Liberals and National Labour, but with the former in a preponderant majority. From a pre-war strength of 418, Chamberlain's support had plummeted to 281 at the end of the Norway debate on the night of Wednesday, 8 May 1940. Forty-one of the Government's normal supporters had voted against it and around eighty abstained. Only five backbenchers had spoken up for the Prime Minister. When Chamberlain made his disastrous appeal, 'I call on my friends to support us in the Lobby tonight', he laid himself open to Lloyd George's accusation of putting personal interests before those of the nation. Lady Alexandra, and many other observers, felt this gaffe 'more than anything turned the tide against him'.

One of the five backbenchers to speak up for him, the Liberal Nationalist George Lambert had asked: 'Who is to be Prime Minister? ... Dr Goebbels could not have done better than the House of Commons has done.'[7] Jim Thomas believed that the Foreign Secretary, Lord Halifax, was 'favourite at the moment but I hear the usual rumour that he won't think of it. Very much persuasion is needed. Winston, of course, a runner and I have a hunch that Anthony [Eden] might step in – but this is an outside chance.'

Therefore, it was by no means certain that Churchill would be chosen and a great shock to many Tories when he was. One of the celebrated Tennant sisters, Nancy, was married to Tommy Dugdale, Tory MP for the North Riding of Yorkshire, who had served in Baldwin's Downing Street and had also spent five years in that bastion of Chamberlainite orthodoxy, the National Government Whips' Office, before joining the Yorkshire Hussars Yeomanry in Palestine in January 1940. The letters his wife sent him give an invaluable insight into Chamberlainite Tory thinking, and her family and social connections with senior politicians gave her access to all the latest political gossip. Two days after the Prime Minister's resignation broadcast, she wrote to her husband: 'Neville spoke and spoke *so* well. I had a *real* shock at his resignation – it seemed to knock the bottom out of the home situation – I can't believe he has gone – the household was plunged into gloom as I was – and to think of Winston getting it!'[8]

When Lady Alexandra Metcalfe, a friend of Lord Halifax's, heard on the radio that Churchill was to be Prime Minister, the news 'evoked a "Thank God" from me'. However, this was solely on the grounds that she knew Halifax did not want the job, but 'from every other point of view I think he would have been more dependable and better than

Winston. One can't talk of them in the same breath and England would have had a man at the helm of whom she could have been justly proud. I am terrified of Winston, the only thing to be said is, he is preferable to L[loyd] G[eorge].'

This feeling was general amongst Conservatives. Chamberlain had won a majority of eighty-one at the Norway debate, so constitutionally he did not have to resign. But on Thursday, 9 May, he accepted the underlying logic of the Norway division and decided to go. He held a meeting with Churchill and Halifax at 4.30 p.m., which ascertained that Churchill would succeed. When the news came through on the morning of 10 May that Hitler had attacked in the West, Chamberlain attempted to countermand this. The key man in forcing him out seems to have been the diminutive Air Minister, Sir Kingsley Wood, who made it clear at Cabinet that he could not use the new military situation to change his mind. Only Hoare spoke up for Chamberlain at the Cabinet meeting. Wood had been in contact with Churchill since the debate and suspicious Chamberlainites saw his subsequent appointment as Chancellor of the Exchequer by Churchill as a reward for changing sides.

More extraordinary for Chamberlainites than their hero's fall was that their former arch-enemy, Winston Churchill, should have won the crown he had been so long suspected of coveting. 'I could hardly control myself,' wrote Nancy Dugdale. 'Everyone here, Lady C[urzon]-H[owe], etc., will *hate* it and the country people also. They say "we never thought of him, Lord Halifax, yes, but Mr Churchill, never". First they never thought Neville would go as the debate meant nothing to them and they still have complete confidence in him.' This point was made by the few Chamberlainite backbenchers who spoke in the debate. Sir George Courthorpe had said that his postbag had indicated no desire for a change of Government, and Sir Archibald Southby did not believe the 'minor knock in Norway' was important enough to bring the Government down. Had it been generally recognized that Chamberlain's very survival was on the line, many Tories who abstained in order to give the Government a shock, or to register a protest against Sir John Simon and Sir Samuel Hoare, would have instead dutifully trooped through the 'aye' lobby as they had throughout the previous nine years.

Nancy Dugdale's letter to her husband continued:

W.C. they regard with complete mistrust as you know, and they hate his boasting broadcasts. W.C. is really the counterpart of Goering in England, full of the desire for blood, 'Blitzkrieg' and bloated with ego and over-feeding, the same treachery running through his veins, punctuated by heroics and hot air. I can't tell you how depressed I feel about it.[9]

This negative attitude towards Churchill's wartime broadcasts may sound surprising today, but from political cognoscenti who were used, if not immune, to his rhetoric, there were constant criticisms. After his broadcast to the neutrals of January 1940, Lady Alexandra Metcalfe had written in her diary: 'It is incredible that a man in his position should make such gaffes. His bragging about the war at sea is followed every time by some appalling loss, last time two destroyers, and his voice oozes with port, brandy and the chewed cigar.'

Churchill's undisguised fascination with warfare was considered somewhat bad form by many Tory MPs, a large number of whom had served in the First World War. Chamberlain's denouncer in the Norway debate, Admiral of the Fleet Roger Keyes, had attended the occasion in his uniform, but if all the Government's supporters had worn their Service uniforms, observers would have spotted a general, eleven colonels, five admirals, nine DSOs, eighteen MCs and scores of other veterans in the 'aye' lobby. They were far from being the stay-at-home civilians sometimes depicted. Detailed academic study of those who voted for Chamberlain shows that age, class and safety of Parliamentary seat were all factors in the way MPs acted. Ninety per cent of those Tory knights of the shire over forty-five who represented safe seats voted for Chamberlain. This was the Conservative Party's backbone and they proved some of the most intractable Churchill-sceptics.

Despite their reluctance to vote for him in the Norway division, many of the abstainers, non-attenders and even some rebels were nevertheless still devoted to Chamberlain personally. The high drama of the debate helped induce a feeling of bitterness against the rebels, which took months to subside. A typical example was the taunt of the Chamberlainite loyalist, Kenneth Pickthorn, at the young rebel, Richard Law, son of the former Conservative Prime Minister, who was leaving the Chamber after the debate: 'Well, I expect you'll get your reward!'[10] His suspicions seemed to be confirmed when Law received a ministerial post at the War Office soon afterwards.

When the House met on 13 May, after the Whitsun recess, a Chamberlainite backlash was well under way. William Spens, Chairman of the Tory backbenchers' 1922 committee, told the arch-Chamberlainite Under-Secretary at the Foreign Office, Rab Butler, that 'three-quarters' of Tory MPs were 'ready to put Chamberlain back'.[11] A number had come under severe pressure from their constituencies to support Chamberlain.

The Aldershot News of 10 May provides a typical example of the way much of the Tory local press reacted to the Norway debate. Lord Wolmer, heir to the Earldom of Selborne, had voted against Chamberlain and, according to the paper:

> When he cast his vote of no confidence in the Government he was far from representing the views of those who sent him to the House of Commons, and as a result of this action he will cease to be regarded as MP for Aldershot. His egotistical action has hurt the Conservatives of this area deeply, and henceforth to them his name is mud.

Many people thought that the rebels acted as they had from self-serving or egotistical motives. The Whips' nickname for the anti-appeasement group around Eden was 'Glamour Boys'. As Sir Victor Raikes wrote to a fellow Chamberlainite loyalist, Alan Lennox-Boyd, on 10 May, 'The new political orientation rather depresses me.... Anyway the late Prime Minister's critics are doing well out of it, so some people should be pleased.' The impression quickly got around that the new Government, as Raikes put it, 'is in fact ... deliberately composed of anti-Munichites'.[12] However, this was far from the truth, as two-thirds of Chamberlain's ministers were reappointed by Churchill and only twelve senior posts went to newcomers. Nevertheless, the sense of betrayal amongst Chamberlainites was acute.

This mood was well articulated by a letter of commiseration written to Sir John Simon, who had been exiled to the Lord Chancellorship:

> I think a good many people are beginning to feel rather ashamed of the House of Commons debate last week and of the newspaper and the BBC-induced hysteria over the comparatively minor Norwegian campaign which began the trouble.... You seem to have had *several* fifth columnists in the Government – apart from the cuckoos!... I am quite certain that it will not be long before the country realises what it has owed to Mr Chamberlain and yourself in recent years.[13]

Another correspondent, the historian and political biographer J.A. Spender, explained how he was advising

> all my friends to bury their hatchets and give full and generous support to Churchill – something very different from what some of them called 'support' when Chamberlain was Prime Minister.... Churchill for the time being is very popular but, as all the advertisers and word-pullers agree, popularity cannot be maintained at a high level except by constant effort.[14]

A recurring theme in the hundreds of letters which Chamberlain received after his resignation was that the game was by no means over.

Rab Butler wrote: 'I hope you will always realise the strength and number of your friends and how much we count on your presence in the Government.' Chamberlain was still Leader of the Party, and Butler feared that 'without a sure touch so much may be swept away.... I am sure that times will come when I and my friends will need these great qualities of yours ... whatever the future might bring and wherever your influence may be required.' It was not the letter of a man who had given up all hope of his master returning. He was articulating the views of many Chamberlainites when, in a subtle critique of Churchill's friends and confidants, he added: 'There are certain virtues and values which those of us, who have been associated with authority since 1931, hold dear, which we are sure you will perpetuate.'[15]

The sense of dozens of such letters of support for Chamberlain is best summed up by that from the backbencher Captain Edward Cobb: 'The fact that you were prepared to serve the new P.M. resolves the doubts of a good many of us who had been doubtful of whether we would like to receive the Whip in these circumstances. If he is good enough for you he must be good enough for us.' One MP, Patrick Donner, wrote to say that, 'if we lose altogether the only leader we have – and there is no other – the standards of value in the party will disappear and with them the reason for continuance'. Sir Archibald Geddes said, 'So far I have met no-one in the Regiment who would like to see Winston PM.'

Walter Liddall, who had set up a 'Loyalty to Leader' group in the Parliamentary Party, wrote to assure Chamberlain that every member of it would support him 'not for a day or month, but always'. This turned out to be no exaggeration. Even Hoare got a number of consoling letters. Leslie Hore-Belisha wrote to him: 'It won't be for long!' John Moore-Brabazon told him, 'this is *not* the last war administration by a long way'.[16] He was wrong, but these were not the sentiments of men who had totally reconciled themselves to the new regime. Many were afraid that their political careers would be stymied by Churchill taking revenge for the catcalls and humiliations to which various Tories had subjected him during the Wilderness Years. The first manifestation of the Chamberlainites' unaltered loyalties came on 13 May, when only the Labour benches applauded Churchill's first entry into the Chamber as Prime Minister. Loud and prolonged Tory cheers greeted Chamberlain when he took his seat on the Front Bench next to the new Prime Minister.

The Chamberlainites' sense of scepticism and resentment against Churchill, which was to metamorphosize into support and eventually devotion, is fully documented in the newly discovered diary of Captain

Charles Waterhouse. 'A true blue Tory, a country gentleman, a Life Guard in the First World War', Waterhouse had been MP for South-East Leicester since 1924.[17] A Derbyshire landowner, Great War MC, Deputy-Lieutenant of the county and Justice of the Peace, Waterhouse was the epitome of the traditional shire Tory. He had been a Whip since 1935 and, after the outbreak of war, was appointed Assistant Postmaster-General. The significance of his diary lies in the extent to which it reflects the views of mainstream Conservatives as they gradually reconciled themselves to Churchill. Waterhouse was a close friend of the Chief and Deputy Chief Whips, David Margesson and James Stuart, and nobody could better personify the Conservative Party as it was cajoled, persuaded, bribed and charmed into eventual support for the new Prime Minister.

Waterhouse's attitude towards the Norway debate was characteristically forthright. Written at 1.45 a.m., on his return from the Commons to his flat in Lowndes Square, he recorded:

> Division 281 against 200 with I estimate 45 of our wettest voting with the Opposition – the usual crowd of Anglo-American – general disgruntled – sacked – aspirant – Glamour, with a few well-meaning sentimentalists and amateur strategists thrown in.... I do not see that [Chamberlain] has any course but resignation. He cannot stand the strain of war against half the world, two Opposition parties and a considerable section of his own. Hitler will thank Thor for our quislings.[18]

The language of treachery – 'quislings', 'fifth columnists', etc. – was freely used by the Chamberlainites in describing the Norway rebels. One of them, Maurice Hely-Hutchinson, told the Norway rebel, Somerset de Chair, that his friends were like 'parachutist troops who had descended behind the lines in Conservative uniform'.[19]

Waterhouse wound up his diary entry on that momentous night:

> We gave the PM a great reception when he left the House after the division but all this is clearly having an effect on him. W.C. after his bloody-mindedness of a fortnight ago seems definitely to have changed his fickle mind and tonight put in heavy blows in defence of the Government position.

The 'bloody-mindedness' reference was probably to Churchill's recent demand for a greater say in the running of the war. Having originally intended to go for four days' fishing on the Kelso over Whitsun with his neighbour Lord Belper, the political situation meant that Waterhouse had reluctantly to be in London on Saturday, 11 May.

Waterhouse wrote when he got back:

> Neville Chamberlain announced on the 9 p.m. wireless that as the Socialists

had refused to serve under him he had agreed to serve under Winston Churchill. If ever there was a mark of real greatness it is this ... the PM is prepared for the nation's sake to serve under one who until lately – very lately – was first an open opponent and then a possibly not over-loyal colleague. So be it.

This was a suspicion many MPs had about the new Prime Minister. Despite his conspicuously vigorous defence of the Government in the debate, when some assumed his own career may also have been on the line, Chamberlainites wondered whether Churchill had been working behind the scenes to make himself Prime Minister. He had not intrigued, unless taking advice from Kingsley Wood not to bow to pressure from those who wanted Halifax can be counted. Churchill reacted angrily against even his closest friends who gloated too publicly at Chamberlain's downfall, and was zealous in observing all the proprieties towards his predecessor.

Waterhouse's estimation of the new Prime Minister was typical:

Winston has his ambition and thank God Chamberlain is there to keep the country straight. I do not think that W.C. will be comfortable as leader, his mind is essentially critical and volcanic and he is used to proposing and propounding schemes and ideas and for having these schemes critically examined and as a rule gracefully withdrawing them. Such is not the role of a PM.

Halifax echoed these misgivings, writing to Lady Alexandra Metcalfe from his suite in the Dorchester on 13 May: 'I don't think WSC will be a very good PM though I think the country will think he gives them a fillip.'

It was to the composition of Churchill's coalition that Tories immediately addressed themselves, in a mood to have their anxieties and suspicions confirmed. 'As always must happen after such an upheaval he will from group loyalty have to give office to a considerable number of people such as Bob Boothby who have brains but lack character and, in that particular case, decency,' assumed Waterhouse. This also worried Nancy Dugdale, who warned her husband: 'Now all those reptile satellites – Duff Cooper – Bob Boothby – Brendan Bracken, etc. – will ooze into jobs they are utterly unfitted for. All we are fighting to uphold will go out of public life. I regard this as a greater disaster than the invasion of the Low Countries.' That, she considered, was merely 'the inevitable unrolling of "Mein Kampf"'.

References to standards of public life were a common theme amongst Chamberlainites. They considered that what Butler had called their 'virtues and values' were under threat from the Churchillian and

'Glamour Boy' adventurers, who supposedly had lower standards of political decency. 'The crooks are on top as they were in the last war,' wrote Baldwin's confidant, Lord Davidson. 'We must keep our powder dry!' Halifax also believed that 'the gangsters will shortly be in complete control'.[20] Churchill's friends, associates and fellow anti-appeasers of the Wilderness Years were cordially detested by the Tory knights.

As well as Duff Cooper, the only minister to resign over Munich; Brendan Bracken, Churchill's widely distrusted right-hand man, whose murky Irish background made Tories suspicious; and Robert Boothby, the flamboyant free-thinking anti-appeaser; there was Churchill's son-in-law, Duncan Sandys, whose use of leaked information over rearmament had infuriated the Party; and most of all the press magnate, Lord Beaverbrook, whom Tories disliked as a thrusting colonial. They had decried the anti-Baldwin campaigns of arguably the most powerful popular newspaper in the history of Fleet Street. All of these friends of Churchill aroused the ire of the Respectable Tendency, who dreaded their entry into the Government.

Another anti-appeaser whose inclusion in the Government was bound to anger Chamberlainites was Harold Macmillan. A Keynesian intellectual who had supported the Master of Balliol against Quintin Hogg, the official Conservative candidate in the post-Munich Oxford by-election, Macmillan had infuriated the Respectable Tendency by his triumphalist attitude at the Norway debate when he, according to Waterhouse, 'stood up like a madly grinning schoolboy yelling abuse at the PM'.[21] With behaviour which Lady Alexandra Metcalfe found 'horrible', Macmillan had attempted to sing 'Rule Britannia', until he was angrily shouted down by the Chamberlainites standing around him.

The formation of Churchill's coalition in the week after 10 May 1940 was a delicate juggling act carried out with great dexterity. The spoils were divided in such a way as to leave every group, if not content, at least unable to complain overmuch. Most important for Churchill's survival, it accorded the Chamberlainites just enough senior places to remove their immediate discontent, yet not enough to give them overall control of the ministry. The linchpin in its formation, as with so much in politics since 1931, was the Government Chief Whip, Captain David Margesson. He had first joined the Whips' Office in 1924, becoming its Chief in November 1931. He more than deserved his reputation as the toughest Chief Whip in British political history. Tall, gaunt and a keen huntsman, Margesson was the grandson of Lord Buckingham and the Respectable Tendency's sergeant-major.

He used to put in sixteen hours a day in the Commons and made it his business to know all the hopes, fears and foibles of the National Government MPs. More martinet than shepherd, 'many of his own party looked upon him as a bully ... anybody of his own side who went into the wrong lobby he considered deserved to be carpeted or treated rough. You were either for the Government or against; there was no half-way house with him.'[22] One young MP remembered how, having rebelled on a vote over India in the early 1930s, he was summoned to the Chief Whip's room. After writing for an entire minute, Margesson finally looked up and demanded: 'What the hell do you mean by voting against the Government last night?' Although the MP answered bravely, he never made even junior ministerial rank.[23]

In *Guilty Men*, the left-wing journalists' polemic against the Chamberlainites which was published in July 1940, Margesson rated an entire chapter to himself. The ex-minister, Walter Elliot, told his wife that he thought the book 'exhibited a guillotine temper'. It explained how Margesson would isolate rebels: 'If the cad won't play the game, well he must be sent to Coventry. The other fellows shun and spurn him.' Churchill well knew the treatment; Margesson's period of primacy during the MacDonald, Baldwin and Chamberlain Premierships coincided exactly with Churchill's Wilderness Years. 'His task was to keep the Conservative dissidents isolated,' says a leading historian of the period, 'to put them under constant pressure from the party organisations in their constituencies, to divert patronage away from them, and to make sure their ostracism by the bulk of the party was as complete as he could make it.'[24]

In mid-1939 the Whips plotted to have Churchill de-selected before the general election which had to be called before June 1940. As Jim Thomas wrote to 'Bobbety' Cranborne that summer, after Lord Camrose's failed *Daily Telegraph* campaign to get Churchill into the Cabinet:

> The Whips are hopeless, hopeless, hopeless and Tommy [Dugdale] the worst. He said to me yesterday that the increased majority at Caerphilly [by-election] had knocked Camrose on the head and that it showed the PM's popularity and now all could be prepared for the General Election next October. I said what about the war next week? But he said that the only thing that would make war certain would be Winston in the Cabinet. Managed to keep my temper....[25]

Three days before the Norway debate, Thomas wrote to Cranborne, who was ill, reporting how 'the Whips were endeavouring to throw the responsibility [for the Norway campaign] on Winston, but they eventually thought it wiser to make use of him'.[26] During the debate, Attlee accused the Conservatives of allowing their loyalty to the Chief Whip to 'overcome their loyalty to the real needs of the country'. When the vote proved him wrong, it was Margesson who had finally and sorrowfully to tell Chamberlain that he had no option but to resign. At the meeting to decide whether Halifax or Churchill should succeed him Margesson said that 'he found a growing feeling in the Labour Party' of opposition to having a Prime Minister from the House of Lords. This information may have helped ease Churchill into the pole position Halifax had left open for him.

Yet Churchill's accession did not automatically entail Margesson's eclipse, as many expected. *Guilty Men* had pointed out how 'in every Ministerial shuffle of the last five years, the Tory Chief Whip has been to the fore', and such was the strength of the Chamberlainites in the Commons that May 1940 proved no exception. As Samuel Hoare noted at the time, 'David Margesson in the centre of everything. Max [Beaverbrook]'s opinion: A clever rogue.'[27] After his fall, Hoare thought Chamberlain had been too much influenced by Margesson, 'his evil genius'. The Fouché of the National Government, Margesson quickly came to terms with the new regime, and the alacrity with which he, like Kingsley Wood, adapted himself to the changed political circumstances was soon to arouse the ire and distrust of some dyed-in-the-wool Chamberlainites. Lady Alexandra Metcalfe had noted during the Norway debate that 'either [the Whips] have got [no backbenchers] to support them or David Margesson is to blame'. Meanwhile, Jock Colville was noting in his diary that Margesson, 'owing to the reconstruction, has landed in the enemy camp, I suppose'.[28]

The senior government posts largely chose themselves. Labour took two places in the War Cabinet with the Party's Leader and Deputy Leader, Clement Attlee and Arthur Greenwood, becoming Ministers without Portfolio. Having been vetoed by Labour for the posts of Chancellor of the Exchequer or Leader of the House, Chamberlain became Lord President of the Council. Halifax stayed on as Foreign Secretary and Churchill became Minister of Defence as well as Prime Minister. The only senior Chamberlainite to be dismissed altogether was Hoare, who considered himself very hard done by. He begged Churchill for the Viceroyalty of India, but was in the end fobbed off with the Madrid Embassy. He then immediately began haggling for an extra £2,000 in special allowances, coincidentally the same sum he was secretly receiving annually from Beaverbrook for political services rendered.

It is a sign of Churchill's perceived weakness that Sir John Simon, the Tweedledum of appeasement to Hoare's Tweedledee, was allowed to become Lord Chancellor. It helped that he was the leader of the small National Liberal Party. On the second day of the Norway debate Lord Dunglass had offered to sacrifice both Simon and Hoare to propitiate Tory malcontents. Despite this, Simon was given the Woolsack by Churchill and spent the rest of the war performing worthy tasks such as chairing a royal commission on the birth rate and passing legal reforms on frustrated contracts.

Further indication of the new Prime Minister's political weakness vis-à-vis the Chamberlainites was his decision to allow Sir Horace Wilson to stay on as head of the Civil Service and Permanent Secretary to the Treasury. Although civil servants do not normally lose their positions as a result of changes of government, Wilson had been Chamberlain's *éminence grise* and was despised by the Churchillians as the Svengali of appeasement. He was turfed out of his office in No. 10 by Randolph Churchill and Brendan Bracken on the first day of Churchill's Premiership. After Wilson's belongings were thrown into the corridor during the lunch hour, Lord Dunglass remarked to a friend that afternoon, 'the advance troops are on the sofa'.[29] Wilson was, however, allowed to keep his powerful jobs until his retirement in July 1942, although his recommendations about his successor were then ignored.

Only one of Chamberlain's ministers actually refused to serve under Churchill. Oliver Stanley was the son of the Lord Derby whom the new Prime Minister had accused of cheating during the Indian constitutional struggle. He had become War Minister after Hore-Belisha was sacked in January 1940. But having clashed repeatedly with Churchill, his naval opposite number, during the Phoney War, he felt, as he told fellow Tory MP Victor Cazalet on 21 May, 'that my personal relations with the new Prime Minister were such that it would not have been honest of me to take the job which was offered me'. Two days later he wrote to Chamberlain: 'I only hope that the country will not have to pay a terrible penalty for the mistake it made,' adding, as did so many of Chamberlain's correspondents: 'I hope some day I may be serving under you again.'[30]

A rumour quickly went around that Churchill had offered Stanley the Dominions Office in so rude a way that he could not but refuse it.[31] What is certain is that on the day it was offered, Halifax – who was keen to have as many friends and supporters in the Government as possible to counterbalance the Churchillians – lunched with Stanley and his wife, Lady Maureen. She was the daughter of Halifax's friend Lord Londonderry and was anxious that her husband should accept Churchill's offer. But, according to Halifax, 'He was very stunt about it; the principal ground being that he could not serve Winston loyally having seen so much of him in the last two months. It would never work.' Nevertheless, Halifax 'exhorted him a good deal and made him promise to see Neville before seeing Winston. This he did, but to my surprise when I saw Neville in the evening he told me that he also had concurred with Oliver on the whole, his reasons being that Oliver would be able to steady the boat in the House of Commons from outside. So that is that.'[32]

When Halifax was shown a further list of government appointees which came out on 15 May, he was 'sorry not to see Eddie Devonshire's name, and puzzled.... He may have refused!' That day Colville had been ordered to telephone Devonshire, whom Churchill thought 'not bad as Dukes go', to say that his 'services were no longer required'. Yet two days later Devonshire became Parliamentary Secretary at the India Office. It is, however, indicative that Halifax's immediate assumption was that this aristocrat may also have spurned Churchill. Halifax also tried to persuade another friend to serve in the coalition. Alan Lennox-Boyd was a zealous Chamberlainite who had made an anti-Czech aside in a speech during the Munich crisis and had once been offered a decoration by Franco. He felt that it was incumbent on him to resign and join the navy. Bracken wrote to him: 'Your reasons for refusing office do you honour. You will have a bigger chance when this awful war is over.'[33] The only other minister of service age, Lennox-Boyd's cousin by marriage, Lord Dufferin, also refused office in order to join up.

With the Dutch surrender on 14 May and the Germans piercing the French line at Sedan the same day, Churchill was too busy to attend to the junior ministerial posts, which were therefore hacked out between Bracken and Margesson. Despite claiming to Hoare that he was 'a mere bellhop', Bracken played a vital role in the formation of the Government. There was no love lost between him and the Chief Whip, who had hitherto marginalized him politically. Bracken ordered a young official on Churchill's staff at the Admiralty, Bernard Sendall, to 'keep a close eye on every move the Chief Whip makes'. In the emergency Churchill did not ask Chamberlain to vacate No. 10 immediately, but conducted the war from the Admiralty before finally moving on 14 June. This had the added advantage of helping to soften the blow for Chamberlain.

Sendall remembers being instructed to 'let Bracken know whenever

Margesson was in the Admiralty so he could come over straight away and put a spoke in the Chief Whip's wheels'.[34] There is some evidence that Margesson did not fight as hard for all Chamberlainites during the reconstruction as might been have expected. Bracken told Macmillan that 'Margesson would say, "Strike him out. He's no good at all." "Why then", Brendan would ask, "did you appoint him?" "Oh well," Margesson said, "he was useful at the time." '[35]

Some Chamberlainite wag distributed a circular around the Commons on the last night of the Norway debate satirizing a future Churchill Government. Their apprehensions can be detected beneath the fifth-form humour: Prime Minister was 'The Rt Hon. Instant Purchill', Lord Chancellor was 'Sir Stifford Craps', 'Lord Privy Squeal' was 'Mr Bootboy', Secretary of State for Air was 'Rt Hon. Arthur Deadwood', and so on.[36] In the end the Chamberlainites did well. Labour had only sixteen ministers in the Government, against fifty-two Conservatives. The following National Government ministers found Cabinet-ranking posts in the coalition: Chamberlain and Halifax, together with Sir John Anderson, Ernest Brown, Lord Caldecote, Ronald Cross, Sir Andrew Duncan, Lord Hankey, Robert Hudson, Malcolm MacDonald, William 'Shakes' Morrison, Herwald Ramsbotham, Sir John Reith, Sir John Simon, Lord Tryon and Sir William Womersley, almost all of whom were Chamberlain devotees. Despite this impressive list of reappointments, however, they were far from mollified.

Reith wrote in his diary: 'how filthy this treatment – and what a rotten government.... A dirty business every way.' The staunchly Chamberlainite editor of *The Times*, Geoffrey Dawson, sarcastically recorded the appointment of 'colourful Kingsley Wood' to the Exchequer and commented on the jobs for Leo Amery at the India Office, Duff Cooper at the Ministry of Information and Lord Lloyd at Colonies: 'too many friends!'[37] Geoffrey Shakespeare, a National Liberal MP, wrote to his party leader, Simon: 'We all feel deeply that the new government ... necessary as it may be to secure the co-operation of Labour – should have been launched on a wave of pettiness and spite.' For Nancy Dugdale the appointments of Wood, Duff Cooper and Churchill's old friend, the Liberal leader Sir Archibald Sinclair, to the Air Ministry, 'makes me sick'. She was not alone amongst Chamberlainites in blaming Margesson for bringing the 'W.C. element into public life.... I can't bear to think of Winston's overweening ambition being satisfied.'

Chamberlain's former Minister for the Co-ordination of Defence, Lord Chatfield, told Hoare: 'Winston seems indeed to have challenged fate by the selection of some of his colleagues. I am really glad I am out of the picture and only a faraway memory. You will soon be in harness again'. Halifax recorded Victor Cazalet's 'horror at the appointment of Beaverbrook to look after the production of aircraft'. The Chamberlainite minister, Euan Wallace, put Duff Cooper's inclusion in the Government solely down to his wife, the famous socialite beauty Lady Diana.[38] Halifax gave Churchill little credit for having to construct a government in the middle of a battle:

> Apart from the merits of his appointments he seems to me to have been incredibly rough in his method of handling those he was going to drop! Merely a message through his secretary! And in two cases at least that I know, the person concerned first saw it in the paper and heard it on the wireless. I think even in war things should be done differently to that. He's an odd creature.[39]

Some Churchillians and Edenites also looked upon the make-up of the coalition as a defeat. Bracken had to mollify Boothby – whose years of devotion to Churchill during the Wilderness Years had been rewarded with a mere Parliamentary Secretaryship at the Ministry of Food – by emphasizing: 'This is a stop-gap government formed during a whizzing crisis. Many changes will have to be made later.' After Jim Thomas had been appointed to an overwhelmingly Chamberlainite-dominated Whips' Office, he reported to Cranborne, his old friend and fellow Edenite, that he had been 'assailed all day by our indignant [Eden] group over the Whips appointments and my own but feel that, personally, I must swallow this tiresome position as I cannot bother Winston with so petty a matter whilst others are fighting the most decisive battle of the War'. He could not help adding, 'unless you think we should protest against an obvious party move'. He had been appointed as a token rebel in a Whips' Office which consisted of the same Chamberlainite zealots as before: James Stuart, Patrick Munro, Patrick Buchan-Hepburn, William Boulton, Robert Grimston and Sir James Edmondson. It was also partly a move to silence him, as by convention Whips do not speak in the House.

'I must say David Himmler has "bowled us a quick one",' Thomas continued. He had been promised that he was going to be a senior enough Whip 'to have some influence with David [Margesson]' and was going to 'be supported by a "sound" junior Whip for help'. Eden had been given the same promise, that 'all the old lot would be cleared out'. Yet 'the next thing I knew was to read the appointments on the tape last night and find all the old gang kept!!' He explained it by saying: 'Brendan was ill and Winston, not unnaturally, conducting the war, so David, presumably, rushed things through.' He concluded to Cranborne: 'The group are upset and feel let down. Yet I don't see quite how they can do anything.... At least I shall have my foot in the door if I am not in the room, but it will be unpleasant and uphill work.'[40]

Churchill made vigorous use of the Honours system in attempting to drum up support for his Government, remove awkward customers and create vacancies in the Commons. Bracken was under no illusions as to the power which control over the Honours system could give the executive and he made sure that people knew how closely he, as PPS to the Prime Minister, was personally involved in the decision-making process. 'When MPs wished to indicate that they had suffered a change of heart since the days when Mr Chamberlain had been their only true prophet and Mr Churchill a noisy brawler kicking up an ungentlemanly fuss in the political wastelands which were his proper home', it was to Bracken that they had to make their supplications.

For the moment, however, that was not happening. When the question arose of Churchill taking over the Leadership of the Party from Chamberlain, he was shrewd enough to eschew it, writing to Chamberlain on 16 May: 'I am, of course, a Conservative. But, as Prime Minister of a National government formed on the widest basis, and comprising the three parties, I feel that it would be better for me not to undertake the Leadership of any one political party.'[41] He made great efforts not to antagonize the man whom the majority of by far the largest party in the Commons still saw as their spiritual, as well as titular, leader.

'During the early days of his premiership', recalled the civil servant Lawrence Burgis about the War Cabinet meetings he attended, 'one thing struck me most forceably and that was the courtesy and deference with which Churchill treated Neville Chamberlain.' This he ascribed to Churchill's 'capacity really to forgive and really to forget', but it might just as convincingly be put down to sensible politics. As Lloyd George's secretary put it more starkly in mid-June 1940, 'The plain fact is that Winston is afraid of Chamberlain'.[42] Good manners, as the matronly saying goes, cost nothing; but snubbing Chamberlain in the six months after he took office might have cost Churchill his Premiership.

In 1966 a well-informed but anonymous correspondent wrote to *The Times* correcting the sentence in Margesson's obituary which stated that Churchill had been 'magnanimous' in reappointing the Chief Whip. 'In the early days it was the unswerving allegiance of Chamberlain and Margesson which rallied the Conservatives in the House of Commons behind [Churchill]. Had he begun by dismissing the Chief Whip the support he in fact received would have been much less readily given.'[43] Considering that some Tories wrote to Chamberlain after the Norway debate to say how reluctant they were to take the Churchill Government's Whip, this was no exaggeration.

For Churchill a potentially dangerous myth was emerging amongst Chamberlainites which questioned his loyalty during the Phoney War. As Waterhouse noted on 12 May, 'Cabinet making is going full blast – there is every appearance to those closest up that much thought has been given and not a few preliminary arrangements made in advance.' For him, as for so many of the Respectable Tendency, the ultimate bogeyman was Lord Beaverbrook. This Canadian adventurer personified everything they disliked and distrusted in politics. He had opposed their hero Stanley Baldwin throughout the 1930s and, despite having been a keen appeaser, was just the sort of dynamic outsider whom they could be relied upon to despise and even fear.

> The exact fitting of the puzzle matters little [wrote Waterhouse]; what does matter terribly is that behind and through the whole issue is a sinister little figure ... who will I believe eventually figure in the administration. If one sells one's soul to the devil one must at some time pay the price, but it is hard to make the country share in the outlay.

It was doubtless Beaverbrook, amongst some others, to whom the Chamberlainite ex-minister Euan Wallace was referring when he, Oliver Stanley and Patrick Buchan-Hepburn remonstrated to Bracken about some appointments, 'of no importance in themselves, which will for personal reasons simply infuriate the overwhelming majority of the Tory Party'. They 'implored' Bracken, who must have known that under slightly different circumstances he too would have been included in the list, 'for the sake of the future, to do what he could to prevent a "spoils" policy being pushed too far'.[44] Wallace himself was offered the post of First Commissioner of Works on the understanding that he would also accept a peerage. He refused, believing it better not 'to take the irrevocable step of becoming a peer and thus depriving myself of any chance of returning to active work in the House of Commons'. Instead, he took up the important non-political post of Senior Regional Commissioner for London's Civil Defence.

His decision was not unconnected with Stanley's refusal of office, as is clear from his diary entry of 26 May. After Wallace had motored up from Dover to dine with the Duff Coopers, 'Bracken joined us afterwards and gave us a lot of interesting information about the formation of the present government.' One piece which directly affected Wallace, and helped sow the seeds of his distrust of Margesson, was that for the decision to appoint Sir John Reith to Wallace's job at the Ministry of Transport 'the initiative came from the Chief Whip!' Bracken and Duff Cooper did their best to persuade Wallace to change his decision not to join the Government, on the rather weak grounds that 'the House of Lords, both present and prospective, would provide greater opportunities for high office after the war'. But it was the fact that 'they were equally sure that Oliver [Stanley] was wrong not to accept office' which led Wallace to the conclusion that 'my original view remains unshaken'.[45]

The mood in the Whips' Office was equally wary of the new regime. According to Waterhouse's diary, the Deputy Chief Whip, James Stuart, 'views the whole box of tricks with the greatest possible misgiving and will get out of the Whips' Office if he can. He has already written at length to Chamberlain but David very naturally wants him to stop in.' Waterhouse himself daily expected the sack: 'I ... have been interested in my departmental work and shall be very sorry to leave it but politically it will be much better to watch this racket from the outside.'[46]

Nancy Dugdale felt much the same about her husband, writing to him on 15 May:

> For the first time I have felt glad for you that you have shaken the dust of politics off your feet. Beaverbrook, Duff Cooper – Rob Hudson as Minister of Agriculture ... I'm just waiting for the 9 p.m. news to hear Bob Boothby has got a job to bring up the rear of reptiles ... 9.30 – I knew it! He has an Under-Secretaryship! And Harold Macmillan ... War always throws up the dregs.... Really Harold Macmillan and Bob Boothby as bedfellows is a new one on me!

Her husband would doubtless have picked up the reference to Macmillan's wife, who was also Boothby's mistress, which would have been missed by army censors. However, the concluding sentence of her letter permitted no misinterpretation: 'I suppose one must hide one's loathing although it is very hard to do.'

Far from instilling a spirit of unity, the military reverses on the Continent provided fresh fuel for the Chamberlainites' invective, little realizing at the beginning that they would be blamed. After reading how Rotterdam had fallen to fifth columnists and parachutists, and that the Germans had crossed the River Maas at Maastricht, Waterhouse allowed himself a dig against Churchill: 'I hope the new P.M. in his effort to fix up his friends at home will not for long neglect his enemies abroad.' As for the reason for Chamberlain's fall:

> Norway, having served its purpose, is now forgotten. The *Express* yesterday referred to it as an 'incident' and the 'wisdom' of our withdrawal has been commented on. When this business is all fixed it will be instructive to re-read the Hansards of Tuesday and Wednesday [the Norway debate] and note the number of things said by the various quislings which they will shortly wish had never passed their lips.

Waterhouse also noted how many MPs came up to him in the Smoking Room to apologize for their behaviour during the Norway debate: 'People who voted against [Chamberlain] on Wednesday are endeavouring to explain their vote away.' Many had not expected to bring down the Government. One Tory rebel, Somerset de Chair, who was proud to have voted against Chamberlain 'while the decrepit old Tories, clinging to their hopes of knighthoods and peerages, carried the day', believed the result 'should be close enough to shake the Government till its teeth rattle without shaking it right off the Front Bench'.[47] When he saw Kingsley Wood and Sir John Anderson on the Government Front Bench four days later, he likened it to 'the solicitor and the undertaker both returning to the funeral'.

Back in the Smoking Room the Chamberlainite reaction against Margesson was well under way. Five senior backbenchers – Robert Smith, Hon. Ralph Beaumont, Edward Cobb, the former PPS to Oliver Stanley, John Crowder and Alexander Erskine-Hill, a senior member of the 1922 Executive – told Waterhouse that 'they thought David had passed his time of usefulness'. Among the criticisms levelled at him was that he was 'out of touch' and had 'gone over to Winston'. Waterhouse duly reported this whispering campaign against their Chief to the Whips' Office.

Tory resentment against the media came out in Waterhouse's sarcastic comment that 'The BBC have just had a talk by a "North countryman" boosting the new Government. I never heard anything of this sort about the old one. I wonder why.' Scepticism about the new Prime Minister was rife. 'I hope Winston won't lead us into anything too rash,' wrote Halifax's son, Charles Wood, MP for York, from Palestine; 'I can't really see what difference except perhaps psychologically the new Government will make.' He echoed the by then prevailing view: 'They seemed to have behaved shamefully in the House of Commons.'[48] John Colville, Erskine-Hill's father-in-law and Chamberlain's Scottish Secretary (who was not reappointed to Churchill's Government), complained to his wife that Churchill was 'no gentleman'.[49]

Waterhouse was predictably caustic about the middle-ranking appointments when they came through on 14 May. 'Some of the changes are surprising, others just beyond comprehension stupid. No one is more likely to precipitate trouble in India than Amery, Rob Hudson was doing well in shipping and knows absolutely damn all about agriculture, Ronnie Cross was doing well in Economic Warfare and knows nothing about shipping,' he began. After lunch that day he spent half an hour talking to a fellow Derbyshire JP and Deputy-Lieutenant, Colonel John Gretton, about why he had abstained. Gretton told him that despite his great respect for Chamberlain, he did it because 'Simon, Sam [Hoare] and [Minister of Supply Leslie] Burgin had to be shifted'. He also vouchsafed the opinion that 'David M should and must go; if he didn't the party would split'. Gretton thought that either Dugdale or Stuart would make a good replacement.

To his genuine surprise – as opposed to that which politicians often feign on such occasions – Waterhouse was called to No. 10 at noon on 17 May to be asked to stay on as Assistant Postmaster-General. The breadth of political opinion in the coalition is illustrated by those whom he found waiting in the lobby when he arrived, namely the right-wing Tory Henry Page Croft, the socialist 'Red Ellen' Wilkinson, the Liberal barrister Dingle Foot and the Chamberlainite loyalist Victor Warrender.

When Churchill appointed a friend, Harcourt Johnstone, to the Government, he managed to hurt the *amour propre* of the Liberals. Their Chief Whip, Sir Percy Harris, recorded in his memoirs that, 'What was resented by my colleagues was not so much that they had not been included, but that it had been thought necessary to go outside to fill a ministerial post.'[50] Johnstone was appointed Minister of Overseas Trade without being either a business expert or even an MP, although he was a Liberal. Tall, Whiggish and elegant, 'Crinks' Johnstone was 'reputed to have more waistcoats than anyone else'. A legendary *bon vivant*, he allegedly died from over-eating.

Johnstone was not appreciated by the more hard-nosed Chamberlainites. When he was eventually elected to Parliament unopposed and took his seat in the Commons, there was not a murmur of support from any Member. 'I never remember such an entry,' wrote Waterhouse. 'Winston was there to see the advent of his personally selected tame member.' In the debates which followed, as Harris related with some satisfaction, 'the younger Tories took pleasure in ragging him and asking him awkward questions'. The explanation for his appointment was simply that like Lord Sherwood and James de Rothschild, who also at different times became ministers, Churchill enjoyed their company, as was witnessed by their membership of The Other Club.

Contrary to Jock Colville's claim, by late May the Tory Establishment was no more reconciled to the new Government than they had been a fortnight before. Robert Bruce Lockhart, who used to write 'Londoners' Diary' for Beaverbrook's *Evening Standard* but was then working in the Political Intelligence Department of the Foreign Office, noted in his diary how, on 21 May, the Manchester Tory MP and former captain of Lancashire County Cricket Club, Peter Eckersley, 'who is anti-Winston', told him that the 'revolt was a farce and will do no good. Winston won't last five months! Opposition from Tories is already beginning.' Within three months Eckersley himself was dead, killed on active service in the Air Division of the Royal Navy Volunteer Reserve during the Battle of Britain.

Anyone tempted to take his opposition to Churchill or the war too far received a shot across the bows on 22 May, when the Speaker announced the arrest of a Tory MP, Captain Archibald Maule Ramsay, under the anti-fascist emergency legislation Regulation 18B. Ramsay's outspoken anti-war and pro-Nazi opinions earned him four-and-a-half years' detention in Brixton Prison. The National Liberal MP and Colwyn Bay GP, Sir Henry Morris-Jones, remembered how Ramsay's 'sincerity, earnestness and depth of belief were unquestionable.... He was a likeable character, and it was a source of regret to his friends that he had to pay so severe a penalty for his views.'[51] Source of regret or not, it acted as a salutary lesson to other MPs – such as Cyril Culverwell – who shared his anti-war views. There were in all a dozen Tory MPs who belonged to Ramsay's Right Club; some, like Mavis Tate, had rebelled in the Norway debate, but the majority had voted for Chamberlain.

'Yesterday the House was as breezy as a girls' school,' wrote Waterhouse on 22 May. ' "All is lost" sort of attitude in evidence in many quarters.' The Tory MP, Roy Wise, was passing around 'a typical rumour that the U.S. and Italy were about to produce peace terms giving Germany Poland, Czechoslovakia and Colonies, Italy half Tunisia and Gibraltar to be internationalised!' When on 22 May the new Government met the House for the first time, there was 'a rather acrimonious argument about who should sit where' as there was no official Opposition. The only party not in the Government was James Maxton's 'Three Card Trick' of Independent Labour MPs, whose demand to occupy the entire

Opposition Front Bench was unsurprisingly turned down.

On 23 May Richard Law wrote to his fellow Norway rebel Lord Wolmer:

> My impression from the very outside fringe of things is that the new Government – or rather the new elements in it – are fighting a war on two fronts, against Hitler and against enemies much nearer home. I did not like the House yesterday at all. I wish Winston weren't such a child in these matters.[52]

Nancy Dugdale agreed about the coalition's difficulties. 'As to the Government,' she wrote to Tommy on 24 May, 'nobody I have talked to likes it ... they hate "the wild man" and don't trust him. They are for the first time really concerned about the War. Those who know think the Government beyond words.' She was at least able to take solace from the fact that the Zionist Baffy Dugdale, who was in love with Nancy's sister's husband, the Health Minister Walter Elliot, had suffered a reverse. According to Nancy, Baffy hated the Colonial Secretary, Malcolm MacDonald, 'as he is anti-Semitic', and had been 'praying and scheming to get Malcolm removed'. When in the reconstruction MacDonald was moved to the Ministry of Health, thereby displacing Elliot, Nancy crowed that he was 'out of the whole show and she is furious! The old bitch!'[53]

The end of May and the first days of June saw the miracle of the BEF's evacuation from Dunkirk. According to one historian of the coalition, 'The backing of many Tory MPs was conditional upon there being no direct clash of loyalty involving the Party Leader.... Dunkirk, we must conclude, was a deliverance for Churchill as it was for the British nation.'[54] The sense of relief that the army was back safely soon turned into a hunt for scapegoats. Chamberlain and the 'Old Gang' proved ideal targets, and they were blamed for the defeat. Their sudden unpopularity was stoked by the bestseller *Guilty Men*, co-written by three Beaverbrook journalists including Michael Foot. Combined with the concurrent surge in Churchill's popularity, this evaporation of public support for Chamberlain proved more than anything else the spur for uncommitted Tories to switch allegiances away from the Chamberlainites. However, the rearguard action fought by the Chamberlainite rump was far longer, tougher and more bitter than is now supposed.

Ambitious MPs concerned about their careers did not miss the signs of the Prime Minister's hugely increased popularity after Dunkirk. One Chamberlainite, Sir Frank Sanderson – who had the *savoir-faire* to keep old press cuttings with headlines like 'Sir Frank Says Hitler's Policy is One of Peace' – addressed the annual dinner of the Ealing Primrose League on 1 June 1940. 'There is not a more loyal man in this country than myself in regard to the late Prime Minister and still leader of our Party – Neville Chamberlain,' he said, to two apologetic little claps from a lady and gentleman in the back row as the rest of the audience sat in silence. After a moment he continued: 'But there comes a time when a specialist brain must needs fill a special position.' At this reference to Churchill, recorded the *Middlesex County Times*, Ealing Town Hall erupted into loud and prolonged applause. Conservative MPs could not but appreciate the implications of this and hundreds of similar manifestations of the national change of mood.[55]

On 4 June, the Dunkirk evacuation completed, Churchill delivered his sublime 'We shall fight on the beaches' speech to the House of Commons. There were complaints. France was still in the war, if only for another fortnight, and his veiled references to her possible surrender worried MPs. In the House, Euan Wallace noted that 'there was some controversy in the Smoking Room afterwards about his double reference to fighting alone'. Cecil King of the *Daily Mirror* quoted from his diary for 4 June how Lloyd George had told him 'Churchill's reception in the House was very half-hearted, he got far less applause than was usually accorded to Chamberlain in spite of his magnificent speech'. The Tories were still refusing to give their wholehearted support despite the gravity of the situation and the glory of his oratory. Indeed, for some, the more magnificent his rhetoric, the more suspicious they became. This was not confined to the politicians. On 16 May 1940 Colville had recorded how his fellow No. 10 Private Secretaries had said of a message from Churchill that it was just 'blasted rhetoric.... He is still thinking of his books.'

On 5 June, after Duff Cooper had experienced a particularly tough time at the despatch box, Wallace recorded Walter Elliot's conclusion that the coalition's 'honeymoon is coming to an end'.[56] In fact, the heat was now being turned up on Chamberlain. Writing to his sisters, Ida and Hilda, Chamberlain referred to 'a party meeting every evening at the Reform Club under the chairmanship of Clement Davies, that treacherous Welshman'.[57] Amery, Macmillan and Boothby sometimes attended in order to orchestrate Chamberlain's removal from office. But Churchill would have none of it, telling Chamberlain somewhat hyperbolically that 'we had gone in together and would if necessary go down together'.

Churchill knew the Parliamentary mathematics remained unaltered whatever happened to Chamberlain's reputation outside Parliament. The Conservatives had won a landslide victory in the 1935 general election, and as the political truce called at the outbreak of war prohibited any contested by-elections by the major parties, they enjoyed an automatic in-built preponderance for the remainder of the war. Churchill had no real option but to stand by Chamberlain, the ultimate guarantor of his Premiership. Their personal relationship was developing well, and Churchill entrusted his predecessor with ever more important tasks on the Home Front, which he knew would be carried out with loyalty and thoroughness.

Cecil King believed that 'time and the Nation are so clearly against the Tory backbenchers that Churchill can defy them and get away with it'. But the Prime Minister himself could not risk it. A lifetime in politics had taught him how fickle opinion could be. Churchill exerted himself and managed to stop the anti-Chamberlain press pogrom almost overnight. He warned Cecil King that, 'If Chamberlain is forced out, all his associates will go, and he will have to resign as jointly responsible with them for the policy of the Cabinet since the outbreak of War. He says that if the newspapers continue with their attacks on Chamberlain on Wednesday [5 June 1940] morning there will be no Government.'[58]

On 7 June he made his point again. A secret session debate was due on Tuesday, 11 June, and attacks on Chamberlain were expected to materialize there. Churchill told King:

> The men who had supported Chamberlain and hounded [him] were still MPs. Chamberlain had got the biggest cheer when they met the House after forming the War Administration. A General Election is not possible during a War and so the present House of Commons, however unrepresentative of feeling in the country, had to be reckoned with as the ultimate source of power for the duration. If Churchill trampled on these men, as he could trample on them, they would set themselves against him and in such internecine strife lay the Germans' best chance of victory.

He would 'not run a Government of revenge', knowing that anyhow 'they were everywhere, not only in the political world, but among the fighting Service Chiefs and the Civil Service chiefs. To clean all these out would be a task impossible in the disastrous state in which we find ourselves.'[59]

His suspicions about the threat of 'internecine strife' were fully confirmed in a letter written by the Chamberlainites' adjutant, the Chairman of the 1922 Committee, William Spens, to *The Times* on Monday, 10 June, the day before the proposed secret session. It said that the Conservatives wished 'to support the present government.... But if others should be so reckless of the national interest as to launch the suggested attack, we should have no alternative but to defend ourselves.' Waterhouse, too, confirms that the Chamberlainites were ready to risk breaking the coalition in defence of their leader. 'Dear me, what this poor country has to suffer to attain political unity,' he had written on 6 June. 'The PM has failings and merits but those around him are a mean despicable lot of envious scamps. The PM's views on Government are completely oriental – you helped me so of course this country shall help you and your best line is to damn your predecessor to heaps.'[60]

Later on 6 June, he added: 'I have rarely felt a more profound disgust about affairs than I do just now. I have no doubt about the War.... But what a pity it is that in a state of emergency the cads come out on top and the country acclaims them. One can take no pride in being a very honourable member of such a company.' He was angered by the way Duff Cooper's Ministry of Information was 'running a political racket. No name of any Minister other than those of the anti-Chamberlain group is mentioned on the wireless if it can possibly be avoided.' Churchill's confidants were still a major bugbear for him:

> It takes the heart out of one to think that the PM relies for inspiration and to a large extent for guidance at such critical times on such notoriously shifty and unreliable fools as Beaverbrook, Lloyd George, Brendan B[racken], Crinks Johnstone and Louis Spears. Baldwin spoke more than truth when he said that our task was as much to make democracy safe for the world as the reverse.[61]

The secret session did not take place, as Italy's entry into the war on 10 June gave the Government a pretext to cancel it. This also prevented the public airing of Chamberlainite complaints that Mussolini could have been bought off back in 1935 had he not been pushed into the German camp by Eden. The political correspondent of the *News Chronicle*, David Keir, the husband of Tory MP Thelma Cazalet, fulminated against the gag imposed upon him by the Labour leadership in accordance with Churchill's orders, and wrote in his diary on 11 June: 'The more I think of the position, the more uncertain the future of Winston's present Government is. It is a second-class Cabinet.'[62]

By 14 June the Germans were in Paris, and two days later Marshal Pétain replaced Paul Reynaud as French Prime Minister and began to sue for peace. On 18 June Churchill made his 'Finest Hour' speech. One might have assumed that this was the moment when all British politicians would bury their hatchets and fall in behind him, but still the doubts and mutterings continued. The Labour Minister for Economic Warfare, Hugh Dalton, noted after the speech: 'It is noticeable how he is much more loudly cheered by the Labour Party than by the general body of Tory supporters. The relative silence of these latter is regarded by some as "sinister".'

Dalton asked his PPS, John Wilmot, to ascertain Chamberlainite opinion and heard that 'many Tories feel the Labour Party has much too large a share, both in offices and the determination of Government policy'. Dalton thought that 'there is some danger in this situation and it must be watched. One very obvious conclusion is that we must not push the Old Man out of the Government. For he would then become a centre of disaffection and a rallying-point for real opposition.' Dalton thought that it was better to 'leave him where he is, as a decaying hostage'.

Waterhouse commented on the 'Finest Hour' speech: 'He was not in his best form. He was inclined to be hesitant to start with and introduced some rather cheap jibes and jeers which seemed to me ill-suited to the gravity of the moment.' Writing to her husband the same day, Nancy Dugdale reported a conversation she had had with Lord Dunglass and the Whip, Patrick Munro, at Prunier's Restaurant: 'Alec said in the last fortnight, and indeed since W came in, the H of C had stunk in the nostrils of the decent people. The kind of people surrounding W are the scum and the peak came when Brendan was made a PC! For what services rendered heaven knows.' Dunglass told Nancy how 'the lobbying against Neville is terrific', but 'that was stopped'. He added that

> they are endeavouring to keep a remnant of cleanliness in public life. Jim Thomas has joined them in the Whips office and he's being quite good so far. Pat said in reply to my asking what he thought of the Government and David M who has most undoubtedly served God and Mammon with equal ease, Pat said that they just *never* allow themselves to think about it.[63]

She confirmed that Lady Wilson had told her that Sir Horace was 'always getting ill-mannered messages from WC to the effect that he is only to do what he is told and to keep his place etc.'. Both Wilson (who was godfather to the Dugdales' son) and Dunglass told her 'that W.C. consults N.C. about *nothing*, neither the small or large things and he tells him nothing'. She concluded by relating an incident when the week before Duff Cooper had got 'really *very* drunk indeed' and had 'hissed hate and was *awful* ... the night after Italy came into the War and he delivered his shameful and outrageously stupid broadcast, I felt ashamed to be English'.

The (largely unfounded) criticism of Churchill for not consulting Chamberlain enough was echoed by Halifax, who, walking to the Foreign Office with Victor Cazalet in early June, complained that the Prime Minister 'is getting very arrogant and hates criticism of any kind ... it is almost impossible to get five minutes conversation with him'.[64] Lack of access to Churchill was a constant complaint of Chamberlainites, who, as Mrs Dugdale wrote, resented the fact that at No. 10, '[Professor Frederick] Lindemann arrived in the vanguard and reigns there, [Sir Desmond] Morton, a very doubtful Civil Servant, reigns, Max B[eaverbrook] and Bob B[oothby] are always there at 10.30 p.m. every night, they all foregather ... carouse and talk.' Waterhouse believed that he had come across a 'plan' for a triumvirate of Churchill, Lloyd George and Ernest Bevin to run the war and commented, 'in spite of our peril the rats are gnawing at the bung-hole of the Ship of State'.

The general mood amongst Tory backbenchers in mid-June 1940 was probably close to that articulated by the irascible MP for Newcastle North, Cuthbert Headlam, who wrote in his diary about Churchill:

I am not one of his admirers – by which I mean that I have never believed in his judgment or his fitness for the office which he now holds – but this does not imply that I do not admire his courage, his abilities, his quickness of uptake and his fervent patriotism. In many ways he is the right man for the present situation.

There was, as with so many Tories, a proviso: 'That he does not run amok as an amateur strategist.'[65]

Churchill was fully conscious of the way many backbenchers still felt, and at the end of his speech-notes for the secret session on 20 June he confronted it head on. 'Lastly, say a word about ourselves,' they read. 'How the new Government was formed. Tell the story Chamberlain's actions. Imperative there should be loyalty, union among men who have joined hands. Otherwise no means of standing the shocks and strains which are coming. I have a right to depend loyalty to the Administration and feel we have only one enemy to face.'[66] This was probably a reference to the continued attacks on Chamberlain, for as Waterhouse had recorded the night before, 'the anti-Chamberlain hunt proceeds in spite of all, but the PM has counter-attacked twice in the H of C. If Neville is turned out then indeed we shall face dangers. His counsel is wise and calm.'[67]

On 22 June Vichy France signed an armistice with Germany, the terms of which arrived in London two days later, to general consternation. Again, instead of forging national cohesion, it encouraged a renewed offensive to force Chamberlain from office. This was conducted from Amery's house in Eaton Square. One of Hore-Belisha's followers in the Commons, Henry Morris-Jones, recorded on 26 June: 'Important move. LlG, H-B and others met at Amery's house for five hours. Move to make LlG PM.' It would have been ironic if this really had been the purpose of the meeting, as it had been in that same first-floor drawing-room at 112 Eaton Square that Lloyd George's downfall had been plotted eighteen years earlier, but Morris-Jones had got it wrong. The intention was to force Chamberlain from office, and Waterhouse's more accurate information that Clement Davies, Amery, Boothby and Lord Salisbury were behind the move shows that the Chamberlainites were alive to the threat.

It is an indication of the suspicion the Chamberlainites were feeling by late June that even the introduction of the new Member for Croydon, Henry Willink, by Harry Crookshank and Harold Macmillan could be interpreted by Waterhouse as 'clearly meant as a kick at the Whips' Office'.[68] Waterhouse was wrong in this, although Whips did usually introduce new Members after by-elections; but Macmillan and Crookshank had been at school with Willink.

Old wounds had not healed, as is shown by Waterhouse's dismissal of Admiral Keyes's defence of the King of the Belgians, that 'it savours too much of an attempt to explain his own failure to keep Leopold on the rails, after the rubbish he talked in the Norwegian debate'. June 1940 also saw the Chamberlainite Chairman of the Select Committee on National Expenditure, Sir John Wardlaw-Milne, being criticized by Churchill for allowing his powerful Committee to range outside its terms of reference and become 'as much a centre for the criticism of organisational and administrative incompetence as for the examination of expenditure' – something the Prime Minister was not prepared to tolerate. The massive expenditure which the war was beginning to generate, quite out of all proportion to peacetime levels, was causing increasing worry to those financially orthodox Tories who considered 'sound money' and budget-balancing central Conservative tenets. They feared that Britain was bankrupting herself, and that Churchill was not interested in preventing socialism entering by the back door. The assumption that, whoever won, Britain would be 'bust' after the war was common amongst Chamberlainites, and Wardlaw-Milne's Committee became a focal point for the expression of these fears.

With breathtaking gall, Waterhouse ruminated on 30 June: 'Looking back one may well wonder first if N.C. could not have held the French to the job [i.e. in the war]. The French politician cannot understand men like him and Halifax. They talk a different language, their minds run in different ways. They command respect and possibly even fear.' It took a true Chamberlainite zealot still to believe this in late June 1940, but Waterhouse continued about the French:

When faced by others, for example Louis Spears who went out [to France] with the PM, or Beaverbrook or [the Labour First Lord of the Admiralty A.V.] Alexander, they must feel themselves on much surer ground. 'Here', one can imagine them saying, 'are some sly dogs come to put something over us – we shall see!' And of course [the French] being far slyer and more adept at such rackets, our racketeers are outplayed.

On 2 July Waterhouse wrote: 'The House of Commons is a hell of a place. No one intends to be defeatist but a more lugubrious lot of blighters it would be hard to find. With a few examples, among whom Jock Erskine stands out, everyone gives the impression that things are so damned bad we will be lucky if we survive.' Dining with Margesson and Stuart he heard that 'folk are not pleased about the evacuation of the Channel Islands. Much comment on the "fight on the beaches, fight on the shores" speech.' So even that, the most memorable of all the Churchillian wartime orations, was criticized at the time by Tory backbenchers. Waterhouse was soon complaining that 'the Channel Islands evacuation does not seem to have been a British Epic'.

Early July also saw Clement Davies's Reform Club and Leo Amery's Eaton Square plots to force Chamberlain out of the Government come to a head. They took a Commons committee room for the afternoon of Wednesday, 3 July, and invited all backbench MPs along to discuss 'further strengthening the present Government', a clear anti-Chamberlain code. But William Spens told his colleagues on the 1922 Committee that he intended to attend the meeting to disrupt it. He then led dozens of the Chamberlainite faithful to the room where Aneurin Bevan, in Morris-Jones's opinion 'the worst one of all to introduce such a motion', was proposing 'to remove the Old Gang'. It soon 'turned out rowdy' and, according to Bruce Lockhart, who got his information from A.V. Alexander's PPS, Rex Fletcher, 'the meeting ended in a dog-fight with everyone shouting for or against Chamberlain'. Sheer weight of numbers prevailed and, as Beaverbrook reported to Hoare in Madrid, the meeting 'was a fiasco'. A satisfied Chamberlain told his sisters on Sunday, 7 July, that 'my friends turned up in force and bullied Clem and his friends till they dropped their resolution and adjourned'. It was an indication to the Executive both of the numbers of loyal Chamberlainites and their undiminished readiness to protect their chief.

For all his deprecation of the movement to Hoare, to whom he wrote 'the attack on Neville and the "Men of Munich" comes to nothing', Beaverbrook was involved in the affair.[69] Wallace recorded how the Chamberlainite Jay Llewellin, the Parliamentary Secretary at Beaverbrook's Ministry of Aircraft Production, had been 'sounded out' by his Chief 'on the desirability of getting rid of "the Men of Munich"'. Llewellin sardonically replied that

it might have some points to recommend it as the pressing need at the moment appeared to be a strong and well-organised Opposition; if Chamberlain were driven out, the Conservative party would go with him and thus provide the necessary alternative government to an Administration which he thought would not last more than six months.

Churchill took a dim view of his friends' anti-Chamberlain plots. According to Baffy Dugdale, 'he accused Bob [Boothby] of being one of those people "intriguing" against Neville', saying, 'you went to Amery's house the other night. You have no right to go there.'[70] He threatened his old friend that 'if he did not mind his own business he might find that he had no business to mind'. Boothby thought 'the danger' was 'that the Old Gang will be pulled down and, if things are not going right with the war, Winston will fall with them'. But by 15 July Chamberlain could write to Hoare that 'the campaign for the elimination of the "Old Gang" and particularly your humble servant, though it has not yet come to an end, seems nevertheless to be petering out'. Although, according to Colville, Churchill 'never countenances a word against Chamberlain', he was willing to make jokes about Baldwin. When told that the Germans had bombed one of Baldwin's factories, Churchill remarked: 'Very ungrateful of them.'

When, on 30 June, Leo Amery and Randolph Churchill expressed the view that Chamberlain 'ought to be punished', the Prime Minister answered: 'We don't want to punish anybody – except the enemy.' Chamberlain owed his successor a debt for this support, and he resolved to pay it. At the end of June the political correspondent of the *Financial News*, Paul Einzig, wrote to Chamberlain to complain about the lack of support his followers were giving the Prime Minister. As he later wrote in his memoirs:

For nearly two months after the advent of Churchill the overwhelming majority of Tory backbenchers, whatever their inner feelings may have been, gave no outward evidence of their support for him. Indeed on many occasions they went out of their way to demonstrate their unwillingness to do so. There was strong resentment amongst them over the appointment of some Tory 'rebels' – looked upon as 'traitors' by orthodox Tories – to Ministerial posts, and over the removal of a number of loyal Chamberlainite Ministers to make room for these 'rebels'.[71]

That much is common knowledge, but Einzig – who daily watched the Commons debates from the Gallery – believed that

> most Conservative Members felt, moreover, that any demonstration of their support to the new PM would be disloyal to his predecessor owing to the circumstances in which the change of Government came about ... they demonstrated their resentment by their sullen silence whenever Churchill entered the Chamber or rose to make a speech. This negative attitude became even more strikingly evident whenever Churchill sat down after concluding one of his historic speeches ... most Tory backbenchers remained sitting and silent.

Einzig also thought that this attitude had 'led many influential Americans to the conclusion that the Tory majority was not behind Churchill in his determination to fight on against heavy odds'.[72]

Einzig told Chamberlain of these suspicions, adding that at least one foreign correspondent believed that the Tory behaviour constituted nothing less than 'a deliberate and organised demonstration against the Prime Minister'. He concluded: 'I know for a fact that on more than one occasion several ambassadors and important press correspondents left the House under the impression that the PM could not rely on the support of the Conservative majority.' Chamberlain replied to this letter, naturally denying that there was any 'want of loyalty to the Prime Minister among the Conservative backbenchers', but tacitly admitting that 'at the present time they are very deeply impressed with the gravity of the situation and they are in no mood to make extravagant demonstrations of any kind'. He went on to assure Einzig of 'my determination not to tolerate anything in the nature of half-hearted support'. More significantly, he told the correspondent that he would 'undertake to see that your impression is not confirmed by anything more serious'.[73]

When a couple of days later, on 4 July, Churchill announced that the Vichy Fleet had been sunk by the Royal Navy at Oran, the Whips had been at work and, when he sat down, according to Einzig, something remarkable happened. The Chief Whip, Margesson, rose to his feet. Turning towards the Tory backbenchers, he waved his Order Papers in a gesture clearly conveying that they too should rise. At his signal all the Conservatives, behind the Treasury bench and below the gangway ... rose to a man and burst into enthusiastic cheering at the top of their voices.

Churchill wept. Einzig was convinced that this demonstration of support was orchestrated, as only the day before in the Commons the Tories had 'pointedly cold-shouldered' the Prime Minister.

Einzig was perhaps playing down the drama and intense sense of relief of the occasion, whilst over-emphasizing his own role in alerting Chamberlain to the problem, but, 'On the evidence of my own eyes and several of my colleagues – all trained observers of Parliamentary proceedings and forewarned by me what to look out for – with whom I compared notes immediately after the scene, I am satisfied without a shadow of a doubt that ... the Tory change was not spontaneous.'[74] He believed that it was 'unquestionable that the Tories had risen to cheer Churchill some seconds after Labour' in response to a signal by Margesson. This incident bore all the signs of Chamberlain asking his 'friends', via Margesson, to be more overt in their support of his successor as Prime Minister.

In his war memoirs, Churchill certainly considered that speech a watershed in his relations with the Tory Party. He reminisced how

the House was very silent during the recital but at the end there occurred a scene unique in my own experience. Everybody seemed to stand up all round, cheering, for what seemed a long time. Up till this moment the Conservative Party had treated me with some reserve and it was from the Labour benches that I received the warmest welcome when I entered the House or rose on serious occasions. But now all joined in solemn stentorian accord.[75]

One historian of the Churchill Government believes that the Oran demonstration proved that the 'Conservatives had at last reconciled themselves to the coalition'.[76] However, it seems that even that support had been stage-managed, and there were still serious doubts about Churchill on the benches behind him.

The same evening, Harry Crookshank dined at White's with Chamberlain's former Agriculture Minister, Sir Reginald Dorman-Smith. He recorded how Dorman-Smith was 'very worried about Home Defence. Had seen Winston whom he thought complacent and a lot of whiskies and soda.'[77] Churchill's drinking was a regular gripe of Chamberlainites. 'I happened to meet [Field Marshal Sir] Philip Chetwode at luncheon,' Halifax wrote to Chamberlain at about this time, 'who led me aside and said, "Do stop Winston – he's drinking too much." You said you might have it in mind to say a word. Philip's evidence was quite good.'[78] We may wonder whether their concern was wholly genuine, or part of the general air of moral superiority the Chamberlainites tended to affect towards Churchill.

On 6 July Beaverbrook explained to his placeman Hoare: 'The Government's standing with the public is not as it was. They are criticised in the newspapers over the use of manpower and a supposed lack of energy and direction in organising home defence.' Although he considered such criticism ill-founded, it 'reflects a general discontent'.[79] Hoare also received a letter from his former PPS and devotee, John Moore-Brabazon, written on the same day. 'Between ourselves,' it began, 'Winston is getting more Chamberlain than Chamberlain and nobody, I understand, can approach him and nobody can say a word to him.' Moore-Brabazon, who had been Churchill's PPS twenty years previously, believed that 'Winston's position is so over-poweringly strong that he can do anything he likes in reconstruction, but it is a pity he imagines that they are a sort of immaculate Front Bench unable to be improved and inviolate.' He thought secret sessions 'very dull', but 'a good thing as Members can let off steam and without them ... a sort of barrier occurs between the House and the Executive which is mischievous'.

Moore-Brabazon, who was sacked as Minister of Aircraft Production in 1942 after publicly making the very Chamberlainite observation that the Russo-German conflict 'suited us', was one of the first and very few to be critical of Churchill in the 1950s. In his autobiography he wrote that the meetings of the committee which co-ordinated the Battle of the Atlantic

> were the most unpleasant meetings I have ever attended ... the way Churchill treated everyone was almost unbearable. He usually appeared after his early afternoon sleep in the vilest of tempers.... He behaved as if he were a bullying schoolmaster. Everyone, in his opinion, was a halfwit; if anyone said anything he was jumped on and snubbed.

He finished by saying that Graham Sutherland's scathing portrait of the Prime Minister, which Lady Churchill later secretly destroyed, 'exactly portrays the man as he appeared to the committee whose unfortunate duty it was to attend'.[80]

By the third week of July, criticism at last began to lessen. Even the curmudgeonly Headlam described Churchill's radio broadcast of 14 July as 'less bombastic than usual and full of vim'. Waterhouse called the decision to send the Duke of Windsor to the Bahamas 'a much criticised Winstonianism', but supported the wide emergency powers that the Government took for itself in the case of invasion. He called the leading opponent of these measures, Sir Richard Acland, 'that miserable tapeworm' and considered that 'a little bit of Hitler's "just-a-po" [Gestapo], as Winston called it, would do them good'.

The decision on 18 July to close the Burma Road, which reinforced Nationalist China against the Japanese, was deeply unpopular. But even though Churchill took this decision against Halifax's advice, such was his popularity that, as the Ministry of Information reported, the public's view was that 'the Munich men are at it again'.[81] As Walter Elliot wrote to his wife the day it came into effect, 'the nation is sore, and alarmed, and will "take it out of" any scapegoats that it can think of', meaning himself and his fellow Chamberlainites. Butler's PPS, Chips Channon, recorded on 21 July: 'Our reign is slowly ending; I shall regret its close, although I have hardly ever been in complete sympathy with it.'[82] At the time of Munich Channon had written of his 'love' for Chamberlain, but by late July 1940 even he was distancing himself.

Butler better appreciated the power the Chamberlainites still wielded and wrote to Hoare: '[Labour War Cabinet member Arthur] Greenwood talks openly of the danger of alienating the Tory Party since they are the majority in the House.' Recalling the experience of the failed Davies/Amery attempted coup against Chamberlain, he added: 'If intrigues or attacks ... grow to any great extent all we have to do is pull the string of the toy dog of the 1922 Committee and make it bark. After a few staccato utterances it becomes clear that the Government depends upon the Tory squires for their majority.'[83] If he had not become a politician, Rab would have made a fine political journalist.

Euan Wallace noted on 23 July that 'we are gradually moving back towards a Parliamentary opposition'. Kingsley Wood's budget that day, which had put a shilling on income tax and introduced a purchase tax, was unpopular with the Tory right. Waterhouse, however, was content with the general political situation, so long as Chamberlain and Halifax were there to restrain Churchill:

> The three men who are at the head of affairs here today make a powerful combination. Edward Halifax deeply religious almost a mystic, not perhaps very practical-minded but a great moral strength; Neville Chamberlain not devout but certainly a man of high moral purpose and strong religious conviction, practical and analytic and above all clear-headed to a degree, and no less important capable of equally clear argument; Winston Churchill

dynamic, explosive, brilliant in exposition and forceful in argument and I hope in action almost ruthless.[84]

Churchill himself approved of this collective view of his Government, telling the *Manchester Guardian* journalist, W.P. Crozier, on 26 July how much he had liked an article which took this line. 'You see, after all,' he said, 'Chamberlain and those other people represent the Conservative Party which has a great majority in the House of Commons and they must be shown some consideration.' He was, despite his popularity in the country, very alive to potential weakness in the event of continued military reverses. 'I owe something to Chamberlain, you know. When he resigned he could have advised the King to send for Halifax and he didn't.... Chamberlain works very well with me and I can tell you this – he's no intriguer.'[85]

Someone who definitely was an intriguer, Rab Butler, nearly came to grief when Churchill discovered that he had had a disloyal conversation with a neutral on 17 July. Butler had told the Swedish Minister in London, Björn Prytz, that 'no "diehards" would be allowed to stand in the way' of a compromise peace with Germany if one was felt desirable, and, in an even more direct reference to Churchill, that 'common sense and not bravado' would dictate British policy in that field. All Churchill did was to administer a light rap across Butler's knuckles, telling Halifax that his junior minister had 'held odd language' with Prytz, which he read because Swedish telegraph traffic was being intercepted. Had Butler occupied a lower place in the Chamberlainite pantheon, it is likely that his reprimand would have been more severe. He himself half expected to be sacked over it.

Chamberlain still inspired great loyalty. 'There are many of us who date our hope of victory from the day when you exploded the myth of collective security with the speech on "midsummer madness",' wrote Dunglass to Chamberlain on 29 July, 'and many more who saw in the faces of those people who greeted you in Munich and London a deep longing for peace, the strength of which could not be long denied.' As Chamberlain's PPS, Dunglass had flown to Munich with him and wanted to let the ex-Prime Minister know how 'the younger generation understood all this and would always be grateful to you and will turn to you again for help and guidance in building a better and happier world'. He concluded by chivalrously assuring his master: 'If ever I can be a help to you in any way you only have to give the word and I will come.'[86] It was, however, at about this time that Chamberlain discovered that he had terminal cancer.

Meanwhile, Waterhouse was busily engaged on fighting Chamberlain's battles in Parliament. 'All the most despicable elements are being the most vocal,' he wrote on 25 July about the attacks by the left-wing Labour MPs, Samuel Silverman, George Strauss and Aneurin Bevan. In his opinion they 'would credit no decent assembly anywhere' and were 'asserting their undoubted power of speech to the national ill'. The Tory MP, Vyvyan Adams, who was conducting a personal crusade against Margesson, also came in for Waterhouse's vitriol. 'Two or three weeks of quiescence', wrote Waterhouse of the Battle of Britain period, 'destroys the morale and balance of this House of Commons in a most remarkable way – a way which speaks ill of the longevity of the system and the safety of the nation.'

When at the end of July Churchill said that he wanted a foreign affairs debate conducted in secret session, no fewer than 109 MPs voted against his proposal. Party politics returned with a vengeance when, on the last day of the month, the 1922 Committee was shown a leaflet which had been circulating in Birmingham claiming that Government successes were due mainly to Labour ministers. 'Great indignation was expressed,' recorded Wallace. Headlam believed: 'There is of course a "Party truce" but it is only observed by one side. Every speech made by the Labour people in the House of Commons is a Party speech and is propaganda.' The unspoken criticism was that by continually emphasizing the national side of the coalition, Churchill was allowing a situation to develop in which, as Headlam put it, 'everything we ought to stand for will go by default'.[87]

On 6 August Italian troops advanced into British Somaliland. Nevertheless Churchill's popularity was at its height, with one Gallup Poll recording an 88 per cent approval rating. However much the politicians continued to squabble, the public at least were solid. Just as during the Peloponnesian War Pericles's enemies attacked him through his friends, advisers and mistress rather than directly, so the Chamberlainites began to harry Churchill's friends and confidants at this period of his political apotheosis. Headlam recorded on 1 August how 'Everyone agrees that personally [Beaverbrook] is a crook and laments the influence he is supposed to have over Winston.' The very next day the Canadian outsider was appointed to the War Cabinet, which worried people further.

Waterhouse approved of the attacks on Duff Cooper, noting how 'there has been a hue and cry against the Ministry of Information and especially against enquiring agents sent to spy out feeling in the country. These sixty ladies and gentlemen led by Mr Vyvyan Adams, a Communist, have been dubbed "Cooper's Snoopers" by the *Daily Herald*, a name which must stick.'[88] In the same entry he recorded Chamberlain's intestinal operation 'for a mild form of stoppage', but continued that 'mercifully he took it in time and there have been good reports on his progress'.

Even as the Battle of Britain reached its height – in the week of 11–18 August – the politicking went on. Morris-Jones wrote in his diary, after a conversation with Hore-Belisha, that 'there was defeatism about. Winston listened many times daily to the pessimism of the General Staff.'[89] Hore-Belisha had his secretary (a Miss Sloane) read a transcript of a speech of Eden's which he thought showed 'no emphatic confidence'. The sacked War Minister believed

> the Tory party in the House were not interested in the War, were afraid for their possessions and of the rise of Labour ... they might one day bring peace terms upon us and D[avid] M[argesson] would get his legions into the lobby in favour of it even though the country was dead against it. It might be a *fait accompli* and Hitler would stiffen his terms the next day and insist on a Government of his own like Pétain's.[90]

Beaverbrook shared this fear and, on 14 August, wrote of the leading candidate for the Pétain role, Lloyd George: 'The public are divided into two camps over that statesman; there are the people who think that Winston should bring him in and other people who think Hitler will put him in.' He applied a similarly paradoxical assessment to Hore-Belisha, who, he thought, 'is in a dilemma. He cannot make up his mind whether to attempt to smash his way into the Government by attacking it or whether to wheedle his way in by praising it.'[91] When on the same day Kingsley Wood backed down on his budget commitment to extend purchase tax to newspapers and books, Waterhouse reacted cynically: 'Beaverbrook clearly has not got into the Cabinet for nothing!'

On 15 August 180 German planes were shot down. More than any other, that day allowed the country to glimpse victory in the Battle of Britain. Returning from Fighter Command HQ at Stanmore in north London, Churchill instructed Colville to telephone the good news to Chamberlain in the country, who was 'overcome with joy'. Yet even on that great day the politicians were disputing amongst themselves and against Churchill. An Independent MP, Austin Hopkinson, asked him why he refused to give details about the composition of Lord Swinton's new Home Defence (Security) Executive, which was designed to 'ensure action' was taken against fifth columnists.[92] Hopkinson said that he objected to Swinton's 'activities on behalf of big business in politics' – which Waterhouse considered 'a clear charge of corruption'. An angry Prime Minister snapped back that, 'if my honourable friend had paid half the attention to the full and very respectful statement which I have made to the House that he was accustomed to obstructing my efforts to get this country properly defended before the War, I would not have to answer his question at all'.[93] Hopkinson asked for the Speaker's protection from this 'gross and lying innuendo' and other Members cried 'withdraw' at the Prime Minister.

Churchill continued: 'Far from withdrawing what I said, I will take the liberty of sending him a copy of one of his interventions in Debate, which I looked up only last night, in which he did his utmost to discredit me when I was doing my utmost for the country.' Waterhouse thought a 'hit well below the belt', but Churchill 'had my sympathy – those who start free fights must expect as good, and, when W.C. is their antagonist, better than they give'. Hopkinson replied: 'I recently looked up the same thing myself and discovered that intervention fully justified up to the hilt.' The reference was to a speech of Hopkinson's on 21 May 1936, in which he accused Churchill of promoting air rearmament partly as an anti-Baldwin manoeuvre. One might have thought that, of all days, 15 August 1940 was an inauspicious day to bring up that particular *canard*.

According to Waterhouse, the House 'warmed to the fight, notably Hore-Belisha, [the Liberal MP Edgar] Granville and Clement Davies, with many Liberals and socialists against the P.M.'. The Labour MP, Ernest Thurtle, 'in due course piped up with the remark that many of those complaining most were lukewarm about the prosecution of the War'. Bevan, in a reply recorded by Waterhouse but not Hansard, called Thurtle a pimp.

> Thurtle complained and asked for a withdrawal of this 'foul and offensive term', but the Speaker seems to have resigned himself to his fate of sitting in the House with liars and pimps, neither of which are apparently unparliamentary innuendoes, and merely said he thought 'it is time that this unedifying incident ceased'. The Prime Minister then got up and gave news of a defeat and retreat in Somaliland about which none of these noisy patriots seemed to care a damn.[94]

There were two sub-plots to this sordid behaviour, which, as Waterhouse wrote, 'showed the House of Commons at its most despicable' during the RAF's finest hour. The first was that 'unhappily the real object is a mean hunt of Swinton by Hoppy', and the second was 'a political capital hunt' by the Liberal MP, Geoffrey Mander, and the Labour MPs, Richard Stokes

and Aneurin Bevan, against Sir Joseph Ball. A former MI6 agent and
Director of Research at Conservative Central Office, Ball had been
appointed Deputy Chairman of Swinton's Committee as Chamberlain's
nominee. In the 1930s he had headed a 'dirty tricks' department, which
had run clandestine operations against Churchill. So the Prime Minister
found himself defending the Chamberlainite Philip Swinton and an old
antagonist, Ball. He got little thanks from the latter, who was 'still pro-
Chamberlain and rather pro-peace',[95] according to Bruce Lockhart, who
met him at the Sports Club eight days later.

The news that Churchill intended to give the United States ninety-
nine-year leases on certain Caribbean and Newfoundland military bases
went down very badly with the Tory imperialist right. The House was
anyhow 'languid', which Colville put down to their not being used to
sitting during August. Waterhouse 'did not like' the way 'in which news
was prefaced by an assurance that of course there was no question of a
cession – possibly a distinction but not a material difference'. On further
consideration he was 'glad it had been done, sorry it had to be done'.
Somerset de Chair agreed and was 'profoundly disturbed at his calmly
handing our strategic bases to USA', reasoning that 'after three generations no American politician is going to give them back'. When he
remonstrated with Churchill, he was told: 'I would sooner they had them
than a lot of Wops. . . . We cannot expect to hold everything.'[96] A motion
de Chair tabled to shorten the length of the leases was signed by a roll-
call of the senior Chamberlainites on the Tory right: Lord Winterton,
Sir Herbert Williams, the recently elected Major-General Sir Frederick
Sykes, Sir Ernest Graham-Little, Right Club member Lord Edmund
Crichton-Stuart and John Stourton amongst them. No longer in the
Government, Alan Lennox-Boyd was also able to sign.

Three days later Crozier interviewed Hore-Belisha, who told him that
he 'was afraid that Churchill would be prevented' from reconstructing the
Government according to merit, 'by the claims of the Tory Party machine
and by the dictatorship exercised by Captain Margesson. It would be
"monstrous" if the principle of party balance in the Government had to be
so rigidly maintained that Churchill could not choose the best man for the
jobs and this was now to be feared.' According to Crozier, Hore-Belisha
'clearly implied that Churchill would like to make certain appointments
but could not do so, or was likely to be prevented from doing so, by Captain
Margesson and the "machine"'. This could easily be written off as the
self-serving explanation of a disappointed ex-minister, who could neither
forgive nor forget his sacking at Chamberlain's hands eight months earlier.

But the very next day Crozier saw Beaverbrook, who told him that the Prime Minister had 'wanted to bring Herbert Morrison into the War Cabinet recently but the Tory "machine" would not let him'.

According to Beaverbrook, Kingsley Wood, Margesson and others decided that Morrison 'would disturb the balance of parties in the War Cabinet and they would not have it'. When it was suggested that Beaverbrook himself was acceptable as a War Cabinet member because he was a Tory, he roared with laughter and answered, 'Well, I'll tell you one thing, Mr Crozier, I'm not nearly such a conservative as Herbert Morrison!'

The underlying fact is clear: even on the day that the Luftwaffe began its all-night raids on London, Churchill was constrained by the Tory hierarchy over whom he could or could not appoint to his War Cabinet. Far from halting their internecine feuding when the nation was in danger, the politicians went on with their jockeying and criticizing unabated. Churchill might have been forgiven for wondering what he could possibly do to win the unqualified support of his Party.

By early September rumours were circulating 'that Winston is going to lead the Tory Party and he will when in the saddle get rid of the Munich Men'.[97] The evidence for this was the adoption of his son Randolph for the vacant Preston seat, as well as the now-public knowledge that Chamberlain was seriously ill. On 5 September Chips Channon wrote:

> In the House, Winston ... spoke at some length, but he was not at his best, and evoked little enthusiasm; the House has become accustomed to his high-flown rhetoric and thinks that he jokes too much: it is true that he is rarely serious about even sacred things, such as loss of life, and he betrays too easily how he is enjoying power.

Over the years politicians had become inured to Churchill's rhetoric in a way that ordinary radio listeners were not. Practised nit-pickers, they were the last group of people in the country to be overwhelmed by his personality and leadership.

Chamberlain's operation for cancer on 9 September convinced him that 'any ideas which may have been in my mind about possibilities of further political activity and even a possibility of another Premiership after the War have gone'. Nancy Dugdale was at the same time telling her husband that, although 'Winston is enormously popular', his coalition was 'definitely unpopular and I believe that ... the House of Commons is very out of gear'. Shakes Morrison, a Chamberlainite former minister, told her that 'the PM's star was waning' and Ernest Bevin was 'training to be the next PM'.[98]

The resentment of the Chamberlainites died hard, and they made spirited and determined efforts to continue trying to see the May 1940 crisis in a traditional left/right context long after everyone else realized that the terms of reference in British politics had undergone a profound change. In September 1940 the Duke of Devonshire voiced his suspicion that before May, 'Herbert M[orrison] as near as possible as he could told the workers to slack till their leaders were taken into the Government'. When the news broke that Chamberlain had cancer, Channon's first thought was that 'the leadership of the Party must then become Rab's, if there is a Conservative Party'. However, one Chamberlainite MP, Rear-Admiral Tufton Beamish, recorded how at the secret session on 17 September, two days after London had suffered one of its heaviest bombing raids in which 103 German planes had been shot down, 'The PM played upon the House like a skilled musician on an instrument and everybody seemed content to give him complete power.'[99]

Yet Churchill's speech at the secret session had once again to wind up with a plea 'to the House to show its consideration to Ministers.... We really are doing our very best.... I ask therefore for the indulgence of the House and for its support in not requiring too many sittings in the next month or two.' Waterhouse kept one of the Whips' notices he had received that week 'as an example of things the House thought it should discuss at this stage of the World War'. It included a two-line Whip for a debate on a 'scheme for Physical Recreation of young people'. As Waterhouse commented on the Blitz's effect on this keenness for debates, 'Needless to say London bombing changed their views!'

On 19 September Chamberlain had to leave London in order to be able to sleep. He offered to resign as Lord President of the Council, telling Halifax: 'I feel awfully bad about deserting you.' Churchill refused the offer, but after the military setback at Dakar on 23 September – when British and Free French forces were humiliatingly repulsed from the Vichyite capital of French West Africa – Churchill swiftly changed his mind. He took the precaution of having Margesson rewrite Chamberlain's resignation letter omitting certain words, which he feared made it sound as if he was asking for the resignation, something the Chamberlainites would not have welcomed.

The Dakar fiasco provided a perfect opportunity for critics of the Prime Minister to emerge from the woodwork and attack him directly, something the exigencies of the national emergency had not allowed in the previous couple of months. The alacrity with which they grabbed it shows the depth of the latent hostility still felt by Chamberlainites towards him and his regime. Victor Cazalet noted how 'all Winston's bad characteristics are now coming out'. Headlam wrote: 'it all beats me, and the whole thing smells of Winston! An affair of this kind, unless it is a success, is worse than useless and decidedly bad for our prestige, if we still possess any of that commodity so far as our "planning" is concerned.' Patrick Hannon wrote to Churchill to say that, in his constituency, 'the feeling of criticism and resentment is acute. Frankly the Dakar retreat is regarded as a cardinal blunder: more grave and far-reaching than the recall of our expeditionary force from Norway.' He went so far as to record his 'suspicion that there is want of foresight and vision in high places'.[100] Even Lord Salisbury, whose Watching Committee had been zealous supporters of Churchill during the Phoney War, admitted to 'a feeling of uneasiness'.[101]

Channon wondered whether Dakar was 'just a Winstonian scheme in his earlier, rasher manner', and believed it 'revealed the PM to be as incautious as ever. It is a deplorable affair and feeling in the Carlton Club is running high against him'. Admiral Beamish thought that, in the House of Commons, Churchill 'managed to slide across the Dakar incident with some adroitness but many had doubts and I am confident a grave error has been made'. All this fulminating against what was, in the wider context of the war, merely a sideshow of a sideshow, shows how sceptical they still were about Churchill and how ready to criticize him, even in the month when Britain lost 160,000 tons of shipping and the Blitz was approaching its height.

Halifax privately distanced himself from the Dakar decision, telling Chamberlain: 'As you know I have never been awfully happy about it. ... I think some of the enthusiasts showed their hopes to become master.'[102] Even 'Cassandra' in the *Daily Mirror* was moved to warn: 'It's going to be hard to convince us that Mr Churchill has feet of clay, but we can't stand a great deal more of this.'[103] Waterhouse's view was that 'politically we can thank our stars that we have no opposition to face in the House. This fiasco could not be easily defended.' It was hardly surprising, therefore, with all the talk of Dakar as being reminiscent of the Dardanelles adventure of 1915, that Churchill became, as Halifax put it, 'frightfully excited' over the criticism and accepted Chamberlain's resignation in order to reshuffle the Government.

Salisbury's Watching Committee – which had played a crucial role in bringing down Chamberlain but had become almost moribund during Churchill's Premiership – was resuscitated by Dakar. Writing to the Tory MP, Paul Emrys-Evans, who had rebelled over Norway, Salisbury

Lord Mountbatten, Nehru and Lady Mountbatten, New Delhi, 1947

Appearing on the balcony at Buckingham Palace after Munich in response to shouts of 'We want Chamberlain!': the Prime Minister and Mrs Chamberlain with the King and Queen.

The National Government Whips' Office, July 1938: the bastion of Chamberlainite orthodoxy. Back row, left to right: Patrick Munro, Sir Albert Edmonson, Robert Grimston, Major John Herbert, Major George Harvie-Watt, Stephen Furness. Front row, left to right: Major Thomas Dugdale, Lieutenant-Colonel Charles Kerr, Captain David Margesson, Neville Chamberlain, Captain the Hon. James Stuart, the Hon. Arthur Hope, Captain Charles Waterhouse

The Norway debate, Tuesday, 7 May 1940: Neville Chamberlain faces the camera. Sitting beside him can be seen Winston Churchill, Sir Samuel Hoare and Sir John Simon. These unique photographs were taken surreptitiously by Tory MP John Moore-Brabazon, with a hidden Minox camera

'All behind you, Winston' – although these ministers were, what did the Tory backbenchers really think? David Low cartoon, *Evening Standard*, 14 May 1940. Front row, left to right: Churchill, Clement Attlee, Ernest Bevin, Herbert Morrison, Leo Amery; behind, left to right: Neville Chamberlain, Arthur Greenwood, Lord Halifax, Archibald Sinclair, Duff Cooper, A. V. Alexander, Anthony Eden

Sir Walter Monckton at the Ministry of Information, 1940

Arthur Bryant, 'patriotic' historian, at home with his first wife, October 1934

complained that the Government's 'outside appearance is certainly one of infirmity of purpose leading to futility' and announced that 'getting rid of' the First Sea Lord, Dudley Pound, was the top Watching Committee objective.[104] Salisbury went so far as to wonder whether Churchill could be more than just a 'defensive' Prime Minister. 'The construction of an offensive policy', he wrote to Lord ('Top') Wolmer, 'is really on a wholly different footing from what he has done hitherto since he has been PM – it may be ill-contrived and too late, or too early, or in the wrong direction.'[105]

Another question which was causing concern on the Tory right was the massive cost of the war, running at £9 million per day. Salisbury wanted the Watching Committee to 'press for some check upon what I hear to be absolutely reckless expenditure incurred in order, I suspect, to keep the working-class in good temper! An outrageous motive, an insult to the working-class, and, of course, hopeless as an ultimate policy!' Headlam found the spending levels 'grotesque', and it was a constant irritant to the Chamberlainites that it 'means higher and higher taxation', although constructive suggestions about how to fight a cut-price war were few.

The reshuffle following Chamberlain's resignation took place on 3 October, but could not be as extensive as Churchill wished, owing to Halifax's refusal to leave the Foreign Office. Churchill did bring Oliver Lyttelton from outside politics into the Presidency of the Board of Trade. When attempting to find a constituency, Lyttelton met Lord Windlesham, the Vice-Chairman of the Conservative Party, to discuss the vacant Wrekin seat. Windlesham asked him whether his candidature 'was backed by Winston' and, when he was told that it was, said Churchill's support was 'a great mistake but it can't be helped'.[106] Bracken was furious when he heard about this, but the hierarchy of the voluntary side of the Party was uniformly Chamberlainite. The Party Treasurer, Lord Marchwood, had even considered refusing to continue in office when Chamberlain fell, until persuaded by Margesson.[107] In the event, Wolmer, an MP with a courtesy title, was elevated to the House of Lords during his father's lifetime by Writ of Acceleration, thereby releasing the Aldershot constituency – to which Lyttelton was now elected.

Waterhouse's comment on Bevin's becoming Minister of Labour harked back to September 1939: 'One cannot put out of one's mind the fact that these same men refused to help when Neville called on them last autumn. Are they *first* Britons or socialist politicians?' Thomas Inskip's departure from active politics – like Simon he went to a high legal post with a peerage – was long expected and enabled the Edenite Lord Cranborne to take over the Colonial Office and vacate the distinctly less prestigious Paymaster-Generalship he had received in May. As with Wolmer, Cranborne was three months later given a peerage in his own right in order to strengthen the coalition in the Lords. With characteristic ill-grace Headlam explained Cranborne's promotion as 'a reward for having stuck to Eden'. With much more accuracy he explained Sir John Reith's peerage as 'due to the fact that he has been a complete failure in the Commons'.[108] This was the first reshuffle since May, and the Churchillians had made only modest advances over the Chamberlainites.

Waterhouse considered his hero's resignation

> a catastrophe comparable to Dunkirk. Halifax will be the lone White Man in the Cabinet capable of taking a straight and balanced view, but he cannot be an adequate counter-poise able to steady and therefore bring out the best in the PM.

He added that Margesson

> said the other evening that the first reactions of W[inston] are almost always wrong but he was ready to have this ... pointed out to him and reverse or modify his views on reflection. It is clearly therefore all-important that someone should be at hand to put his reflective powers under way; one can't imagine Attlee, Greenwood or Beaverbrook cast for such a part.

In fact, barring Halifax, the Chamberlainites had no contenders for the job and willingly battened on to the colourless Sir John Anderson, who had taken Chamberlain's place as Lord President of the Council and who, Waterhouse thought, 'would be an acquisition to the Cabinet'.

Chamberlain thought so too for, as he told Halifax:

> I have been very anxious about the reconstruction, but David Margesson has been here today and what he had told me has immensely relieved my mind. The changes will strengthen the Cabinet enormously and the fact that you remain at the F.O. will comfort many who will be sorrowful over my departure.

He could not forbear one slightly quizzical comment to his old friend about Churchill's hasty acceptance of the resignation that had been refused before Dakar: 'the invitation which came upon me so suddenly was so unexpected that one could not at first feel sure of its implications'.[109]

Lloyd George was disappointed not to be appointed to the Cabinet after his arch-enemy Chamberlain's departure, but consoled himself by confiding to his private secretary: 'I shall wait until Winston is bust.'[110] It may have been about this time, too, that Baldwin reputedly told

Cazalet: 'My time is not yet. It may come soon. At present I am low and Winston is high. Who knows how soon the positions may be reversed?'[111] Certainly Channon, four days after recognizing that 'the Churchill regime will never offer me anything', went back on the offensive against the 'Glamour Boys'. According to him, 'now so prominent and powerful, after being fallow for so long, [they] are a makeshift and shoddy lot. Their only merit has been long subservience to Winston.'[112]

On 8 October Randolph Churchill took his seat in the House. He was introduced by Margesson. Waterhouse felt that

> one would have expected it to be an occasion of a remarkable demonstration. In fact the remarkable circumstance was the absence of any enthusiasm. The affair was treated more as a joke than a rather triumphal moment in the P.M.'s life. But the House is that way inclined. Its opinions are not very consistent and I fear it will not be long before the acclamations which have cheered Winston the attacker and successor of the hated Neville will be heard no more when not Winston the rebel but Churchill the Conservative Party Leader faces the House. From his own point of view I think he has made a mistake.

Waterhouse was referring to Churchill's decision to accept the Leadership of the Conservative Party, given up by the dying Chamberlain. Far from being reconciled to Churchill by the time of the sinking of the French fleet in early July 1940, as most historians have suggested, the Tory Party was still suspicious of him. In October a man with his ear so close to the Tory ground as Waterhouse could remark that, 'Everyone realises the inevitability of the change ... but no one pretends to like it.' There had long been 'a simmering dislike of Churchill' in the 1922 Committee, and this resurfaced at their meeting held just before the leadership election in Caxton Hall, Westminster, which took place at 4.30 p.m. on 9 October.[113] Beamish records how, at that meeting, 'some malcontents made the best they could of their promises to accept as our new leader the PM', considering Sir Archibald Southby, Sir Herbert Williams, Austin Hopkinson 'and some others' as people who 'professionally oppose the P.M.'.

The criticisms at the 1922 Committee meeting centred on Margesson, who was felt by some to be 'too aloof'.[114] Waterhouse records how 'a frontal attack on David developed. He was roundly accused of failing to keep the leaders in touch with the feeling in the Party.' Waterhouse admitted that Margesson 'possibly failed to put the Party's views strongly enough to influence policy', but in his defence argued that

> he has proved himself an extraordinarily capable party manager and at the

moment it is more than usually important that he should be at the PM's elbow, to keep some semblance of sanity in political arrangements and prevent for example an attempt to drop Halifax and put Anthony [Eden] back in the F.O., and in humbler spheres make Clement Davies Parliamentary Secretary for Works and Buildings.

The 1922 Committee agreed that 'it was the sense of the Committee that it would be highly undesirable that any proposals other than the election of leaders should be discussed at the Party meeting'. There had been talk of a deputy leader being proposed – Eden, Shakes Morrison and Butler all having been mentioned – but the Churchillian hierarchy were keen to avoid this happening.[15]

Clementine Churchill did not want her husband to become Party Leader, but to remain instead a purely national figure. However, Beaverbrook and Bracken – using Lloyd George's fate in 1922 to show what happened to 'national' figures without party backing – made him see the sense of it. One does not turn down the leadership of the majority party lightly and Churchill knew that the Tories needed him as much as he them. Beaverbrook also 'pointed out the danger of divided loyalties, of possible complaints against Churchill by Conservative backbenchers' if anyone else was allowed to take Chamberlain's mantle.[16] By taking on the Leadership, Churchill was paradoxically showing how politically weak he still perceived himself to be.

It was at this time that the young Chamberlainite MP, George Harvie-Watt, showed Churchill around his anti-aircraft unit stationed at Redhill. He remembered how

the PM started talking politics to me. There had been a meeting of the Conservative Party to elect a leader and there were some cliques in the Party who said that Churchill should not become leader and that he would be in a stronger position without too strong a Party attachment.... The PM asked me what I thought about these developments at Westminster. I said it would be fatal if he did not lead the Conservative Party.... He was still suspicious of them and of their attitude to him before the war. I said ... essentially he must have a majority and I was sure this majority could only come from the Conservative Party. He questioned me a lot about the strength of ministers and what influence they wielded. I replied that if you have a strong army of MPs under you, ministers could be won over or crushed, if necessary. He seemed to appreciate my arguments and thanked me very much.[17]

Harvie-Watt little realized that he was being sounded out as a potential PPS for Churchill, precisely because of his Chamberlainite connections.

At the Caxton Hall meeting of the Conservative Party on 9 October Halifax took the chair, thanked Chamberlain and proposed Churchill as the new Leader. These were put together, in an 'omnibus' resolution, so that no Tory could vote in favour of the first and against the second, as Waterhouse suspected some Tory MPs would have liked. Just prior to leaving for the Hall, Halifax wrote to Lady Alexandra Metcalfe to say that he found his speech 'very difficult to do', but the next day he said he had been told that he 'had not put my foot in the rather boggy ground!' According to Crookshank, Halifax made 'a beautifully phrased speech', treading the careful line between praise for the two men. Beamish noted how he 'paid a wonderful tribute to Mr Chamberlain who was not present, very firmly and in fine language he praised Neville C. for his efforts to keep peace and gain time ... to overcome the madness of our people in their almost criminal unreadiness for inevitable war'. No verbatim record exists of what Halifax said, but the first half was clearly an apologia for appeasement.

He then spoke for a much shorter period about Churchill, and eventually put the resolution to the vote. In the national emergency, let alone the absence of alternative candidates, it is hardly surprising that nobody actually voted against. Instead, the electoral college, consisting of Tory MPs, peers in receipt of the Conservative Whip and Executive Committee members of the National Union, elected Churchill *nemine contradictente*. This, as Beamish pointed out, was not the same as unanimously, because it meant 'that some did not vote for or against, but they were few'.

Churchill then entered the Hall to 'a good but not tempestuous welcome'. He gave 'a good speech of acceptance', lasting about ten minutes and, in Wallace's opinion, 'hitting exactly the right note as usual'.[118] He certainly hit a right-wing note, concentrating on those subjects – the Empire, the left-wing threat and so on – most likely to appeal to Chamberlainites. Indeed, as he had put it in rather different circumstances three decades earlier, he served up 'sentiment by the bucketful, patriotism by the Imperial pint'. He naturally paid an extravagant tribute to his predecessor, emphasizing 'how close had been his work' with Chamberlain over the previous thirteen months, and how their 'friendship had grown'. He then dealt frankly with Tory concerns about his personality, chaffing himself 'gently about his alleged fickleness'. For a speech of acceptance for the leadership of a party on which he had 'ratted' and 're-ratted', it was a masterpiece.

The extent to which he was willing to appease the Tory right can be perceived from the statement that 'his basic belief in and support of the imperial outlook was his main incentive to accept the leadership'.[119] After that 'he stressed the importance of speaking with authority on behalf of the Party and the organisation in the Cabinet'.[120] Beamish noted: 'He realises that there are dangerous influences at work in the socialist and further left parties. Every trade union and the co-operative movement and the rather cowardly ... pseudo-intelligent left movements are using every minute to promote their pestilential views.[121]

Yet not everyone was impressed. Beamish sat next to the Chamberlainite MP, Sir John Power, who 'blamed [Churchill's] Ten-Year Rule' for British military unpreparedness, and when leaving the Hall, Kenneth Pickthorn told him that Churchill was 'a word-spinner, a second-rate rhetorician'. Pickthorn's son remembers how his father 'thought Churchill's judgment fearful. Right to the end he thought him a disastrous war leader, albeit a vigorous personality. He thought Churchill pretty invariably chose the wrong course of action.'[122] Halifax wrote to Chamberlain after the meeting that he had been touched by the 'evident personal feeling of real sorrow and regret and regard for you. Nor was there any doubt as to the overwhelming sense of the meeting as to what you had done to keep the peace of the world as long as you could.'

It had been agreed when the 1922 Committee met before the Caxton Hall election that a deputation led by its Chairman, William Spens, would 'interview' Churchill after his election 'and express to him the hope of the Committee that there might be in the future as close as possible a liaison between the Party and its leader': coded criticism of Margesson. At the next meeting of the Committee there was further talk about the 'importance of consulting opinion in the Party before controversial legislation ... was introduced'.[123] According to Waterhouse, the deputation had suggested that Tommy Dugdale be recalled from Palestine to take Margesson's place.

After the deputation had left, Churchill reassured the worried Chief Whip that 'he had listened carefully and that was all he intended to do'. For the time being Churchill found Margesson too useful an ally to replace with a Chamberlainite loyalist such as Dugdale. When Channon met Churchill in the House the day after the Caxton Hall meeting, he wondered 'why he always bows and withdraws into himself when he is aware of hostility ... he seems to contract, suddenly to look smaller and his famous charm is overclouded by an angry taurine look'. Churchill was, for all his Olympian efforts, leading a party which was still at soul Chamberlainite.

The same day Morris-Jones noted how it was a 'curious House. Conservatives seemed to have lost all interest although numerically they are in overwhelming majority. Labour – a party of 200 – are both dominant in the government and in opposition as far as the House is concerned.' This fact, despite Churchill's vigorous anti-socialist remarks at his adoption meeting, was a constant irritant for Tory backbenchers. The Conservative Party organization effectively went into hibernation during the war, with no propaganda, conference, constituency organization, regional activity or local agents, and the Party faithful always feared that Labour was stealing a march on them. They also suspected that they could hardly look to Churchill to rectify this, although he was eventually to pay heavily for it in the 1945 general election.

This criticism of the lack of party organization, together with the belief that whilst there was an electoral truce there was precious little political truce, cropped up regularly in the complaints of Chamberlainites.[124] As the Chamberlainite MP for Totnes, Major Rayner, told the 1922 Committee, to general endorsement, 'all over the country the Conservative cause was being allowed to go by default'. They particularly resented 'socialist' Ministry of Information speakers being sent to give talks in their constituencies, for which they blamed Duff Cooper.

On the night of 14 October one of the centres of Tory discontent disappeared when the Carlton Club was destroyed. Some junior ministers were having a pre-prandial glass of sherry with Margesson in the smoking-room when the ceiling suddenly collapsed. About thirty people were dining there, with another forty in the smoking-room. The building had received a direct hit. Despite all this, everyone (including the numerous club servants) escaped alive – which, in Headlam's words, 'seems to indicate that God approves of Conservative legislators'. Equally, it may have reflected divine retribution against Churchill's detractors.

Meanwhile, the campaign to remove Margesson and replace him with a more committed Chamberlainite was gathering pace. On 18 October Sir John Simon's former PPS, John Crowder, wrote to Nancy Dugdale asking her to pass on to her husband the news that, as far as the Party was concerned, 'many of us feel that the Chief Whip has for some time ignored the feelings and wishes of the backbench members of the Conservative Party and that advice given to the late PM was certainly not good'. He believed that

> things have gone from bad to worse since 'Winston' became PM. I have seen [Conservative Central Office Chairman Sir Douglas] Hacking twice and explained that there was no one to whom we could go to discuss matters concerning the Home Front such as Finance, the activities of the Ministry of

Information, the future policy of the Conservative Party, etc. He agreed the position was difficult.

He went on to say that at a recent meeting of the 1922 Committee, he had suggested that Dugdale be recalled and 'this remark was greeted with loud applause from all parts of the room and other speakers agreed and said we badly wanted him back'. This was because 'we could all trust him'. The implication was that having 'sold out' to Churchill, the Tories could no longer trust Margesson, and in particular they had their suspicions about his behaviour at the time of the Norway debate. Sir Horace Wilson deprecated any early expectations Dugdale might have of replacing the man he codenamed 'King Zog': 'I don't see any weakening in K.Z.'s position ... he has the confidence, apparently, of the Emperor.' He told Nancy Dugdale that, if her husband were recalled, he 'should be astonished.... It would indeed be a sign of grace, at present lacking!'

To boost her hopes came another letter from Crowder on 27 October, saying, 'in my opinion it is essential to get him home if we want the Conservative Party to survive. I am working closely with Erskine-Hill and others.' These 'others' included Lady Davidson, the Tory MP wife of Baldwin's confidant and Chamberlain's friend J.C.C. Davidson. Although the Chamberlainites acknowledged that 'certain quarters', in particular Bracken, did not want Dugdale to return, 'I can assure you that as far as I can gauge the feeling, eighty per cent of the backbenchers of the Party want him back'. Crowder concluded: 'That is really the position as I see it but I will urge my friends to make "Winston" cable to him if possible.'[125]

Sir Horace Wilson wrote to Mrs Dugdale again the next day about a letter she had written Eden about her husband's recall, wondering 'whether he has sense enough to see that Tommy could be useful *to him* here'. But an extravagant attack by Vyvyan Adams against Margesson in the Commons served only to strengthen the Chief Whip's embattled position, as Churchill could hardly be seen to bow to such overt pressure. As Wilson noted, 'the V. Adams business was just silly ... and only cements D.M. in again'. He added: 'Actually the H of C is very much out of the picture now and likely to remain so; nobody takes any note of it, for we are in a stage during which various dictators make their speeches via "loudspeakers" and the echo of one is distorted by the next!'

An indication of how carefully Churchill still felt he needed to tread when confronted with Chamberlainite sensibilities can be seen in the kid-glove treatment given to the Duchess of Atholl's request of 16 October to be allowed back into the Conservative Party. The first woman to hold office in a Conservative government, she had been a zealous anti-appeaser, and the Tory Whip had been withdrawn from her for six months in 1935. She gave it up altogether in April 1938 and, after Munich, resigned from Parliament in order to contest her Perth and Kinross seat as an Independent at a by-election. Churchill wrote a letter in her support. This provoked a violent row between James Stuart and Churchill, which neither had forgotten. Despite the Duchess's letter, which said 'I now feel that with you as Leader I can once more work for the Conservative Party', Churchill was wary about accepting her back into the Tory fold for fear of angering the Chamberlainites.

He passed it on to Margesson, who predictably minuted that 'the letter which she sends is not suitable for publication and would tend to foment trouble within the Party in Scotland'.[126] The political secretary to James Stuart, the Scottish Whip, had written, ironically enough from Atholl Crescent in Edinburgh, that, if published in its present form, the Duchess's letter 'indirectly would amount to a slap in the face to Mr Chamberlain'. Margesson therefore drafted another, in which he placed the blame for the breach squarely on the Duchess. Churchill sent it to her for signing, saying that any other wording 'might raise some controversial questions within the Party'. After she signed it Margesson easily brushed off the question of her re-entering Parliament, which she never did.

On 18 October Beamish had 'a weary hour' with Henrietta Bower, daughter of Lord Strickland and wife of the Tory MP and Norway rebel, Commander Robert Bower. She was 'inciting me to attack the PM and get the Board of Admiralty changed and replaced by young blood'. Beamish merely promised to 'watch things'.[127] More important to Tory MPs was the Irish Government's refusal to allow the Royal Navy to use the 'Treaty' ports of Lough Swilly, Berehaven and Queenstown. These naval bases had belonged to the United Kingdom from the time of the Anglo-Irish Treaty of 1922 until Malcolm MacDonald had ceded them in 1938, and were in a strategically vital position for the anti-U-boat offensive. Many MPs believed Churchill was showing uncharacteristic weakness in not threatening Eire to secure their return.

Beamish, who as an admiral probably appreciated the ports' strategic value more than most, concluded: 'what a race, what a tribe of blind, revengeful outcasts not worthy to survive.... I believe the majority in Southern Ireland would welcome our reoccupation.' Headlam was also soon complaining: 'I hope that Winston now realises what a mess he was party to when he surrendered to [Prime Minister Eamon] de Valera in the first instance,' conveniently forgetting that in 1938 Churchill had vigorously opposed MacDonald's handing back the ports which he himself, as Colonial Secretary, had secured from the Irish negotiators in 1922.[128] The campaign over the Irish ports made some strange bedfellows; one of the people who worked hard 'to raise public opinion as to the threat' was Oscar Wilde's former friend, Lord Alfred Douglas.

No sooner had Churchill weathered this storm than another blew up, one which filled Chamberlainites with barely disguised glee. It was discovered that Bob Boothby had been a potential beneficiary when advocating the unfreezing of Czech assets. This appearance of corruption by one of Churchill's closest friends and confidants delighted many Chamberlainites who had resented Boothby's part in that summer's plots against their leader. It fitted in perfectly with their perception of themselves as morally superior to the 'gangsters' who had taken over in May and a tangible air of 'I told you so' pervaded their correspondence and diary entries.

Waterhouse noted that 'the Boothby affair in detail does not look pretty' and asked rhetorically, 'What can one expect?' Beamish wrote of Boothby's contact in the affair, Richard Weineger: 'He is a trader in finance and thinks in no other terms than money and is ready as Jews have always been to pull up his stumps and flit to safer places with his wealth.' Anti-Semitism of this sort was rife amongst politicians of the day. When Lord Woolton, the Minister of Food, complained that month that the Labour MP, Colonel Harry Nathan, had been given a peerage solely so that Bevin could take his Wandsworth seat, he seemed to regret this more because Nathan was Jewish than because of the political gerrymandering involved.

Churchill felt unable to do anything more than distance himself from his former lieutenant – something for which Boothby was never to forgive him. Boothby's biographer, in a recent book, has put this down to the fact that 'Churchill was politically in the hands of the Conservative machine, which, although Churchill was temporarily beyond its reach, was out for revenge against one of its most independent spirits; and [Churchill] was quite prepared to sacrifice an old friend for his own interests.'[129] Telling Woolton that 'Boothby had much capacity but no virtue', the Prime Minister appointed a Select Committee to investigate the affair. The Chairman was Waterhouse's friend and neighbour, Colonel John Gretton, 'a passionate Chamberlainite and supporter of Munich'. According to the biography, Boothby 'detected in Gretton's appointment the hand of the Whips' Office, particularly that of Stuart, and he may have been right'.

Boothby only agreed to suspension from his post as Parliamentary Secretary at the Ministry of Food on the urging of his Chamberlainite PPS Leslie Pym, who, his diary states, had advocated this course of action in conjunction with Margesson.[130] Nancy Dugdale crowed when she heard how Boothby 'has had to resign his position as Ministry of Food bottle washer. I was so delighted as you know my opinion of him. Perhaps the bad ones will gradually come to the surface and be ejected.' It is impossible, considering the vigour and enthusiasm with which the Select Committee hounded Boothby, not to detect a note of personal malice amongst his prosecutors.

After a secret session debate in late October 1940, Morris-Jones noted that the 'House very concerned and restive over our war efforts. We are just about holding our own against the whole world.' The U-boat campaign had been intensified and Britain, answering Greece's call for aid against Italy, had now postponed her long-awaited Middle Eastern offensive. In such dire circumstances Margesson's complaint to Woolton that 'Churchill is not really interested, in spite of his long experience, in any of the civil or social problems' may be seen as rather beside the point. Far from all coalescing around the national leader, Kingsley Wood told Woolton that 'the number of people who think they are the future P.M. of this country is quite amazing'.[131]

Maritime losses, including that of HMS *Jervis Bay* on 5 November, and a worsening food situation added to Churchill's troubles. On Guy Fawkes Day Harold Nicolson sensed a 'wave of defeatism'. Lord Woolton could discern 'no personal loyalty to Churchill' amongst his colleagues and, on the same day, the Prime Minister managed to anger Headlam by giving 'very grave figures' for those killed in air raids − 4,558 that month − 'but he made light of them'.[132] On 6 November Churchill announced that the Commons would henceforth sit in Church House rather than the Palace of Westminster. According to Headlam, 'the House took none too kindly to this.... Members are complaining openly that Winston trades on his position, on his immense following in the country, though his popularity is on the decline but it is still high. Yet the country does not want a dictator.' On 10 May 1941 a bomb destroyed the House of Commons Chamber.

When the Commons met at Church House, Morris-Jones complained that 'everything seemed very strange. We sat on chairs.... Acoustics not good.' There was a smoking-room, but no Members' room, library or other facilities. This had the unintended advantage for the Government that there was less space for malcontents to congregate informally. Nothing, however, was allowed to lessen the intrigue going on outside, and on 7 November the Tory MP, Beverley Baxter, wrote to Bracken about 'a private dinner at the Savoy the other night', given by Hore-Belisha. 'The purpose of the affair was to inflame opposition against the PM,' claimed Baxter.[133] Churchill was sent this report and passed it on to Beaverbrook for his comments. In fact the dinner, which took place in the 'Patience' room there, had no such purpose, but Churchill's sense of vulnerability and irritation could only have been heightened by such snippets of intelligence.[134]

It was probably this frustration that led him to be, according to the Australian paper *Truth*, 'sarcastic' in answering the Chamberlainite MP, William Craven-Ellis, who had said in Parliament that there was a growing feeling amongst the public that the country was not being properly mobilized for total war. Considering that in January 1939 Craven-Ellis had reassured an audience that he was 'satisfied that this country can and will be kept out of war this year', he would perhaps have been better advised not to have criticized Churchill over the war effort.[135]

On 11 November 1940 the Royal Navy attacked and crippled the Italian fleet at Taranto. Much relieved, Churchill told Channon before announcing the news in the Commons that 'we have some sugar for the birds this time'. Perhaps it was their flightiness and twittering that led him to choose that metaphor for his backbenchers. The news won him little respite. Only two days later Lord Kemsley, the Chairman of Allied Newspapers and Editor-in-Chief of the *Sunday Times*, told Woolton that 'people have become very critical of Churchill: whilst fully recognising that he represented the spirit of the nation and made marvellous speeches, they were beginning to doubt the quality of the government – in which, of course they are quite right'. The newspaper magnate went on to surmise that, 'if there had been an Opposition, the government would have gone over Dakar, but the whole trouble was that there was no alternative P.M'.[136]

In the adjournment debate on 12 November, Vyvyan Adams renewed his attack on Margesson, describing his reign as Chief Whip as an 'evil, unhappy tyranny'. In that philippic he said, 'the power for evil is still there, sitting just by the mace ... whispering his counsels in the ear of the Prime Minister'. Adams alleged that 'if anyone over the last nine years deserved a title, it was necessary to approach the Right Honourable and Gallant gentleman on all fours'. Quintin Hogg came to Margesson's defence, rather illogically claiming that Adams's words were 'really a deliberate and vicious attack on the Prime Minister who is responsible for the appointment'.[137] Sir Eugene Ramsden, a senior backbencher who had seconded his fellow Chamberlainite Sir George Courthorpe's proposal of Churchill as Leader of the Party the month before, told Nancy Dugdale that 'people are sick of D.M. and the general feeling is that he should go'.

On 12 November the Commons heard Churchill's panegyric on Chamberlain, who had died three days before. Beamish uncharitably considered it 'flawless as a rhetorical effort, but a close examination reveals a clear intention to make the late P.M. shoulder the blame for what has happened and to buttress his own efforts past and present'. He thought Churchill employed 'deliberate faint praise', and concluded: 'no wonder some men distrust the P.M. for his capacity for cajolery and fervent persuasive English'. Churchill had been fortunate, felt Beamish: he 'became P.M. at a very perfect moment. I incline to the feeling that had Churchill been P.M. in 1938 or before we should have slid into war unprepared or disunited.' Of Chamberlain he thought: 'it takes a great-hearted man to accept with perfect loyalty service under a·man such as Churchill when he has been the cause of your downfall'.[138] This was the rewriting of history on a grand scale.

The funeral at Westminster Abbey on 14 November 1940 was an emotional experience for Chamberlainites. Waterhouse was 'sick to see the solemn humbugging expressions on the faces of some of those who had made his last months a hell'. Colville 'noticed the look of blank indifference, almost of disdain, on Duff Cooper's face, the boredom of Bevin. Only Anderson and Hankey sang the hymns.' Channon felt that 'some seemed to be gloating', but admitted that 'Winston ... had the decency to cry', which was not in itself perhaps too much of a tribute from the most lachrymose Prime Minister since Lord Goderich. There were many occasions when Churchillian tears were shed during the war, but none were more politically felicitous than these.

Chamberlain's old foe Lloyd George honourably declined to be a pall-bearer – a position to which his status as an ex-Prime Minister entitled him. Sir Kingsley Wood, the man who put paid to Chamberlain's hopes of staying on as Prime Minister on the morning of 10 May 1940, accepted. He thus buried Chamberlain in both the corporeal and political sense. In the House of Commons on 12 November, Churchill had lauded his predecessor's 'love of peace, the toil for peace, the strive for peace, the pursuit of peace, even at great peril ... to save the world from the awful, devastating struggle in which we are now engaged'. It is unlikely that this eulogy to his old foe would necessarily have been so warm had the Chamberlainites not still been so prominent in his Government.

'As I expected,' wrote Beamish in mid-November, 'the House of Commons having got over the Chamberlain eruption and Churchill's rise to power is steadily sorting itself out and becoming critical and some of those displaced such as Belisha, [National Labour former minister Kenneth] Lindsay, etc., are gathering courage and sniping at their successors'. Lord Salisbury, at least, felt that as far as the Watching Committee was concerned, Taranto 'possibly makes any interventions' – over the deficiencies of First Sea Lord Admiral Pound, the loss of HMS *Glorious* and the failure at Dakar – 'at this moment inopportune'.[39]

In stark contrast to the rock-solid national belief in victory, the House of Commons was less certain. On 19 November Morris-Jones noted in his diary that 'several Members consider that we cannot get a victory over Germany, that the best we can expect is a stalemate'. It may have been the British people's 'Finest Hour', but the same cannot be said for the politicians.

Woolton wrote in his diary on 20 November 1940:

> Chamberlain succeeded in getting a personal allegiance from members of his government, because although he was not strong he was absolutely reliable and trustworthy. There is no allegiance to Churchill; there is nobody in the government whom the public would trust. Halifax belongs to the Old Munich School; Anderson has no imagination and little human sympathy; Greenwood [is an] economic philanderer in Government, the victim of theories. Bevin will blow himself out – he is very vain, I don't trust Beaverbrook, LG ... no one trusts either! It isn't the government of this country that's going to win the war – it's the people.

Woolton suspected Beaverbrook's *Express* newspapers were becoming critical of Churchill, with John Gordon writing in the mass-circulation *Sunday Express* even after Taranto: 'Don't sit on the safety valve too long. ... You promised us hammer blows on Italy, Mr Churchill. Strike them!'

Cazalet considered Churchill to be 'either very much under the influence or very frightened of Beaverbrook, who ... is now becoming a public danger'. He reasoned that 'once, of course, you have people like B. in the government you are bound to have to pay the price'. On 27 November, after a lunch at the Dorchester for those MPs serving in the forces, Cazalet, who had fallen out with Churchill over India in the

1930s, noticed that 'Winston is very bad at *tête-à-tête* talk.... He keeps very strange hours and is a very bad chairman at Cabinet meetings. He takes no notice of the agenda until about the last five minutes.'[140] Cazalet was not, of course, a member of the War Cabinet, but we can easily detect the source of this unflattering information: he and Halifax walked to the Foreign Office from Eaton Square together every Wednesday morning.

By late November criticisms were not coming solely from Chamberlainites such as Cazalet; on the 28th even the Liberal MP, Clement Davies, was complaining to his fellow Welshman Lloyd George that 'the government had a really bad time yesterday ... the House was seething.... I am afraid Winston is so absorbed in playing the part of Marlborough, Nelson and Trenchard that he has no time for the more mundane things. Last night Members came to ask me to put down a motion for radical reconstruction.' He had also sensed 'general dissatisfaction with regard to production and labour', and considered Bevin to have 'failed miserably'. The shipping situation was 'almost horrifying', and Greenwood – who had a drink problem – was 'appalling, even worse than he was three months ago'.[141] The same day Abraham Lyons, Tory MP for Leicester, suggested to Headlam that 'we should get together and form a group'. He was turned down: 'I hardly know the man but he is a King's Counsel (Jew of course) and said to be honest and clever'. On the train home the previous weekend Headlam had sat next to the Labour MP, William Lunn, who 'was intensely gloomy at the prospect of war and our prospects'.[142]

December 1940 began badly, and Headlam found 'that a lot of people are dissatisfied with the government'. Shipping losses, supposedly bad production figures and the threat of communism in the dockyards all contributed to this mood amongst MPs, but, as the only vocal opposition leaders were Hore-Belisha and Lord Winterton, Headlam could not 'see how an effective group can be formed'. General Wavell's victory against the Italians at Sidi Barrani on 8 December, and the Eighth Army's subsequent drive along the North African littoral over the next three months, saved Churchill's prestige. One historian believes the victory in Libya 'may have given Churchill the confidence he needed to bring Eden into the Foreign Office in place of Halifax' on 23 December.

The change in the political scene was not lost on Sir Horace Wilson, the former power behind Chamberlain's throne, who told Nancy Dugdale:

It is a good thing that the Libyan move came, for we are all getting very depressed by the combination of December weather and shipping losses and political conditions. If the rumour is true that we are going to be governed by W[inston], the B[eaver], & Ll[oyd] G[eorge] − a trinity − I am afraid I shall become a sore trial to my friends! But of course we shall all wake up presently and find we have been in a fearful dream.[143]

Many such rumours abounded that the war administration would be shared between Churchill and two other triumvirs, whose identities changed regularly but often revolved around Bevin, Beaverbrook and Lloyd George.

The death of the British Ambassador in Washington, Lord Lothian, on 12 December gave Churchill an ideal opportunity to reconstruct the Government. He had long wished to bring Eden into the Foreign Office, but as *de facto* leader of the Chamberlainites, Halifax had hitherto been able to refuse to move. Now at last there was somewhere viable for him to be sent and, politically strengthened by Wavell's continued victories against the Italians, Churchill sent Halifax to the Washington Embassy. This occasioned considerable private disquiet amongst Chamberlainites, but Churchill had couched the offer in terms of Halifax's public duty and there was no outright opposition. The true reason for the reshuffle, believed James Stuart, was that 'Winston ... knew he could bully Anthony, but not Halifax'.[144] Cazalet suspected that 'Winston wanted H. out of the country so that Ll[oyd] G[eorge] might join the Government − what a gang'. The editor of *The Times*, Halifax's close friend Geoffrey Dawson, said: 'I distrust the sponsors of the plan.' Waterhouse believed the change 'moves from the War Cabinet the last link with really honest sanity'. He did not think that Halifax could be spared, whereas Eden could.

One of the arguments Lady Halifax put to Churchill against the proposal was that 'although W.C. was at the height of his popularity, P.M.s sometimes get unpopular and he might want Edward's support and help'. According to Halifax, this 'impressed' Churchill, who nevertheless stuck to the plan. Waterhouse heard a half-true rumour that 'Halifax was ordered out without an option'. Once he was gone, 'the field is nicely cleared here. Some of us are wondering just where all this is going to land us.' As one of the three people whom Churchill consulted about the appointment was Kingsley Wood, that ex-Chamberlainite may thus have been instrumental in 'dishing' both his former leaders. Indeed, Churchill may only have asked him because, as Colville noted in late August, he had 'proved himself the perfect yes-man'.[145]

Meanwhile, the 1922 Committee had come to the conclusion that its Chairman, William Spens, was 'too amiable a man to lead the fight for influence and position which clearly lay before it'.[146] He was persuaded to resign, as he put it, 'to preserve party unity', and the younger and more ambitious Tory MP for Edinburgh, Alexander Erskine-Hill, took over. No sooner was he in the chair than he heard from Margesson that the Prime Minister was contemplating, in the interests of coalition unity, 'asking Cabinet ministers not to address Party committees such as the 1922'. This direct affront to Tory backbenchers was precisely the sort of move they had been predicting and, at the 1922 Executive, 'strong opposition was expressed by all members present'.[147]

By 22 January 1941 Erskine-Hill had seen off the threat, although to save the Government embarrassment it was agreed that 'an "all Party" meeting should be held occasionally'. The new Chairman had won his spurs. On the same day 120 Tory backbenchers crammed into a committee room to hear Beaverbrook address them. In the opinion of the historian of 'The '22', the tussle 'reveals the awareness of the Committee's elected leaders that they had the power to contest Prime Ministerial decisions provided there was the will'.[148]

After Halifax left the Foreign Office on 23 December, David Margesson took Eden's place at the War Office. He had been 'badly wounded' politically since the 1922 Committee had expressed 'no confidence' in him in mid-October. 'These last few months have been very trying and painful,' he wrote to his old boss Stanley Baldwin some time later, 'but then political upheavals are always like that.' The Labour MP for Southwark, John Martin, believed that Margesson had been sent to the War Office '(a) because Winston rather likes his martial temper and (b) to placate the Chamberlainites and to prevent them feeling that they are to be gradually excluded from the Government'.[149]

Martin was making an error common to those outside the Tories' innermost councils; by December 1940 Margesson was no longer considered a card-carrying Chamberlainite. Churchill, who owed him a debt dating from the previous May, had found the ex-Chief Whip a senior ministry in the teeth of criticism mounted by Chamberlainites from whom Margesson had distanced himself ever since he decided that Churchill represented the future. He had appreciated that it was the duty of a Chief Whip to serve the Prime Minister of the day, not his predecessor. Nevertheless, he only took on the War Office reluctantly, telling Baldwin:

> I was *so* happy in the Whips room, I hated to leave. It had become a second home to me. No one was more surprised than I was when Winston asked me to come here. I advanced every reason good and bad why he should not

make the appointment ... but in the end he came back to his old vomit and naturally I could hold out no longer. In wartime one has to do what one is told.[150]

That letter to Baldwin, of late March 1941, also contains possibly the only written account of the May crisis by Margesson. By then his view was that 'the country took the view (rightly I think) that you can't fight a war on a division of political opinion ... so no matter how big a majority we had in the fateful division, or if the House had not divided at all, the result would have been the same, the Government was doomed'. This was certainly not the view of true-believers such as Waterhouse, who would have pointed out (correctly) that 'the country' had not been involved in the purely Parliamentary coup of the previous May. After Margesson left the Whips' Office, nearly three weeks elapsed before a replacement was found, during which time the relative merits of his deputy, the Scottish aristocrat James Stuart, and the Yorkshire landowner, Tommy Dugdale, were considered, whilst their respective supporters canvassed for them.

According to Stuart's memoirs, his eventual appointment represented a defeat for Churchill, showing that the Party could still impose its wishes on the Prime Minister even in early 1941. One of Churchill's worries was that the new Chief Whip might attempt to block Beaverbrook's appointment to new posts or in other ways try to dilute the Prime Ministerial influence. Churchill had actually sent for Dugdale from Palestine before he was finally persuaded to accept Stuart. Yet even Dugdale, as his wife's letters imply, was a severe Churchill-sceptic.

One of Dugdale's supporters, John Crowder, thought that 'James Stuart's appointment is only temporary for a few months', but in fact he held the post for the rest of the war. Crowder believed it was 'very popular. It is thought that he will stand up for Conservative principles and if necessary take a strong line with the P.M. ... Anyhow he will see that the views of the backbenchers are considered.'[151] There had been no question of a Churchillian rather than a neo-Chamberlainite taking the post. Jim Thomas wrote to the diplomat, Rex Leeper, that there was 'no chance of his being made Chief Whip [as] the Munich influence was still too strong'.[152] Waterhouse believed that had Thomas got the job, it 'would I imagine have finally disrupted the Party'.

Meeting the 1922 Committee on 29 January 1941, the new Chief Whip said that he 'wished to co-operate in every way with the Committee'. He soon found that it 'was useful to him ... it provided him with a buttress when his duties put him at variance with the Prime Minister or the Cabinet, making his difficult personal position less exposed'.[153] In his autobiography, which was published after Churchill's death, Stuart wrote:

> I will not pretend that when I was appointed my first six months were either agreeable or smooth. The simple, basic reason was that my P.M. did not like me and had not wanted me as successor to David Margesson.... I had had in the Chamberlain days a head-on clash, with strong words on both sides, and it was not forgotten.

Margesson had told him that in the discussion over the new Chief Whip, 'there had been some quite heated arguments, running on, as was Mr Churchill's habit, into the night-watches'.[154]

When Churchill decided to accept Stuart, he saw him alone in the Cabinet room and told him that, while he appreciated 'that many in the Party, and some members of the Government, were not kindly disposed' to Beaverbrook, he rated his old friend highly and 'wanted him to take on more responsibilities'. The struggle had begun. Stuart's secretary, Charles Harris, told him later that 'he was afraid "they" would "get me down" and break me ... my life as Chief Whip was at first, like Gilbert's policeman, "not a happy one" '. His autobiography discreetly mentioned that 'by no means all of' the Tory backbenchers were happy about some of the men at the top, 'usually because they had doubts about their past political histories'.[155]

This was transparent Tory code for Chamberlainite disquiet over Churchillians such as Beaverbrook, Duff Cooper and Bracken. Stuart 'sat through many hours of acrimonious arguments, sometimes alone as the link with the "top" trying to reconcile the two sides: I lost a lot of sleep in those years, but a Whip has to get used to that.' But, if the Chamberlainite backbenchers were bad, 'nothing in those first six months compared with the difficulty of my relationship with my own Leader and Prime Minister.... I sincerely believe that the Prime Minister would not have minded if I had felt myself forced to resign or if he had felt himself able to get rid of me.' The row over Churchill's support in 1938 for the Duchess of Atholl had not been forgotten, and it was not until July 1941 that Stuart felt confident of his boss's backing and esteem − which was, incidentally, the time that Churchill came at last to feel himself completely safe politically. Even then, Stuart believed, his master was 'not an easy man to work for or serve; far from it. He was argumentative, he wanted his own way ... he was a bit of a bully.'[156]

After only a week in Britain in January 1941, Franklin Roosevelt's adviser, Harry Hopkins, wrote back to Washington reporting that

'Churchill is the Government in every sense of the word – Labour trusts him – the army, navy and air force are behind him to a man. The politicians and upper crust pretend to like him.'[57] They did not, however, even have to pretend to like his friends and when, in January 1941, Bob Boothby made his *apologia* for the Czech assets affair in the Commons, 'the House heard him in dead silence'.[58] Headlam recorded the general opinion of the speech as 'far too much a special pleading', as though in the circumstances it could have been anything else. Many Tory backbenchers, unashamedly delighted at the demise of the 'Glamour Boy' who had taunted them for so long, thought 'he ought to make "a gesture" and join up ... it is the obvious thing to do'.

Dining in Waterhouse's flat in Lowndes Square in mid-January 1941 were Rab Butler and Ralph Assheton, the Lancashire landowner and Chamberlainite MP for Rushcliffe. Their conversation turned to the future of the Chamberlain faction, as well as the Party itself. Waterhouse felt

> that some of us must have some idea of what we are going to try and attain when all this is over or we will find ourselves a host without direction, and will then shortly cease to be a host at all. Our Party has too sound a basis to suffer the sort of eclipse of the Liberals in 1918–24 but we might have a serious temporary set-back which would be a major national disaster.

As a foreboding of the 1945 general election defeat and the onset of post-war socialism, this was impressively prophetic.

February 1941 saw yet another spat between the Prime Minister and the Chamberlainites, this time over Churchill's practice of sending potential political opponents abroad. Churchill, who had joked of Horace Wilson that 'if he comes [to No. 10] any more ... I'll make him Governor of Greenland!', had sent Halifax into exile two months earlier.[59]

Churchill wanted, as Baffy Dugdale put it, to have the National Labour MP and Chamberlainite minister, Malcolm MacDonald, 'banished to Canada' as High Commissioner. Beverley Baxter told Hoare in Madrid that he found the appointment 'astonishing ... the general feeling is that now the official Labour Party is supporting Winston, he wants to liquidate the National Labour platoon altogether'. Baxter, acknowledging that 'Churchill and Beaverbrook have no love for the Conservative Party', said that before he died the Colonial Secretary, Lord Lloyd, had feared that Churchill and Beaverbrook might form 'a new central party' with Bevin, and as a result 'he was very anxious about the future of the Conservative Party.'

In order to allow MacDonald to continue as an MP, legislation had
to be introduced which would permit the Executive to issue certificates
which would override the normal rules of disqualification for MPs
accepting 'offices of profit under the Crown'. Chamberlainites both spoke
and voted against the Disqualification (Temporary Provisions) Bill on its
Second Reading. Although the main opponents came from the 'awkward
squad', Kenneth Pickthorn, Lord Winterton and Austin Hopkinson, it
was the Independent Labour Party MP, John McGovern, who put the
case most bluntly, warning that the measure would help Churchill 'create
around himself a servile force, making Parliament a paid institution to
keep the Government and Prime Minister in office'. Many Chamberlainites agreed that this process would only be aggravated by a Bill which
allowed MacDonald to be, in Waterhouse's characteristically direct
phrase, 'kicked out'. During the debate on 27 February, Churchill's
speech was interrupted. According to Headlam, 'Winston is apparently
very angry with some of us for venturing to criticise his measure which
is being introduced in order to enable Winston to get rid of young
MacDonald (or anyone else) . . .'

By declaring that he regarded the vote on the measure as one of
confidence in his ministry, Churchill displayed, in Headlam's opinion, 'a
very childish exhibition of temper'. MacDonald, the son of the former
Prime Minister, was deluged with letters from friends disapproving the
move, all more or less along the lines of one which read: 'this Government
can ill afford to lose you, one of the few people [we] genuinely trust. It
looks as if none but "yes" men are wanted!'[160] From Washington Lord
Halifax noted 'the feeling' among political *cognoscenti* 'about Winston
sending Malcolm to Ottawa. I deprecated it when Winston first mentioned
the idea. He doesn't think much of him – He's wrong; but he's not at
all Winston's type! (Any more than I am!)'[161] Over both the cession of
the Irish Treaty ports in 1938 and the Palestine White Paper in 1939
Churchill had vigorously opposed policies MacDonald had championed.

A Select Committee was appointed under Sir Dennis Herbert, the
Conservative Deputy Speaker and Chairman of the Ways and Means
Committee, to examine the whole question of disqualification. His report
turned out to be so complex that the Government was able to ignore its
recommendations.[162] With Hoare in Madrid, Halifax in Washington and
MacDonald in Ottawa the scene was set for a number of other such
banishments. Chamberlain's former Agriculture Minister, Sir Reginald
Dorman-Smith, was sent out to govern Burma as soon as the legislation
was passed; later in the war Churchill sent Lord Swinton off to be

Minister Resident in West Africa and, much against his will, Colonel John Colville to be Governor of Bombay.

Churchill's attempt to exile his noisiest and most persistent critic in the Party, the Tory MP for Horsham, Lord Winterton, failed, however. The holder of an Irish peerage, Winterton was not debarred from sitting in the House of Commons. He refused the Governor-Generalship of South Africa in February 1941, despite Churchill telling him, 'It is a wonderful climate, you can sleep outside under a wagon any time.'[163] Instead, in Headlam's words, the rebel 'plugs away at the idea of forming an alternative national Government'.

Parliament was in any case becoming less powerful a forum as the war progressed. Some 200 MPs were in government service in some form or other by February 1941 and another 116 were serving in the armed forces. They alone constituted a majority of the 615 members of the Commons. Parliament had fewer sittings during shorter sessions and was soon on a three-day week. The usual number of 180 Bills per session dropped to less than one-third of that total, and the dominance of the Executive was further emphasized by the gradual winding up of many Standing Committees.[164] Many MPs left London altogether during the Blitz, and the House rarely saw full attendance levels.

The behaviour of one Chamberlainite MP, William Crawford Greene, has been recorded by his nephew Nigel Logan in a poem entitled 'His War'.

> My uncle had his part to play
> When at our house he came to stay.
> When bombing raids on London started,
> From Eaton Place he soon departed.
> He came along with retinue,
> For MPs have a lot to do.
> He sat for Worcester, so he said,
> But actually he lay in bed.
> Perhaps he kindly thought it best
> To let his chauffeur have a rest.
> The Rolls waited outside all day,
> But never took him on his way.
> In sleep till five, he passed his days,
> His nights in alcoholic haze,
> And in this war, when young men died,
> He lay in bed and never tried
> The cause of England to advance
> When all seemed lost, along with France.
> And once he even did confide,

'We should have backed the other side.'
What adjectives would rightly fit
Such conduct? – Château-bottled shit.

Political insiders may have spotted what was happening in the Party
by looking at the choices constituencies were making in seats such as
Dorset South, which was left vacant by Lord Cranborne's elevation to
the Lords. The popular historian and journalist, Sir Charles Petrie, had
got on to the short-list. He had been a propagandist of appeasement
and biographer of the Chamberlain family, and would under normal
circumstances have cruised into the safe Tory seat. In February 1941,
however, the local Party instead chose the maverick Lord Hinchingbrooke – who held a courtesy title, was a serving officer and a great
admirer of Churchill.

The Prime Minister was still acutely conscious of the need to keep
'balance' in his coalition. He told Waterhouse, when offering him the
Parliamentary Secretaryship at the Board of Trade on 6 February 1941,
that, 'We have been having a good time, we shall take Benghazi in a
day or two but during the next six months we shall suffer great dangers
and great trials. We must be united.' Waterhouse recalled how when 'a
proposed appointment might upset the balance' of his ministry, Churchill
said, 'I well appreciate the necessity of preserving the piebald complexion
of my pony.' When 'an extreme socialist' called Wilfred Paling took the
recently demised Lord Tryon's place as Parliamentary Secretary at the
Ministry of Pensions, in order 'to maintain the equipoise of the national
effort' Churchill appointed the Duke of Norfolk to the junior Agriculture
position vacated by Lord Moyne (who moved to the Colonial Office,
which had been left empty by the death of Lord Lloyd).

As Churchill had predicted, the Eighth Army captured Benghazi on
6 February. British troops invaded Abyssinia early in March. Despite all
this Hore-Belisha told Morris-Jones that he 'does not consider we are
winning the war and is anti-Churchill'. Channon still privately called
his house, where Rab Butler was lodging, 'the Belgravian Citadel of
Chamberlain Conservatism'. In late March the journalist, W.P. Crozier,
described Churchill's 'great domination.... He's quite indispensable and
everyone knows it.' That was not to say, however, that people were not
privately thinking 'that it is a pity there is not some person (or persons)
in the Cabinet who could go and take him firmly by the arm and say,
"Look here, you simply must look into this!"'

As Churchill had also predicted, Britain entered 'great dangers and
great trials' in April 1941. The decision to send 60,000 troops to Greece

had the Chamberlainite MP, Jay Llewellin, telling Beaverbrook, as he was going off to attend a War Cabinet: 'Remember three words: Gallipoli – Narvik – Dunkirk.'[165] Sure enough, when the army had to be evacuated soon after it had landed, Churchill's critics quickly re-emerged. Wavell evacuated Benghazi on the 7th, Coventry was blitzed the next day later and on the 20th Rommel attacked Tobruk. It was a black period, but rather than displaying self-discipline and at last giving Churchill the national unity he needed – and after eleven months of leadership surely had a right to expect – Chamberlainites and others instead heaped criticism on him and his Government.

Beamish attended an informal meeting of senior Chamberlainite backbenchers on 23 April (St George's Day), after the evacuation of Greece had been ordered. Among others there were present Colonel Edward Wickham (Margesson's PPS), Malcolm McCorquodale, Sir Douglas Thomson (PPS to Ronald Cross), Sir George Davies, Sir Percy Hurd and Sir Malcolm Robertson, all but the last of whom had voted for Chamberlain at the Norway debate. They expressed 'the same anxiety' over 'the bad patch'. They spoke of 'if we pull through' and 'if we win'.[166] Channon recorded how 'The House of Commons is restive and the Government's popularity is declining, but the Prime Minister's position seems secure.' Hore-Belisha leapt at the opportunity to bring up the old canard of the Prime Minister's drinking, telling Morris-Jones that he 'regards the P.M. as a danger. He says he has no judgment and predicts when some calamity will arise as a result of his change of strategy. He lunched with the P.M. today; plum pudding mixed with wine and later brandy. P.M. took him to his deep dug-out which was full of whisky bottles, etc!'

A motion of 'no confidence' in Churchill's Government was called for 7 May 1941, where there were, in Beamish's phrase, 'the usual speeches by ex-Ministers who had been tried and found wanting and a few wanting to be tried, some who are very trying and still others who might almost be described as wanting'. Lloyd George and Hore-Belisha led the attack, which only served to solidify Tory support for Churchill. Beamish's dislike of Hore-Belisha ('a potent and pungent Jew') seems to have been primarily on racial grounds. He also described the Government's Labour critic, Emanuel Shinwell, as 'a clever poisonous Socialist Polish Jew ... very far from an honest man and an Englishman.'[167]

During the debate Channon thought that 'Winston looked uncomfortable.' Harold Nicolson was happier: 'Members are a bit defeatist. But Winston cheers them up. Yesterday it was rather like a hen-coop of wet

hens: today they all strutted like bantams.'[168] Beaverbrook believed that
whilst there were 'no politics at home, it is true that there are still
politicians with their ambitions and rivalries'. Clearly no national danger
was too great for these to be indulged to the full. Although hardly any
MPs actually voted for the motion, Waterhouse thought

> the House in a very fractious mood. Ready to find fault at every turn. Hore-
> Belisha, Shinwell, Winterton, each with small groups about them, Herbert
> Williams, Archie Southby and others of our friends are restive. Erskine-Hill
> and what he calls 'the boys', by which he means his 1922 Committee
> Executive, are extremely active.

The difference between the rock-solid allegiance of the nation and the
intrigues, cabalism and disloyalty of the politicians could not have been
more marked.

What Colville called Churchill's 'My patience fails, go out and govern
New South Wales' attitude towards foreign postings returned in May
when the Shipping Minister and former senior Chamberlainite Whip,
Ronald Cross, was dispatched to Australia as High Commissioner.
Channon joked that on present showing Rab 'would soon be sent to the
Falkland Islands'. This proved too close to the bone for Butler to be
much amused. In fact, within ten weeks he was prised out of the Foreign
Office and moved to the wartime political equivalent of Port Stanley,
the Board of Education.

The criticism that Churchill was surrounded by 'yes-men', an accusation which Lloyd George forcibly made in the 'no confidence' motion
on 7 May, was reiterated by the Australian Prime Minister, Sir Robert
Menzies, who confirmed to Halifax what Lady Alexandra Metcalfe had
been telling him about 'the complete yes-man attitude of the Cabinet'.
Lord Hankey was also telling Samuel Hoare, in a letter marked 'VERY
SECRET', how

> the P.M. still appears to keep his hold on Parliament and public. He has a
> wonderful genius for inducing the public to accept bad news. But the position
> is not what it was. Ll[oyd] G[eorge]'s warning about the P.M., for all his
> genius, having made the mistake of surrounding himself with 'yes-men' has
> set people talking, and Winston's speech, which was tantamount to admitting
> that they are 'yes-men' and that this was necessary to get things done, did
> not lessen the talk. There is a good deal of murmuring and one hears repeated
> a saying attributed to A.J.B[alfour] that [Churchill] is a 'genius without
> judgment'. Although the façade is almost as strong as ever I fear that the
> structure behind is not quite as sound as it was.[169]

When Rudolf Hess landed in Scotland on 10 May 1941, there were 'orders from Churchill to play down' the news and, despite the obvious propaganda advantages that could have been scored, 'Britain did nothing.'[170] The Prime Minister was probably more concerned at the possible re-emergence of a pro-peace lobby than in scoring a few easy propaganda points. Complaints continued throughout May 1941. Headlam deprecated the acceptance of Labour's amendments to the Trades Disputes Act, which had been pressed on the Government by the TUC, as 'sheer blackmail, which I have no doubt Winston and Beaverbrook would pay quite willingly'.

It was in May, too, that Lady Astor revealed to her friend Pauline Spender-Clay that she had 'begged the PM to strengthen the Government on the Home Front. They have let twelve cities be bombed and burnt before they brought in State Fire Service. It seems to me monstrous.' The news that Haile Selassie had been reinstated in Abyssinia that month provoked another Tory MP to comment that it was 'rather laughable that after nearly two years of War all we can show for it in the way of successful accomplishment is the restoration of a black potentate with a somewhat murky past!'[171] Meanwhile, the National Liberal, Hore-Belisha, was still 'vitriolic about the Government. The country would soon wake up and realise that speeches were not victories ... and that we were drugged with Winston's oratory.'

The German invasion of Crete on 20 May 1941, followed by the British evacuation within eleven days, led the diplomat, Oliver Harvey, to write to the anti-appeasement Tory MP, Paul Emrys-Evans, that Churchill must take the blame, and if he fell there were only Lloyd George and Beaverbrook to take his place. This left him 'worried' and 'disquietened'. Emrys-Evans meanwhile wished to shift the blame on to Margesson at the War Office, telling Cranborne: 'He is essentially a yes-man – dangerous in peace and war.' Over a bottle of 1870 Château Margaux, the diplomat, Roger Makins, told his Chamberlainite MP father, Sir Ernest, that 'we made a botch of the defence of Crete and were not properly prepared though we knew it was coming and might have given the Huns a real knock'.[172] Channon recorded how 'on all sides one hears increasing criticism of Churchill. He is undergoing a noticeable slump in popularity and many of his enemies, long silenced by his personal popularity, are once more vocal. Crete has been a great blow to him.'

According to Waterhouse, the latest joke in the House of Commons was that the initials BEF stood for Back Every Fortnight. He could not help reflecting that 'Neville Chamberlain was hounded out because we were beaten in Norway. Since then France, Libya, Greece and Crete have to be added to the fearful list and none of the last three have the excuses of the first two.' Having already noted that 'his position is no longer a quite such unassailable pinnacle as a few months ago', Waterhouse allowed himself to speculate on Churchill's future: 'It will be interesting to see how Winston's prestige weathers the storm and who if anyone will be thrown to the wolves ... someone must have made a fearful hash, unless we are prepared to admit the inadmissible – that we cannot fight Huns.'[173] By mid-June Salisbury's Watching Committee 'were agreed in deploring Winston's relations with the Chiefs of Staff. With all his brilliance and services [the Chiefs] evidently considered that this is a most formidable blemish.'[174]

Later in June, Bracken paid off an old score by engineering the dismissal of the Conservative Party Vice-Chairman in charge of candidates, Lord Windlesham, the person who had the previous October told Oliver Lyttelton that it was 'unfortunate' that Churchill was backing him for the Wrekin seat. Windlesham vetted prospective Parliamentary candidates and was thus in a crucial position to influence the political orientation of the Party. He made it clear that he did not want to leave, but eventually reluctantly had to agree, telling the Prime Minister: 'I have, of course, no alternative but to comply with your request.' He asked for a few minutes' interview with Churchill to be told how he had failed, but was merely informed that the Party would be 'reverting to the practice' of having a Whip as Vice-Chairman.[175] The job went to Tommy Dugdale, who had been languishing in the Whips' Office since being brought back from Palestine in vain. When Jim Thomas was asked to the farewell luncheon for his old antagonist, the pro-appeasement Windlesham, 'a remnant of decency made me say no'.

Windlesham's sacking was the precursor to a Churchillian Night of the Long Knives, which took place on 20 July 1941. This showed that, for the first time since becoming Prime Minister a full fourteen months before, Churchill at last felt himself politically safe. The large-scale promotion of his friends and supporters over Chamberlainites occasioned plenty of complaints and resentment in the Party, but no outright rebellion. Besides 'those snarling and contemptible Conservatives', whom Robert Bruce Lockhart described even a year later as being 'out to down Winston', there was no seriously dangerous resistance to the Prime Minister for the rest of the war. The 20th of July reconstruction – which took place almost entirely within Tory ranks – therefore represents the final victory in a long *sotto voce* war of attrition fought between Churchill and the Chamberlainite Tory Establishment, and proves that the Prime Minister at last felt secure enough to model his coalition according to his own tastes.

Bracken became Minister of Information, replacing Duff Cooper, who had widely been considered a failure. Bracken's first action there was to sack the Chamberlainite Lord Davidson as Controller of Production. He did this at a press conference without first informing his victim. Lady Davidson, the Tory MP for Hemel Hempstead, remarked that 'nobody would have expected that mountebank Brendan Bracken not to take the opportunity of getting rid of John for political reasons'. Dugdale told her, however, that 'it would have been foolish at this stage to make a fuss about it'.[176] Instead of being dropped altogether, Duff Cooper was given Maurice Hankey's post as Chancellor of the Duchy of Lancaster, and sent to co-ordinate the defence of Singapore, where he had no more luck than he had had at Information. The Chamberlainite stalwart Hankey was demoted to the Paymaster-Generalship, which had been left vacant since Cranborne had moved to the Dominions Office the previous October.

With Butler sent off to the Board of Education, a post released by awarding a peerage to the Chamberlainite Herwald Ramsbotham, who as Lord Soulbury spent the rest of the war as Chairman of the Assistance Board, Butler's key position at the Foreign Office was taken by Richard Law, whose Norway rebellion had enraged many Chamberlainites. Churchill's old friend Hugh Seely – a member of the Other Club – was appointed Parliamentary Secretary to the Air Ministry and awarded a peerage.

The Labour MP, Ernest Thurtle – who had been described as a 'pimp' by Aneurin Bevan for defending Churchill – became junior Information Minister, replacing the National Labour MP, Harold Nicolson, who left government never to return. The team at Information was considered to have failed, and Labour were demanding a greater number of ministerial posts than they had been able to secure in May. As a consolation prize, Nicolson became a Governor of the BBC under the terms of Churchill's House of Commons Disqualification (Temporary Provisions) Act of the previous February. He was not consoled.

By far the most criticized promotion was that of Churchill's son-in-law, Duncan Sandys, who took Law's place as Financial Secretary to the War Office. 'I imagine the inner circle of the Conservative Party will have words to say to the P.M. on this matter,' thought Woolton. Sure enough, three days later the Chamberlainite Ian Orr-Ewing brought up

the whole matter at the 1922 Committee. He 'viewed [Sandys's] appointment with some dissatisfaction', and the mood of the meeting also went
against Cooper, who was described as 'dangerous'. When Sandys next
entered the Commons Chamber, he 'was received in ominous silence'.
The joke went around that it was hard on Churchill's other son-in-law,
the stand-up comedian, Vic Oliver, that *he* had not got anything in the
reshuffle.

The reconstruction was not a total Churchillian whitewash. Jim
Thomas's attempt to have Emrys-Evans moved into the Whips' Office
did not 'manage to get very far'. As he told Cranborne, 'I am one against
eight.' The appointment of the Chamberlainite George Harvie-Watt to
Bracken's post as the Prime Minister's PPS also met with some approval.
Harvie-Watt was proposed because he 'was friendly with all the Chamber-
lain followers, which was important'.[77] This, even eight months after
Chamberlain had died.

On becoming his PPS, Harvie-Watt was told by Churchill: 'What I
want is for you to keep the flies off the meat. It becomes bad if they are
allowed to settle even for a moment. I am the meat and you must show
me the warning light when troubles arise in the Parliamentary and
political scene.' Bracken had been a vital aid during the May 1940 crisis,
but the political scene had altered significantly by the summer of 1941
and Churchill showed great percipience in appointing a Chamberlainite
to such a sensitive post.

Headlam was predictably cynical about the reshuffle. The news that
Cooper was going out to co-ordinate operations in the Far East meant

> no doubt he will be heavily paid and be allowed to take [Lady] Diana with
> him to cast a glow East of Suez. He has failed in every job he has been given,
> is clearly incompetent as an administrator, but belongs to the Winston Clique.
> B. Bracken succeeds him.... Young Law succeeds Rab and Duncan Sandys
> goes to the W.O. So the family and friends are well looked after by Winston
> in the old, unabashed, Whig manner of the 18th century – and we are all
> supposed to say 'how right and proper'![178]

The long guerrilla warfare between Churchillians and Chamberlainites
had ended in victory for the former. No national crisis had proved so
perilous as to silence the mutterings and moans of the dispossessed group.
When the nation outside Parliament unified to meet the Nazi threat,
imposing upon itself an extraordinary self-discipline, their elected representatives schemed, criticized and joined cabals to withhold full-hearted
support from the coalition. This phenomenon was perfectly summed up
by Channon, who, after the 'no confidence' motion of 6 May 1941,

'despaired of England and of democracy all day, and yet I seldom enjoyed a day more, thanks to the intrigues'.

Apart from those few months in the summer of 1940 when the British people expected invasion daily, Parliamentary cabals became more outspoken as the military situation became more desperate. Some may consider these mutterings – which were rarely heard far beyond the Palace of Westminster – as an encouraging sign that Britain remained a functioning pluralist democracy even in her darkest hour. But, despite Colville's assertion that after fourteen days of Churchill's leadership the Establishment had coalesced behind Churchill, it is clear that the Respectable Tendency actually spent fourteen months putting Party before country, and love of intrigue before both.

4

Churchill, Race and the 'Magpie Society'

It was during the Premiership of Winston Churchill forty years ago that Britain took her first steps towards becoming a multi-racial society. This is not without a certain irony, as although racist views were almost universally held until around the end of the 1950s, Churchill was more profoundly racist than most.

In quite such a zealous child of the Empire – he was a true believer for longer than almost all his contemporaries – anything else would have been astonishing. Churchill's racial assumptions occupied a prime place both in his political philosophy and in his views on international relations. He was a convinced white – not to say Anglo-Saxon – supremacist and thought in terms of race to a degree that was remarkable even by the standards of his own time. He spoke of certain races with a virulent Anglo-Saxon triumphalism which was wholly lacking in other twentieth-century Prime Ministers, and in a way which even as early as the 1920s shocked some Cabinet colleagues.

The purpose of this chapter is not to make spurious and anachronistic value judgments about Churchill's lack of political correctness, still less to criticize him for assumptions which were overall to work more for Britain's benefit – especially in 1940 – than to her detriment, but to ask objectively how and why he of all Prime Ministers allowed Britain to start to become a multi-racial society.

Churchill's views about human superiority and inferiority were not confined to ethnicity. In the early part of the century he dabbled in eugenics and in 1906, warned:

The unnatural and increasingly rapid growth of the feeble-minded and insane

211

classes, coupled as it is with steady restriction among all the thrifty, energetic and superior stocks, constitutes a national and race danger which it is impossible to exaggerate. I feel that the source from which the stream of madness is fed should be cut off and sealed before another year has passed.[1]

He instructed his officials to look into the possibility of enforced sterilization, promising that after 'a simple surgical operation, they could be permitted to live freely in the world without causing much inconvenience to others'.

Churchill expanded on this proposal when staying with the writer Wilfrid Scawen Blunt in 1912, prompting the following diary entry:

> Winston is also a strong eugenicist. He told us he had himself drafted the Bill which is to give power to shutting up people of weak intellects and so prevent their breeding ... many would ask to be sterilised as a condition of having their liberty restored ... without something of the sort the race must decay. It is decaying rapidly, but would be stopped by some such means.[2]

Much of the eugenics canon was taken for granted by Churchill's contemporaries across the political spectrum, and it was for him not too large a step from assuming a hierarchy in human worth to a belief in the superiority of certain racial groupings over others.

'I have a keen aboriginal desire to kill several of these odious dervishes,' Churchill wrote to his mother during the 1898 Sudan campaign. 'I anticipate enjoying the exercise very much.'[3] Such views may have been typical of his time, but what is remarkable is for how long he stuck to them and how little they altered throughout his long political career. In *My African Journey*, the account of his 1907 visit to East Africa whilst Under-Secretary at the Colonial Office, Churchill believed that the British officer class was, 'in all that constitutes fitness to direct, as superior to the Buganda as Mr Wells' Martians would have been to us'. The Buganda tribe were themselves, according to Churchill, the primary one of the region. They benefited from his general policy to 'encourage, as far as may be in our power, a careful patient discrimination between different classes of coloured men'.[4] On that trip Churchill thought the Kenyan Kikuyu 'light-hearted, tractable if brutish children ... capable of being instructed'. Africans in general were 'less crudely animals' when they wore clothes. After declaring, 'No man has a right to be idle', he charitably added, 'and I do not exempt the African.'

As Colonial Secretary fourteen years later, Churchill averred that 'the Indians of East Africa are mainly of a very low class of coolies, and the idea that they should be put on equality with the Europeans is revolting to every white man throughout British East Africa'. His Cabinet colleague, Edwin Montagu, said that he expected to hear such a view from a 'fanatical' white settler, but not from a minister of the Crown.[5] Churchill's adviser on intelligence matters, Major Desmond Morton, wrote that to Churchill 'all Germans were Nazees, all Italians organ-grinders ... *en masse* the Bedu is a dirty, cowardly cut-throat, with very primitive passions indeed and about as trustworthy as a King Cobra'.[6] Furthermore, Negroes were 'niggers' or 'blackamoors', Arabs were 'worthless', Chinese were 'chinks' or 'pigtails', Indians were 'babus' (a contemptuous term for clerks), and South African black tribes were 'Hottentots'.[7] Not all Churchill's racial characterizations were negative, however. He believed the Jews to be 'the most formidable and the most remarkable race which has ever appeared in the world'. He felt an instinctive affinity for their genius as well as a historian's respect for their trials, and he supported Jewish aspirations whenever they did not clash with those of the Empire. He may have inherited his philo-Semitism from his father, but he certainly gave it new lustre in his own life. One commentator has recently maintained that his lack of anti-Semitism meant that Churchill was not racist, but another has pointed out that his 'particular veneration of Jewish people was simply another facet of his racism'.[8]

In general Churchill found Indians 'the beastliest people in the world, next to the Germans'.[9] During the 1943 Bengal famine, in which over a million Indians died, he reassured his Secretary of State for India, Leo Amery, that they would nevertheless continue to breed 'like rabbits'. After such an outburst in August 1944 Amery was prompted to tell the Prime Minister that he 'didn't see much difference between his outlook and Hitler's.[10] When in June 1944 the Cabinet considered constitutional reform in Ceylon, Amery recorded that 'Winston muttered and growled and mumbled for a quarter of an hour or more in order to ventilate his emotions of disgust at anything that could extend self-government to brown people'.[11]

Churchill's doctor, Lord Moran, believed his master 'thinks only of the colour of their skins: it is when he talks of India or China that you remember that he is a Victorian'. In his conversations with Blunt it was clear that it was 'the civilising mission of the British race' that drove his imperialism rather than any economic benefits which the Empire might bring. 'If the British people will have a great Empire, if any ray of true glory is to fall upon it,' he had told the National Liberal Club in January 1908, 'they will need an imperial race to support the burden.' In a speech he delivered at the Royal Albert Hall in March 1931, Churchill argued that Britain had brought to India a civilization 'far above anything they could possibly have achieved themselves or could maintain'.

As the great tribal leader of 1940, his glorious speeches were peppered with references to the British race. During the Second World War he unerringly put the interests of the white man over those of the black. In 1942 the Labour MP, Tom Driberg, questioned the Prime Minister in the House of Commons about the 'introduction in some parts of Britain of discrimination against negro troops'. Churchill did nothing to discourage racial segregation, which was both widespread and officially recognized in the American armed forces based in the United Kingdom. When he was told that a black official at the Colonial Office had always lunched at a certain restaurant from which now, because it was being patronized by white American officers, he had been barred, the Prime Minister replied: 'That's alright: if he takes a banjo with him they'll think he's one of the band'.[12] During one wartime discussion over India, Rab Butler recorded how Churchill 'launched into a most horrible attack on the baboos, saying that they were gross, dirty and corrupt'.[13] In support of the Anglo-American Alliance, the Prime Minister continually stressed the racial superiority of the English-speaking peoples. At a lunch in the White House in September 1943, for example, he 'said why be apologetic about Anglo-Saxon superiority; that they were superior'.[14]

Neither did this attitude abate with time. Sir David Hunt, his Private Secretary during the early period of his 'Indian Summer' Premiership, recalls how 'Churchill was on the whole rather anti-black. I remember him sending a telegram to [South African Prime Minister] Dr Malan and asking me whether he should say sardonically, "My dear Mr President, *Alles sal reg kom* (Everything will be all right). Keep on skelping the kaffirs!" he'd joke'.[15] In January 1952, after an Egyptian crowd attacked the BOAC offices in Cairo, he described them to Eden as 'lower than the most degraded savages now known'.[16] During the build-up to the Korean War, he told a friend dismissively when informed of the vast size of the Chinese Red Army: 'Four million pigtails don't make an army.' The very week he left office in April 1955 he was asked whether he had seen the film *Carmen Jones*. According to Lord Moran's diaries.

Winston replied that he didn't like 'blackamoors' and had walked out early in the proceedings. He asked, a little irrelevantly, what happened when blacks got measles. Could the rash be spotted? When he was told that there was a very high mortality among Negroes from measles he growled, 'Well, there are plenty left, they've a high rate of production'.[17]

Indisputably then, Churchill, along with the vast majority of his contemporaries – including such left-wingers as Hugh Dalton and Sidney and Beatrice Webb – was an unrepentant racist. Whilst his attitudes may have been common until around the 1950s, they were expressed with a virulence which would not have been found in contemporaries such as Baldwin or Chamberlain. His very longevity in government meant that by the end he was getting out of touch. 'When you learn to think of a race as inferior beings,' he told his doctor on a train to New York in January 1952, 'it is difficult to get rid of that way of thinking.'[18] Churchill introduced his Colonial Secretary, Alan Lennox-Boyd, to the Secretary-General of NATO, the Belgian Henri Spaak, with the words: 'Meet the Colonial Secretary; he looks after Southern Rhodesia [he did not] .... In Southern Rhodesia many locals have a vote but no black Rhodesian can drive a train; in your Congo they have no vote but all races can drive trains.' Lennox-Boyd said that Churchill 'left no doubt which destiny he preferred'.[19] He and others in the Cabinet sometimes despaired of the Prime Minister's racial assumptions, coming as they did from a man a quarter of a century older than them. 'Are you aware,' Churchill once rang Lennox-Boyd in the early hours of the morning to enquire, 'that a British sailor was birched by order of a Chink?'

How was it, then, that under Churchill's Premiership Britain began to take in ever-increasing numbers of immigrants from the West Indies, India, Pakistan and Ceylon? It has famously been argued that the Empire was acquired 'in a fit of absence of mind'. Equally, the post-imperial implosion took place without any concerted plan to promote it. Certainly, there was no premeditated political programme, and no one argued that large-scale New Commonwealth immigration should be encouraged in order to make Britain a better place.

Despite the various conspiracy theories from both right and left, no evidence has emerged to suggest that this arose from a deliberate policy designed to flood the labour market. It was not a policy but a complete lack of one which best explains the phenomenon. Neither was the electorate ever consulted over the significant demographic change about to happen. The issue did not begin to appear in electoral manifestos until long afterwards. If anything, the British Isles were considered at the time to be too overcrowded, with one of the globe's highest densities of population.

The Labour Government's British Nationality Act of 1948 – the first attempt to define British citizenship – was drawn up at the height of enthusiasm for the concept of 'Commonwealth'. As India became independent and moved towards becoming a republic, a structure was considered necessary in the period of the heightening Cold War which would both bind the ex-Dominions to Britain for security and trade reasons and act as a fig-leaf to cover the nakedness of her post-imperial weakness. All political parties embraced 'the Commonwealth ideal' with a fervour and naïveté which may seem absurd today. The Act supplanted common allegiance to the Crown – something India abandoned in 1951 – with the amorphous concept of separate citizenships for the Commonwealth states, plus the status of 'Commonwealth citizen' which gave rights equivalent to those of any British subject. This effectively gave over eight hundred million Commonwealth citizens the perfectly legal right to reside in the United Kingdom.

The holes in Labour's cumbersome legislation allowed hundreds of thousands to enter Britain. America, a nation created by immigrants, had no wish to receive more West Indians; this culminated in the restrictive McCarran–Walter Immigration Act of 1952. Stagnation threatened Jamaica and other Caribbean economies, whereas in Britain there was full employment. Cheap travel, by sea and later by air, made access easier. Lastly, Britain's welfare system provided more and better benefits than anything which could be expected elsewhere in the Commonwealth.

The *Empire Windrush*, a former German pleasure steamer, docked at Tilbury in June 1948. The 492 West Indian immigrants it brought marked the beginning of New Commonwealth immigration. There had, of course, been coloured people living in England, notably in London and Liverpool, since the eighteenth century. During June 1919 several people had been killed in a series of vicious race riots in Liverpool, where over seven hundred blacks had to be removed to Bridewell Prison for their own safety. During the war there had also been some ugly brawls in Liverpool dance halls, but overall the story of the black presence in Britain had been harmonious. Although the numbers stepping off the *Empire Windrush*, and ships like her, were not considered significant in the early years, it was the concentration of immigrants in largely working-class inner-city areas such as Brixton, Stepney, Notting Hill Gate and Bethnal Green which was soon to invite official attention.

Cabinet papers show that it was the Labour Government which first considered closing the legislative loophole that gave so many people right of residence in Britain. Two days after the *Empire Windrush* docked, eleven Labour MPs wrote to the Prime Minister, Clement Attlee, protesting that 'an influx of coloured people domiciled here is likely to impair the harmony, strength and cohesion of our public and social life'. When assessing liberal Tory arguments that no action could be taken for fear of Labour opposition, we must remember that the call for restrictions initially came from Labour members themselves. A Cabinet committee under the Labour Home Secretary, James Chuter Ede, was set up in June 1950 to investigate 'ways which might be adopted to check the immigration into this country of coloured people from British colonial territories'.[20] It was only much later that, despite complaints from Labour's natural constituents, trade unionists and inner-city working-class inhabitants, 'at the elite level there was agreement on not limiting such immigration'.[21]

In his report to the Cabinet on 22 February 1951, Ede explained that, whilst no restriction on numbers was necessary for the time being, any substantial inflow 'might produce a situation in the United Kingdom rendering legislation for its control essential'. The Cabinet Committee's secretary, Sir Alan Atkinson, remembers how 'there was a strong disposition among some people to hope that it was an unreal problem and that any problems were temporary ones'. Nevertheless, there were a few doubters, such as Mr J. Keith, the welfare officer at the Colonial Office, who as early as 1952 – before large-scale immigration had begun – was reporting that 'it would be better to stop the influx now to forestall future difficulties'.[22] Such advice was systematically ignored, downgraded or even circumvented by Tory politicians, although it was never contradicted or denied.

Churchill's return to Downing Street in October 1951 coincided with a sea-change in the way racial issues were viewed. Whereas Attlee's Cabinet in 1947 could hear the First Lord of the Admiralty explain how 'British soldiers would not take kindly to service under coloured officers and discipline would be undermined', and Mrs Attlee would complain about coloured people at a party at the Dorchester Hotel, saying, 'I suppose one should enjoy entertaining them but I must say I find it awfully difficult', by the early 1950s the language of race had subtly changed.[23] This was not the result of anything which had taken place in Britain, but because of developments in America and South Africa.

The American and South African experiences – where indigenous blacks were demanding civil rights and the franchise – were radically different from that of Britain, where the debate centred solely on rights of residence. Nevertheless, the phraseology and perceived moral implications of America and South Africa were introduced into the British arena, bringing with them an impassioned rhetoric which quickly replaced rational analysis. No matter how far removed the actual experiences of Alabama or the Transvaal were from those of Liverpool, the language had changed. All too often it moved from the logical to the absurd, as when in a debate in the House of Lords the problems of Notting Hill Gate were equated with those of Little Rock, Arkansas.[24] This was partly the result of America's cultural and political dominance after the Second World War, but also because, as consciousness about racial issues increased, the starker images of the civil rights struggle in America and South Africa tended to eclipse the more mundane British experience.

Statistics for the early period are unreliable as the Home Office did not initially keep figures, but most studies agree that during Churchill's Premiership, immigration from the New Commonwealth climbed from roughly 3,000 in 1953 to 11,000 in 1954 and 42,650 in 1955. After he left office, it rose to 46,800 in 1956, dropped to 42,400 in 1957, and did not reach that level again until 1960 when 57,700 entered the United Kingdom. In 1961, 136,400 arrived and in the first six months of 1962, before restrictions were imposed, an additional 95,000.[25] It was, therefore, during Churchill's time in office that the line on the graph achieved its 'take-off' point.

There had, of course, been relatively large-scale immigration into Britain often before. Huguenots in the seventeenth century, then Poles, Italians, Irish and Jews in the nineteenth had all arrived in significant numbers relative to the indigenous population. In 1900 there were 54,310 'aliens' living in the borough of Stepney alone. They also tended to congregate together in inner-city areas. However, these earlier immigrant waves were different from those of the mid-twentieth century. This is not because of the crude reason of skin pigmentation, but because earlier immigrants often came as a result of political or religious persecution and were usually from highly skilled groups who brought special expertise needed by the British economy.

The New Commonwealth immigrants, on the other hand, arrived at a period of full employment and took largely blue-collar jobs which would either have been done by the indigenous population or phased out altogether by labour-saving innovations. One of the unquantifiable by-products of immigration is the extent to which cheap labour slowed up the drive for greater productivity in British industry, to the long-term detriment of the entire economy. At a time when Britain desperately needed to move from labour- to capital-intensive structures, immigration held her back.

None of Churchill's former ministers interviewed for this book failed to express regret that the loophole in the 1948 Act had not been closed earlier. The Cabinet and Cabinet Committee papers on the subject which are now available in the Public Records Office show how short-term political expediency guided the various Conservative Governments' attitude towards the issue throughout the 1950s. These papers point to irresolution and wishful thinking as the principal characteristics of the liberal Tory response to an issue which, with a little foresight and resolution, could easily have been nipped in the bud.

The first time it arose in Churchill's Cabinet was on 25 November 1952, as the last item on the agenda – even after the question of compensation for part-time clerks in magistrates' courts. The Prime Minister asked 'whether the Post Office were employing larger numbers of coloured workers. If so, there was some risk that difficult social problems would be created.' The Postmaster-General, Lord De La Warr, looked into the matter and reported that the Post Office trade unions 'raised no objection to the employment of coloured people in basic grades'.[26] But – as was probably intended all along – he also 'raised the whole issue ... of whether coloured subjects of the Commonwealth and Empire should be admitted to the country from now on'.

At this the Home Secretary, David Maxwell Fyfe, said: 'Legislation would be necessary before coloured British subjects could be deprived of their traditional freedom to enter this country.' He added that the Attlee Government had 'recognised some of the risks involved' and had thought there was a case for an enquiry 'to establish the facts of the situation, including any special difficulties to which the presence of substantial numbers of coloured people in particular localities (for example, the East End of London and Liverpool) were giving rise in practice'.[27]

'There is little worse in death or life, than David Patrick Maxwell Fyfe' went a popular ditty on the Northern Circuit. He was a hard-working, ambitious barrister, with 'a considerable intellect, excelling more in its retentive than its creative faculties'.[28] There were times when he could be tough on social issues, such as when he told Bob Boothby, who was lobbying for reform of the homosexuality laws: 'I am not going down in history as the man who made sodomy legal.' His great moment had come when, after the American prosecutor at the Nuremberg Trials had mismanaged the cross-examination of Hermann Goering and allowed the Reichsmarschal to gain the upper hand, Maxwell Fyfe re-established mastery through patient, detailed and incisive questioning, forcing the chief surviving Nazi to condemn himself.

He had accepted the post of Home Secretary from Churchill on the understanding that he would become Lord Chancellor on the retirement of Lord Simonds, so his time at the Home Office was intended to be an uncontroversial interlude. By the time of the Cabinet debate over immigration he was keen to ensure that nothing upset his smooth path to the Woolsack. His vanity even allowed him to think of himself as a possible future Prime Minister – which in a Cabinet that included Eden, Butler and Macmillan was patently absurd. In the event, his hopes for a quiet life at the Home Office were destroyed by the Craig–Bentley case, the ramifications of which endure to this day. The appointment of an inter-departmental committee to investigate the question of coloured immigration was, therefore, probably the best that could be expected from a man who was essentially, in the opinion of the Colonial Secretary, Oliver Lyttelton, 'an unimaginative plodder'.[29]

The appointment of a Civil Service committee is often a Whitehall delaying tactic, and the Home Office's snappily titled 'Working Party on the Social and Economic Problems Arising from the Growing Influx into the United Kingdom of Coloured Workers from other Commonwealth Countries' was no exception. It took no fewer than thirteen months to deliberate. When Maxwell Fyfe circulated its report to Cabinet in January 1954 that 'there is no effective means of stopping this influx without legislation', he was telling them nothing they had not known in 1952. The report of the Working Party, which came out in late December 1953, contradicts the popularly held view that the British Government pursued a deliberate policy of encouraging immigration in order to rectify the labour shortage. It stated that:

> the unskilled workers who form the majority are difficult to place because they are on the whole physically unsuited to heavy manual work, particularly outdoors in winter, or in hot conditions underground, and appear to be generally lacking in stamina. ... They are more volatile in temperament than white workers and more easily provoked to violence. ... Coloured workers are said to be slow mentally, and the speed of work in modern factories is said to be quite beyond their capacity.[30]

Maxwell Fyfe explained to the Cabinet how the various West Indian territories had been 'unwilling to put restrictions on the issue of passports to British subjects who appear to be entitled to them'. In his opinion to alter that was 'not politically practical'. It was hardly surprising that all efforts to persuade the West Indian Governments themselves to retard emigration ran up against the rock of their self-interest; they were effectively exporting unemployment and, when the immigrants sent money back to their families, importing capital.

'We were playing a very delicate game with the Government of Jamaica, being most anxious not to offend them,' says one of Churchill's ministers closely concerned with the issue, 'yet equally wanting to impose some sort of voluntary control over the flow of immigrants. In fact, the Jamaican Government refused to set any sort of informal quota on the number of passports issued to would-be immigrants.'[31] As Churchill's Private Secretary at the time recalls, 'It all depended on travel being very expensive.'[32]

Maxwell Fyfe made it clear that 'there is no power to prevent these people entering, no matter how much the number may increase,' adding that 'there was already evidence of some racial feeling in those districts, for example, in London, Liverpool and Manchester where there were concentrations of coloured people'. Nevertheless, according to him, 'the political and administrative difficulties' which were likely to arise did not justify any action.

When the Cabinet considered his report a few days later, Maxwell Fyfe again argued that with only 40,000 coloured people then resident in Britain, 'he did not believe that the problem had yet assumed sufficient proportions to justify legislation which would involve a reversal of our traditional practice and would antagonise liberal opinion'.[33] Had the Cabinet known that within four decades that number would have increased seventy-five-fold, they would have doubtless been more willing to antagonize liberals. The Commonwealth Relations Secretary, Lord Swinton, pointed out that all other Commonwealth countries had legislative restrictions on the immigration of British subjects. He argued that it was, therefore, unlikely that 'Commonwealth opinion would be disturbed if powers were taken to deport from this country British subjects from overseas'.

So far the debate was conducted entirely in terms of bringing the United Kingdom's immigration and deportation laws into line with the practice of the rest of the Commonwealth and the rest of the world. As one minister pointed out in the general discussion, 'it was no longer incumbent on the UK to follow a policy more liberal than that in force in other Commonwealth countries'. Churchill's own contribution to the discussion was characteristically forthright. 'The rapid improvement in communications,' he warned his colleagues, 'was likely to lead to the continuing increase in the number of coloured people coming to this country, and their presence here would sooner or later come to be resented by large sections of the British people.' But he went on to say that, in his opinion, 'the problem had not yet assumed sufficient proportions to enable the Government to take adequate counter-measures'.

Having assumed the issue shelved, the Government was forced to readdress it in early March 1954 owing to pressure exerted by MPs in response to constituents' concerns. The major problem, reported Maxwell Fyfe, was that 'large numbers of coloured people are living on National Assistance' and that tenancies of old properties were being acquired by coloured people, who, 'by their conduct, made life difficult for white people living in the same building or area ... the result is that the white people leave and the accommodation is then converted to furnished lettings for coloured people, with serious overcrowding and exploitation'.

The Government's immediate worry was a Parliamentary question which had been put down by the Labour MP for Swindon, Thomas Reid, asking 'the Prime Minister if, in view of the ever-increasing immigration of overseas British subjects into Britain regardless of economic and other circumstance he will appoint a committee to report on the matter, which is causing widespread interest'. He believed that 'a large number, if not the majority, of Opposition members shared his point of view'. Even if his optimism were misplaced, it is clear that action by the Churchill ministry over immigration in 1954 or 1955 would have split the Labour Party had it decided to oppose the measures. Churchill, however, merely stalled Reid by saying: 'This matter is engaging continuous thought and study but I am not convinced this subject would serve a useful purpose at the present time.'[34] After his stroke in July 1953, Churchill was a very different beast from the man of 'Action This Day'. The Government then had ten days in which to formulate a response to Reid.

In a Cabinet memorandum of 8 March, Maxwell Fyfe argued that Reid's question could easily be shrugged off, and reiterated the 'serious difficulties involved in contemplating action which would undoubtedly land the Government in some political controversy ... the Government cannot well be expected to take action which would stir up so much trouble'. He admitted that 'there is no indication that this problem will not continue to grow and the longer it is left the more difficult and dangerous it may become'. None the less, he concluded that 'the question is not yet sufficiently acute and we should not, therefore, add to our difficulties'.

This is a prime example of the reactive politics which characterized the liberal Toryism of the 1950s and 1960s. Prescience and pre-emptive action were always at a discount, and all too often sacrificed to short-term expediency and the craving for consensus. As a result of their failure to grasp the political nettle, the Churchill and Eden Governments presided over the start of a significant alteration of the country, a change for which there was neither governmental enthusiasm nor any sign of popular support.

Part of the problem lay in the huge difference between those who were taking – or in this case refusing to take – the decisions over immigration and those upon whom the consequences of those decisions would fall. Of the seven Home Office ministers between October 1951 and January 1957 all were public school products and all but one Oxbridge-educated. A majority sat for rural constituencies and had homes far removed from the areas which were beginning to bear the brunt of immigration. It fell for the most part upon ordinary working people at the bottom of the jobs and housing markets to pay the price for the Commonwealth idealism of their social superiors. The addresses given in *Who's Who* record David Maxwell Fyfe as living in Withyam, Sussex, Gwilym Lloyd George in Baker Street, David Llewellyn in Glamorgan, Sir Hugh Vere Huntly Duff Munro-Lucas-Tooth of Tean-anich in Fordingbridge, Hampshire, Lord Lloyd in Hertfordshire, Lord Mancroft in Montagu Square and William Deedes in Aldington, Kent. No Home Office minister, indeed virtually no Conservative MP, actually himself lived in the environments which were starting to alter drastically as a result of mass immigration.

Some, like David Llewellyn, the Parliamentary Under-Secretary at the Home Office after the 1951 election, were men of impeccably liberal credentials. He was 'essentially an old-fashioned liberal or even radical, who sat uneasily on the Tory benches, though he identified with Macmillan's "Middle Way" brand of corporatist Conservatism'. He was later to publish an admiring biography of Aneurin Bevan and, in a classic example of paternalist Toryism, explained his involvement in politics thus: 'As a member of a coal-owning family, I felt I had a debt towards those to whom I owed ... privilege I had not earned.'[35] It is these worthy sentiments which have throughout history impelled patricians towards politics. The enormous social difference between governors and governed had not been a malign force in the past. As officers in the two wars they had never taken care of themselves before their men, and had indeed managed to establish a genuine sympathy with them. Yet over the question of immigration a profound gap opened up and widened between the opinions of the governors and the governed.

In time their distance, lack of interest and unwillingness to solve it rebounded against the Tory paternalists. In the 1960s their attitude over immigration helped to break the habit of social deference within the Conservative Party and end the long domination of the upper and upper-middle classes. Recognizing that Tory grandees could no longer be relied upon to act in their best interests, ordinary Conservative voters and constituency activists began to turn to people of their own social background. Since 1964 the Conservative leadership has been a lower-middle- to middle-middle-class sinecure, largely because ordinary people felt that their social superiors did not appreciate their point of view over important issues. Such was the price paid by the traditional elite for their Commonwealth enthusiasm and social progressivism. As no less a liberal Tory thinker than Lord Gilmour has commented on the immigration issue, 'the failure of politicians of all parties to respond earlier to the fears and discontent that were being expressed in the country did much to diminish public faith in British institutions'.[36]

In the Cabinet discussion of March 1954 on Maxwell Fyfe's paper, 'some ministers' expressed the view that 'the coloured population in this country was increasing rapidly, and in ten or fifteen years' time it might have reached unmanageable proportions'. They believed that, at the very least, 'serious thought might have to be given to the possibility of taking power to control the entry into this country of British subjects belonging to other parts of the Commonwealth'. Maxwell Fyfe, Lord Swinton and Oliver Lyttelton were deputed to look into this.

It was at this point, exasperated by the prevarication and subtle Whitehall footwork of the liberals, that the fifth Marquess of Salisbury stepped in. Grandson of the great Tory Prime Minister and possessor of 'a hair-trigger conscience', 'Bobbety' Salisbury had resigned over appeasement with Anthony Eden in 1938. He was later to resign over a similar issue: from Harold Macmillan's Cabinet in protest over policy in Cyprus. In 1954 he was Lord President of the Council, a Cabinet Minister without Portfolio. He was universally regarded as the keeper of the Conservative Party's conscience – no easy task in any era.

'Salisbury's charm and courtesy clothed a will of steel,' commented his *Times* obituary in 1972. 'He stood in awe of no man. ... He affirmed his beliefs with a patrician serenity which was sometimes mistaken for arrogance. ... But there was nothing pompous about "Bobbety".'[37] Having no constituency but History to address, Salisbury pursued his case in Cabinet in an unfailingly open and forthright way. Where his opponents on the immigration issue tended to use bureaucratic inertia and a (probably misplaced) fear of the electoral implications to bury initiatives over immigration, Salisbury merely restated his arguments forcefully and concisely in Cabinet. His methods were Cecilian, theirs Sicilian.

Whereas men like the Health Minister, Iain Macleod – whom Salisbury was later to depict as 'too clever by half' – concluded that large-scale immigration was acceptable because of its technical and economic implications, the Marquess – a Burkean Tory taught to consider the interests of 'generations yet unborn' – could see beyond such short-term trends. 'He was suspicious of over-cleverness in politicians, though he was no mean tactician himself. His intellectual honesty and instinct for public service were part of his Cecil heritage, deeply rooted as it is in a long religious tradition.' He was concerned about the problems of cultural assimilation and agreed with Churchill's remark to Sir Hugh Foot, the Governor of Jamaica, that, if it continued unabated, 'we would have a magpie society: that would never do'.[38] The Cecils are in politics to look beyond the immediate electoral or financial consequences of a policy. Here was a shining exception to the rule that the Tory grandees were getting out of touch with the aspirations of ordinary people.

As the name suggests, the Commonwealth Relations Office was concerned with ensuring the best possible relations between Britain and her former dominions. Its Secretary of State, Swinton, was thus cast in the role of appeaser-in-chief of the Commonwealth. His department argued that bringing British immigration policy into line with the rest of Commonwealth practice would inevitably arouse their ire. As Churchill's Private Secretary put it, 'The difficulty was that the minute we said we've got to keep these black chaps out, the whole Commonwealth lark would have blown up ... it would have meant a fundamental change in the nature of the Queen's dominions, and relations between Commonwealth countries.'[39]

Writing to Lyttelton on 19 March 1954, Swinton said that whilst he did not mind looking into the question of deportation for criminal immigrants, he was against acquiring powers to control immigration as such. He concluded: 'If Bobbety does not wish to press his views any further, the three of us could put in a paper to Cabinet setting out our reasons for recommending against the restriction of immigration.'[40]

But Salisbury certainly *did* wish to press his views. The next day he wrote Swinton a long letter from his home, Hatfield House. Over the question of acquiring deportation powers he said:

> I should not be satisfied with the legislation which you suggest. I feel that it would be only tinkering with what is really becoming a fundamental problem

for us all, though it is only beginning to push its ugly head above the surface of politics. The figures which we have been given make it clear that we are faced with a problem which, though at present it may be only a cloud the size of a man's hand, may easily come to fill the whole political horizon. ... With each year that passes, and with the general improvement with methods of transportation, the flow increases. Indeed, if something is not done to check it now, I should not be at all surprised if the problem became quite unmanageable in twenty or thirty years' time. We might well be faced with very much the same type of appalling issue that is now causing such great difficulties for the United States. The main causes of this sudden inflow of blacks is of course the Welfare State. So long as the antiquated rule obtains that any British subject can come into this country without any limitation at all, these people will pour in to take advantage of our social services and other amenities, and we shall have no protection at all.

Salisbury, who in his time had been Colonial Secretary, Commonwealth Relations Secretary and twice Dominions Secretary, appreciated how the discussion about deportation powers was a red herring. 'It is not for me merely a question of whether criminal negroes should be allowed in or not,' he pointed out, 'it is a question whether great quantities of negroes, criminal or not, should be allowed to come.' He suggested that a Commonwealth conference should be called to establish a uniform immigration policy. To the argument that 'this is likely to cause friction with the Indians' he said that we should not 'allow ourselves to be deterred by comparatively limited questions of that kind'; he concluded that 'we should recognize that this coloured problem is potentially of a fundamental nature for the future of our country'. He ended his letter by calling for 'far more far-reaching action' than the deportation Bill which Swinton had been proposing.[41]

Swinton replied three days later, suggesting that 'we ought to get this thoroughly thrashed out before we go back to Cabinet'. He did not believe a Commonwealth conference would help, 'because if the subject is raised it cannot be confined to selected issues, but gives the Asiatic Commonwealth countries a chance to raise all their grievances, not only against South Africa, but Australia and New Zealand as well'. He went on to suggest that the Labour Party be brought into the consultative process, as 'nothing would be worse than to put half the Commonwealth and all the Labour Party against us on a difficult issue'. This negative attitude did not extend to Lyttelton, who wrote to Swinton on 31 March agreeing with Salisbury that deportation legislation would not 'in any way solve the problem'. He wanted restrictions imposed, such as a £500 deposit to be put down by the immigrants, 'if there is to be any means of controlling the increasing flow of coloured people who come here largely to enjoy the benefits of the Welfare State'.[42]

Lyttelton asked officials to draw up a list of all the restrictions the various colonial governments imposed on immigrants. This showed that many refused to accept 'persons who are likely to become a public charge', 'illiterates', those 'deemed by the Minister to be undesirable' or had 'unsuitable standards or habits of life', and many places operated quota systems and dictation tests. Jamaica itself, for example, prohibited immigrants 'who are likely to become a charge on public funds by reason of infirmity of body or mind or ill-health or who is not in possession of sufficient means to support himself or such of his dependents as he shall bring with him to the island'. These were far more draconian than the restrictions Salisbury had in mind.

Lyttelton discovered that the following territories operated an entry permit system, or required prior permission before entry for residents was allowed: Aden, Ascension Island, the Bahamas, Bermuda, Borneo, British Honduras, British Solomon Islands, Brunei, Cyprus, the Falkland Islands, the Gold Coast, Kenya, the Leeward Islands, Malaya, Malta, the New Hebrides, Nigeria, Nyasaland, St Helena, Sarawak, Sierra Leone, Singapore, Somaliland, Tanganyika, Trinidad and Tobago, Uganda, the Windward Islands and Zanzibar. Yet British ministers were too faint-hearted to incur the supposed odium of the Commonwealth by adding the United Kingdom to the list.

On 12 April 1954 Salisbury, Maxwell Fyfe, Swinton and Lyttelton sat down to another informal meeting at the Home Office. They discussed whether a £25 deposit for those with no guaranteed employment would prove 'a sufficient deterrent' and the Salisbury–Lyttelton axis clearly got the better of the argument, as the minutes record that 'it was thought to be desirable to have powers of restriction upon entry'. A Working Party was set up under the chairmanship of a senior Home Office official, Mr W.H. Cornish, which, unlike the earlier groups, took only a month to report. It stated that £25 would prove no deterrent at all, suggested a £100 minimum, but concluded, as usual, that only legislation to bring British practice into line with the rest of the Commonwealth could provide a practical, long-term answer.

This sent the politicians back to the drawing-board, and six whole months passed in deliberation, during which the rate of increase of arrival was growing exponentially. At Cabinet in mid-October 1954 Churchill served notice on Maxwell Fyfe that another long delay would not be acceptable because 'the problems arising from the immigration of coloured people into the UK required urgent and serious consideration'.[43] Six weeks later the new Home Secretary, Gwilym Lloyd George, the son of the former Prime Minister, presented a memorandum to Cabinet. It began by admitting that since the Civil Service had first looked into the problem, 'the flow of immigrants, mainly from the West Indies, has greatly increased.'[44] He went on to explain that 'Colonial Governments cannot be expected to control this flow and no limit to the numbers likely to come here, especially from Jamaica, is in sight ... as the law stands there is no means of putting any limit on the number of Commonwealth citizens from overseas who may choose to settle here.'

Part of the explanation for government inaction in the face of such a situation lies in the tremendous prestige of the Civil Service in the 1950s. Whereas Maxwell Fyfe had been able to hold his own against Sir Frank Newsam, the Permanent Under-Secretary at the Home Office, Lloyd George was 'dominated' by him.[45] Newsam had been at the Office since 1948 and was one of Whitehall's toughest operators. 'A doer rather than a thinker, he originated few ideas' is one historian's verdict on him, and he was certainly not about to break Civil Service precedent and pre-empt an issue that was generally seen as inevitable but still some time off. Meanwhile, the Governor of Jamaica, Sir Hugh Foot, was reduced merely to keeping the Home Office informed of every boatload which set sail, with numbers aboard and dates of leaving dock. The Commonwealth Relations Office was warned that should restrictions be introduced, 'there might well be a chance of the governments of India and Pakistan introducing retaliatory restrictions against the entry or residence of members of the British business community'.[46]

Concluding that 'increased public discussion' was tending towards the opinion that 'the extent of the present immigration is causing many to revise their opinion and to favour some sort of control', Lloyd George suggested in November 1954 that another departmental committee be set up, yet again with Labour Party representation, since 'this is not a matter of party politics but is one of national concern'. The next day Swinton produced a memorandum complaining that 'any action which may weaken the ties which help to bind the Commonwealth together is a matter of direct interest to the UK ... we must expect to be criticized by the public and press in those countries'.[47] The essentially racial argument underlying this whole debate was kept as submerged as possible by the anodyne language of the Cabinet minutes, but was starkly put by Swinton, who pointed out the paradox that 'we shall welcome the comparatively few good young Canadians or New Zealanders who wish to work here, while restricting an excessive number of West Indians or West Africans'.

The Cabinet discussed this memorandum the next day and heard the Home Secretary state that 'the gathering momentum of this movement made it a matter of some urgency that the Government should provide themselves with means of controlling it'. Nevertheless, it was decided that pressure of Parliamentary time made it impossible to legislate that session, so Lloyd George was invited merely to submit proposals for the new committee, which would be chaired by one of the Great and the Good. The Warden of All Souls, the Master of Balliol and Lord Crawford were all mooted. The Cabinet seemed to prefer Lord Radcliffe, the effects of whose previous report concerning Commonwealth citizens has been seen in Chapter 2. The rest of the committee was to have been selected on the classically Whitehall basis of tokenism and Buggins's Turn. It would consist of three MPs (one from each party), a TUC representative, 'one person (preferably a woman) well known as a social worker', an economist, 'one person familiar with Commonwealth problems' and 'at least one of the members should be chosen from Scotland and one from Wales'. Cabinet right-wingers feared that any such committee would have an in-built liberal bias which would make it unlikely to reach the conclusions for which it was set up.

At the next Cabinet on 8 December 1954 ministers duly expressed the view that any such committee

> was bound to include some members who would be opposed in principle to any action which might appear discriminatory in character. At best, therefore, the Government would be likely to find itself obliged to act in disregard of a minority report, whilst at worst the Committee's recommendations might make it impracticable for the Government to take any action.[48]

Over two years had passed since Churchill had brought up the subject, and a combination of bureaucratic inertia, political procrastination and funk was still stymying all impetus for action.

A relatively uncontroversial amendment to the 1948 Nationality Act bringing immigration procedure into line with the rest of the Commonwealth was all that was needed. It was legislation which even the newly appointed and liberal Colonial Secretary, Alan Lennox-Boyd, had earlier admitted was inevitable. He had circularised the Cabinet with a memorandum which began: 'It is virtually certain that this Government or its successor will be driven by events and by the pressure of popular opinion to enact legislation controlling the immigration into this country of British subjects from overseas.' Despite admitting again that, in the end, 'the Government will be obliged to impose control', Lennox-Boyd nevertheless regarded 'any discriminatory legislation as open to the gravest objections'.

Lloyd George, however, had already written to Swinton saying that he was convinced that they should push ahead 'without the delay involved by further correspondence. The P.M. is pressing for the matter to be brought before the Cabinet.'[49] At the Cabinet meeting on 8 December, he stated that 'there appeared to be a surprisingly wide body of opinion in favour of immediate action'. He and Lennox-Boyd were instructed to produce draft legislation. It took over a month for Lloyd George even to report that the preparation of a Bill was in hand, by which time all eyes were on the prospect of Churchill's retirement and the forthcoming general election.

The *Spectator*'s new editor-proprietor, Ian Gilmour, brought up the immigration issue in January, February and March 1955. This drew Churchill's attention, and Gilmour's book *Inside Right* records what happened next:

> Not all politicians lacked foresight. In Downing Street shortly before he gave up the Premiership, Sir Winston Churchill questioned me about the attitude of the *Spectator* to the arrival of immigrants from the West Indies. After expressing some measure of approval [of what Gilmour had told him], Churchill said, 'I think it is the most important subject facing this country, but I cannot get any of my ministers to take any notice.[50]

One minister who did was Oliver Lyttelton. He told the Kenyan businessman, Sir Alfred Vincent, at about the same time: 'You are quite right about the colour problem in England. If it is not tackled, which it will be, we may easily get a situation of great proportions in twenty-five years.'[51] But in the main Churchill was right, for in the words of the junior minister there, Sir Hugh Munro-Lucas-Tooth, 'it was not a problem to which the Home Office devoted much time.[52]

This only changed as a result of the public and Parliamentary pressure for action which was gradually building up. The issue had first arisen in the House of Commons in June 1953, when Thomas Reid had asked Maxwell Fyfe how many immigrants had taken permanent residence in Britain since 1945. He was told that such information was not available. A month later he asked whether the Home Office would keep statistics in future, to which Maxwell Fyfe replied that he had no powers even to obtain the information for them.[53] Reid, who had spent twenty-five years in the Ceylon Civil Service and was a former Financial Commissioner of the Seychelles, could in no sense be written off as a Little Englander.

Churchill's personal views on the subject were first hinted at in Parliament in February 1954, when he was asked during Prime Minister's Questions whether he 'would instruct all ministers to take action within their ministerial and departmental powers to prevent the operation and continuation of the colour bar'. He replied: 'The laws and customs of this country upon this subject are well known and I am advised there is no need for new instructions.' When Labour's Philip Noel-Baker questioned him further, Churchill merely replied: 'I will certainly bear that and many other factors in mind.'[54]

Contrary to Government hopes, the subject still failed to recede. The movement to introduce reciprocal legislation to replace the unilateral right of unrestricted entry was gathering pace in both Houses of Parliament. In April 1954 Lord Listowel, the Labour peer, organized a meeting between some of his concerned colleagues and Charles Carstairs, Assistant Under-Secretary in the Colonial Office. He told the official that 'the public did not know the facts' – which would not have come as a surprise to Carstairs as they had studiously avoided collecting, collating and publicizing them. He added that 'the situation would be likely to become worse if full employment slacked off and it would therefore be better to tackle the question now, as a bipartisan affair'.[55] As the last Secretary of State for India and the man who, together with Mountbatten in Delhi, had implemented Indian independence from London, Listowel's credentials as a friend of the Commonwealth could hardly have been bettered. But after eight months of waiting he was so frustrated with the situation that he put down a measure in the House of Lords urging the Government to instigate immediate action, because 'during any delay which may occur the problem is getting worse'.[56]

At the same time as the Carstairs meeting in the Lords, the Tory MP, Bernard Braine, wrote to Maxwell Fyfe to say that he was setting up a 'ginger group' to warn ministers that 'colour consciousness would grow if the coloured community here increased in size'.[57] As it was still considered a Commonwealth rather than a Home Office matter, Swinton was deputed to write to Braine to say: 'The fact that we are wisely keeping quiet on this subject does not mean that we are not doing a lot of work on it.' This had been the Government line throughout the summer and autumn of 1954, as pressure gradually built up. In May 1954 Maxwell Fyfe was told by the Tory MP, Sir Waldron Smithers, that 720 Jamaicans had just set sail and asked if 'it was the policy of Her

Majesty's Government to facilitate the export of large unemployment to Britain'. The Home Secretary was reduced to agreeing: 'I think it would be safe to conclude ... that the number of immigrants is increasing.'

In June 1954, in answer to a request from Smithers to consider legislation 'on the lines of the system in force in the Dominions and in foreign countries', he deployed a yet more anodyne block: 'Very wide and complex issues are involved and I regret that I am not in a position to say when a conclusion will be reached.'[58] Harold Watkinson of the Ministry of Labour told the Tory MP, William Steward, in October that no statistics were available for the number of immigrants in receipt of unemployment benefit. When a week later another Conservative, Peter Remnant, asked whether it was true that National Assistance could be drawn by immigrants within a matter of days after getting off the boat, the question was passed from department to department before being finally answered in the affirmative.

The first Parliamentary debate on the issue finally took place on Guy Fawkes Day 1954, when the MP for Sheffield and former Labour minister, John Hynd, managed to secure a thirty-minute adjournment debate. 'Members have put down a series of questions in the past and have had most unsatisfactory answers,' he told the House, 'or answers which do not show that the Government have any apprehension about the scope of the problem, or are doing anything about it.' The fact that this came from a Labour former Chancellor of the Duchy of Lancaster is instructive. For it was Labour's natural constituency, the urban working class and trade unionists, who were expected to bear the brunt of large-scale New Commonwealth immigration; and, as a former Pensions Minister, Hynd understood the resentment many ordinary people were beginning to express against those who were drawing welfare benefits without having first contributed anything to the public exchequer.

'One day recently no less than seven hundred embarked from Jamaica without ... any prospect of work, of housing accommodation, or anything else,' said Hynd during the debate, adding, 'there are several hundred millions of British subjects of different races and colours in various parts of the world and it would not be possible to accept the implications of that argument if the problem got out of hand'. As a socialist, he pointed out that it was not a racial but a resources question, which in time of labour shortages might seem less acute, but the situation could not be expected to last for ever. This point was addressed by Salisbury and Lyttelton, but by virtually no one else in government. Whilst immigration may have made economic sense in a period of full employment, it was short-sighted not to have considered what would take place when – as happened all too quickly – the boom ended.

'What would happen should there be a recession in employment nobody knows,' warned Hynd. This high level of Labour interest in restricting immigration makes a mockery of the liberal Tory refrain that legislation to bring British practice into line with the rest of the world would necessarily have been dangerous for the Conservatives. It was nearly another decade before Hugh Gaitskell's Labour Party opposed immigration controls, and even later than that, as Richard Crossman recorded, 'It has been quite clear that immigration is the greatest potential vote loser for the Labour Party if we are seen to be permitting a flood of immigrants to come in and blight the central areas in all our cities.'[59]

At the November 1954 debate, Hynd was at pains to point out that 'if there is a sudden influx of outsiders, whether they be Jamaicans, Poles, Welshmen or Irishmen, it upsets the balance'. The results had already been seen in his constituency with inter-racial knife fights in the Sheffield dance halls. Fully aware of the way the Government was likely to deal with him, Hynd insisted that it would not be enough for the Colonial Office minister, Henry Hopkinson, to produce the standard soft-soap answer. He demanded that Hopkinson should not 'merely reply by ... saying that the Government are fully conscious of the problem and that it is under active consideration. That is not enough.'[60] Despite privately being in favour of controls, when he stood up Hopkinson had to give precisely the delaying answers Hynd had feared: 'I can assure the House that this matter and the problems arising from it are receiving very careful attention on the part of the Government.'

When asked by Marcus Lipton, the Labour MP for the Brixton division of Lambeth, whether pressure was being put on the Government of Jamaica to discourage emigration, Hopkinson answered: 'I really must get on for I have very little time.' Later in the debate he summoned up the shade of Palmerston, proclaiming: 'We still take pride that a man can say *Civis Britannicus Sum*, whatever his colour may be, and we take pride in the fact that if he wants he can come to the Mother Country.' The difference between 1854 and 1954, however, was that Don Pacifico did not ask to reside in Great Britain, but stayed in Athens. Now 800 million could legitimately claim right of residence and, as Hopkinson agreed, 'additional transport facilities have been made available simply because there is demand for them'. Keen competition between shipping lines for the growing immigration trade had led to drastic cuts in the price of tickets to Britain.

At one point as the debate progressed Hopkinson tried to argue that it 'is not a matter I can properly discuss', because it raised 'all sorts of different questions and involves legislation'. On the problems of what would happen to recently employed coloured workers who would be laid off during an economic down-turn, Hopkinson said: 'the principle of last in, first out would tend to apply. But in the present circumstances of a high level of employment, I feel that this subject is academic and that there is no advantage in my going into it in greater detail today.' A slightly farcical point was reached later when he informed the House that, in order to reconcile the local residents of Lambeth and North Kensington to their new neighbours, 'tea parties have been arranged'. When the Tory MP, Sir Edward Keeling, asked whether a statement about an inter-departmental committee would be given before Christmas, Hopkinson stalled again: 'We are giving this what is described as "active" consideration.'[61] No representative from the Home Office was even present at the debate. Hopkinson had been placed in an impossible position by the Government, and attempted manfully to defend a difficult brief.

On 8 November 1954 Lloyd George told a Tory MP that it was 'not possible to give an estimate' of how many Jamaicans were then resident in the UK. In mid-December 1954 Reid asked Lloyd George if he would speedily introduce legislation giving the Government

> control over the immigration to this overcrowded island of aliens, and citizens of British Dominions and Dependencies, of whom the latter can now enter regardless of their health record, means of subsistence, character record, habits, culture, education, need for them economically or otherwise, or of the wishes of the British people.

The Home Secretary brushed this off by saying that he was 'not yet able to make a statement'.[62]

When finally the Government did agree to a Committee of Inquiry, the Cabinet Secretary told Churchill that it was intended 'not to find a solution (for it is evident what form control must take), but to enlist a sufficient body of public support for the legislation that would be needed'. In Cabinet on 13 January 1955, as the last item on the agenda, 'there was general agreement that the social consequences of the increase in flow of West Indian immigrants into this country were sufficiently serious to compel the Government to take such action as was open to them, or at least to make their attitude on the matter clear to the public'. It was agreed that a White Paper should be drafted describing the existing restrictions on British subjects in the rest of the Commonwealth. One explanation for governmental inaction was that, in the words of one of Churchill's ministers most closely involved in the decision-making process:

> We never thought for a moment ... that anybody other than Caribbean people would be involved, and never conceived that hundreds of thousands of Hindus from India, Moslems from Pakistan, as well as blacks from Africa itself would be applying to come in. In fact ... we were at that moment just stalling and hoping for the best.[63]

Other explanations that have been given almost defy satire. One of Churchill's Private Secretaries has pointed out that 'at the time it seemed a very good idea to get bus conductors and stuff', and one of the junior ministers of the day complained that, without New Commonwealth immigration, it was becoming 'hard to find somebody to carry your bags at the station'.[64]

In January 1955 the subject of immigration suddenly reappeared on the Cabinet agenda when the Tory MP, Cyril Osborne, decided to introduce a Private Member's Bill on the subject under the Ten Minute Rule. His threat was serious, coming as it did simultaneously with Birmingham City Council's warning to the Cabinet of the 'serious housing problems resulting from the concentration of large numbers of coloured immigrants in slum houses'. The liberals in Cabinet called for yet another Committee of Inquiry, whereupon one unnamed Cabinet minister – probably either Salisbury or Lyttelton – expostulated that, after studying the subject since 1952, 'it was already clear that there was urgent need for legislation to restrict the admission of coloured immigrants to this country and that the Government would be amply justified in introducing a bill for this purpose'.[65]

When four days later the terms of Osborne's proposed Bill – 'To regulate the admission into the UK of persons not belonging to the British Isles' – were published, the Cabinet decided that it should abstain and other ministers should either follow suit or vote in favour. The Chief Whip was instructed to tell the rest of the Government that they 'should refrain from voting against the proposal'. This was the ideal situation for a Government which wanted restrictions introduced but was wary of being seen to initiate action themselves. It effectively shifted responsibility for action from them on to a private member, and was the nearest Britain got to closing the open-door policy.

Osborne never presented his Bill to the House, for reasons which remain unclear. The *Spectator* reported – in a leader entitled 'Avoiding a

Problem' – that he was ill, adding that this 'will not save the Government from the duty of facing the facts'.[66] But this is exactly what it did do. The Cabinet minutes certainly imply that Osborne had been put under pressure, partly because of the approaching general election, not 'to proceed with this project'. They go on to record that although the Bill 'would at least have provided for the expression of public and parliamentary opinion on the subject', the Government could congratulate itself on the 'immediate advantage' of not embarrassing Princess Margaret during her visit to the West Indies. This had 'made the present an inopportune moment to initiate action in this matter'.[67] The Princess was due to celebrate the tercentenary of Crown sovereignty over Jamaica.

It is not inconceivable that Osborne was persuaded to feign his illness so as not to embarrass the Princess during the celebrations. Osborne's papers were destroyed after his death in 1969, so we cannot know exactly what happened. But, whatever the reason for it, the only opportunity Parliament had to vote on immigration was lost and a major ethnological alteration of the nation thus took place without any democratic ratification whatever.

Neither was the Government preoccupied with any other great events at that time. The items on the Cabinet agenda were usually the banal, administrative topics every Government has to get through. Apart from the surrender of Mau Mau, early 1955 saw very little else happening in politics. The line that the liberals used that the Government was too busy to devote Parliamentary time to restricting immigration was a smoke-screen. It was only political code: a general election was approaching and issues likely to be controversial were best avoided.

The draft White Paper setting out the rest of the Commonwealth's immigration policies was circulated to the Cabinet in mid-February 1955. This was considered a prerequisite for any legislation, as it would obviate the argument that Britain was doing anything unique in seeking to restrict immigration. It showed how in some Commonwealth countries 'steps were taken to exclude British subjects who were not of European origin by administrative methods which lacked the support of any statutory authority'. This put the Government in a quandary: any White Paper would expose racial discrimination by 'White' Commonwealth countries, and they 'might not welcome disclosure of the fact'.[68] Equally obviously, however, its purpose 'could not be achieved if it concealed the fact'. In the end no White Paper appeared, as it was feared one might 'embarrass the white Commonwealth countries'.[69]

The sixteen-page report did show, however, that in Canada the

Governor-General was empowered to prohibit entry by dint of 'nationality, citizenship, ethnic group, occupation, class or geographical area of origin'. Similarly, 'non-European British subjects are not generally permitted to take up permanent residence in Australia, though there is no statutory authority for their exclusion'. Their entry was controlled by the use of medical and dictation tests, of which the latter could be demanded 'in any prescribed European language'. New Zealand, as well as prohibiting 'idiots or imbeciles, persons suffering from a loathsome or contagious disease', also had provisions to exclude 'persons who are descended from Aboriginal natives of any Dominion, or any British Colonial territory'. These were a few of the countries which, the liberal Tories in Cabinet were arguing, would take the moral high ground against Britain should she try to restrict coloured immigration.

The issue did not recede in the dying days of Churchill's Premiership, as opponents of restrictions had hoped. In March 1955 the Tory MP, Frederick Burden, asked Harold Watkinson, the Parliamentary Secretary at the Ministry of Labour and National Service, whether 'immigrants ordinarily resident in this country and who are not nationals of, or resident in, any other country' would be called up for National Service. The minister answered that 'we should create more difficulties than is worthwhile if we attempted in peacetime to call up compulsorily men who are not British subjects' but only 'Commonwealth citizens'. Burden considered it scandalous that 'young men who come to live here, who have no other country, who enjoy the benefits of all our services, including education, and who certainly will become British citizens when they are no longer liable to call-up, are not doing their duty in the same way as British citizens who do theirs'.

As the *Spectator* put it at the time, 'Plainly, the whole question is rapidly qualifying to be described as "an issue" ... this is something which everything possible must be done to avert.' The magazine accepted that the Government was reluctant to abandon the doctrine of common citizenship between the UK and the Colonial Empire, 'but doctrines cannot always take precedence over facts'.[70] That, however, was precisely what was happening. By early 1955 Churchill was in no state to embark upon a crusade which he had systematically postponed until then. He was an old man in no hurry. Sir David Hunt has explained, 'There were some subjects in which he took great interest and others which he would only touch with the greatest reluctance.'[71] Despite his repeated warnings about the dangers, Churchill put action to deal with immigration in the latter category.

The Prime Minister would sometimes tell advisers: 'This is a democratic Government, these matters must be decided by the Cabinet as a whole; I cannot possible settle them on my own authority.' This, believes Hunt, was often only a case of his 'using impeccable constitutional maxims as another method of deferring a decision'. Churchill's last Private Secretary, Anthony Montague Browne, believes: 'He was simply too tired to deal with the immigration problem. He could only concentrate on a few big issues at a time – like the Russians – and the rest of the time he could only give a steer and not see it through.'[72] Contrary to what an embittered Lord Boothby was to allege, Churchill was not 'gaga' at the end of his Premiership; he could still make magnificent speeches on big issues, but he was eighty and tired.

One of the men who worked closely with Churchill during the war, Sir Ian Jacob, put it perfectly when he said that, contrary to the popular impression :

> He was never keen on making a decision on matters that did not demand immediate action. Unless one had to be made he liked to discuss the pros and cons at length and would then adjourn the meeting for further thought ... then there would be a period of private discussion, further documents either in the form of minutes or of memoranda trying to strengthen the case of those who wanted action, and perhaps of more meetings.

If this were true of wartime, how much more was it the case when there was no immediate urgency? Certainly, as Hunt discovered, 'when handling controversial points he wanted to be sure that everything was exactly right, that everyone who should have been consulted had had his say and that all the consequences of the proposal had been thought out'.[73] Over the immigration question this meant that three years were spent deliberating, during which the unintended influx turned from a trickle into a flood.

The entire process, which for good or ill has transformed large areas of urban Britain, was carried out without reference to the wishes of the British people as a whole, let alone those living in the areas likely to be most affected. As Ian Gilmour has stated in his political credo *Inside Right*:

> British politicians of all parties in the Fifties and early Sixties showed themselves to be lamentably short-sighted on these questions ... the great immigration took place without the British people feeling they had been consulted, an omission which has produced much natural resentment. ... The failure of politicians of all parties to respond earlier to the fear and

discontent that were being expressed in the country did much to diminish public faith in British institutions.[74]

The last time Churchill's Cabinet debated the matter was three weeks before he left office, when it was agreed that a discussion at the Central Council of Conservative Associations would be 'a useful opportunity for ventilating the conflicting views which are held on this subject. There would be no need for the Government to give any indication of their attitude on this occasion.'[75] As was perhaps obvious to all, Churchill's departure as Prime Minister meant that what impetus there had been for tackling the problem vanished almost completely. Despite having won the May 1955 general election handsomely, Eden abandoned the idea of a Committee of Inquiry in June.

The Eden ministry then discussed the issue fitfully, before burying it altogether at a Cabinet meeting on 3 November 1955. This was not before Salisbury had proposed a 'guest-worker' system, advocating 'the possibility of admitting Colonial immigrants for temporary employment for a period not exceeding five years. This might meet the need for labour with less prejudice to long-term social considerations.'[76] This idea was turned down by a Cabinet committee chaired by the Lord Chancellor – who was none other than Sir David Maxwell Fyfe, now Lord Kilmuir. Apart from Salisbury and the Attorney-General, Sir Reginald Manningham-Buller, the other members were the three leading liberals on the issue, Alec Douglas-Home, the Commonwealth Secretary; Lennox-Boyd at Colonies; and Iain Macleod, the Minister of Labour. Salisbury dissented from their conclusion, finding himself in a minority of one.

One idea Lennox-Boyd advanced seemed to call into question his liberal credentials, however. This was for 'internal colonialism', in which he argued that 'the preferable course was to try by other means to disperse the colonial immigrants more evenly over the United Kingdom', by sending them to governmentally designated areas to avoid their congregation in urban ghettoes. The enforcement of this extraordinary plan would presumably have required some sort of pass laws.

On the night of 24 August 1958, and again a week later, the race issue escaped from the domain of inter-departmental working groups and Cabinet committees to spill out on to the streets. In the first major civil disturbances in Britain since the Cable Street Riot of 1936, mobs of 700 in Notting Hill and 4,000 in Nottingham were involved in full-scale race riots, in which 140 arrests were made. George Rogers, the Labour MP for Notting Hill, had a fairly crude explanation. 'For years white people have been tolerant,' he said, 'now their tempers are up.' In polls taken afterwards, 80 per cent of people favoured immigration restrictions. Three years later Gallup reported over two-thirds of the public still supported controls, which were eventually introduced in 1961. But in the words of Lord Hailsham, 'by that time the damage had been done'.[77]

There was more than a whiff of post-imperial 'guilt' in the attitude that many liberals took on the immigration question. In May 1955 a don at Hertford College, Oxford, had written to the *Spectator* arguing that: 'We still owe the Negro race a great debt for the crimes of our slave-trading forefathers, perhaps we should pay it off in this way.' (A letter the next week pointed out that the Royal Navy had stamped out the slave trade, which 'could never had persisted so long as it did without the active connivance of Africans themselves'.) After the Notting Hill riots Father Trevor Huddleston wrote to *The Times* saying that 'we should do something to redress the balance' of centuries of having 'indulged in the white colonisation of Africa to our advantage'.

This argument did not cut much ice with Salisbury, after whose grandfather the capital of Rhodesia was named. In the House of Lords debate on the riots he pointed out that eighty years earlier Central Africa had been depopulated by tribal warfare and the local slave trade, whereas in 1958 colonialism had brought a large measure of peace and justice. 'We have nothing to apologise for in our colonial record,' he said, adding that he thought this 'hypothetical moral debt' was of 'doubtful validity'. West Indian Governments were busy 'transferring their surplus population into this small over-crowded island which already has a population of more than fifty million'. He continued: 'There are many hundreds of millions within the boundaries of the Commonwealth and the Empire who are not so fortunate as us and who enjoy a far lower standard of living than we do. Are we going to open our doors to all of them?'[78]

This point was not answered. The nearest person to address it was Lord Pakenham (later the Earl of Longford), who said that 'We as Christians are all in the position of the Good Samaritan – everyone is our neighbour.' A devout Anglican, Salisbury was not about to be trumped by this, and answered: 'There are restrictions in existence in all the colonies and practically ... in all members of the Commonwealth as well. I did not think you could have a fundamental Christian principle which applied to the United Kingdom alone.'

It took another three years, and the expense of a great deal of political capital, for the Macmillan Government to introduce immigration restrictions in 1961. By then the Labour Party's attitude on race had so altered that Hugh Gaitskell was able to mount a tough opposition – something that would have been impossible seven or eight years before. By that time, however, the pass had been sold. For good or ill but certainly for ever, Britain had become what Churchill had feared, 'a magpie society'.

5

Walter Monckton and the 'Retreat from Reality'

Walter Monckton was a charmer. His was not an oleaginous, sycophantic charm, but one which sprang from a genuine interest in the lives of others. As his Private Secretary, Conrad Heron, remembered years later, 'when he turned it on you, you weren't conscious of it until afterwards'. Of the hundred or so people Lord Birkenhead interviewed for his 1969 official biography of Monckton, dozens referred to this charm, the great majority saying that it was in no way superficial, but the honest expression of a completely natural character. He rarely criticized anyone, or said much which his listeners did not care to hear; he was a good listener and must have had one of the highest boredom thresholds of anyone in politics. His favourite political weapon was always the velvet glove. This has been put down to the fact that he was 'so genuinely kind that he did not want to hurt other people's feelings'.[1]

The man whom David Margesson, the Chief Whip, called 'the old oil can' was thus considered the ideal person to conduct Churchill's policy of appeasement towards the trade unions during his 'Indian Summer' Premiership of 1951–5. It was a policy dictated by sheer political expediency, and led directly to the wage-induced inflation, union militancy and series of industrial relations catastrophes which plagued Britain in the 1960s and 1970s.

Monckton was born into an old Kentish family in January 1891. His ability to identify with both sides of every argument manifested itself at Harrow when he asked his friend and future best man, Eric Long, to second him in a debate on John Morley's Indian reforms. As the day of the debate approached, Monckton changed sides. Long recalled that this left him 'in an awkward position ... he could never make up his mind on which side of the Conservative fence he wanted to be'.[2]

A minor member of the brilliant pre-Great War Oxford generation, which also included Patrick Shaw-Stewart, Philip Guedalla and the Grenfells, Monckton became President of the Union in 1913. A friend remembered how 'he had not the brilliance and epigram of Raymond Asquith or Ronald Knox, but he had a very taking, persuasive way of speaking'. Winning the Presidency of the largely Radical Union was an impressive achievement for a Tory, but one of his Balliol contemporaries believed: 'Walter was at heart a suppressed Radical ... a tremendous mixer, never getting involved in any particular clique, and always open to everyone.'[3]

On the outbreak of the First World War, Monckton joined the Royal West Kent Regiment and served in the trenches for four years. He was awarded the Military Cross in June 1919. Demobilized the previous month, he was called to the Bar by the Inner Temple. There he pioneered the 'conversational' school of advocacy. As a barrister friend described it, 'no histrionics, no affectations or mannerisms, no cross-examination'. In court he removed the monocle which he wore both on the hunting field and in the trenches, for fear that it might be mistaken for a pose. His method with witnesses was the antithesis of the Marshall-Hall style of theatrical cross-examination, and was no less effective for it. Instead of hectoring, he exuded charm and persuasiveness. His courteous manner often lulled witnesses into admissions that might have eluded a more aggressive or flamboyant cross-examiner. Monckton took silk in 1930 and his successes include some of the great events of inter-war legal history, including the Budget Leaking Tribunal of 1936 and the Croydon Typhoid Enquiry of 1938.

He had an excellent memory, a voracious application for work and an incisive brain. Heron remembered how he 'told me he used to work right through the night once a week when a barrister. He had an extraordinary capacity for getting through paper quickly and economically, going straight to the guts of the issue. ... He was the best departmental civil servant of us all.'[4]

In 1932 Monckton became Attorney-General to the Duchy of Cornwall, as a result of his Oxford friendship with the Prince of Wales. It was in this capacity that he advised King Edward VIII on the legal, financial and constitutional aspects of the Abdication four years later. If ever his ability to see both sides of an argument was needed, it was then. Just as he had had a 'good' war, so he also managed a 'good' Abdication crisis, and was one of the few to emerge from it with enhanced stature. It was Monckton who drafted the Instrument of Abdication and he managed afterwards to keep in both with the Windsors and the new King and Queen. His knighthood was the first George VI bestowed, within a month of becoming King.

The royal family's decision not to grant the Duchess the style 'Her Royal Highness' made no difference to Monckton. 'He made his wife curtsey to Wallis,' remembers a friend of the Windsors, who – like Monckton – attended their wedding, 'saying, "it does no harm, and makes the little man so happy," and he always bowed to her himself.'[5] When criticized over this, he used to explain: 'I find my head bows easily.'

One of the lawyers whom Monckton saw regularly during the crisis, Sir Ulick Alexander, told Birkenhead that 'the Duke liked Walter, but he had it up against him for accepting the KCVO too quickly. This made the Duke think Walter was too pro the new King. . . . Mrs Simpson quite liked Walter, but she also held the knighthood against him.' Their doubts about where his sympathies lay may have been understandable, for as Baldwin's adviser, J.C.C. Davidson, told Birkenhead, 'There were those in the little King's entourage who were ready to do all they could to see that the Duke did well out of the transaction, but these tales are best left untold. Monckton was never of their number.'[6] When Baldwin's other confidant, Tom Jones, wrote to Lady Grigg two days before the Abdication, he reported that Monckton had been 'invaluable' to the Prime Minister. Baldwin wrote to Monckton after the announcement of the 1937 New Year's Honours List to say, 'sometimes things happen (but seldom I fear) which seem so in accord with what is eternally fitting that one's wavering faith is propped up afresh. Such is your KCVO and I rejoice.'

Monckton continued to advise the Duke and Duchess after the Abdication, occasionally helping them out of difficult situations. He invariably urged the Duke to adopt the line of least resistance, and managed to persuade him not to resign his style of HRH when the Duchess was refused hers. In late July 1940 Monckton was instrumental in persuading the Duke to leave Portugal and take up his Governorship of the Bahamas. He was always discreet about the Abdication, despite occasionally deploying it as a conversational weapon. Once in the Ministry of Labour, when the Chief Industrial Commissioner was threatening to resign over a climb-down with the unions, 'he spoke of his life and told him about the Duke and Duchess of Windsor'. He well appreciated the fascination which the story held for people. When trying to establish good relations with another member of the Reparations Mission in Moscow in 1945, he 'told him about episodes of his life and about the Abdication'. It worked every time.

Like so many others, Monckton thoroughly approved of Chamberlain's policy of appeasement towards Germany. At one point in the late 1930s, Margesson offered him the vacant safe Tory seat of Tonbridge, but he turned it down. After Hitler's seizure of Prague in March 1939, Chamberlain told Monckton how 'your letter, coming at this time of discouragement, gave me great pleasure and comfort'.[7] On the outbreak of war, Monckton was appointed Director-General of the Press and Censorship Bureau in the Ministry of Information. Fleet Street soon responded to his charm, and he wrote to Sir Horace Wilson during the Phoney War that 'the Press is like a young horse, to be ridden with good hands and a light curb'.

The advent of Churchill in May 1940 saw another offer of a Parliamentary seat, which he again refused. A confidant of both Edward VIII and Baldwin, offered seats in Parliament by both Chamberlain and Churchill, friendly with characters as antipathetic as Lord Halifax and Lord Beaverbrook, Brendan Bracken and Stafford Cripps, Monckton was clearly far more than just, as Harold Nicolson said of him, 'a very exceptional official in very exceptional circumstances'. He became Director-General of the entire Ministry of Information in December 1940.

One of the reasons why he refused the option of a political career may have been because, despite outward appearances, he was not really a Tory. Although he cultivated a non-political image, Monckton was moving significantly to the left. The 'suppressed Radicalism' of his Balliol days found expression in his correspondence with Cripps, the ascetic, carrot-juice-drinking high-priest of the Labour left, who was then Ambassador to the USSR.

Their letters show how far down the road to a neo-socialist 'New Jerusalem' Monckton was prepared to go. In mid-August 1940 he had discussed with Halifax 'the need for some statement as to our purpose for the new world after the war'. Halifax was characteristically sceptical, noting that 'it strikes me as slightly academic until you know how much of the old world is going to survive'. But Monckton was 'pretty emphatic that the demand for something of the kind is wide and substantial'.[8] Just what he had in mind can be seen from his correspondence with Cripps, which would have surprised Conservatives with its overtly left-wing assumptions, Utopian even by the standards of the day.

Writing to Cripps during an air raid in September 1940, Monckton spoke of 'showing now that we mean to get rid of the rotten parts of the established system here'.[9] He went on: 'There are signs in the "Daily Worker" and in some bits of the East End of dissatisfaction with the Government, but they don't amount to anything much yet.' Cripps answered that:

> What has temporarily brought Russia and Germany together is because historically they are both an attempt to get away from an effete civilisation which the countries we represent are desperately trying to cling on to and to revivify. It is indeed a revolutionary war and we are on the side of the past − for the moment ... it will be more difficult then to make any change without a revolution ... if only we would act in time to create a new order. But why preach to the converted![10]

The extent to which Monckton had been converted to a form of socialism can be seen from his letter to the Labour moderate, A.V. Alexander, in November 1940, in which he said: 'in point of fact I am not nor have I ever been in politics and ... such political views as I had might not agree with yours because I was a follower of Sir Stafford Cripps'.[11] Hitherto Monckton has been considered an exemplar of the apolitical, practical statesman. In fact, he exemplified John Maynard Keynes's maxim that 'practical men, who believe themselves to be quite exempt from any intellectual influences, are usually the slaves of some defunct economist'. In Monckton's case the economist was Keynes himself, a fact fully borne out by his period as Minister of Labour in the 1950s.

In late 1940 Monckton help draft a Ministry of Information statement entitled 'What We Are Fighting For', which shows how far his views had progressed leftwards. It was packed with 'New Jerusalem' war aims, such as 'the political Rights of Man and the political Rights of Nations' and 'the Brotherhood of Man'. It proclaimed that 'we are fighting for the New Order ... the liberation of mankind ... social justice'. There was no mention of the things Tories felt that they were fighting for − a chastened Germany, Polish and Czech independence, King and country. 'Our New Order, our planned Social State, must set the world free from ... the fear of poverty,' it trumpeted.

The rest of the statement which Monckton sanctioned contained undiluted socialist propaganda; it is small wonder that backbench Conservative MPs were railing against the Ministry of Information at the time. It claimed that:

The social conscience of the whole people has been aroused. The wartime controls must form a part of a thorough overhaul of our whole economic and social machinery. . . . We must cease thinking in terms of risk and profit; we must think only in terms of the needs to be met. . . . For the workers of Great Britain there must be greater security, increased partnership in industry, more fruitful leisure.[12]

When J.B. Priestley set up 'The 1941 Committee' in the first half of that year, Monckton told Cripps that he 'attended some of the earlier meetings and found general agreement with the obvious expediency of eliminating as far as possible the profit, property and privilege motives, and replacing them by something worthier'. Priestley proved too much of a *prima donna* for much to be done, but Monckton was soon 'seeing people outside [the Committee] who want to form a critical ginger group inside the Government'. When Cripps made two copies of the War Aims he wanted incorporated into the Government's Statement, he sent one of them to Monckton, who duly circulated Cripps's document around his friends in the coalition. It received predictably short shrift from Lord Cranborne, who believed 'the remedy, in democratic states at any rate, seems already in the hands of the people − if they don't like capitalists, they shouldn't elect capitalists − neither Cripps nor we can compel them to vote against their predilections'.

Monckton's own predilections were obvious, and the claims of his official biographer that 'his political opinions were entirely cross-bench' must now be taken with a pillar of salt.[13] By June 1941 Monckton was urging Cripps to return to London:

I fear that too long a stay in [Russia] might injure your prospects of leading us all a little later on. The fact is that there is no satisfactory successor to Winston. . . . Anthony [Eden] is too conventional a thinker to make a great leader. . . . I have discussed you as leader with the most diverse people . . . I find them all attracted by the possibility.[14]

The next month Monckton left the Ministry of Information and went to Cairo as Director-General of British Propaganda in the Middle East, stopping off in Moscow to visit Cripps on the way.

Whilst serving in Cairo, Monckton had the opportunity to draw up a second Instrument of Abdication, this time for King Farouk of Egypt. Although it was never signed, Monckton later remarked that, like Edward VIII, Farouk had complained about the pen. Monckton returned to London in May 1942, where he undertook a number of quasi-governmental public duties for which he was awarded the KCMG in 1944. The previous October, as Chairman of the National Policy for Industry Committee, he stated in a report that:

> The responsibility for those directing industry is to hold a just balance between the varying interests of the public as consumers, the staff and workmen as employees, and the stockholders as investors, and to make the highest possible contribution to the well-being of the nation as a whole.

While not actually mentioning Uncle Tom Cobley and all, this must rank as one of the more platitudinous of wartime policy documents.

Despite the pinkness of his views, Monckton continued to be asked by the Conservatives to stand for Parliament. He turned down an offer to represent Holborn in January 1945 because, as he informed Bracken, 'on domestic issues I should, I think, be expected to plump for the removal of controls on a wider scale than the Labour Party would approve', and he was not keen on doing that. Furthermore, 'my approach to the question of nationalisation ... is that ... in the case of mines either nationalisation or regionalisation is likely to prove more efficient', and he would be inclined to vote in favour. He would thus be 'embarrassed and uncomfortable' standing as a Conservative.[5] Six days later, Cripps wrote to ask whether he would prefer to stand for Labour; but in order to preserve his 'apolitical' stance and continue his career at the Bar unhampered, he refused that too.

Monckton recorded in his unpublished autobiography how, in May 1945, Churchill 'said he would like me to ... join his government. I said that I wasn't a Conservative, and that I should feel difficulty about that. He said that he knew that, and did not think it made any difference.' He thus became Solicitor-General in the Conservative's 'Caretaker' Government. His son, Gilbert, who had himself won the Military Cross in 1940, wrote to ask, 'Where will you stand, and under what colours?' Monckton accepted the legal post, but, reluctant to declare himself a Conservative, did not seek a seat in the Commons. He was spared any further embarrassment by the Government's defeat in the 1945 general election.

This willingness to promote non-Conservatives may seem strange today, but in the context of 1945, when ideological Conservatism was in headlong retreat before the forces of collectivism, Churchill was zealous to appear a national rather than a party figure. The legal posts were in any event far less overtly political, and even in 1951 Churchill seemed to think that they could be done part-time. This attitude towards 'apolitical' ministers, however, still pertained amongst Tories even after Labour's nationalization programme and the creation of the Welfare State between 1945 and 1951. There was nothing underhand about Monckton's position; he always let the Conservatives know exactly how little he sympathized with their philosophy, but so fearful were they of proclaiming the benefits of free market economics and the non-socialist alternative that they leapt at the opportunity of employing him and other non-Conservatives. The result was that in the 1951–5 Churchill Government there were a great number of ministers in key 'Overlord' posts who had no ideological star to guide them, and who proved political failures.

In January 1946 Monckton went to India to advise his client, the Nizam of Hyderabad – then the richest man in the world – as the sub-continent lurched towards independence. The Princes, who ruled over one-third of the territory and a quarter of the population, faced political oblivion if they were unable to come to an arrangement with Congress, which was increasingly looking like the heir apparent to a unified India. A major problem for Monckton was the intractability and vanity of the Nizam. Hyderabad may have had more inhabitants than Canada and more territory than the United Kingdom, but her ruler acted as though the opposite were true. The Princes had fought loyally for the Crown in two world wars, when Congress leaders in the Second had been impri-soned for preaching non-cooperation. This led Monckton, as he wrote to a sympathetic Churchill in May 1946, to 'wonder if we must always be driven to let down our friends and appease our enemies'.

As late as July 1942 the Viceroy had declared that Britain would implement the Government's 'inviolate and inviolable' treaty obligations towards the Princes and, as Monckton put it to Churchill in September 1946, they 'cannot believe that after the greatest victory in history the British people are prepared voluntarily to abandon their heritage in India and their obligations to their Indian friends'. When he was brought to realize that this was precisely what was intended, Monckton had swiftly to change his tune, and he was soon effectively presenting a third Instrument of Abdication to a royal pen. By April 1948 Mountbatten was gloating to Lord Ismay that:

Walter's attitude on arrival absolutely amazed me, I must say ... he tried exactly the same tactics ... of threatening to put Winston and Max Beav-erbrook personally on, to show up some anticipated action which neither Nehru nor I even knew about. But now he is playing 100% (and, incidentally, stayed with me at Government House up to the 17th) and so there is just a chance of pulling something off together.[16]

The 'anticipated action' Mountbatten referred to may have been

Monckton's request to Churchill to start 'contemplating the sending of British troops to fight for the Princes against the rest of India'. By the time independence was in sight, however, Monckton – exasperated by the Nizam – had little alternative but to counsel appeasement. On 5 August 1947 Mountbatten told his staff that 'Sir Walter Monckton had reported that his conversations with the Nizam were going well. He was coming round slowly.' But it proved too slowly, and, through no fault of Monckton's, India eventually invaded Hyderabad in September 1948. As he told Butler, 'it reminded me of the Nazis'.[17]

As might have been expected for a charmer with phenomenal powers of persuasion, Monckton was hugely popular with women. His first marriage, to Polly, the daughter of Sir Thomas Colyer-Fergusson, took place whilst he was still an undergraduate. They had a son and daughter to whom they were devoted, but during the 1930s the couple drifted apart and a formal separation came in 1940. During the 1930s and early 1940s Monckton exercised a fascination over women as diverse as a married hunting acquaintance nicknamed 'the old grey mare', the actress Leonora Corbett, and later on a Mrs Mary Newall who organized his private office in Cairo, and whom he installed in a villa near the Pyramids. He obtained a divorce from Polly in 1947 and married Lady Carlisle, whom he had met in India when she was Director of the Women's Royal Auxiliary Corps. Divorce was a serious matter in 1947 – and was probably the reason Monckton never became Lord Chief Justice – but both he and Lady Carlisle found happiness and were never to regret it. Polly was at first devastated by his behaviour, but eventually forgave him on her deathbed.[18] There was clearly a passionate quality to Walter Monckton not immediately evident from the somewhat dour photographs of him.

On his return from India Monckton devoted himself to the law, appearing for the sinister Dr Thomas Ley in the famous Chalk Pit Murder case. He eventually became one of the best-paid barristers in the country, earning the vast sum of £60,000 a year by 1951. Public duty continued to call, however, and in February 1951 Churchill persuaded him to take the recently demised Oliver Stanley's safe seat of Bristol West. His political views had changed remarkably little since the war, but just enough over such issues as nationalization for him to be able to stand as a Conservative with a clear conscience. He was, as he states in his autobiography, 'in opposition to the Socialist programme, though not by any means a Conservative, fully committed to the Party'.[19] As it was the Attorney-Generalship for which he was earmarked, this lukewarm attitude was not considered a problem. But events, as so often in politics, turned out differently.

During the October 1951 general election campaign the Shadow Minister of Labour, David Maxwell Fyfe, gave a radio broadcast in which he repeated the long-standing Conservative pledge not to undertake any legislative action in the field of industrial relations, 'without prior union agreement'. Instead of this extraordinary self-denying ordinance being welcomed, such was the perceived power of the union movement at the time that, in the words of a leading historian of the period, 'uproar ensued'.[20] The Labour politicians Herbert Morrison and Patrick Gordon Walker made great political capital out of it, alleging that the phrase implied reforms were being contemplated. The incident, as well as 'stiffening Churchill's resolve to avoid trouble with the unions at all costs', meant that after the election was won, Maxwell Fyfe became Home Secretary instead of Minister of Labour.

Calling it 'the worst job in the Cabinet', Churchill told Monckton that it was his duty to take on the Ministry of Labour portfolio, and he is believed to have also given assurances that he would become Lord Chief Justice after Lord Goddard retired. Churchill had a number of trade union skeletons in his cupboard, most notably his supposedly over-zealous actions at Tonypandy and during the 1926 General Strike. In his autobiography, Monckton recalled how 'Winston's riding orders to me were that ... he wanted me to do my best to preserve industrial peace. I said that I should seek to do that by trying to bring justice ... without worrying about Party policy.'[21] But this noble aim of 'Peace with Honour' swiftly degenerated into 'Peace at any Price'.

'Monckton had direct orders from Churchill to appease the unions,' remembers the Prime Minister's Private Secretary, Sir David Hunt. 'He was certainly directly ordered by Churchill to go to extravagant lengths.' This he did, with ultimately disastrous results for post-war industrial relations. Although the Conservatives had a seventeen-seat majority, they acted as though they had scraped home. Despite Disraeli's famous comment, which Churchill made his own, that 'One is Enough', the new Prime Minister felt himself politically insecure. He wanted a quiet life during his 'Indian Summer' Premiership. As he told Jock Colville, his priorities were 'houses and meat and not being scuppered'. By this he meant building council houses, derationing food and not being brought down by an economic downturn caused by industrial unrest. These were fine ends, but in the event the massive house-building programme impeded industrial regeneration, food was derationed over-cautiously, and the unions were appeased for far longer than was necessary for the Government to avoid being 'scuppered'.

Eleven years earlier, during the Blitz, Churchill had said to Colville that 'he did not wish to lead a Party struggle or a class struggle against the Labour leaders who were now serving him so well ... he was determined not to prolong his career into a period of reconstruction'. Yet there he was in 1951, presiding over just such a period, with such a concern for his place in history – which was, of course, completely safe anyhow – that he was not about to jeopardize it by confronting the unions. During the election campaign, when issues arose such as 'contracting out' of the political levy, secret ballots and abolishing the closed shop, Churchill suggested that they be 'left to common sense and the British way of settling things'.

The 1945 general election result had broken his and the Conservative Party's political nerve. They drew false conclusions from that landslide, believing it represented a sea-change in the political views of the British people. Privately they agreed with the Labour minister Sir Hartley Shawcross's triumphalist pronouncement of April 1946 that 'We are the masters at the moment – and not only for the moment but for a very long time to come.'[22] This arose from a failure fully to appreciate the historical factors that were at work, let alone the way the electoral system exaggerated the swing. Labour polled fewer than twelve million votes in 1945, less than the Tories achieved in the next five elections despite a comparably-sized electorate.

Therefore, Britons had not suddenly been converted to socialism in 1945 – as the Tory leadership feared and suspected. They had merely abandoned the Conservatives temporarily – the Party of appeasement and the Depression, which polled fewer than ten million votes. The Conservative-dominated National Government's last victory had been ten years earlier and had itself been a landslide, as had the one before. The February 1950 election brought something nearer the equilibrium which was to be the norm for nearly a quarter of a century, during which both major parties polled between 11.4 million and 13.8 million votes in the subsequent seven elections.

Instead of treating it as the freak result it was, an entire generation of Tory politicians was emasculated by the 1945 election result, especially over the issues of nationalization, the growth of the state and trade union reform. They failed to learn the lesson of what an extra two and a half million Conservative voters between the 1945 and the 1951 elections meant, and instead ceded the intellectual high-ground to the collectivists for a quarter of a century and settled down to manage imperial and commercial decline. This allowed the 'ratchet effect' to pertain throughout the 1950s, 1960s and 1970s, whereby each incoming Tory Government merely preserved the shifts to the left made by the previous Labour one.

Conservatism was thus reduced to trying to administer the enlarged state more efficiently. The only industry properly returned to the private sector by the Churchill Government was road haulage, the nationalization of which was considered a particularly hubristic socialist move. When the iron and steel industries were denationalized in 1953, they effectively continued to be run centrally via the Iron and Steel Board. Lion-hearted on the battlefields of two wars, the Tory MPs of the period became invertebrates on the shop floors of Britain. The difference between physical and moral courage has rarely been more marked than in the liberal Tory response to British post-war socialist advances.

For Churchill, brought up with imperial grandeur and deeply nostalgic for his exhilarating world role of 1940–5, disputes between electricians and their employers, or over lock-outs in Dundee printing works, were quarrels in a faraway country between people of whom he knew nothing. He wanted to dedicate himself to the grand vision of ending the Cold War and dispelling the 'warmonger' image which the *Daily Mirror* had created. Few appreciated then that the agenda had changed; national greatness in the post-war world would be measured by such mundane criteria as productivity, competitiveness and exports rather than by navies and empires. Industrial relations should have come at least as high on the Cabinet agenda as international relations, but only our defeated foes and new competitors had those priorities.

By 1951 the assumption had been allowed to take root that trade unions constituted far more than merely another industrial special interest group, albeit one that performed the useful and necessary function of fighting exploitation. Instead of being seen as sectional organizations, whose duty was solely to secure the best possible deal for their members largely regardless of macro-economic factors, they had been accorded a quasi-governmental role. This practice had grown up naturally during the war and 'winning the peace by the same methods as winning the war' was a slogan to which Tories paid almost as much lip-service as socialists.

The leaders of the major trade unions were Establishment figures of huge *gravitas*. They have accurately been described as 'salt-of-the-earth types with silver hair and watch chains'.[23] Monckton swiftly established the most cordial personal relationships with the traditional leaders – men such as Sir Vincent Tewson, General Secretary of the Trades Union Congress (TUC), Arthur Deakin, head of the Transport and General Workers Union (TGWU) since 1940, and Tom Williamson of the General and Municipal Workers – all of whom were responsible and impressive figures. In common with many other Tory politicians who had served in the armed forces, Monckton saw them as the non-commissioned officers of industry whose job it was to relay commands to the men. But Brendan Bracken had already noticed by February 1951 that, as he told the American Ambassador, 'the Trade Union leaders, who are the real proprietors of the Government, have lost their grip on what is called "organised labour" '.[24]

During Monckton's time a more abrasive and radical leadership was to emerge, but except to expert eyes such as Bracken's this was not generally evident early on. It was not until Frank Cousins's election to the General Secretaryship of the TGWU in 1956 that what had been taking place all over the country on the shop floor became evident to all. Power was in the process of passing from the heavy watch-chained mandarins of the wartime Union establishment to the more politically radical shop stewards, and this dangerous process was greatly aided by Monckton's appeasement policy.

As Heron puts it about this period, 'The leaders were being squeezed out as the local people brought home more bacon ... rats were eating away hard at the fabric of the Trade Unions.'[25] The great safeguard against this process would have been the introduction of secret ballots both before strikes and for the election of union officials. But such was the movement's perceived power in the early 1950s that the Conservatives felt unable unilaterally to institute any reforms. Instead, they asked for the movement's permission before doing anything, a process akin to asking foreigners permission to alter foreign policy or consulting criminals over changes in sentencing procedure.

Much of the moral authority which the unions possessed sprang from the general perception that they had played a vital role in winning the war. While on a national level it is true that their support was invaluable, even in this area liberal Tories tended to look at the phenomenon through rose-tinted spectacles. This was partly the fault of the wartime propaganda machine, which for reasons of morale constantly laid emphasis on positive industrial relations stories, playing down the negative ones.

Between 1939 and 1945 the Ministry of Labour kept a Trades Disputes Book, which detailed the date, cause, number of workers involved, duration, eventual result and aggregate number of working days lost for every work stoppage in the period.[26] These were meticulously listed by occupation, district and number of firms involved. Although at a national level the trade unions did not sanction every stoppage, especially after Ernest Bevin became Minister of Labour in May 1940, on the ground union officials were often involved in them. The Book shows how, even during the Battle of Britain and the Blitz, there were continual strikes – even in industries absolutely central to national survival such as aircraft production and shipbuilding. After the war the Ministry also commissioned an in-house survey entitled 'Strikes and Lock-outs 1939–45', which makes astonishing reading. It proves that, despite Bevin's declaration of 4 June 1940 that 'in this period of national emergency it is imperative that there should be no stoppage of work owing to trade disputes', they were in fact constant.[27]

In the First World War there had been an average of 814 stoppages per annum, but in the Second this nearly doubled to 1,527 despite the far more immediate danger to Britain. Nearly a million working days were lost to strikes in 1940, and this rose to over 3.7 million by 1944. That year – which also saw D-Day and the Battle of the Bulge – there were 2,194 stoppages, some lasting up to twenty weeks in length. Neither were wages the main reason for disputes; 'working arrangements, rules and discipline' explained 30.7 per cent of them, and 'employment of particular classes of persons' accounted for another 10.5 per cent.

When the Conditions of Employment and National Arbitration Order had been instituted on 25 July 1940 in an attempt to instil industrial discipline, the Chief Industrial Commissioner at the Ministry of Labour, Sir Frederick Leggatt, was worried that it would be flouted. By September 1940 – when Britain was under daily threat of invasion – he felt that, with the London dockers and Clyde shipbuilders both on strike, 'intervention of any kind at the wrong moment may greatly embitter the situation'. Leggatt stressed 'the need for patience, especially in the case of dockers. Compulsion or even the threat of it might lead to widespread stoppages.'[28] By September the Order was effectively a dead-letter and by April 1941 the police were instructed not to support employers who attempted to invoke it.

On 21 May 1940 – as the BEF was on the retreat on the Continent – 144 men at the Blantyre colliery outside Glasgow struck over 'a disagreement between machinemen as to which employee should take over cutting work in a new section'. Whilst the small boats were ferrying troops of the BEF back from the Dunkirk beaches nine days later, seventy maintenance staff at the A.V. Roe aircraft works in Manchester downed tools in protest over the dismissal of an employee accused of 'falsification of the recording of his time of arrival at work'. No fewer than 4,426 days were lost at the De Havilland aircraft construction factory in Edgware between 6 and 24 August 1940 – when the Battle of Britain was at its height – over the 'transfer of four capstan fitters from the firm to other work of national importance'. The shipbuilding industry – upon which the survival of the nation also depended – saw strikes take place in July, September and October 1940 in Hartlepool, Plymouth and South Shields.

Because of the censorship of newspaper reporting, and the desperate need for good propaganda during the national emergency, such facts were not allowed to enter the public consciousness. Yet trade union officials were usually implicated in this perilous withdrawal of labour. Demarcation, unionization, pay, and all the normal peacetime disputes carried on, admittedly at a lower intensity, but almost as though the nation was not in mortal danger. Some of the reasons over which Scottish miners saw fit to strike in 1940 included: 'alleged inaccuracy of a weighing machine', 'against employment of brushers at coalface when facemen were unemployed', 'refusal to work with non-unionists', 'dispute arising out of workpeople's incorrect impression that a workman who had been transferred at his own request from one job to another had been dismissed', and 'demand that certain people who worked during a stoppage in the previous day should be suspended for one day'.

Some of these strikes dragged on for long periods. In April and May 1941 – when Coventry was blitzed, Rommel attacked Tobruk, the Germans seized Crete and HMS *Hood* was sunk – there was a five-week stoppage by engineers 'for the reinstatement of an employee dismissed for bad timekeeping'. The Ministry of Information managed to play down – or sometimes censor altogether – these incidents which were so damaging to the war effort. It depicted organized labour as having been uniformly selfless during the war, a myth that was to cost the nation dear. In fact, the industrial proletariat had been crudely bought off; between October 1938 and July 1945, according to Ministry of Labour figures, earnings levels for a wide range of major industries and services increased by as much as 80 per cent.[29]

The myth operated particularly strongly on the liberal wing of the Conservative Party, and found its most potent expression forty years later, in Harold Macmillan's famous maiden speech to the House of Lords on 13 November 1984. There he said that the miners' strike was being fought by 'the best men in the world', the Durham miners. 'They beat the Kaiser's army and they beat Hitler's army. They never gave in,' he said. In fact, in the same month that Captain Macmillan of the Grenadier Guards received his first wound in the First World War, September 1915, Durham miners – whose reserved occupation status excused them military service – were on strike at Gateshead, Seaton Delaval and Hebburn collieries. In the fortnight before his second wounding on 26 June 1916, 4,815 working days were lost by hewers, stokemen, shifters, putters and surfacemen striking for higher wages in County Durham. And when Macmillan was recovering from being shot in the hand in September 1916, 'the best men in the world' were withdrawing their labour, with 2,022 men affected directly and indirectly. Bishop Auckland in County Durham saw strikes taking place during the Battle of the Somme costing no less than 8,711 working days, over wage rates greatly in excess of what Captain Macmillan's men were receiving for a job involving a good deal more hardship and danger, and no right to strike.[30]

In 1951 Churchill chose a Government which was the least recognizably Conservative in history. Several Cabinet ministers – Lords Cherwell, Ismay, Leathers and Alexander, and Walter Monckton among them – came from outside politics altogether. Lord Asquith and Marshal of the RAF Lord Portal were also invited to join but declined. Other ministers, such as Lords De La Warr, Simonds and Reading, Sir Arthur Salter and Gwilym Lloyd George, had political origins outside the Party. Talented free-marketeer Conservatives, such as Ralph Assheton and Oliver Lyttelton, were either exiled to non-economic posts or did not receive the call-up at all. Despite the slogan on which they fought the election, 'Set the People Free', when it came to an all-embracing policy of removing wartime controls this most liberal and pragmatic of modern Tory Governments, in the words of one study, 'actively discouraged both innovation and critical thinking'.[31]

Monckton's PPS during his time at the Ministry of Labour, Ian Orr-Ewing, remembers being

staggered on the very first day [there] when he said to me: 'I have to tell you that I am expendable. If the Government or I do anything which rocks the boat in our relations with the trade unions I will resign.' He made it quite clear to me that he had been put in there to appease the unions and to build bridges.[32]

The first Chief Industrial Commissioner at the Ministry, Sir Robert

Gould, believed Monckton 'did not want to be too politically committed because of the possibility of his becoming Lord Chief Justice'.[33] Monckton could only achieve this on the retirement of Lord Goddard, who did not want a divorcee in such a senior legal post. Monckton's campaign to outlast him was perhaps inevitably dubbed 'Waiting for Goddard' by the press. This desire to become Britain's top judge added to his determination to avoid political controversy during his time at the Ministry.

Churchill came to power during an acute balance-of-payments crisis and this, combined with the great power of the trade unions, the promises made during the election campaign and the Government's small majority, ensured that Monckton had little room to manoeuvre even had he wished to. It was felt by the Government that quite apart from the political implications, any production lost through strikes would cost more than the money paid out in increased wage settlements. Like predatory beasts, the unions could smell this fear. Yet even after 1953, when the economic conditions had improved, Monckton stuck rigidly to the line of least resistance, not only acquiescing in successive union demands, but even actively anticipating them. Furthermore, he consistently failed to look into ways of limiting their powers. Nothing was allowed to interfere with the close personal relationships he had built up with the union grandees. Aneurin Bevan used to joke with union leaders about what a pushover Monckton was, and in July 1953 Arthur Deakin even said: 'We have been able to do things that were difficult to do under our own people.'[34]

This was the heyday of consensus politics and Monckton tended to get on better with his front bench opposite number Alfred Robens than with his own backbenchers, some of whom soon began to find the levels of his concessions increasingly unpalatable. Heron remembers how the practice by which Robens asked Parliamentary questions which had been planted by Monckton reached such a stage that he would sometimes be sent to the Commons to put down a question on Robens's behalf.[35]

Tewson told Birkenhead that 'when things were becoming difficult over a matter on which Walter and I were in agreement, Walter would say in confidence, "I shall have trouble with my own people" ' – thus echoing the words Deakin had used to describe the Labour Party. The Conservative Minister of Labour and the TUC General Secretary would then agree a formula which would outmanoeuvre both employers and Tory backbenchers. This cosy relationship which Monckton had established had its price. As Heron remembers:

The line the Government took was dictated by the great and good of the unions, and they didn't want Government interference. The introduction of secret ballots was considered outside Monckton's remit. If you started making legislative requirements in the mining unions, for example, it would have broken the relationship between Monckton and them.

This was a course Monckton would never contemplate; the resultant special status for the NUM in post-war industrial relations was not to be broken until 1984–5.

In early 1952 Sir Wilfred Neden, the Chief Industrial Commissioner at the Ministry, planned to combat the national shortage of skilled workers by introducing government retraining initiatives. The unions, however, gave the idea a cool response and, as 'Monckton had a precise remit to ensure there were no difficulties with the unions, this effectively prohibited him from being an innovator', so the idea was shelved.[36] All it took was a raised eyebrow from union leaders. The Workers' Charter and the Industrial Charter, policy documents drawn up by the Conservatives when in Opposition, were quietly dropped by Monckton when in office.

The impartial role between employer and employee which Monckton wished to adopt meant that the Government

> refrained from commenting on the substance of a dispute, even if it was widely held that the union claim was unrealistic. It meant that when an Inquiry reported, its recommendations were pressed on the parties as a basis of settlement even if ministers privately disagreed with them. More often than not, this entailed leaning on the employers to increase their last offer.[37]

Monckton was thus not even really impartial; the relations he enjoyed with the British Employers' Confederation were good, 'but not nearly so close as with their union counterparts'.[38]

Monckton argued vigorously against derationing and the lowering of food subsidies. According to Orr-Ewing, Monckton 'was horrified that it might destroy his relations with the unions. In fact there was not a tremor, not a ripple when it happened.' Scare stories abounded that eggs would cost a shilling each if derationed and when, in March 1952, the Cabinet discussed cutting subsidies, in 'a comparatively mild budget', Monckton argued vigorously against the proposal. When bread was derationed, he considered it almost a resignation issue.

May 1952 saw the Chancellor of the Exchequer, Rab Butler, propose a scheme to link wage increases to productivity. He addressed the Ministry of Labour's National Joint Advisory Council – a quango which brought together trade unionists and employers – to warn of the dangers to exports of high wage increases. A 10 per cent rise in wages in manufacturing industry, he told them, without any corresponding increase in productivity, raised export prices by 4.5 per cent. These truths were creating industrial co-operation for competitors such as Germany and Japan, but in Britain charges of naïveté were levelled against Butler. Also, as Anthony Seldon, the historian of the 1951–5 ministry, points out, 'Treasury anxiety ... carried little sway with Churchill.'[39] Butler, for whom politics was often only the art of the plausible, did not press his points. As he was later cynically to tell a historian of Monckton's appeasement policy towards the unions, 'it was extremely convenient. It didn't do me any harm.'

The official history of the communist-dominated Electrical Trade Union (ETU) shows what little effect Butler's warnings had. The 1952 wage round, which culminated in the first national dispute in the industry since the war, was conducted by its General Secretary, Walter Stevens, for the ETU, and a Mr Penwill for the employers. When Penwill

said that unfortunately everyone had to take into account the new Tory Government's appeals for wage restraint as witnessed by meetings between the Employers Federations, the TUC and the Chancellor, Stevens said that he was not going to allow the employers to get away with that: they used to want automatic linking to the cost of living index. Suddenly they had other priorities.[40]

In the end the TUC General Council formally rejected Butler's proposals, saying that they 'preferred not to risk novel experiments in peacetime and under the aegis of a Conservative Government'.[41]

When, in July, Monckton attempted to refer back the increases which had been fixed by twelve Wages Councils – following a precedent set by George Isaacs, Attlee's Minister of Labour – the Economic Committee of the TUC went direct to Churchill. In a humiliating climb-down, the Government not only 'assured them that the proposal would be approved', but were also obliged to disavow any future intention 'of interfering in any of the functions of the Wages Councils'. As Butler was later to put it, 'my wages policy was governed by Walter's friendship with the leaders ... it can justly be said that weaknesses were often shown and too many concessions were made'.[42]

One who disagreed with this analysis was Harold Watkinson, Monckton's ambitious Parliamentary Secretary at the Ministry. He 'did not think that the price paid was too high', justifying this with a statement typical of liberal Tories of the period: 'It was a trend and politicians cannot alter trends – to bring the trade unions into close relations with the Government.' In 1976 Watkinson published a book entitled *Blueprint for Survival*, the subtitle of which posed the question: 'What Has Gone Wrong in Industrial Britain Since the War?' For an answer he needed to have looked no further than his own memoirs, in which Watkinson claimed that if the unions *were* being appeased, 'then it was Winston who decreed it, not Walter Monckton'.[43]

Watkinson, who entered the Ministry of Labour in May 1952, wrote that 'if it had been possible in 1951 to persuade the unions ... to consider putting the national interest above the immediate wage demands of their members – then British industry might have led the world in the postwar drive for recovery'. He remembered how 'it was vaguely felt that exhortation would achieve what was in reality an industrial revolution'. Although he believes 'some draconian measures' were desperately required, he claims Monckton's health was not up to presenting them to the Cabinet. There is precious little evidence to suggest that any such measures ever existed. In a rare *mea culpa* in the book, Watkinson admits that both employers and unions 'needed the spur of legal sanctions if anything was to be achieved. ... We did not provide it. ... In the pressing immediacy of our day-to-day industrial relations problems we just could not manage the time or quiet thought to work it out.'

Despite a 'general acceptance that Britain's techniques and public utilities lagged far behind competitors, particularly the United States', 1952 saw the abolition of the Anglo-American Productivity Council, and its replacement by the far less influential British Productivity Council. Since 1948 the A-APC had attempted to introduce modern production methods into British industry, but in doing so had incurred the ire of the unions because of the perceived threat to jobs. The Ministry of Labour did little to give its successor any teeth, for, as Orr-Ewing remembers, 'Just as the Ministry of Education is full of ex-National Union of Teachers people, so too the Ministry of Labour had fully gone native and was full of staunch trade union types. Few people not of that ilk would have opted to join such a boring echo-chamber.'

As a conciliator in industrial disputes, the Ministry followed, in Heron's words, 'the wartime policy, which was to split the difference. Everyone knew how it worked. There was a long tradition of resorting to Committees of Inquiry as a knee-jerk reaction. A recommendation would come which always gave both sides something.' The knowledge of this encouraged the unions to make higher demands, so the difference, once split, would automatically be higher, regardless of profit or productivity. Another practice which became fully established during Monckton's time was that of using 'comparability'. 'Today the market is the accepted touchstone as to what people should receive,' remembers Heron, 'but then "comparability" was in vogue. In an economy as sectionalized and diverse as ours, there was never any difficulty in looking elsewhere to find people being paid better for a roughly comparable job. The concept dates from the war.'

Many assumptions that were prejudicial to Britain's economic success can be traced back to wartime thinking. The spirit of individual enterprise and initiative, which was lauded on the field of battle, now looked dangerously like profiteering when exhibited on the Home Front in peacetime. After so much 'New Jerusalem' Utopian criticism of the profit motive, it took Britain far longer to adjust back to the realities of commerce than rival economies. As one leading post-war industrialist has put it:

> The old Conservative Party was profoundly ill at ease with industry, commerce and free markets. For years the intellectuals who created the environment for Conservative thinking, people such as Arnold Toynbee, Arthur Bryant, George Trevelyan and so many others, were hostile to industrialisation. They variously described industry as philistine, competition as predatory, commerce as debased and considered the whole thing as rather vulgar.[44]

Macmillan stated that 'Toryism has always been a form of paternal socialism'. Lord Hinchingbrooke, representing the Tory Reform Committee, announced that, 'True conservative opinion is horrified at the damage done to this country since the last War by individualist businessmen'; and Quintin Hogg criticized *laissez-faire* as 'an ungodly and rapacious scramble for ill-gotten gains'. Monckton's policy of appeasement towards the unions was part of this general mood amongst liberal Tories.

With the end of the Korean War came a fall in commodity prices, and Britain's economic performance began to improve. Yet in the summer of 1953 there was a marked increase in industrial unrest, spearheaded by the ETU. The previous year's talks between Penwill and Stevens had dragged on to November 1952, when the employers had granted a large rise and conceded the principle of paid holidays for all. 'The union', as its biographer has put it, 'thought this too represented simply an "interim" payment and resubmitted a claim for increased wages in May 1953.' These talks stalled and consequently the union's Executive planned strikes set to hit ten selected sites. At this point 'the Ministry immediately stepped in' and, after the union refused to accept arbitration, Monckton appointed a Court of Inquiry.

These Courts were set up almost as an automatic response throughout Monckton's time as Minister. Instead of free collective bargaining between employers, the Government involved itself in proceedings as early as possible, appointing judges with an unspoken brief to 'split the difference'. This did not dampen the unions' hyperbole, which was to become a stock feature of post-war industrial relations. At the ETU policy conference at Margate, Stevens called the strike 'a story of struggle which will go down in the annals of history as one of the most important demonstrations of militancy and solidarity that the Union Movement has ever known'. Guerrilla strikes – usually against companies with national defence implications – were called on national, local and company level for one-day, weekly or indefinite periods. Lord Holderness, the Minister of Power from 1959 to 1963, remembers how, in his time, 'everyone was very frightened of the ETU, which we felt could bring the country to its knees. We should have stood firmer then. ... No one really handled it until Margaret [Thatcher] came along.'[45]

At the TUC Conference at Margate in October 1953 the ETU, along with two other unions, submitted the resolution that: 'Policies of so-called "restraint" or "moderation" are condemned.' Churchill's response to the dispute was described in the diary of his doctor, Lord Moran. The Prime Minister 'began questioning me about electricity, is it nationalised? ... He rang for a secretary: "Is electricity nationalised?" he demanded. The Private Secretary, David Pitblado, thought it was. "Make certain," he said impatiently. "Find out the exact position." ' The position was that Attlee had nationalized the electricity industry in 1947. When Moran asked if the strike would "hold up everything", Churchill replied: 'Oh no, it can't go on for long. It would cause too much annoyance and interference with people's lives. I mean to take a hand.' He went on to explain: 'Walter Monckton has gone on holiday.... He is worn out by giving way.' Monckton, who expended a great deal of nervous energy in the negotiations, came close to breakdown several times during his period at the Ministry.

Monckton did not attend the Conservative Party Conference in Scarborough in October 1953. The official reason was because it clashed with a speech he was giving to the Institute of Personnel Management at Harrogate, but it was in fact because he feared that indulging in party politics 'might jeopardise his relations with the unions'.[46] Many local constituency associations put forward motions to the Conference which were critical of the closed shop, union victimization and restrictive practices, and which supported secret ballots and compulsory votes before strike action. The motion which was eventually chosen for debate was anodyne even by the standards of Tory Party conferences.

In his speech to the Conference, Churchill went out of his way to emphasize that 'there is no aspect of our social policy that our successful, capable and tactful Minister of Labour Sir Walter Monckton – or even if need be myself – would not readily discuss with responsible leaders of the TUC'.[47] As William Deedes, who entered the Government the next year, remembers, 'The unions were a serious threat to industry. They had to be fixed, settled, because we did not have the strength to deal with them. A heavy use of tranquillizers was prescribed.'[48]

When in December 1952 Watkinson had produced his 'Industrial Code' on job security and incentives, it soon became clear that, despite pressure from Conservative trade unionists, no action on the closed shop or postal balloting would be taken. The reason for this was to be found in an internal Conservative Central Office memorandum entitled 'Points of Vulnerability'. This was circulated just before the 1955 general election. It explained that 'though the closed shop has been spreading over the last few years, the Government is reluctant to upset the Unions about it'.[49]

Monckton continued to benefit from the fawning attitude adopted by the press. When he had settled the engineering pay dispute in October 1952, by conceding almost exactly what the unions demanded, he was deluged with praise. Under a front-page headline 'Triumph for Sir Walter', the *Daily Mail* commented that it was 'his greatest success so far ... he has kept the peace in industry'. The *Daily Express* agreed: 'The triumph of Sir Walter Monckton is not a matter of opinion. It is demonstrated by the evidence, the Trade Unions get along with him very well.'

A pattern was set for future disputes. Paeans of praise greeted Monckton's every retreat, with hardly a voice raised against. Only the *Spectator* and the *Economist* ran sceptical articles about the phenomenon, pointing both to the ill-effect on the unions of receiving such regular Danegeld, as well as the wage-induced inflation which was being stoked up. But in the rest of Fleet Street the mere appointment of a Court of Inquiry by Monckton would draw admiring press comment for his 'statesmanship' and 'diplomatic skills'.

Even had he wanted to be tough, Monckton was constrained by Churchill's overriding desire to avoid trouble. As the Scottish Secretary, James Stuart, remembered, the Prime Minister

stopped Walter taking any action which meant firmness, He did this whenever there was a threatened strike and ... delayed our recovery by several years by thus preventing a show-down. When Winston wanted a Minister to take on an awkward debate ... Walter would always say that it would upset his relations with the trade union leaders.[50]

An insight into Ministry of Labour thinking during this period can be found in the suggested replies for ministers to the resolutions submitted by constituents for debate at the Conservative Party Conference in October 1953. On the question of secret ballots before strike action, the Ministry advised that it was 'a matter best left to the discretion of the trade union leaders'. Legislation would, according to the civil servants, 'do more harm than good; not only would it weaken the authority of trade union officials, but it would also be singularly resented by the trade union movement as a whole'. In fact, as was shown in the early 1980s, secret balloting tended to encourage moderation and brought increased authority for trade union officials through increased democratic legitimacy.

The next resolution was dismissed as 'merely an expression of dislike of the closed-shop principle. As such it seems harmless, as long as it is made clear that this is a matter to be dealt with by both sides of industry and not for Government intervention either by legislation or otherwise.' It was ludicrous to expect unions voluntarily to end the system whereby employees were forced to join a union as a condition of employment. The third resolution called for an end to restrictive practices, but the Ministry felt that, 'since it merely calls upon both sides to condemn such practices, it seems unobjectionable'. The question of profit-sharing schemes to increase efficiency in nationalized industries was ruled out because 'the TUC is not generally in favour'.

If any industrial dispute typifies Monckton's overall approach, it was the threatened rail strike of December 1953. Late in that year the engineering and shipbuilding employers had rejected a demand for 15 per cent wage increases, submitted at a time when inflation was in the low single digits. The Engineering and Allied Employers' National Federation had twice asked Monckton not to interfere in the bargaining process, arguing that a wage increase of that order would be seriously inflationary. Nevertheless, he had set up two Courts of Inquiry (under the same chairman) which decided upon a 5 per cent increase. By the end of 1953 the electricians and miners had all refused to be bound by arbitration.

In July 1953 the three main rail unions had also submitted a 15 per cent increase, which was rejected by the Railways Transport Commission – the body which managed the industry – and in November the matter came before the Railway Staff National Arbitration Tribunal. On 3 December this in-house body recommended an across-the-board increase of four shillings per week. The General Secretary of the NUR rejected this as 'meagre', and a national strike was called for 20 December. Monckton immediately instituted a Court of Inquiry and, in three days of hearings, Lord Justice Morris heard the usual demands for parity with other nationalized industries and 'restoration of differentials'.

The prospect of a strike over Christmas sent politicians and the press into an extraordinary state of funk. Without breaching the Transport Commission's constitution, which required that the railways broke even each year, the employers could not afford to pay large increases, even if they felt them justified. Railwaymen were considered to be generally underpaid, but made up in total job security what they lost in remuneration. To demand a 15 per cent rise during a period of such low inflation was clearly absurd. Monckton summoned the employers and unions to the Ministry.

He found these negotiations 'harder than the Abdication'. He told Heron: 'Then there were very few players and you could easily get their views, but when there were three unions, two Ministries, the Transport Commission and Number Ten all with changing views, it was nerve-racking. There was also far more waiting.' However, it was not all work. Neden remembered how 'with a stupid trade union delegation, although charming in their presence, Monckton saw through them, and laughed at them afterwards'.[51]

The NUR, ASLEF and TSSA had the last laugh in December 1953, however. Churchill's stance was simple. 'We cannot have a railway strike, it would be so disturbing to all of us,' he told Butler. 'You will never get home, nobody will be able to see their wives.' Butler's argument that 'we should not have wage increases which we could not afford' was waved aside by Monckton, who, in Butler's words, 'averted the crisis in masterly fashion and was much praised'. The *Economist* summed up the essential elements of this masterliness as 'sympathy, patience and funk'. The Tribunal's face was saved by its original four shilling across-the-board increase being kept, but on top of that the unions won the right to a further award. According to the *Daily Telegraph*, the union spokesmen 'made no secret of the fact that they expect their eventual increase, in terms of annual cost, to be between two and three times the amount of the award. In practical effect, therefore, the award has been over-ruled under a threat of force.'

In the end the railwaymen were given, on top of the immediate four shillings a week, another award within two months, which amounted to roughly an extra three shillings, as well as a re-examination of the entire wages structure, which effectively meant further increases after that.[52] This had the double effect of encouraging unions in other industries, which were led to expect similar largesse, as well as spurring the railway unions, who came back for more with an identical threat the following Christmas. As Kipling put it, 'We've proved it again and again, that if once you have paid him the Danegeld, you never get rid of the Dane.'

Shortly after Monckton ordered Sir Brian Robertson, the Chairman of the Transport Commission, to give in to the unions' demands on 16 December, Churchill rang Butler at midnight to tell him: 'Walter and I have settled the railway strike so you won't be troubled any more.' When Butler asked him 'on what terms have you settled it', the Prime Minister replied: 'Theirs, old cock! We did not like to keep you up.' As Butler laconically remarked at the way Churchill and Monckton had excluded the Treasury during the negotiations, 'I was up nearly every night until one o'clock doing my boxes. Of course I could have been present.'[53]

Harry Crookshank wrote to Monckton after the strike had been averted wondering whether a dangerous precedent had been set. He feared the Treasury strategy of an equilibrium between wages and prices was in tatters. Nigel Fisher, a Tory MP and the biographer of Iain Macleod, Monckton's successor as Minister of Labour, thought that

> to some Conservatives, [Monckton's] policy appeared to be little short of appeasement in the face of union pressure. It certainly contributed to wage-cost inflation, and his settlements in the railways strikes in 1953 and 1954 would have forced any private company out of business. In practice, the broad impression he created was that of taking the difference between the unions' claim and the employers' offer.

Fisher nevertheless regarded Monckton as 'a man of great ability and infinite charm, and I cannot remember any senior member of the Government who was more liked and respected'.[54]

As usual, Monckton was deluged with congratulations from his colleagues, the press and the general public. 'Well done!' wrote Derick Heathcoat Amory from the Ministry of Agriculture on New Year's Day 1954:

> Many congratulations. The Report has landed us with some embarrassing long-term problems ... because in practice in one way or another I suppose we should have to support the railways. But having once gone ahead with the Court of Inquiry – obviously the only possible course – we clearly had to

follow their conclusions. ... We all of us felt – as usual – complete confidence in your judgment throughout.

The *Daily Telegraph* leader on the subject was entitled 'His Triumph'. It asked: 'Was this a Conservative Minister earning the heart-felt plaudits, without exception, of socialist ex-Ministers and MPs?' Only the *Economist* failed to join in, arguing that 'Sir Walter's triumph is one more retreat from reality.'

Monckton's health broke after the strike was resolved, and he went to hospital in January 1954 with eczema, gout and nervous exhaustion. As Tom Williamson, Chairman of the trade union section on the National Joint Advisory Council, put it, 'he was always conscious that if any serious trouble broke out he would be held responsible, and was therefore continuously under a great strain'. Taking Monckton's place to face the Conservative Party's Labour Committee on 26 January 1954, Watkinson heard demands from backbenchers for the imposition of secret ballots before strikes and for the Agricultural Wages Board to be brought under ministerial control. Before these two issues reappeared in the 1922 Committee, Watkinson had his civil servants draw up reasons why they should be blocked. The latter was rejected for the simple reason that 'the opposition of the trade unions could be relied upon'.

Although Monckton welcomed the idea of permanent machinery to settle industrial disputes, during his time 'the unions were unenthusiastic and the plans came to nothing'. Equally it was felt that any action over legal immunities, a Royal Commission, secret ballots, wage settlements policy, restrictive practices or the closed shop 'would have needed the active consent of the unions'.[55]

Industrial peace had to be bought regardless of the ability of industry to pay – and the private sector was immediately and adversely affected by the unions' victories in the public sector. The financial journalist Samuel Brittan, in his book *Steering the Economy*, considered that

all the Ministry of Labour's energies were devoted to bringing the two sides together even at the cost of highly inflationary settlements. Appeasement did trade union members little good in the long run, as higher wages were largely cancelled out in higher prices. Indeed, British workers were paying until 1967 for the Monckton policy, which by pricing British goods out of world markets slowed down the growth of the whole economy.[56]

The Government did not have the excuse of not knowing where the policy would lead. Brittan believes: 'The Treasury's Economic Survey for 1954 – a remarkably good one – was one of the first published documents to draw attention to Britain's falling share in world trade.' It warned that:

> if in present conditions the price of our exports generally were to be pushed up by a rise in internal costs, we should be taking a short-cut to national bankruptcy. Our competitive power would be disastrously weakened and the consequent worsening of the Balance of Payments would destroy for the time being any chances of a future improvement in the standard of living.

Yet in his pre-election budget speech in April 1955, Butler had to admit that in 1953–4 wages and salaries had gone up by three times output. On that road economic madness lay.

The logic of the railwaymen's victory was not lost on unions in other industries, and 1954 saw a significant rise in the number of days lost in strikes. These leapt from 1.4 million in 1950 to 2.5 million in 1954. No fewer than 3.8 million days were lost in 1955. As with the appeasement of inter-war Germany, treating the unions with kid gloves had the opposite effect of what was intended. Yet still the bouquets arrived. After Monckton had 'solved' the dock strike in November 1954 by giving the dockers almost everything they wanted, Sir Reginald Manningham-Buller, the Attorney-General, wrote to him: 'My dear Walter, Hooray – Hooray – many congratulations on yet another triumph. I do hope you'll get some peace now and no more of these strikes.' It was a vain hope, for as Christmas approached so did the prospects of the railwaymen coming back for more.

As Lord Woolton, the Chancellor of the Duchy of Lancaster, noted in his diary on 13 December 1954, 'A year ago precisely similar circumstances arose and as a result of the intervention and pressure of the P.M. the Transport Commission gave way. The men got an increase in pay which they regarded as insufficient. A section of them applied for more a few months later. ... The concession started a whole series of demands that have gone on all through the year in other industries.' At the Cabinet meeting called to discuss it, 'The P.M. said that a strike now might ruin our election prospects and also the Budget and his mind went back to the railway strike of 1924 and the subsequent general strike of 1926.' Churchill had long been accused of being anti-union; he was longing to lay that reputation to rest.

Woolton asked Monckton in Cabinet whether the railwaymen 'had used the appointed machinery of arbitration. Monckton said "no", because they knew that if they did they would only get, at most, one shilling or one shilling and sixpence a week; therefore they were determined to demand the 15%.' Woolton went on to recall that at this point Monckton, 'for the first time in my experience – was against giving way', as it would 'start off another series of demands from miners, postmen, engineers, etc.'. He at least had learned the lesson of the previous six months. Nevertheless, Churchill 'was unconvinced. He's frightened of a strike.'[57] Macmillan made the characteristically Machiavellian suggestion of appointing a committee which would put off a strike until after the cold weather. Toby Low, Minister of State at the Board of Trade, remembers: 'It wasn't Monckton who wanted to give into the railwaymen, it was Winston. You've got to carry people with you. ... Winston was an emotional man. He loved the railwaymen.'[58]

Robertson was to tell Birkenhead in 1969 that Monckton 'did counsel him to make a settlement ... if there was a weakness over this it was a collective weakness. Churchill did not want a strike.' One of the very few times the Cabinet was formally consulted on an industrial relations issue was over this threatened strike and they advocated surrender. Woolton himself wanted industrial peace 'even at the risk of entering into compromises that could only have an inflationary effect'. They went into it with their eyes open. As one historian of the period puts it, 'There is no evidence that the Churchill Government faced up, even to the extent that Attlee's had done in 1947–8, to the problem of public industry wages.'[59]

As so often in this period, it was Lord Salisbury who sounded the note of realism. He wrote to Churchill on 9 January 1955 warning that he did not think 'we have, by what we have done, by any means avoided the danger of a further railway strike'. He called for 'the most drastic reorganisation of the railways' to eliminate waste and overmanning, so that 'the [Transport] Commission may be put in a most favourable position to pay its way "taking one year with another"'.[60] As usual his advice was not taken. As Churchill's Private Secretary, David Pitblado, puts it, 'In earlier years Winston had dynamism, but in his last administration he was just keeping things going. ... He feared he'd decline rapidly once out of office.'[61] The same day that Salisbury was writing to the Prime Minister, the Scottish Secretary, James Stuart, told Butler that a remark that the Chancellor had made about Churchill 'being as bad as [NUR General Secretary James] Campbell amused me and was very true. He wanted "Peace in (his) time" at almost any price. He is indeed a queer kind of man.'[62]

It was thus under Monckton that the principle was established that nationalized industries could become a burden on the taxpayer, something which was not originally intended and was to have baleful implications for succeeding decades. When the interim report of Sir James Cameron QC's Board of Inquiry was published on 5 January 1955, it not only recommended 'substantially larger increases than had originally been offered', but also coined the phrase that, as far as the British Transport Commission was concerned, losses on the railways should be transferable from one year to the next. As the report famously put it, 'Having willed the ends, the nation must will the means.' As Stuart told Butler, 'Apparently the taxpayer is under an obligation to foot the bill of any nationalised industry whether they work and try to put their house in order – or not. The Act of Nationalisation said the opposite – to my mind. . . . It does seem to me that there ought to be some sort of stopper on the taxpayer's liability.' But his suggestion of a royal commission to look into the implications for the taxpayer was ignored, with disastrous results for the Exchequer during the 1960s and 1970s.

Orr-Ewing found it 'amazing that the Treasury allowed the Transport Commission to take on losses year on year' – which soon meant year *after* year. 'I was very surprised the Treasury never raised its head with those big inflationary wage rises and the British Transport Commission decision.' But Butler had been outmanoeuvred by Churchill and Monckton. The award was predicated upon 'comparability' and not upon the employer's ability to pay. Indeed, one historian of the industrial dispute tribunals, arbitration bodies and Ministry of Labour conciliators of the 1950s has dubbed all of them 'agents of inflation'.[63]

Neither should we assume that the Cameron Report was necessarily wholly impartial. Orr-Ewing recalls how 'Walter used to fix inquiries, so they found as you wanted. The idea of an independent inquiry is rubbish.'[64] Birkenhead was told by another insider, William Webber of the TUC's General Council, that, 'It has been stated that the Government exercises no influence on arbitrators. . . . Nevertheless it is remarkable how similar results have been. In 1953 many cases taken to arbitration resulted in a flat rate increase.' Neden threatened to resign after the December 1954 capitulation to the rail unions. He found that 'he did not get much help from Walter when things had gone too far. He could not recall one instance when Walter had really got tough on them.' Monckton charmed Neden into staying.

The railwaymen wanted parity with profitable private industry, and as 'the inquiries and settlements built up remorselessly, a pattern of comparability which had not been envisaged by the architects of nationalisation' emerged – which was to cause problems for all future Governments until the early 1980s. Neither was the Transport Commission particularly keen to hold settlements down once the principle had been established that the taxpayer would pick up the bill. Robertson told Birkenhead how his Deputy Chairman at the Commission had been Sir John Benstead, a former General Secretary with the NUR, and another important figure there was William Allen, a former General Secretary of ASLEF. By 1969 Robertson was willing to admit that 'it was perhaps open to question having railway trade unionists on his staff'.

British management in the immediate post-war period was almost as pusillanimous towards trade union demands as the Government itself. 'National Joint Advisory Council meetings became rather like a family tea party,' remembered Sir George Pollock, the Director-General of the British Employers' Federation from 1954 to 1965. Speaking in 1969, after the collapse of Labour's trade union policy, 'In Place of Strife', he told Birkenhead that 'Nothing happened, but nobody particularly wanted anything to happen at that time. . . . [It was not] fully appreciated that concessions in the cause of industrial peace would leapfrog into the situation we get now.'

Employers increasingly left relations with the workforce to the unions, and Jack Jones, then a district secretary in the Confederation of Ship-building and Engineering Unions, noticed how, during this period, 'a reluctance to face the workpeople applied to most industrialists with whom I had dealings'.[65] This was also true of Conservative politicians. As one of Monckton's successors has put it, 'Sheer ignorance of the realities of working-class life was responsible for a lot of Tory mistakes over the trade unions. In order to find out what working people thought they asked the trade union leaders!'[66]

After Cameron reported that the British Transport Commission, already in debt, should finance an increase, Monckton was immediately deluged with congratulations. 'Once again the Monckton magic has worked,' trumpeted the *Star*. Even the Queen sent a telegram praising his 'patience and powers of persuasion'. The Tory MP, Anthony Nutting, called it 'magnificent in every way', and the Warden of All Souls congratulated him on 'your repeated and miraculous personal triumphs'.

Once again the *Economist* was almost alone in pointing out that the emperor had no clothes. It explained how overmanned the railways were and argued that, 'by sweeping away restrictive practices and cutting down an inflated labour force, railwaymen could have been enabled to earn a much bigger increase'. They believed the Government should fight 'restrictionism, feather-bedding and neo-Luddite obstinacy'. The time had come to 'jettison the precepts of the emollient administration that have been found particularly useful over the last three years'. Instead, however, the Ministry was run by 'a policy-less mediator, more or less "akin to the Attorney-General", as one left-wing newspaper admiringly described Sir Walter Monckton last week'.[67]

This was the point at which the Government – having survived the dangerous first two years, in which the first priority had been to ensure that the wheels of industry kept turning – should have changed course. This was, however, simply not a policy over which Monckton, who prized his genuine friendships with the union leaders, could have presided. As the *New Statesman* – the paper referred to by the *Economist* – put it, 'he cannot, one suspects, be other than charming now – he has done it so often that the smile, the warm handshake, the caressing interest in everything that is said have become like something out of a Pavlov text-book'. According to the magazine:

> The tap is turned, the warm spray plays gently. It is as deliberate, as unsubtle as that ... he thinks that everyone is worth the effort. ... His real achievement as Minister of Labour is that he always sought to act as if he were one of the Law Officers of the Crown. Lacking any capacity for political passion, he has made it as nearly an unpolitical office as any man could.[68]

This was part of the problem. In Germany, Konrad Adenauer and Ludwig Erhard were achieving incredible advances in productivity and efficiency. Britain desperately needed someone to crack employer and employee heads together, and that man was not Walter Monckton. The only legislation with which he troubled the Statute Book during his period as Minister of Labour embraced regulations stating the hours during which bread could be baked. Although he had shown a new-found willingness to stand up to the rail unions in December 1954, it had not taken much persuasion from Churchill for him to give in to them. This would have been the ideal time for Monckton to move to the post of Lord Chief Justice which he so much coveted – but still Goddard hung on. Churchill refused his offer of resignation over ill-health and instead, on doctor's orders, Monckton took a two-month rest from mid-January 1955.

Union leaders were becoming 'deeply worried about the way power was draining down to the shop floor'. The London dock strikes of September 1954 had shown, according to Monckton's Private Secretary, 'how poor the unions were at putting their own house in order, the leaders were split from the chaps on the ground. Deakin tried but failed.'

This was welcomed by the younger, more militant generation of trade unionist such as Jack Jones. In his autobiography, *Union Man*, Jones recorded how Deakin 'held firmly to the view that workers should get no special advantage from nationalisation, which should be seen only as "serving the nation" '. It was a notion Jones found risible and much of the book is devoted to explaining how he and other young radicals outmanoeuvred the TUC top brass. This would have been halted by legislation introducing secret ballots and industrial democracy, but, ironically enough, this was blocked at every stage by the union leaders themselves.

Frank Chapple also remembers how after the communists took control of the ETU in the late 1940s:

> there was less and less consultation with the members, even those who, like me, helped the leadership by rigging meetings and ballots. The [Communist] Party group ... didn't have the members, but at any ETU conference they had the platform in their grip and enough of my kind on the floor to see that what they wanted was secured.[69]

In May 1956 the *Daily Mirror* brought out a special supplement on the trade unions. This estimated that only about one in sixty of the 216,000 ETU members was a communist, yet the country's ninth largest union was completely dominated by them. The General Secretary, Frank Foulkes, who had two years earlier been returned unopposed under the union's byzantine election rules, declared: 'I am a communist and proud of it.'

The *Mirror* supplement, which was researched by the twenty-five-year-old Gerald Kaufman, explained how non-unionists were not allowed to replace lightbulbs in offices. The job could only be done by authorized, card-carrying ETU members:

> The correct union practice is that first an electrician is summoned to diagnose the trouble. He then calls an assistant who brings a new bulb and, if necessary, a pair of step-ladders. The assistant hands the bulb to his mate who then inserts it in the socket. Testing takes place (flicking the switch) and, if satisfactory, the pair of them retire.

When Churchill left office in April 1955, it was during a newspaper strike, which meant that, much to his chagrin, no eulogies appeared about his long career in politics. This was, understandably, one of the few strikes in which Churchill intervened personally, but to no effect. After Eden comfortably won the May 1955 general election, he asked Monckton to stay on at the Ministry of Labour. No sooner was the election over than the railwaymen struck yet again and Monckton was forced to take emergency powers to deal with the crisis. Even this step was not taken, however, without the prior permission of senior TUC leaders. With dockers, miners, busmen and lightermen also coming out, Monckton had to work as hard as ever to settle.

Churchill, who assumed a tough stance on the issue once he had retired, wrote to Eden on 31 May to say that:

> Firmness in the rail strike is vital. It can only be based on patience at the outset. The national response may be overwhelming ... the timing of the strike by its leaders so as to try to hit the holiday-makers will be judged very cruel. Personally, I have always had a great liking for engine-drivers, and am astonished at their behaviour.[70]

He went on to say that although volunteers could efficiently and safely drive locomotives, 'this, however, would raise grave issues with the TUC'. By 14 June Monckton had bought off the strike. Unlike Neden, who thought they had once again been over-conciliatory, the press and public deluged Monckton with plaudits. The day after the strike was settled he was inundated with congratulations by everyone: from Irene, Baroness Ravensdale, to Miss Riley of 27, The Drive, Wallington, Surrey, 'and all her friends who travel with her on the 8.30 from Wallington'.

Oliver Lyttelton told Birkenhead much later how Monckton's 'profession had accustomed him to not saying "no". It was necessary to have peace with the unions, but after that he ought to have been relieved. He was excellent until the time came for him to say "no".' Lyttelton had a number of trade union friends, who told him frankly that 'we are getting a bit more than we ought.'[71] Shawcross also considered that 'it was arguable that on Winston's instructions he went too far ... that it would have been better to have had a show-down'. Yet even in November 1955, Butler was telling the Cabinet that the best way to instil 'restraint in industrial relations and wage claims' was 'to consider whether contact between the Government and the TUC could be improved'. There was simply no stomach for a confrontation.

Unpalatable though it may sound, in terms of inducing a sense of discipline in industrial relations Heron was correct when he said that 'there's no substitute for a bit of unemployment in the market'. As a future Employment Secretary was to say of the 1950s economy, 'There was no labour shortage, just massive over-manning.'[72] Government initiatives to deal with this were not instituted, largely out of fear of opposition from the trade unions.

At the Conservative Conference in Bournemouth in October 1955, the motions submitted by constituency associations once again reflected concern from the Tory grass-roots about industrial relations. Clapham wanted 'a period of reflection before a recommendation to strike is implemented', Eastleigh deplored secondary picketing, Walford proposed 'a secret ballot system of voting', Arundel attempted to draw attention to the 'ultimately disastrous effect of unchecked and unrealistic demands for higher wages, without a proportionate increase in productivity'. But predictably the motion chosen for 'debate' in the end was one which 'welcomes the initiative taken by the Prime Minister and the Minister of Labour in discussing with the British Employers' Federation, Trade Unions and nationalised industries, ways and means of avoiding recourse to strike action'.[73]

Although many of the strikes in 1955 came as a result of inter-union rivalry – the newspaper strike, for example, was about who should represent the printing maintenance men in negotiations with the employers – Monckton did nothing to induce the unions to reform themselves. By 1955 Gallup polls were showing that even a majority of Labour supporters thought the Government was erring on the side of weakness. Pressure grew for statutory ballots before strikes to become official, unofficial strikes to be declared illegal, compulsory arbitration before all disputes, and a Committee of Inquiry into political extremism in the trade union movement, but these were all turned down by Monckton out of hand. The reason was that he 'was apparently satisfied ... to carry on in the traditional way'.[74]

When Monckton finally left the Ministry in December 1955, after over four years at the post, Goddard – now seventy-nine – was still holding on as Lord Chief Justice, so Monckton elected to become Secretary of State for Defence. What should have been a quiet time for him turned out very differently when the Suez crisis erupted seven months later. Perhaps predictably, considering his previous career, Monckton was a leading 'dove' in the Cabinet, and along with Butler let it privately be known that he disapproved of the use of force. When asked by David Astor, the editor of the *Observer*, why he did not resign, he said: 'I owe my position to Anthony. It would be an act of betrayal. I can't be the person who knifes him and brings him down.'[75]

He resolved instead to accept Eden's offer to become Paymaster-General on health grounds, whilst remaining in the Cabinet. When a fellow Suez-sceptic, Lord Mountbatten, demanded an explanation, he said that 'by staying in the Cabinet I can hold the hot-heads', although there is little evidence of his having achieved that.[76] None the less, it was an honourable

stance to take. As he modestly wrote about the decision over armed intervention, 'inasmuch as my opinion was not shared by any of my colleagues,
a certain measure of humility demanded restraint in action on my part'.
Lady Monckton told Birkenhead that 'he had no intention of rocking the
boat'. Aneurin Bevan used to say that at the time of Suez, 'Tory shame was
only slightly alleviated by Walter Monckton – and then they didn't know
whether to wear him as a gas-mask or a jock strap.'.

Monckton left politics at the same time as Eden, in January 1957, and,
still unable to become Lord Chief Justice through Goddard's tenacity,
took over the Chairmanship of the Midland Bank. Having five years
earlier exchanged his £60,000 per annum for a Cabinet minister's
£5,000, he had every right to try to increase his fortune. At the Midland he
introduced many innovations to encourage popular capitalism. Personal
cheque-book accounts, wider share ownership and the introduction of
personal loans without conventional security were all pioneered under
his Chairmanship. He can legitimately claim to have been an early
proponent of the concept of the 'property-owning democracy', which was
first preached by Eden, but not actually put into practice in any serious
way until many years later.

He also took on various sensitive Establishment tasks, for which his
famous tact and discretion made him well suited. The Duke of Kent's
marriage settlement, Lady Caroline Howard's arrest for shoplifting, the
position of Group Captain Peter Townsend should he have married
Princess Margaret, and the publication of the German documents relating
to the Duke of Windsor's time in Spain and Portugal in 1940, as well as
dozens of other such sensitive issues, all crossed his desk. When in July
1964 a Mrs Joyce Hilda Wachman of 19 Mulberry Walk, Chelsea, wrote
to claim that she was the Duke of Windsor's unacknowledged child, it
was left to Monckton to put her mind at rest. He performed no greater
service for his old master, however, than when in early 1959 he managed
to cover up a potential scandal involving the Duke and Duchess of
Windsor, their private secretary and over a billion French francs of illegal
currency transactions.

In December 1958 the Duke of Windsor discovered that his private
secretary, Victor Waddilove, had been defrauding him on a systematic
basis. It had been going on for years, but the situation was rendered
especially delicate because the money he had stolen had itself been made
by the Duke's and Waddilove's secret dealings in the French currency
black market. Although the Duke had been given special financial
dispensations by both the British and French Governments, these deals,

which broke the strict exchange controls then in operation, were illegal. These now defunct laws were regularly evaded by British subjects who lived or travelled abroad, but probably never on quite the scale the Duke was employing.

At first Waddilove attempted to blame the shortfall on a wholly innocent secretary of the Duke's, who was sacked. But when his employer looked closer into it, whilst Waddilove was on holiday, the full scale of the fraud became clear. The Duke contacted his lawyer, Alan Philpotts of Hunter's, the Lincoln's Inn solicitors, to ask for advice on how he could get rid of Waddilove.

After studying an accountant's report, Philpotts wrote to say that 'it will always, I think, be difficult to say with absolute certainty what may have happened to substantial sums of cash; but there is undoubtedly circumstantial evidence which gives rise to the inference that your Secretary's explanations are unsatisfactory'.[77] Another former secretary to the Duke remembers how Waddilove used to take her to the d'Enghien casino outside Paris, where he would play roulette and baccarat for amounts far in excess of what he was paid by the Windsors.[78]

Philpotts brought Monckton in at an early stage of the affair. Together they gave the Duke three alternatives for dealing with Waddilove. The first, Plan A, was to keep him on whilst a full audit of the Duke's finances was performed. Philpotts pointed out that 'the disadvantages are that confidence may have been destroyed to such an extent that you and the Duchess could never feel comfortable in having him in your employ. Furthermore he may feel even under controls that he has "got away with it" and may try something else.'

Plan B was to 'indicate to the Secretary that ... the only course open is to invite him to tender his resignation [in return] for a year's salary'. Philpotts appreciated that the Duke 'may say that he has ample reserves – however acquired – to make this act on your part unnecessary, but one cannot be certain'. He added that both Monckton and the accountant, Mr Cucksey, approved this course. The third option was simply 'to give him notice'. However, Philpotts and Monckton were 'anxious that the situation should not be created which could give your Secretary a "comeback" which could only open up matters best left unopened'. All his advisers were keen to avoid the prospect of an action being brought by Waddilove against the Duke for wrongful dismissal.

On 15 December 1958, in the middle of these discussion, Waddilove himself wrote to Monckton from 63 The Ridge, Orpington. It was a letter of which Uriah Heep would have been proud:

May I ask your indulgence and valuable time to give me advice ... with the knowledge that your concern is as great as mine for the well-being of my principals. ... I have operated on the black market on their behalf for the past ten years, against my own conscience and the advice of [the Duke's solicitor] the late Sir George Allen. Unfortunately, I did not take that advice and in devotion to my employers continued these illegal operations to please them, and to benefit them to the extent of well over £200,000.

(That amount in the mid-1950s would be worth over £2.5 million in the mid-1990s.)

Waddilove disingenuously continued: 'I am now very worried that with the extension to others of the knowledge of these transactions there may be a leak of information. They have totalled over one and half billion Francs and have only been known to my principals and myself.' Waddilove went on to mention 'the unique status [the Windsors] have financially and diplomatically in France', with the unspoken implication that this would be fatally compromised if any legal action were taken against him. He also informed Monckton that he was protecting the Duke and Duchess because 'my own safety has been and is at stake as well'. Ending his letter saying 'your wisdom and experience is so much greater than mine ... Please forgive me for troubling you', Waddilove asked for an interview.

Turning down an invitation to holiday with Churchill at Marrakesh, Monckton met Waddilove at 11.00 a.m. on 7 January 1959 and attempted to persuade him to resign quietly. Afterwards he told Philpotts that, in his opinion, should Waddilove be dismissed, it would go to court, where 'his justification would depend on going into the very matters which I don't think we can afford to get into. Therefore the only course is to give him adequate notice of money in lieu of notice.' Another interview took place on 23 January, by which time Waddilove was hinting he had been offered a six-figure sum – an astonishing amount for the time – by a national newspaper for his story.

By now the affair had widened to include Sir Edward Peacock, a former director of Barings Bank and also a director of the Bank of England, who was brought in to handle the financial side of whatever was decided. Peacock was a former Receiver-General to the Duchy of Cornwall and had advised the Duke on financial affairs before. Another Barings director, Lord Ashburton, the Receiver-General of the Duchy of Cornwall, was also recruited. They both advised that 'unless Waddilove is left in peace he will take [the newspaper] on'. Monckton recorded in a memorandum that Ashburton 'is going to warn the Queen in vague terms that something may blow up'.[79] Meanwhile, Philpotts wrote a strong letter to the Duke advising him to drop the idea of prosecuting Waddilove.

The negotiations dragged on until May, by which time a thorough investigation of the Duke's finances had been carried out by another former Barings employee, John Masters. In the course of this, Masters had a four-hour interview with Waddilove and, according to Monckton's memorandum of his report, 'the deals in which the Duke has been engaged in French Francs on the black market' had been part of a much wider crime ring. 'It would appear that the sum involved is something like FF 1.5 billions, and that in the last year or two a profit of something like FF 600 million has been shown.' One of the Duke's intermediaries, the banker 'Lacazes, who is now in goal, appears to have been one of the dealers for the Duke'. Furthermore, Loel Guinness, a friend of the Duke's, 'has been advised to keep out of France and is now in Switzerland'. This was because of Guinness's 'own deals on this market on his own account'. To make matters worse, Masters reported that 'on occasions he believes the Duke has done the actual work on the market himself personally'.[80]

The Duke managed further to exacerbate the situation by criticizing his long-time personal banker, Maurice Amiguet of Swiss Bank, 'for not protecting his interests'. As Masters told Monckton, 'Amiguet has in consequence disclosed all that he knows to the Swiss Bank'. On top of that, 'the fact of the Duke's business in the black market is known to Montreal bankers'. The story was beginning to get out. Masters went on to warn Monckton that if, possibly on the advice of his over-litigious American lawyers, the Duke decided to proceed against Waddilove, 'it will be impossible to keep the deals in the French Franc market out of publicity'. Furthermore, the French Finance Minister, Antoine Pinay, 'with the backing of General de Gaulle', was 'at present probing into all these black market deals', and could in any case easily discover the Duke's 'particular instance'. If he did, Masters thought 'that would have an effect on the Duke's present freedom from tax and from death duties'. Monckton immediately picked on this as 'the best point on which to hang advice to the Duke about Waddilove'.[81] In 1939 the Duke of Windsor had refused to return to England to campaign against the war, partly because coming back would have made him liable for British income tax. It was shrewd of Monckton to spot the tax angle as a clinching argument to use with the Duke.

Monckton saw Masters – who had worked for the Duke when he was

Prince of Wales – the day after reading his memorandum. He was told that Ashburton 'has had some more or less informal talk with the Queen's Private Secretary Sir Michael Adeane because he feels that the position and reputation of the Crown may be affected'. Adeane encouraged him to go to Monckton. He in turn would 'persuade the Duke and Duchess to come to London where we can have a full talk'. Whether true or not, the rumour was getting around that Waddilove was now being offered a quarter of a million pounds for his story, but was refusing it for the opportunity of leaving his job without prosecution.

Monckton steered the Duke towards the only sensible conclusion to the affair: Waddilove was paid off and allowed to return to Kent unprosecuted, where he eventually died in July 1991. It is largely due to Monckton that this scandal has never come to light, and in July 1959, in conjunction with Peacock and others, he put the Duke's financial affairs in order, especially over foreign currency exchange. The Windsors continued to be treated as special cases by the French authorities, and on Monckton's advice Peacock was added to their Christmas card list.

The final public service Monckton undertook was to chair the commission which reviewed the constitution of the Central African Federation, a country made up of Nyasaland (now Malawi), Northern Rhodesia (now Zambia) and Southern Rhodesia (now Zimbabwe). The 1955 Conservative Manifesto had stated that: 'We uphold the principle of racial partnership as exemplified in the new Federation of the Rhodesias and Nyasaland so auspiciously launched and increasingly enjoying the confidence of Europeans and Africans.' But by February 1960 the Macmillan Government was bending under what it considered to be serious African pressure to allow Northern Rhodesia the right of secession from the Federation.

Although the Monckton Commission was intended to be 'an educative instrument and a stimulus to discussion rather than an exact blueprint for the future', and was not supposed even to consider the issue of secession, Monckton knew what the British Government expected of him, just as the chairmen of countless industrial relations Committees of Inquiry had known what Monckton expected of them without necessarily having to be told in so many words. As Lord Home, the Commonwealth Relations Secretary at the time, confided to Birkenhead, 'although Monckton did not advocate secession, they suggested that a qualified right of opt out should be given' – which amounted to much the same thing.

Although Sir Roy Welensky, the Federation's Prime Minister, rejected the Report, 'it was a mortal blow to the Federation'. Lyttelton believed that 'at the time evidence of African opposition to the Federation was very slight. Ninety-nine per cent of them did not know there was a Federation, or what it meant.'[82] He thought the appointment of the Commission an error because 'it recommended secession off their own bat'. He believed that it was the British Government's lack of support that destroyed the Federation, which represented a great hope for non-racial democracy in Southern Africa. The result was that the country split up soon afterwards, Malawi and Zambia becoming left-wing, one-party states and Rhodesia eventually unilaterally declaring independence from the British Crown.

There is evidence that Monckton had made up his mind as to what to report before even setting foot in Africa to hear evidence. He had a meeting at the Midland Bank with David Astor, editor of one of the very few papers hostile to the Federation. 'He said he was just off,' recalls Astor; 'he had reached the firm conclusion that Federation was an error.' Monckton was thus canvassing press support for a report which he knew would go beyond his remit and help scupper the Federation. As Home admitted, 'the Government were ... not surprised at the course events took'.

One of the Commission members, Aidan Crawley, told Birkenhead: 'The Federation was never "sold" at all to the Africans by the British Government. British officials ... decided to adopt a neutral attitude towards it. The Africans felt that if these wise men were so indifferent to it the thing must be a wash-out, despite the great economic advantages the Federation brought the Africans of Northern Rhodesia.' Even Iain Macleod, who welcomed its collapse, admitted to Birkenhead in 1969 that 'the advantages of the Federation were indeed great, and some African leaders now say that a federal structure will at some time return for this reason'.

Welensky rejected the Commission's recommendations, but the damage to his country's legitimacy had been done. As Home later agreed:

Welensky could represent the Monckton recommendations as a technical breach of engagements, thus H.M.G. had always assured him that the terms of reference would not include the question of a right of secession and they did recommend a qualified right. To that extent Welensky had a grievance.[83]

This was something of an understatement, considering what Monckton had done to wreck the Federation, albeit for the highest of liberal Tory motives. Macleod believed, 'African leaders always demanded more than they could get, it was a form of negotiation Walter was familiar with from his Ministry of Labour days.' But, as his report showed, Monckton had neither learned nor forgotten anything from that period.

'In industrial relations,' says Frank Chapple, 'if you reward bad behaviour you'll get more of it. The Churchill Government's appeasement policy was based on a fear of the strength of the labour movement. Whatever they did was designed to smooth over and avoid too much of a rough and tumble.' By February 1962 Macmillan was writing to the Australian Prime Minister, Sir Robert Menzies, that 'all the moderate trade union leaders tell me how alarmed they are at the way the Communists are infiltrating into their executives and getting the leading positions'.[84]

A communist until 1957, Chapple remembers how:

> the 1951–6 period had been good for us but bad for democracy. Organisations that are not legitimate, responsible or democratically accountable could wreak havoc on the nation. ... In the branches the militants were working away in groups, elections were rigged, open-air meetings and shows of hands were mis-counted, decent people were discouraged from becoming candidates.

As Minister for Labour during that period, Monckton must bear heavy responsibility for this state of affairs. His legendary charm and powers of persuasion were of little use against growing hard-left intransigence. The emollience he showed, while probably necessary at the very beginning to prove that the Conservatives could work with the unions, ended by sending entirely the wrong messages to organized labour. By the 1960s and 1970s trade union militancy threatened the British economy and even brought down a Conservative Government.

On 21 January 1974 the Prime Minister, Edward Heath, was speaking to five Tory backbenchers in the Smoking Room in the House of Commons. 'Nowadays,' he told them, 'because of the weakness of successive Governments, the unions always believe there is something to go for. It is only when they are convinced there is nothing more that they will sit down and start negotiations.'[85] Five weeks later his majority disappeared in the 'Who Governs Britain?' general election, and within nine months Labour had an overall majority. The Conservatives had been defeated in part by the National Union of Mineworkers and their allies.

One of the backbenchers listening to Heath that day had been Norman Tebbit, who later served as Margaret Thatcher's Secretary of State for Employment. Her Government introduced many of the reforms to limit overweening union power at which Sir Walter Monckton and successive liberal Tory Ministers of Labour had always balked. It was the first time in history that the dragon was slain by the maiden rather than the knight.

6

Patriotism: The Last Refuge of Sir Arthur Bryant

On 19 February 1979 London's literary, political and historical world came together in the Vintners Hall for a dinner to pay tribute to Sir Arthur Bryant CH, CBE, LLD, FRHist.S, FRSL on his eightieth birthday. The author of over forty books, a columnist on the *Illustrated London News* for more than four decades, and knighted by Churchill, Bryant sat between a former Prime Minister and the Archbishop of Canterbury. Other guests included the then Prime Minister, James Callaghan, a brace of Field Marshals, the Chairman of Times Newspapers, half a dozen knights and over two dozen peers and peeresses. The historian Dr A.L. Rowse of All Souls, Oxford, gave one of the many speeches. It was, as one of those present has put it, 'Bryant's apotheosis as the Grand Old Man of British historical writing'.

Shortly after winning the 1945 general election, Clement Attlee asked Churchill what he would be doing in the immediate future. He said that he wanted to write history books, whereupon the Labour leader asked the outgoing Premier to name his favourite living historian. Churchill answered that it was Arthur Bryant, which struck Attlee as a coincidence because he was his too.[1] Bryant's bestselling histories of the Napoleonic Wars had been the literary counterparts of those of Churchill's speeches which had urged the British people to emulate the great heroes of the past. His accounts of Trafalgar and the Peninsula campaigns echoed Churchill's own 'Finest Hour' exhortations about the feats of Drake and Nelson. 'History', as Churchill put it in 1940, 'with its flickering lamp stumbles along the trail of the past, trying to reconstruct its scenes, to revive its echoes, and kindle with pale gleams the passion of former days.' At the time no historian was busier rekindling those passions than Bryant.

Yet Churchill, Attlee and those distinguished guests in the Vintners Hall could not have known what the expiry of the Fifty Year Rule and the subsequent opening of Bryant's private papers can now tell us: that far from being the patriot he so long and loudly proclaimed himself, Bryant was in fact a Nazi sympathizer and fascist fellow-traveller, who only narrowly escaped internment as a potential traitor in 1940. He was also, incidentally, a supreme toady, fraudulent scholar and humbug.

Born in 1899, Bryant was the son of a Court official and grew up at Windsor. His father never held the position there of which Bryant subsequently boasted to clubland acquaintances, but it might have been from that environment that he acquired his talent for flattery. He then went to Harrow, where his Housemaster, Mr Mayo, had many years before taught Churchill. Mayo told Bryant how he had once exclaimed rhetorically to an unruly class: 'I don't know what to do with you boys', only for Churchill's hand to shoot up from the back: 'Please, Sir, teach us!'

At eighteen, Bryant joined the Royal Flying Corps and spent the last eighteen months of the Great War serving in France. From his letters to his parents it is clear that his attitude altered in November 1918 from an intense dislike of all things German to an equally irrational 'radical compassion, even moral envy, for Germany'. So profound was his sympathy with the aspirations of the defeated German people that he was to suspend his critical faculties wherever the former enemy was concerned.[2] It was, of course, a fine Christian reaction to wish magnanimously to appease the conquered foe, but Bryant's sympathies were to go way beyond such decent, acceptable sentiments.

After a period as a teacher, first at Holloway and then as Headmaster of the Cambridge School of Arts and Crafts, Bryant became educational adviser to Conservative Central Office in 1927. He swiftly identified himself with the policies of the Prime Minister, Stanley Baldwin, and two years later published a paean to Baldwinite Toryism called *The Spirit of Conservatism*. It explained, in a glutinous style that Bryant was to make his own, how the spirit of the past – 'that sweet and lovely breath of Conservatism' – could recreate 'a world of genial social hours and loved places, upon which the conservative heart of Everyman can cast anchor'. His political philosophy constantly harked back to a Golden Age, in which Britain basked in Peace and Prosperity, when there was no discontent or civil unrest, and happy ruddy-cheeked yokels tilled the fields, whistling. He was never so rash as to put a date on this supposed period in our history, but it formed the basis of his attacks on anyone – capitalists, Jews, liberals, socialists – who he felt disturbed this eternal idyll. It also inspired his anti-industrial attitudes, for he never appreciated the connection between the manufacturing industry he despised and the rise of the British Empire he admired.

The Spirit of Conservatism also contained patronizing references to the 'alien' Disraeli, who, despite his Jewishness, nevertheless succeeded in becoming a good Tory. His chapter on 'the white man's burden' explained that he did not think democracy worked for everyone, a belief that was later to have sinister implications when he applied it to the Europe of the 1930s. To orientals, for example, the idea of the vote, the ballot and democracy were 'unintelligible'. A brief sideswipe against 'the speculator and jerry-builder' was all he allowed himself in his strictures against capitalism, but it was in his chapter on foreign policy that he gave voice to his most telling hostage to fortune. He stated that the Great War could not have broken out had Germany believed that Britain would fight for Belgian neutrality and thus 'the well-meaning vacillation of certain English statesmen' made possible a war which no nation would otherwise have dared to precipitate.[3] It was a lesson he was completely to forget over the coming decade.

As a sideline, Bryant co-ordinated the Greenwich pageants, huge tableaux which floated along the Thames, with up to three thousand people taking part. Schoolchildren and volunteers dressed in historical costume to represent different episodes of 'Our Island Story' and were watched by the royal family and vast crowds of spectators. His first foray into writing history came in 1931, when he published a revisionist biography of King Charles II. Its central theme was that the King had made Britain safe for Toryism. The Oxford historian, Hugh Trevor-Roper, has called it 'superficial, lacking judgment and, in particular, a toadying book'.[4] It was Bryant's first two works on Samuel Pepys, *The Man in the Making* and *The Years of Peril* (published in 1933 and 1935 respectively), which gained him his reputation as a historian and scholar. This can now be seen to be largely undeserved.

The distinguished historian of the seventeenth century, Dr J.R. Tanner of St John's College, Cambridge, had been writing a life of Pepys when he died in 1931. His well-ordered and voluminous notes took his subject up to 1689, and the Cambridge University Press passed them on to Bryant, whose sole achievement was to write them up into book form. Yet when Bryant's book appeared, Tanner received a cursory

289

acknowledgment, along with nineteen other people and in only the penultimate paragraph of the Preface. The proof that Bryant was not up to the whole job is demonstrated by the fact that his book ends at the point when Tanner's research notes ran out, in 1689 – although Pepys lived for another fourteen years.[5]

In 1934 Bryant wrote *The National Character*, a series of syrupy semi-historical essays, on 'The Country Gentleman', 'The Craftsman', 'The Yeoman Farmer', and so on. It more than merits Sir Jack Plumb's comment that Bryant vulgarized history to a degree that made it no longer credible and 'his failure was of intellect'.[6] Rowse agrees with the latter judgment, believing that Bryant was 'a good historical landscapist but second-rate intellectually'.[7] Of the yeoman farmer, Bryant eulogized 'that blood I think we may call the measure of our common Englishry', inaugurating what was to be a half-century career of chocolate-box history about 'Englishry'. 'If to be proud of one's forefathers and to honour their honest virtues is sentimentality,' wrote this Uriah Heep of historical writing, 'I must plead guilty.'

His other book of that year was a collection of essays on world statesmen entitled *The Man and the Hour: Studies of Six Great Men of Our Time*. He asked Ernest Tennant, the Chairman of the Anglo-German Friendship society, to write the chapter on Hitler. Tennant had already written pro-Nazi articles in the *English Review*, and his piece for Bryant was a predictable panegyric to the Führer ('he is quite a good artist ... he has a good sense of humour and enjoys hearing and telling a good story ... he is not naturally ruthless'). Yet nothing in it could rival the editor's concluding chapter.

In a year which saw the Night of the Long Knives, Bryant wrote that 'Hitler, like all the best Germans, is a mystic', and praised 'the mystic dream of inspired leadership and disciplined unity' in Germany: 'In awakening her, Hitler has shown himself to be a great German.' He likened Hitler's 'vital and passionate quality' of sincerity to that of Cromwell, an analogy he was often to return to in later years. Writing of Mussolini's 'magnificent achievement' and Germany's new 'prophets and heroes', Bryant wound up with the 'It may not do for us, old boy, but they seem to like it' argument. He believed that Germany was 'happy and self-sufficient in her own somewhat mystic conception of life and government', which he thought could exist side by side with neighbours 'who rule their lives on considerations far otherwise'.

Meanwhile, Bryant was editing the quarterly journal of the Bonar Law Conservative College in Ashridge, Hertfordshire. Donated by the former

Tory Prime Minister, Ashridge housed Conservative Party 'think-tanks', conferences and lectures. In the 1930s, its weekend courses on defence and foreign affairs became an intellectual centre for appeasement, whose influence on Tory thinking was more important than the commonly cited scapegoats of Cliveden and All Souls. Senior politicians went there to discuss aspects of government policy with Tory thinkers and Party activists. Bryant was rarely absent, becoming a Governor in 1935.

In the March 1934 issue of *The Ashridge Journal*, Bryant's editorial proudly disclosed that when the Gestapo searched luggage at the Reich's frontiers, 'publications, peanuts, the works of Feuchtwanger, ladies' lingerie and other objects were constantly stripped, surcharged and even burnt, but only "The Ashridge Journal" passes untaxed and unpersecuted'. This was hardly surprising: Bryant rarely allowed a word of criticism of Nazism into his publication.

The Spanish Civil War allowed Bryant to indulge his fondness for both political propaganda and authoritarian regimes. His notes for a letter to Baldwin after a visit to Spain in April 1935 show how Bryant saw Hitler as the defender of Christian civilization. It was a common enough belief at the time; what makes Bryant specially culpable is how long he clung to it.

The year 1936 saw the beginnings of the social advancement Bryant believed he deserved. He was invited to Lady (Sibyl) Colefax's dinner parties, where he found he could butter up important people. His closest friend, Dr A.L. Rowse, emphasizes Bryant's great powers of charm, but always 'felt dear Arthur was a flatterer ... rather indiscriminate in his praise'.[8] His 'instant' biography of George v, which appeared only a month after the King's death, was so gushing that he makes Richard Dimbleby look a dangerous subversive. The forelock-tugging was all topped off with a paean to 'Englishry' which was intended to be mystical but was instead risible. 'The island was bathed in half-faery translucent light' reads a typical sentence describing the King's Jubilee, 'the mean, the shoddy and the cheapjack had suddenly and mysteriously vanished and proud England had again become England'.[9]

A letter Bryant wrote to *The Times* from his rooms in D3 Albany in May 1936 inaugurated his campaign to inveigle himself into the good counsels of the BBC. He wrote that almost from the first moment he entered the building, he was made aware of the 'eager efficiency, cheerfulness, consideration and good manners' of 'every official, high and low'.[10] Sure enough, when the following March it was announced that a talks advisory committee was to be established to discuss BBC policy, Bryant was a member. He was later to use his position to complain that anti-appeasers such as Harold Nicolson were given radio air-time to criticize Chamberlain's foreign policy.

Another bout of unctuousness came in 1937, when *Stanley Baldwin: A Tribute* was published to coincide with the Prime Minister's retirement. In his eulogy to 'one of the greatest Prime Ministers of all time', Bryant took the opportunity to attack those 'hot-heads' who opposed Baldwin over such issues as air rearmament against Germany.[11] In July 1937 Bryant was chosen to run the National Book Association (NBA), a Tory book club designed to rival the Right Book Club, which was itself intended to challenge Victor Gollancz's Left Book Club. Bryant became General Editor, Baldwin himself was the President, and Lords Halifax and Davidson were Vice-Presidents. The Chairman of the Publishing Committee was Walter Hutchinson, and it was based in Paternoster House in the City of London. Membership was free and books cost 2s 6d.

In April 1937 Douglas Jerrold, a director of the *English Review*, had reported to Bryant how the Catholic writer, Arnold Lunn, had asked him if 'this book club of Bryant's is genuinely right-wing, because otherwise I will not write for it'. He was told that it certainly was. The people Bryant had earmarked to contribute books included George Trevelyan, A.P. Herbert, Hugh Cecil, T.S. Eliot, Wyndham Lewis, G.K. Chesterton, André Maurois, Sir Charles Petrie, Keith Feiling, Compton Mackenzie and Sir Basil Liddell Hart, most of whom were moving away from Bryant's type of politics by 1937. In the event, hardly any of them wrote for the NBA, which instead published the rants of men who sailed dangerously close to the fascist wind.

Lunn's own contribution, *Spanish Rehearsal*, came out in 1937. 'I see the soldiers passing through the street,' he wrote in chapter three, 'the note of gay colour in the Phalangist crests and the red berets of the Carlists, and I hear the song of troops on the march: "Up, squadrons and let us conquer, for the dawn is breaking ... ".' Lunn wrote that when the Nationalist General Mola 'rose on the balcony of Burgos, Spain knew that the black night of fear had passed'. Bryant praised the book highly, a major reservation being that he should, whenever possible, refer not to Franco but to Nationalist Spain: 'People think of the former as a dictator and not as a saviour; you have got first to convert them.'[12] Lunn's later NBA books, including *Whither Europe?* published in 1940, attempted to do just that.

To another political contributor, Francis Yeats-Brown, author of *Bengal*

Lancer, Bryant had to commiserate that the time had 'unhappily passed when a current biography of Franco, even if written by you, could have much chance of obtaining sympathy in this deluded country'. Bryant knew precisely what he was getting when he commissioned Yeats-Brown. As early as October 1933, Yeats-Brown's review of *Mein Kampf* spoke of the Nazis' 'ideal of brotherhood, and a soul behind the flaunting swastikas'.[13] He was a member of the National Headquarters branch of Mosley's British Union of Fascists and for the past six years had contributed to the magazine *Fascist Week*.[14] Yeats-Brown, who was soon a regular guest at Bryant's country home, the White House at Claydon in Buckinghamshire, eventually did write a book for the NBA entitled *European Jungle*. It spoke of the Spanish fascists' 'lofty enthusiasm, self-sacrifice and sanctity'.[15] Writing to Bryant just after the *Anschluss* in March 1938, he enthused: 'Dear Arthur, I am just back from Germany and Vienna where I saw Hitler drive in: a historic moment.'

Bryant also wanted the Tory MP, Sir Arnold Wilson, who had 'an admiration for many aspects of the Nazi regime', to write on 'Hitler's Germany', and Evelyn Waugh to discuss the German mandated territories in Africa. Bryant himself was going to write books with such titles as 'St George for England: A Forgotten Ideal' and 'Colonel Blimp Answers Back'. In the end, apart from his own biography of Baldwin and a selection of Baldwin's speeches, the only work to reach the first NBA list was by Admiral Sir Barry Domvile.

In his autobiography, *By and Large*, published in 1936, Domvile had explained that he was

> far from adopting the sloppy sentimental attitude towards the Jewish race which is so popular in this country. ... It is only because the Jews have so thoroughly impregnated big business and the Press in this country that we make such a song about their treatment in Germany. ... if we were not such a tolerant race there would have been trouble long ago.[16]

Domvile even wrote, 'I have a number of Jewish friends whom I like very much, but that does not carry me as far in mawkish sentiment as some of our papers go when sitting in judgment on the Nazis.' When visiting Germany, he was shown around Dachau, coincidentally on the same day as a story appeared 'of a British Jew-boy who had been in a concentration camp'. He made light of this fact. It was this man's second foray into the world of letters that Bryant was responsible for publishing.

Discussing the title of the new book, Bryant wrote to Domvile in July 1937: 'I feel that there are too few people in England who hold our views for us to be able to afford to quarrel.' Lady Domville had to cancel their dinner with Bryant that week 'as the Ribbentrops have to entertain all the sports people who are coming over from Germany'. Domvile was 'convinced that you must become – by some means or other – the Guide, Philosopher and Friend of your people.' The same month another meeting had to be postponed as 'I may have – very probably – to go to Rome in a few days to see M . . . .'.[17] The sailor's clumsy attempt at concealing Mussolini's identity shows that even then Bryant's confederates were aware of the gravity of their activities.

Bryant had close connections with Conservative Central Office and the Chairman there, Douglas Hacking MP, wrote regularly commending his work. In June 1937 Hacking lunched with Noël Coward to try to persuade him to write for Bryant. 'The chairman had heard rumours that he wanted to go into political life,' wrote Sir Patrick Gower, the Chief Publicity Officer at Central Office, who was also at the lunch:

> He also wanted to consult him about some of the Left-wing propaganda that is appearing on the stage, in particular the 'Sybil Thorndike Lewis Casson Company' which is touring the country under the auspices of the TUC giving performances of 'The Six Men of Dorset' based on the story of the Tolpuddle Martyrs. We had a most interesting talk.

They ascertained that although Coward was not contemplating a political career himself, 'his sympathies are entirely with us . . . he said it was only after [*Cavalcade*] had been put on that he realised the value of it from the point of view of National propaganda'. Despite Hacking's overtures, Coward – a staunch anti-Nazi – did not take up the opportunity to write for Bryant.[18]

Later that year came the first glimmerings of a backlash against Bryant's propaganda activities. The anti-appeasement Tory MP, the Duchess of Atholl, wrote to Hacking complaining that the NBA was publishing a book by a White Russian named Korostovetz, whom she believed to be a Nazi agent. Instead of investigating these claims, Hacking passed the letter straight on to Bryant, who replied five months later that 'the Duchess has entirely identified herself with the Communists' position, which, unfortunately, also includes the destruction of Conservatism and all that we mean by civilisation'.[19] Later that month another anti-appeasement Tory MP, Vyvyan Adams, visited Hacking with the Duchess to complain that Yeats-Brown's projected NBA book was 'extremely ill-advised, especially in view of his statement that, in certain circumstances, he would fight against this country. Surely our Party does not want to be associated with this kind of Fascism.' Bryant had no difficulties associating himself with it, even after July 1939 when he was told by Yeats-Brown that the Government had found Yeats-Brown 'too Fascist' to be appointed to a diplomatic post.[20]

Writing in the *Observer* in June 1937, Bryant protested that the fascist and Nazi regimes received a 'torrent of unmeasured and provocative calumny' from the anti-appeasers. He attacked the 'yelling invective, like a pack of fish-wives', which these 'war-mongers' used in order to 'stir up prejudices against Germany'. He went on to predict that it would 'not be the Kaiser whom the man in the street would want to hang after the next war', with the clear implication that it would instead be the likes of Winston Churchill. Bryant made it clear to which of the particular 'foolish Tories' he was referring when he said that they had 'tried to strangle Bolshevism at birth'. Attacking the 'old jingo writ large', he accused Churchill and his friends – although never by name – of 'concealing and perverting the truth for partisan ends. ... They really want another war.'[21]

His philippic pleased Yeats-Brown, who wrote that it 'filled me with delight, also several other people where I was staying for the weekend. Many of us look to you, in these days.' Bryant replied that he had appreciated his letter more than he could say. A fortnight later, writing in the same newspaper, Bryant likened Franco to William of Orange 'and the patriots of our Glorious Revolution', forgetting perhaps that the 1688 Revolution was also bloodless, and that the Whigs did not celebrate their victory by slaughtering 100,000 of their countrymen.

Bryant's information about Spain came direct from Franco's Embassy in London; so his claim that 350,000 people had been 'butchered in cold blood' by the Republicans in Valencia since July 1936 was pure fascist propaganda. Writing to his friend the Spanish Marquess del Moral, in late June 1937, he said that he followed the fight of 'your gallant compatriots, who stand for everything that civilised and Christian people value, with the deepest sympathy'. In September he told his *Observer* readers that the bombardment of Guernica was no more an 'atrocity' than the British bombing of cities like Frankfurt and Mannheim during the Great War, and claimed that Guernica was 'a military objective, full of troops and munitions and a key part of the defences in the operations then in progress'.[22]

The sensible stance for a Briton to take towards the struggle in Spain would have been that of Henry Kissinger towards the Iran–Iraq War: 'A pity they both can't lose.' Instead, Bryant's unquestioning apology for jackboot atrocities was constantly reiterated in his *Illustrated London News* column, 'Our Notebook', which he had taken over from G.K. Chesterton in 1936. The magazine continually extolled Germany's new *autobahns* and featured double-page spreads on her colonial claims. Bryant's cooing articles blended well with the overall tone of this house magazine of appeasement.

In an August 1936 article on the Berlin Olympics, entitled 'Doing in Rome as Rome Does', Bryant took a BBC commentator to task for filling in time during an unexpectedly long address of welcome to Hitler with humorous comments on the seriousness with which the Germans were taking the opening ceremonies. Bryant was outraged that the commentator 'even went on talking during the Führer's brief speech'. Believing that 'the proper pride' the Germans were taking in their 'reformed nationhood' was 'not a fit subject for humour', Bryant even went on to say that British athletes ought to have given Hitler the Nazi salute as they paraded past his box. He could not see why they should not have 'gone a little out of their way to make this friendly gesture to their hosts'.[23]

In a book Bryant published in 1937, entitled (without a trace of irony) *Humanity in Politics*, he said that the fascism of Germany, Hungary, Italy and Spain arose from the desperation of 'peaceable and ordinary folk' who felt it better to die than to see 'every decent rule and tradition of civilisation trampled underfoot by the brute force of a heartless, unthinking mob'. According to him, 'the average Britisher's attitude' towards fascism was 'even more perilous to the peace of the world' than the phenomenon itself.[24] In Bryant's semantics, true fascism had 'no resemblance whatever to the foolish, provocative and completely unnecessary play-acting under the name of Fascism which we know in England'. Bryant considered Mosley to be a laughable Roderick Spode sound-alike rather than a bona fide fascist leader.

According to Bryant, the British did not permit personal liberty and freedom of speech 'when the foundations of our own state ... were threatened by our enemies of twenty years ago'. Here the historian once again gave way to the polemicist. For just as Burke had opposed the war against the American colonists, Charles James Fox had expressed scepticism about the Napoleonic Wars and Lloyd George had stood out against the Boer War, so Ramsay MacDonald had condemned the Great War without any threat of the retribution which the fascists promised against those who followed their consciences.

Bunkum masquerading as history fills the pages of *Humanity in Politics*. There is also a good deal of the anti-capitalist, quasi-national socialism he was to preach throughout his life. 'I have no quarrel with Communism as such,' he argued on page ten. He said that there was something to be said for 'a system of life in which all men automatically share the same goods and amenities instead of competing for them'. Competition and the free market were anathema to Bryant, whose Golden Age was essentially rural, pre-industrial and non-materialistic. As is customary with Utopian political philosophers, he led his own life on very different lines. Bryant was intensely materialistic and acquisitive, collecting valuable pieces of furniture and paintings through shrewd bidding at auction. His popular histories brought in vast royalties, with which he purchased a succession of large and beautiful old houses, including one in Salisbury's Cathedral Close. He had sound financial ability and a good eye for traditional art, and there is little indication that he ever wanted 'all men' to share any of *his* 'goods and amenities'.

As 1938 dawned, Bryant's tone grew more dogmatic and aggressive. In a review of *Thoughts and Talks*, a book about foreign policy by Sir Arnold Wilson, he attacked the 'petulant, shrill-voiced, mean-tempered men' who disagreed with the author, and commended the way Wilson's 'warmth of sympathy and strong sense of the needs of common humanity' made him comprehend 'the ordinary decent Italian or German who wholeheartedly supports the Dictators who have restored their native countries not to liberty, but at any rate to some measure of order, common decency and self-respect'.[25] The sentences got longer as the tone became shriller. A growing contempt for British democracy was also becoming discernible in Bryant's political discourses. He went on to congratulate Wilson for never failing to distinguish democracy 'from the corrupt and racket-ridden sham that so often passes by the name', and condemned 'the plutocratic Christmas revels in our so-called democratic Press'.

In the third volume of his Pepys biography, *The Saviour of the Navy*, published at the time of the Munich Agreement, Bryant ruthlessly twisted historical evidence to fit the political point he was attempting to make. Having earlier identified Franco with William of Orange, he now saw his protagonist, James II, as a Franco-style dictator whom 'the better and more thoughtful' Protestant English had 'called to the throne to save the realm from anarchy and their estates and church from spoliation'. As a result, thought Bryant, they could not complain because he used his power 'to protect the religion which he had openly professed in the days of exile and proscription'.[26] This is yet more historical *legerdemain*, for no-one 'called' James II to the throne; he acceded to it as younger brother and legitimate heir of Charles II.

Bryant's anti-democratic sentiments rose in pitch during the weeks before Munich. Beside a full-page portrait of Chamberlain in the *Illustrated London News* on 3 September 1938, he rhetorically asked whether communism, fascism, Nazism and Phalangism were any less successful than government by 'the vote-catchers and share-pushers of our own despised pluto-democracy or demo-plutocracy'. The next week he predicted that the Sudeten crisis would mean 'as little to our descendants as the Danubian crises of the nineteenth century. . . . It would seem a far lesser disaster for mankind' if Czechoslovakia should vanish altogether under 'the hammer blows of Hitler's army' than if there should be world war. What he refused to consider was Churchill's fear that Czechoslovakia would indeed disappear and there would be a world war as well.

Bryant concluded that there was nothing new about races being subjected to one another: 'It has occurred ever since the world began.'[27] Yet the idea of the Aryan Sudetens being subjected to Slavs revolted him. In the post-Munich issue of *The Ashridge Journal*, he expressed the opinion that the Sudeten Germans had the perfect democratic right to join the Third Reich if they so desired, despite the fact that this ran directly counter to the provisions of the Versailles Treaty.

On the day Chamberlain left for Munich, Bryant advised him to disregard 'the little noisy minority of the extreme Right' whom he believed, in a direct reference to Churchill, had lost contact with reality – 'just as they did during the Constitutional [Abdication] crisis'.[28] He prefaced his remarks by calling himself 'one who has tried, in my small way . . . to waken opinion in this country to a more sympathetic understanding of the German point of view'.

Bryant predictably hailed Munich as a triumph and lost no time in pouring scorn on the anti-appeasers in their hour of defeat. His complacency about German *revanchism* is well illustrated by a letter he sent congratulating a NBA author, W.J. Blyton, on his book *Arrows of Desire*. In his usual gushing way he told the writer how the third chapter had struck him as 'the finest thing of its kind since Burke'. In fact, Blyton had written a book which sought to show, as the author put it in a letter to the publisher at Hutchinson's, how 'Winston is wonderfully eloquent, impressive and wrong. . . . Hitler's Germany is so formed as to tread far less on our toes than the Kaiser's.'

Bryant sought to apologize for the Nazis in an *Illustrated London News* article in the wake of the *Kristallnacht* pogrom of November 1938. Admitting that it was 'a sorry business', he went on to blame the organized anti-Semitic outrages on 'a murderous attack made by a half-crazed Jewish youth who fired at a distinguished representative of Germany'. The Germans were 'virile, manly and heroic', and almost all Bryant could find to criticize them for was 'a curious inability to see things from other people's point of view'. He explained how ten years earlier the Jews had 'lorded it' over the Germans, and they were now getting no more than what had been coming to them. He pursued this argument on 10 December 1938 in another article, entitled 'Is There a Jewish Problem?' 'They have seldom been welcome guests and scarcely ever for long,' he wrote.

Discussing the German Jews, the most highly assimilated in Europe, Bryant argued that in the decade after the Great War, 'it seemed as if the Jews', who constituted a tiny percentage of the German population, 'would soon control the whole of Germany'. The result, according to Bryant, was that 'the German people feel, in fact, that there is no room for them and their very competent Jewish minority in the same house'. Jews should not be welcomed to Britain, however, because of their propensity to take 'an unfair and disproportionate amount of wealth and power'.

In the Christmas 1938 *Ashridge Journal*, Bryant composed a check list of 'Munich: Some Charges and Their Answers', which took an aggressive, anti-Czech line. The Czechs were the 'racial big brothers of the Soviet Union', who had 'maltreated' the Sudeteners and, unlike the English, were 'not a governing race'. Their Aryan minority, on the other hand, 'felt a growing pride in the revival of German consciousness, prosperity and strength under the Führer'. On the issue of whether or not Hitler was bluffing over Munich, Bryant believed a close study of his career did not reveal him as 'the kind of man who threatens what he is not prepared to perform. It is not men like Hitler who are afraid to put things to the test.' Bryant could not have known that Hitler had given orders to withdraw from the Rhineland in 1936 if the French had offered resistance, and was extremely nervous about war breaking out over the Sudetenland before his defences in the west had been completed. He was, in fact, a supreme bluffer.

'Treason', said Talleyrand, 'is a matter of dates.' Whilst it may have been intellectually acceptable to support appeasement at Munich, or even possibly up to March 1939, when Hitler invaded the rump of Czechoslovakia and so brought non-Aryans into his Reich, after that it became a moral issue. The Polish guarantee of April 1939, the Danzig crisis, the invasion of Poland and the Phoney War were all stages along which Britons of almost all opinions gradually joined the consensus that

Hitler had to be stopped. Even such German sympathizers as Philip Conwell-Evans, Ernest Tennant, Thomas Chambers and Lord Mount Temple fell silent at various stages along this *via dolorosa*. Although the evidence naturally gets patchier, it seems clear that Bryant was not weaned off his fellow-travelling until the prospect of arrest stared him in the face in 1940.

January 1939 saw him take the breathtaking step of choosing *Mein Kampf* for his NBA Book of the Month. It was not even an accurate translation, for, as the Duchess of Atholl was quick to point out, it omitted certain parts of the original, such as the reference to France as Germany's 'deadly enemy' which had to be 'smashed'. The translator had also toned down certain phrases, such as those concerning Germany's 'sharpened sword'. One NBA member, a Colonel Lorimer, cancelled his membership in protest against the Editorial Note in which Bryant likened Hitler to another imprisoned writer, John Bunyan. It took Bryant to equate the authors of *The Pilgrim's Progress* and *Mein Kampf*.

Lorimer predicted that 'in time to come the publication of this version of *Mein Kampf* will be quoted as a classic example of propaganda furthered by publishing organisations of the people whom it is designed to mislead'.[29] Following the invasion of Prague in mid-March 1939, Dr Ernst Hanfstaegl, a former friend of Hitler's then in exile, wrote to Bryant from West Kensington to say that he was 'truly glad that a scholar of your name and ability has set himself the task of interpreting the Third Reich to the world'.

It was also about this time that Bryant began his friendship with Henry Drummond-Wolff, a former Conservative MP, rich imperialist and fascist sympathizer. Drummond Wolff was to provide funding for various right-wing projects of Bryant's until 1980. Encouraged by Sir Joseph Ball, the head of the Conservative Research Department, Drummond-Wolff undertook several visits to Germany in 1938 and 1939 for discussions with, amongst others, Goering and his principal adviser, Helmut Wohltat. As his letter to Ball after the fall of Prague indicates, he was almost the last man to whom any measure of secret diplomacy ought to have been entrusted. Writing on 20 March 1939, Drummond-Wolff argued that Britain was opposing Germany

> not in our own vital interests, but through the dictates of the Government of the United States and of international economic forces now centred in the United States in which Jewry has the strongest voice, and close affiliation with the USSR and Communist organisations. The Jews, at the moment, control to a large extent the Roosevelt Administration.[30]

This unquestioning belief in the Bolshevik–Zionist conspiracy had serious implications. On 24 March Drummond-Wolff passed on to Ball – and thus to Chamberlain – the message from Goering that 'any agreement' with Russia directed against Germany would have disastrous consequences 'and force an "encircled" Germany into a major conflagration'. It was into this circle of people that Bryant was keen to insinuate himself. Ball, whose anti-Semitic newspaper *Truth* was engaged in ridiculing Churchill and the anti-appeasers, was another of Bryant's correspondents. Since his papers were burnt some time after the war, it is impossible to ascertain the full extent of Ball's undercover activities.

A letter to *The Times* on the Polish guarantee of early April 1939 shows that Bryant was still keen to pursue 'fresh possibilities' for an Anglo-German understanding. He believed that it could result in 'a higher European order'.[31] Writing to the BBC's Chairman two days later, he suggested that Hitler should be invited to make a radio broadcast direct to the British people, 'stating Germany's case, her needs and her grievances'. Bryant even proposed that Hitler and Mussolini might write introductions to the collection of Chamberlain's speeches, *My Struggle for Peace*, which he was then editing.

Writing the same day to Dr Rosel, a German propaganda official based in London, Bryant described himself as 'one who has been a consistent advocate of Anglo-German friendship ever since the Führer's rise to power, and still is'. When Rosel was about to be expelled from Britain the next month, Bryant wrote to the Home Secretary, Samuel Hoare, saying that Rosel was 'an honest man who, with the natural predilections of his race, has done his best to promote friendly relations between our two peoples'. Bryant's intervention assisted Rosel's case for remaining in Britain, and soon afterwards he thanked him. In the letter, Rosel asked for the return of a copy of Hitler's speeches he had lent the English patriot. Bryant wrote back to ask whether he could keep them a little longer.

When at long last Bryant's views were attacked publicly, he reacted vociferously. On 19 June 1939 G.R. Strauss, a Popular Front MP, stated in a Parliamentary question to R.A. Butler that Bryant should not be allowed to advise the Foreign Office, as his fascist sympathies were 'well known'. 'They may be well known to Mr Strauss,' Bryant wrote to *The Times* the next day, 'but they are certainly not well known to me.' He added that it was standard Communist Party practice to attribute fascist sympathies to opponents 'whom it regards as in any way dangerous to itself and those whose reputation it is determined to blacken'.[32]

Meanwhile, Bryant used his *Illustrated London News* articles to welcome the renewal of sporting links with Italy, and to suggest that the royal family's visit to America would be seen as more significant than what he called 'suburban quarrels between Germans and Poles'. On 24 June he declared that 'Liberty does not consist merely of denouncing Tyranny, any more than horticulture does of deploring and abusing weeds, or even pulling them out.'

June 1939 saw Chamberlain's *éminence grise*, Sir Horace Wilson, asking Bryant to write a long article expressing 'the British point of view' for the German press. In it, he blamed the British for seeing Hitler 'not as the restorer of a great but fallen nation', but as 'a loud-voiced intruder' who threatened world peace for incomprehensible reasons. This was not the Führer's fault; it was because the average Briton did not read the political or foreign news in his newspaper but only paid attention 'to the cricket or football news and racing tips'.

Bryant criticized the Jews because they 'did not minimise their sufferings'. The English did not appreciate the causes of anti-Jewish persecution, 'they only saw defenceless creatures'. The Night of the Long Knives had merely been 'the Führer's drastic method' of preventing a revolution. His 'rapidity of action' had probably saved tens of thousands of lives. Bryant complained that Hitler's introduction of conscription, building of the Luftwaffe and militarization of the Rhineland had all been seen as breaches of the Versailles Treaty by Britons, who failed to appreciate 'how just they may have seemed in equity'. By the time the article was finished, in August 1939, the international situation had worsened so drastically that even Wilson did not think it opportune to publish the article. Like any good hack, Bryant kept it for later use, and it eventually appeared as the Introduction to his grand apologia for Nazism, *Unfinished Victory*, which came out after the outbreak of war.

The details of Bryant's late July 1939 visit to Germany only became available in January 1990, because an official in Harold Wilson's Downing Street had decided in 1968 that their release under the Thirty Year Rule might embarrass the historian. Only the year before, Harold Wilson had raised Bryant to the Companionship of Honour. The news that Bryant had visited Nazi Germany just before the war and described Hitler as 'the great German whom fate has raised up to rescue his people' might well have affected the sales of the patriotic books he was publishing in the 1960s. The papers were therefore reclassified under the rarely used Fifty Year Rule.

The message which Chamberlain had at all costs to get across to the

Nazi Government in the summer of 1939 was that there would be no second Munich over Danzig, and that a German invasion of Poland would inevitably mean world war. Unfortunately Bryant, with his long history of abject grovelling to power, was precisely the wrong man to make this uncompromising point. Sir Walter Scott once wrote that every historian secretly despises himself for never having himself taken part in the great events of which he writes. As a personification of that species of historian so fascinated by power that he fails to discriminate objectively between those wielding it – E.H. Carr's fawning over Stalin was a contemporaneous case – Bryant had long since suspended his critical abilities. In the 1930s many writers and intellectuals were mesmerized by tyrants, and Bryant was one of the worst examples of the phenomenon.

The nature of his trade should have made him more hard-headed and suspicious – cynical, even – about politicians, but in his case the history he wrote was so much of the 'Good Queen Bess/Bad King Richard' school that he failed to exercise these faculties. Had he appreciated that *chiaroscuro* rather than stark colours more often correctly represents the past, his political judgment might have been more acute. There were plenty of pro-appeasement historians – Sir Herbert Butterfield, Arnold Toynbee and George Trevelyan among them – but none so keen to ingratiate himself as Bryant. He wrote his history as he had presented his Greenwich pageants, with lots of colour and easily identifiable heroes and villains. It is noticeable how, when Bryant finally broke with Hitlerism – one of the last public figures to do so – he immediately cast the Führer in the role of devil incarnate, and further cheapened his historical writing by portraying Napoleon as identical.

The genesis of Bryant's visit to Germany was both innocent and typical. Yeats-Brown had brought a party of young German men to Bryant's home for tea. Bryant fondly recalled years later how they had all stood around his eighteenth-century piano singing songs. This led to Bryant receiving a letter from Kurt Blohm, a former Hitler Youth leader who was now desk officer of the British section of the foreign affairs department of Nazi Party Headquarters. His superior was Walther Hewel, a staff officer and close friend of Hitler's. It was a connection Bryant was to come to value. He could not have chosen a more fanatical Nazi; Hewel had gone to prison with Hitler in the 1920s and was to die with him in the Führerbunker in the last days of the war.

On 11 June 1939 Bryant wrote to Chamberlain asking him to meet Blohm. This was refused, but a fortnight later he received a letter from Blohm in Berlin, on 'German-English Friendship Society' writing-paper, to say that if he could be 'of any practical use' in promoting their 'mutual task' of better understanding, Bryant should get in touch. Of the chapters of the book he was in the process of writing, he told Blohm: 'I have a feeling that in some mysterious way I could not explain they were going to have an effect on the future of our two countries.' He believed that he could build 'a bridge of sympathy and refrain' between Britain and Germany.[33] He took the Nazi into his confidence, saying that he 'thought he knew England better than most'. In his opinion, except for 'a few noisy intellectuals' who had no real power in a country that despises intellectuals, 'there is no inherent enmity to Germany'. This was, of course, precisely the wrong message for Nazi Party Headquarters to be given in June 1939. Nothing could have been more encouraging to them than to believe that Britain had not the will to fight for Poland.

Yet Bryant continued, describing Hitler as 'the great German whom fate has raised up to rescue his people from the miseries and humiliations' which he was describing in his book *Unfinished Victory*, the proofs of which he sent to Blohm for his comments. Bryant then said that should Hitler, 'by a supreme act of patience and magnanimity', save the world from war and Bolshevism, 'he would be recognised in this country for the great man that he is'. Bryant declared himself surprised by how often he heard 'common folk over here', whose instinctive perception he believed often surpassed that of the politicians, speaking 'of what the Führer has done for his own people and what he might do for the world if he should prove himself at the eleventh hour to be not a Napoleon but the Unknown Soldier come to life'. It was in this role that Bryant declared he had always viewed Hitler.[34]

Chamberlain allowed Bryant to be informed 'entirely unofficially' that 'he should certainly go to Germany' to meet Blohm. This journey was to be undertaken 'on his own authority and there must be no suggestion in any quarter that he was going at the request of the P.M.' In the notes Bryant made of his trip, he observed 'no obvious militarism', in a country which was six weeks later to pour 200,000 troops into Poland. He was astonished to find that neither of the German trains he caught ran on time.

Bryant had written to the Prime Minister on 3 June saying that his trip would be made at his own expense, and he would appear as an ex-serviceman without the smallest official connection. He would go ostensibly to collect material for his book and as a brief holiday trip, which would not in itself have seemed unusual. He told Chamberlain that he was 'conscious that it will mean risking my professional career and livelihood', but in fact the official secrecy laws have meant that neither was in any way jeopardized.

Bryant spent 9 to 12 July 1939 in Berlin and Salzburg and met Hewel on the 11th and 12th. On the first day he told Hewel that there was no fundamental jealousy or dislike of Germany amongst Britons – 'only fear and dislike of her methods of violence'. The conversation got round to Czechoslovakia, which had been occupied four months before. When Hewel stated that Germany would respect Czechoslovakia's integrity 'under all circumstances', Bryant, reluctant to get into an argument, 'did not pursue this'. Hewel, who picked up Bryant's hotel bill, repeated Hitler's line that all Germany wanted was her rightful place in partnership with Britain as a great power.[35]

The Englishman heard how Poles were 'a highly excitable people in an inferior state of civilisation'. To this Bryant did at least reply that he 'could not help feeling that an affray between Poles and Germans ... must bring Britain in on the side of Poland'. But the point was lost on Hitler, to whom Hewel reported that evening and who, according to Hewel, did not react very favourably. Bryant's report of his talks struck Chamberlain, who passed them on to Lord Halifax, the Foreign Secretary, with marginalia, as having 'an air of frankness and even naïveté'. When Hewel told Bryant that only the night before, Hitler had been speculating in conversation what would have happened if Britain had accepted his earlier offers of collaboration on a basis of equality, Chamberlain annotated briskly, 'He never made any.' Nevertheless, he had his Private Secretary, Arthur Rucker, tell Bryant that he was 'deeply obliged to you and has been reading the report with deep interest' and offered to pay his expenses from Secret Service funds.[36]

As might have been expected, Bryant's visit did nothing to help convince Hitler of the inevitable consequences of attacking Poland, but his statement that the Germans should not attach too much importance to the tone of the British press, and his view that had a general election followed Munich the majority for Chamberlain's policy would have been enormous, were later quoted approvingly by Hitler, who believed that Britain regretted the Polish guarantee and was preparing for a second Munich. Goebbels's diary confirms the impression that they did not expect the British to fight.[37] By not vigorously and repeatedly insisting that the opposite was the case, Bryant did his country a grave disservice.

On his return he discovered a cheque from Lord Davidson made payable to the NBA – which wags were nicknaming the Nazi Book Association – to pay off its debts and wind it up. 'We need not say anything at all about this new money for obvious reasons,' wrote an NBA official.[38] As the world moved towards war, Bryant still failed to alter his opinions about the Third Reich. 'I almost am an admirer of the Doctor's,' he wrote about Goebbels in the *Illustrated London News* after the Nazi–Soviet Pact and a week away from the outbreak of war. In his opinion, Goebbels's diary was 'a most absorbing and thrilling narrative, and a historical novel of the first importance'. He understood the 'outstanding energy' needed to stage the Nuremberg rallies, which he likened to his own Greenwich pageants. Goebbels was 'a neat thinker' to make up the joke that under democracy one counts heads, whereas under Bolshevism one counts them off.

The new Spanish Ambassador, the Duke of Alba, was staying with Bryant in early September 1939. He wrote from the Embassy in Belgrave Square on the 9th: 'I am trying to get you an estimate of the number of people killed by the Reds, but since I want to give you reliable information, it will take a few days still to obtain.'[39] Bryant's method of seeking facts and figures from precisely the most biased sources says little for his historical methods. At one point in the Phoney War, he claimed in the *Illustrated London News* that the Spanish Republicans had massacred 800,000 innocent men, women and children, 'in cold blood of course'. This drew an outraged letter from H.G. Wells demanding his evidence for that figure. As the answer was Alba, Bryant merely answered 'official sources'. This prompted Wells to ask whether Bryant believed Goebbels too. Naturally, he did; Bryant quoted unquestioningly statistics about the Jews that came straight from such Nazis as Kurt Blohm. The background information for his anti-Semitic rant, *Unfinished Victory*, was partly supplied him by Chambers, who got it from 'a few of my personal friends in Germany'. The Germans must have hardly believed their luck that a historian with such good credentials and connections as Bryant should regurgitate their propaganda for them.

Such conduct was, of course, highly unprofessional. Bryant was nevertheless made a Fellow of the Royal Historical Society, a Fellow of the Royal Society of Literature and President of the Royal Society of Authors. He was awarded honorary doctorates by Edinburgh, St Andrews and New Brunswick Universities. He won the *Sunday Times* Gold Medal and Award for Literature in 1950 and the Royal United Services Institute's Chesney Gold Medal in 1955, and was elected to the Council of the Royal Literary Fund. In 1954 he was knighted and in 1967 he became a Companion of Honour. His friend A.L. Rowse, a far superior historian in every respect, has, meanwhile, received no official recognition of any kind.

Just as one might have imagined a period of silence on his part would have been welcome, Bryant flung himself into the anti-war movement. His correspondents in the campaign ranged from the respectable Lord Halifax and Rab Butler, via the pro-peace Lords Queenborough, Westminster, Brocket, Arnold, Rushcliffe, Davies and Buccleuch, to the distinctly shady Domvile, Ball, Yeats-Brown and Drummond-Wolff. From his private papers it is clear that far from becoming reconciled to the war as it progressed, Bryant became disillusioned with the Chamberlain Government for not attempting to make peace with Hitler.

Writing to *The Times* on 7 October 1939, as Hitler's peace proposals were announced, Bryant argued that to achieve the destruction of Nazi Germany at the expense of destroying Christendom would be 'a sterile victory'. Britain was at war, but Bryant still wished to remind readers that Germans regarded the rule of Hitler as 'the sole reason for their emancipation from the miseries of the Versailles era'. He called for a way 'to end the war successfully' without fighting. As earlier with the Jews and Czechs, Bryant began to blame the Poles for provoking the Führer, arguing – with his special insight into the English mind – that there was no enthusiasm 'for the cause of the Polish leaders' outside Westminster, Fleet Street, 'the sheltered West End' and the more prosperous suburbs.[40] For all his sneers at democracy and claims that the rights of opposition did not exist during the Great War, Bryant made full use of his own freedom of speech. With Drummond Wolff's money he started an organization called Union and Reconstruction. This was ostensibly a think-tank for post-war issues, but was in fact an anti-war lobbying organization and propagator for national socialist economic ideas.

He sent long memoranda to Halifax and Butler, while requesting from the latter a chit for an additional petrol allowance. Butler answered: 'I am hoping that you will feel that you have immediate access to me and those I serve if you desire to approach us.' It is not known whether he got his petrol. In mid-October Lord Brocket – who had been impressed by Bryant's pro-peace letter to *The Times* – wrote to say that 'it was such a pleasure to hear all your views and to realize that all the people of England are not yet mad!'[41]

One of Bryant's memoranda from this period declared that Britain should state her war aims in as general a way as possible, so as to avoid the danger of being forced to continue fighting 'when circumstances and public opinion have changed'. He proposed that Britain should proclaim that she was fighting for 'a United States of Europe'. This entity would limit sovereignty in the external affairs of member states. Britain should announce her intention to sign a treaty which would include the 'Lincolnian proviso' that 'once assumed it could not be discarded'. Bryant believed that a declaration of readiness to join such a European union would prevent war and 'appeal to the imagination of the whole world'. The 'new international order' arising from it would have the additional benefit of avoiding having to alter Germany's internal form of government. This was desirable because, according to Bryant, 'our real quarrel' was not with fascism.

Bryant wrote to Butler on 18 October 1939 warning that 'the war-to-the-death element in this country' would bring about a communist Germany. He proposed 'an honourable peace or truce', arguing that although Hitler has broken many offers and promises, 'few of them were accepted at the time by those to whom he made them and none were treated with anything but derision in the popular press of this country'. Germany needed to be told that Britain recognized her right to economic autarchy. Bryant blamed the British press, the Ministry of Information, the BBC and the Admiralty (then presided over by Churchill) for 'inflammatory and needlessly provocative statements' against Germany.

Bryant believed that 'warmongering in the newspapers' did 'quite as much as Hitler to bring about disaster' and had destroyed any chances of success which he believed the Munich settlement might have had. Such claptrap went down well with various noble correspondents such as Lord Davies and the Duke of Buccleuch; the former sent Bryant a letter in November about his own efforts to 'discover contacts in a neutral country through which this idea could be conveyed to people in Germany'.

The peace lobby in the House of Lords had great faith in Bryant's abilities. Lord Brocket wrote to him in mid-January 1940: 'you have such power in your pen that you can sway multitudes', adding that the war 'should be brought to a close as soon as possible ... our policy should be "peace before destruction"'. Bryant had spoken to Lord Halifax on the issue of peace negotiations, and on 18 January 1940, in classic cloak-and-dagger style, he offered to put the Foreign Secretary 'in touch at the earliest possible moment with someone who ... could put you in possession of certain information of which I believe you may possibly be unaware and which might have very great bearing on the possible course of events in the near future'.

Government papers relating to this affair will not be opened to the public until January 2016. From the scraps to be found in Bryant's private papers, however, it seems clear that certain peers, including Lords Brocket and Rushcliffe, had made contact with Goering via a Dane called Mr Bengt Berg, and that Bryant was involved in bringing it to the attention of senior Foreign Office figures. Making private contact with the enemy is, of course, a treasonable offence. Although it went on in a semi-official capacity throughout the Phoney War, Bryant was undoubtedly sailing close to the wind in his quest for a peaceful end to the war against Hitler.

Among Bryant's papers there is a draft letter to Halifax about a telegram relating to a meeting Berg had with 'G', with what he regarded as favourable results. Bryant hoped that the British Government would not insist on a peace which enjoined the restoration of full Polish and Czech independence or substantial disarmament, as he thought this would inevitably mean Hitler's 'own internal downfall'. He also believed that Britain's internal situation was deteriorating and predicted that 'there will be something approaching revolution here before the end of the year'. He told Halifax that travelling around the country he had noticed 'a curious change' in the previous few weeks. He warned the Foreign Secretary that 'there is a growing feeling which I meet everywhere that there is something fundamentally wrong with our present system and that we are fighting to preserve something as evil and destructive as Hitler himself'.

Bryant was fast becoming disillusioned with the former appeasers. Believing himself to have been 'deliberately thwarted' by Halifax, who had sent him a 'brush-off' reply, he wrote to 'Ronnie' Brocket that 'our only course is to go all out for Union and Reconstruction and make the public realise the *real* causes that are so blindly and arrogantly seeking their enslavement and (as we believe) their now certain destruction'. Nothing could be expected from those in authority, he told Brocket, and urged him 'to give every penny you can to Union and Reconstruction to get the truth realised'. He ended with a characteristic touch of flattery, saying that when the peer was able 'to give all your brilliance and energy to get the truth over ... by God, we shall win'.[42]

Brocket's reply shows how out of touch they both had become:

> I feel that we must now redouble our efforts for Peace and I hope you will become a perfect nuisance to Chamberlain, Halifax, Butler and anyone else. What about bearding Winston? Could you knock some sense into his bald head? ... I really believe we may succeed if we press forward all together.

The idea that Bryant could have lobbied Churchill to negotiate for peace with Germany in January 1940 is an indication of how far removed

Bryant and Brocket were from the world of mainstream politics.

A week later Bryant and Drummond-Wolff published *A Declaration of Economic Independence*, which Union and Reconstruction circulated to its friends. Lord Elton read it 'with much interest and a great deal of sympathy'. He supported Bryant's aim to 'substitute British-controlled capital for foreign in the cinema, Press, etc', and wrote to him:

> You are thinking, of course, of Jews. But how would one do it? The Jew would probably be a British Jew, so that, unless you had some sort of Aryan Clause, I don't see how you would work it. ... I am only too ready in some moods to believe in a sinister non-Aryan conspiracy, but normally I remember that ... not many real levers of power are in non-Aryan hands.

Despite appearances, Bryant's own 'sinister Aryan conspiracy' was not peopled exclusively by peers. In January 1940 Yeats-Brown wrote to Bryant congratulating him on yet another policy paper put out by Union and Reconstruction, entitled *Preparations for a Constructive Peace*. Admiral Domvile also wrote to 'My Dear Arthur' asking him to read 'this little paper edited by two friends of ours', which was sadly not to be found in the Bryant archive.

Early February 1940 saw a restoration of interest on Halifax's part in the Berg–Goering connection which Brocket and Bryant had pioneered. He received a letter from the Foreign Secretary which said, 'you may put me in touch with the person you mentioned'. Bryant reactivated Brocket, and on 20 February Halifax wrote to 'My Dear Bryant' asking him to let Berg know 'that the Legation in Copenhagen will forward the letter addressed by him to Brocket'. Bengt Berg, of Halltorp in Sweden and Vedbak in Denmark, was cabled by Brocket, who told him to come to Britain at his expense to meet 'my friend' (i.e. Halifax). Brocket, who in the intervening period had written a letter to the *Daily Sketch* calling for 'an honourable and lasting peace', wrote to Bryant on 18 February to thank him for 'all you did with H. regarding Berg and I hope all goes well'. Bryant had thus been instrumental in passing a pro-peace message from Goering to the British Government during the Phoney War.

In March 1940 Bryant extended his contacts with anti-war peers to the Duke of Westminster and Lord Queenborough, the President of the Royal Society of St George. On 18 April Queenborough sent Bryant a cheque for £1,000, a vast sum in those days, 'to be used entirely at your discretion for any and all the purposes we discussed and which may in your judgment be associated with reconstruction and with those aims which are so close to my heart'. He wrote that he would like to see some quick results, as he was dying, but added, 'it is my intention to supplement this cheque from time to time as funds permit'. Union and Reconstruction, based in York Buildings, Adelphi, soon distributed 7,000 copies of *Britain Awake*! by 'Junius'. This was the pseudonym of Bryant and Drummond-Wolff, and the pamphlet was based on their anti-Semitic *Declaration of Economic Independence*.

Bryant's *Illustrated London News* articles took scant notice of the fact that Britain was now at war with Germany. On 3 February 1940 he had the gall to complain that Goebbels had been 'ably, if unconsciously, assisted by many eminent publicists in this country,' as if Bryant had not himself been of their number. In March he told his readers that Britain had nothing to gain by war with Germany and everything to lose. In mid-April, even after Hitler's invasion of Norway and Denmark, Bryant reached for the rhetorical heights when he recollected how the previous July, 'from the highest tier of the great Olympian stadium at Berlin, I looked down upon the grandiose works of a newer Pharaoh'.[43]

When *Unfinished Victory* was published in April 1940, the Introduction was lifted virtually word for word from the long article Bryant had written for Lord Kemsley the previous July, as though nothing of significance had happened to Anglo-German relations in the intervening period. One must admire his sheer gall in bringing out such a work at such a period, but everything else about it displayed a depravity that far exceeds mere poverty of judgment. Britain had been at war for seven months when the future knight of the realm published this book. It was as pure an apologia for Nazism as it is possible to imagine being published at such a time. In its way it was a monument to British freedom of speech that it was not censored or banned.

The book complained that Hitler's speeches offering Anglo-German co-operation had fallen 'on rather deaf ears'. This the author put down to the fact that the British Labour movement was so antagonized by the persecution of German trade unionists that it 'overlooked the revolutionising reforms that the National Socialist Party was achieving for German labour'. According to Bryant, 'under Hitler's forceful leadership' Germany was regaining 'a just confidence' in herself. He regretted that during *Anschluss* the British public failed to see the cheering Austrian crowds. He waxed lyrical over his July 1939 visit to Germany, recalling a great lake close to the Austrian border where thousands of children rowed and swam in the sunlight, and camped beneath the pine trees, 'their faces gleaming with happiness and health and new-found knowledge of how to live'.[44] The Nazi propagandist film-maker, Leni Riefenstahl, could not have presented Hitler's Germany in a warmer light.

Bryant dismissed the notion that the English people had 'any particular love for the Jews, but they hated cruelty'. Without even the standard reference to his many Jewish friends, Bryant then painted a picture of Nazi anti-Semitic persecution which made it look entirely the fault of the Jews. They took advantage, argued Bryant, of Germany's post-war weakness and, 'since the sun does not shine often on their race, they made hay as fast as they could'. This was done so successfully that by 1938, after five years of persecution, Jews 'still owned ... something like a third of the real property in the Reich'. This mostly fell into their hands through financial trickery during the inflationary years of the 1920s and 1930s. As usual, Bryant had got these absurdly exaggerated statistics direct from Chambers and his 'friends' in Germany, and from other equally tainted sources such as Kurt Blohm and Dr Rosel.

The Jews, continued Bryant, increasing in tempo, cared nothing for national standards or traditions. Instead, they set out to dominate politics, business and the learned professions. In this British equivalent of the *Protocols of the Elders of Zion*, Bryant argued that Jewish control of German wealth and power 'soon lost all relation to their numbers'. All government ministries had their quotas of Jews. The Reichsbank and the large private banks were 'practically controlled' by them. So were the press, the arts and the publishing trades. According to Bryant, 'a telephone conversation between three Jews in ministerial offices' could close down any newspaper in Germany, and this power 'was frequently used'. Furthermore, authorship in Germany 'almost seemed to have become a kind of Hebrew monopoly'. The professional organizations of writers 'were controlled almost entirely by Jews'.[45] It is worth noting Bryant's use of the weasel words 'seems', 'almost' and 'kind of' to allow let-outs should any part of this rant be put under the factual microscope.

As this Jewish stranglehold over German national life developed, Gentiles were excluded from privileged occupations: 'At this time it was not the Aryans who exercised racial discrimination.' The Germans had somehow to rescue their indigenous culture from an alien hand and restore it to their own race. For Jewish culture was 'not the same as that of the long-settled nations of the west. There is a pathos in it and the wanderer's yearning and the outcast's bitter complaint.' Bryant believed that Jews exhibited an 'oriental and passionate enjoyment of the sensuous delight of the hour', that they were intellectually aloof and that they felt nothing but contempt for 'authority and the household gods of more pampered races'.[46]

Since they could not comprehend the countryman's point of view, Jews moved to the towns, 'where quick fortunes were to be had by quick wits'. Bryant was writing at precisely the time when the Nazis were forcing Polish Jews to leave the land they had tilled for centuries and herding them into ghettoes such as Krakow. 'Their inherited instinct was to skim the cream rather than to waste vain time and effort in making enduring things,' he continued. Exponents of the get-rich-quick philosophy, Jews were 'lovers of the flamboyant and the arts of advertisement'. They sneered at the Teutonic virtues of discipline, hard work, thoroughness and craftsmanship. Still claiming a historian's objectivity, Bryant then wrote of 'the migrant type – "Asiatic hoards on the sands of the Mark of Brandenburg"', who seemed, 'with all their invincible vitality and irresponsible opportunism of their race, to be making of a broken nation their washpot'. There was plenty more in this vein, which, owing to copyright laws, unfortunately cannot be quoted directly at greater length. It was unadulterated by any obvious primary research and full of such rhetorical flourishes as: 'Beggars on horseback are seldom popular, least of all with those whom they have thrown out of the saddle.'[47]

Bryant wrote of the German Jews in particular, who comprised some of the most cultivated and assimilated in Europe: 'They were arrogant, they were vulgar and they were vicious.' They made films glorifying 'financial crooks, criminals and prostitutes'. It could only have been a matter of time before the frothing historian brought up sex. Affecting a shocked tone, Bryant reported that Jews dominated 'the innumerable nightspots and vice resorts which mocked the squalid poverty of the German capital'. Their promiscuity 'can seldom have taken a more loathsome and repellent form', especially to those 'brought up in a Christian and traditionalist culture'.

Innocent Germans were thus introduced, presumably against their will, to 'a bewildering degree of sexual promiscuity. ... At private parties mattresses were strewn about and petting was only the beginning.' This took place in literally hundreds of 'cabarets, pleasure resorts and the like ... most of them owned and managed by Jews'. Every perversion, according to Bryant, was 'exploited and stimulated by Jewish caterers who, while seldom sharing such tastes, did not hesitate to turn them to their profits'. Bryant was sedulously drawing a picture of German life between the wars in which his readers were encouraged to sympathize with the Nazis and merely shrug when, at the end of this vicious tirade, he explained that in redressing the balance against the Jews it was an unfortunate German characteristic 'to carry things to extremes'.[48]

When Bryant sent the manuscript of *Unfinished Victory*, to his publishers, Macmillans, one of the editors there, Lovat Dickson, told Harold Macmillan that it could not be published because it clearly condoned fascism. Macmillan – a Conservative MP of whose impeccable anti-appeasement credentials Bryant was privately contemptuous – stoically answered: 'We are publishers, not policemen,' and went ahead.[49] He resolved, however, never to publish Bryant again. It was not long before Bryant's views were to interest policemen as well as publishers.

Bryant sent *Unfinished Victory* to the Duke of Alba, who 'felt, while reading it, that I was in an aeroplane, soaring above the pettiness of the world up into the realms of truth'. Democrats were less impressed. Hugh Trevor-Roper was 'nauseated by it ... it was not merely because it was an "appeasing" book. ... Bryant's work shocked me because it was not a plea for political realism but a plea for Nazism itself. I particularly remember the phrase about the "Cromwellian fervour of the SS" which we were invited to admire.'[50] He also felt:

> The title 'Unfinished Victory' has always seemed to me rather strange, if not sinister. What was the victory that was unfinished? Presumably the completion of the process of appeasement: Hitler's New Order in Europe. That book really determined my view of Bryant, whereas otherwise I only thought of him as a second-rate popular historian.[51]

Nancy Mitford's novel, *Pigeon Pie*, was published at the same time as Bryant's *Unfinished Victory*, in the last days of the Phoney War. In it the heroine complains of her pro-German husband:

> I shall have such an awful grudge against him, don't you see? I do so fearfully think the war is the result of people like him, always rushing off abroad and pretending to those wretched foreigners that England will stand for anything. Cracking them up over here, too; Herr Hitler this and Herr von Ribbentrop that and bulwarks against Bolshevism and so on. Of course the old fellow thought he was making good feeling, and probably he never realised that the chief reason that he loved the Germans was because they buttered him up so much.

All those sentences apply perfectly to Bryant, except the last. It was not because they buttered him up that Bryant admired the Nazis – although they did – but because he liked the combination of nationalism, socialism and discipline in Hitler's political system. Bryant was, in fact, a fascist fellow-traveller who devoted his literary talents to the cause of his country's enemy. England had little need of 'patriots' like him in 1940.

After *Unfinished Victory* was published, according to Rowse, 'his popularity temporarily slumped'. On 10 May 1940 Hitler unleashed *blitzkrieg* in the West and the national mood swung decisively behind Churchill's policy of defiance and away from the appeasing sentiments which Bryant and his friends were still promoting. Realizing the danger of his position, Bryant quickly wound up Union and Reconstruction, whilst continuing to accept financial assistance from Drummond-Wolff, who was complaining a month later that 'I am so depleted financially that I shall have to raise an overdraft as soon as possible'. Drummond-Wolff was unrepentant about Union and Reconstruction, writing to Bryant on 19 May: 'I assure you that I shall not give up. We must press forward as much as we possibly can, but I fear that our little organisation may not be able to continue during the period which we must now expect. ... I do not think we have been or shall be in any way retrograde.'

Bryant's swift dissolution of Union and Reconstruction could not have been better timed. On 23 May fascists began to be rounded up and a number of Bryant's friends and correspondents appeared on Special Branch lists of people to be arrested in the event of a German invasion. Admiral Domvile was interned in Brixton Prison on 7 July, from where he indulged in paranoiac rants about the Jews and 'the mysterious power at work behind the scenes controlling the actions of the figures visibly taking part in the government of the country'. Bryant quickly appreciated the seriousness of his mistake and embarked on a buying spree of *Unfinished Victory*, which as a result is now a collector's item.

It was then that Lovat Dickson approached Trevor-Roper in a semi-official capacity to ask whether he thought Bryant should be interned as a fascist sympathizer under Regulation 18B. The enquiry had originally come from a source inside the Fleet Air Arm. Dickson made it quite clear that the enquiry was as serious as it was highly confidential.[52] Macmillans had published Trevor-Roper's first book, on Archbishop Laud, and it was thought that he may have known other historians of the period. Trevor-Roper's advice was that it would not be necessary to arrest Bryant, as he would doubtless 'change with the times'.

He could not have been more right. By the end of the year, Bryant had brought out a popular history of England from 1840 to 1940 entitled *English Saga*, which became an immediate bestseller. It fed the public's need to see Britain's plight in a broader historical context. It more than made up in patriotism what it lacked in historical rigour. Despite its sentimentality and side-swipes against free enterprise ('the England of the Rationalists and the money-makers has no time to consider the England of "the yeoman and the alehouse on the heath" '), the book helped raise morale during Britain's *annus mirabilis*. It concluded with a passage which would help keep him out of Brixton Prison, in which he described England as 'an island fortress ... fighting a war of redemption, not only for Europe, but for her own soul'. As Rowse put it, 'Arthur went on playing the gramophone records about how wonderful the English people are. ... He got rapidly on the bandwagon with *English Saga*, trying to make it up to Churchill.'[53]

Baldwin 'thought Arthur Bryant had much overdone his case', thus showing that he misunderstood the point of the book. It was written as much to rehabilitate the author in his readers' eyes after *Unfinished Victory* as to argue an intellectual case. Bryant soon found that he had tapped into a vast market of people who wished to find comforting historical parallels for the situation Britain found herself in. Overnight Bryant's *Illustrated London News* articles also wrapped themselves in the Union Jack, and, as Rowse was later to put it, 'he was all for England, and made a most successful career out of his patriotism and singing her praises'.[54] His propensity for adulation was redirected towards Churchill, rather than Hitler, and soon the Prime Minister became the recipient of the honeyed words of Bryant's purple prose style. His belief in the central tenets of national socialism, however, and his desire to replace the profit motive and free market with a form of political economy which harnessed all for the state, never wholly left him.

In *The Ashridge Journal* in November 1940, Bryant wrote of 'the vile and evil things we are fighting'. The rise of Hitler was 'a terrible calamity'. He went on to demand, however, that after the courage of Britain's youths had saved the world from slavery, society would have to be reorganized. Instead of asking whether commercial enterprises would pay, Bryant believed Britain ought 'to revert to a far older and more English question (used in ancient times by our Christian forefathers who made this island great), "will it help to make good and decent men and women?" ' In the guise of historian, Bryant peddled a ludicrously Utopian view of the past. The date of this Golden Age in which 'Christian forefathers' took decisions without reference to commercial implications was kept deliberately vague by Bryant, whose knowledge of the seventeenth century must have told him that even the puritan New World adventurers expected to turn a profit.

In September 1942 Rab Butler invited Bryant, along with others 'who though in general sympathy with the Party faith are not of the machine', such as G.M. Young, Keith Feiling, Arnold Toynbee, Sir Charles Petrie and Geoffrey Dawson, on to 'sub-committees on various aspects of national life' which were being set up to look into the future of Toryism. Bryant was there able to pursue his penchant for nationalist collectivism under a different name. Speaking on 'Reconstruction' at a Foyle's literary tea on 26 May 1943, Bryant delivered an eighteen-page address which was shot through with totalitarian assumptions. He attacked capitalism and materialism, in the name of his quasi-mystical 'Englishry'. Food production, physical security and employment would be taken over and run centrally by the state, in return for 'a daily insistence of a temporal and spiritual authority'. In the course of his rambling talk, Bryant let drop a significant insight into the reasons for his change of political heart in the summer of 1940.

He told his audience in the Rembrandt Hotel that, faced with the ruthless efficiency of Germany and the 'terrific results' totalitarianism had produced in 1940, 'most of us must have had moments ... when we felt tempted' to believe that the fascist system was superior. Yet 'it was not the rigid, ruthless totalitarian system which produced the men and machines that won the Battle of Britain'. Here was the true reason that Bryant lost his faith in the dictators; it was because they lost. His famous patriotism was as thin as the tiny margin of superiority the Spitfires enjoyed over Messerschmitts in the Battle of Britain.

Having scored a great political and financial success with *English Saga*, which had, in Rowse's words, 'caught the mood of the time and reinstated him in the public's favour', Bryant brought out many more patriotic pot-boilers. *Years of Endurance*, published in November 1942, was the story of the early period of the Napoleonic Wars. It drew constant analogies between England's earlier plight and her present. It was excellent wartime propaganda, laboriously emphasizing the similarities between 1804 and 1940 at every opportunity.

Bryant did a superb job in helping to stiffen the people's resolve by putting their sacrifices in historical context. He even attacked those 'unconscious allies or dupes in every decaying eighteenth-century state' who had helped Napoleon. After his overnight *volte face*, Bryant never lacked gall. He did not dedicate *Years of Endurance* to Churchill, as Rowse suggested, because 'he did not feel on strong enough ground for that yet', but to Rowse himself instead. Once it became clear which way the wind was blowing, however, Bryant passed up few opportunities, however tangential, to praise the Prime Minister.

Churchill's return to the Premiership in 1951 was welcomed by Bryant in predictable tones. He called him 'the brave old man' and 'the pilot who weathered the storm of war in 1940'. He also enthused over the choice of St Crispin's Day for the election as 'the right choice, and under the circumstances, the only one possible'.[55] Bryant received a knighthood in 1954. The Prime Minister's retirement the next year elicited more genuflection: 'The brave old man, as he will always be to me and to millions of my contemporaries,' he began. In that article he stated that 'democracy had been failing through its own seemingly inherent defects' in the 1930s, but in 1940 Churchill had 'rallied a neglectful nation and ultimately the whole world behind him'. Bryant was never to admit who had been amongst the most neglectful of the nation at the time. Indeed, he never apologized for his lack of political judgment over Nazism. He even had the nerve, in a private argument after the war about the situation in 1939, to 'place all the blame for the perilous state of the country on to Churchill'.[56]

Having written history as wartime propaganda, a necessary and worthwhile activity at the time, Bryant proved incapable of altering the formula when peace came. It had been immensely commercially successful and he saw no reason to change. Whenever reviewers savaged his work, he smarmed up to them and gave them lunch, prompting his publisher's quip that he had learnt the habit of feeding the hand that bit him. A favourite method of ingratiating himself with people was to send scores of copies of his books, unsolicited and with suitably oily inscriptions, to relative strangers. Ministers, soldiers and members of the royal family, as well as other writers, were favoured in this way. The letters of thanks would then be replied to by Bryant with a letter of thanks for their thanks, and a correspondence was thus entered into.

Such behaviour, combined with a determination never to criticise other writers by name, was, as Rowse admits, 'a good technique for success'. Bryant needed all his talents when his edition of Lord Alanbrooke's diaries, *The Turn of the Tide*, was published in February 1957. Despite his explanation to the Field Marshal that it made Churchill out to be much more real and human than 'the rather boring and infallible image which a stupid propaganda is creating', he only later realized how angry the Churchillians would be at this first crack in the edifice of Churchill's wartime reputation.

When the book was being serialized by the *Sunday Times*, Bryant kept 'pestering' the paper to tone down passages which were 'likely to provoke Winston's displeasure'.[57] On publication Bryant addressed the Foyle's literary lunch at the Dorchester Hotel, attended by Attlee, Sir John Anderson, Admiral Cunningham, Glubb Pasha, Lord Portal, Lady Churchill and Alanbrooke himself. Bryant tried hard to explain how

Churchill's 'impulsiveness' was really 'resistance' and said that had Churchill not been the kind of man he was, 'this country would never have been saved in 1940 and could never have won the war'. Churchill's doctor, Lord Moran, noted in his diary how 'Bryant's panic spread to the other speakers', who all said in their speeches that the book would enhance Churchill's reputation rather than diminish it. None of this fooled the Churchillians and Montgomery wrote to Bryant in early June 1957: 'Winston is very angry indeed about the book'. Portal privately thought Bryant had 'put too many plums in the pudding', and had exaggerated Alanbrooke's influence, and Oliver Lyttelton complained that it 'made out Brookie made no mistakes whatsoever'.[58] That was just Bryant's style; he could write no other way.

In 1960 Bryant published a stomach-churning biography of his spaniel, Jimmy. An acquaintance remembers how Jimmy's 'elaborate bobbing and ducking and generally fawning manner' was reminiscent of his master. His other books written in the 1960s, such as *The Age of Chivalry*, *The Fire and the Rose* and *The Lion and the Unicorn*, seemed to take their titles either from pub signs or Mills and Boon novels. They peddled an 'Alfred-and-the-Cakes' view of history which proved that the only thing worse than dry, inaccessible history written by and for academics was the syrupy, false sort which Bryant served up. Certainly, had publishing success eluded him in Britain, Bryant could have earned a good living in Hollywood writing screenplays for period swashbucklers.

Bryant's opposition to Britain's entry into the Common Market may be thought surprising in one who had earlier advocated a 'Lincolnian' treaty of perpetual European union. There were perfectly reasoned, intelligent arguments against Britain joining, but he did not make them. Instead, he published a book called *A Choice for Destiny*, with chapter headings such as 'Our Ocean History', 'The Painful Plough' and 'Once to Every Man and Nation'. The book did, however, secure him an invitation to meet Lord Beaverbrook to discuss the campaign. Afterwards he wrote to 'thank you for all these things and the hospitality of your beautiful home and woods, and, most of all, for the privilege, and even more, the pleasure of meeting you'.

When Churchill died in 1965, Bryant wrote in the *Illustrated London News*: 'The age of giants is gone forever. For nobody now who can remember 1940 and the Second World War can expect to see in his lifetime anyone of the stature of this colossus of a man.'[59] Did Bryant ever privately wonder what would have happened to the England he so publicly revered had she taken his route in 1940 rather than Churchill's?

It would have required an effort of self-questioning of which he was congenitally incapable. By then his apostasy was complete and he probably could not himself remember the stance he had taken towards Churchill when it had really counted.

In *The Search for Justice*, the third volume of his history of the British people, which was written in 1957 and republished as recently as 1990, Bryant declared that the dictators' New Order was 'constructed on falsehood, menace and violence'. Hitler – rather than 'the great German whom fate has thrown up to rescue his people' or 'the Unknown Soldier come to life' – was by now 'a cruel unappeasable aggressor who tortured racial minorities, who tore up treaties, who ranted and shouted and bullied and, when he was thwarted, would rain death and desolation on peaceful millions'.[60] As Rowse put it, by then 'Arthur knew on which side his bread was buttered'.

Bryant's campaign against coloured immigration, though predictable enough for someone of his views, was also presented in a vernacular least likely to get sympathy or results. In the *Illustrated London News* he argued against 'an influx ... of men and women of alien race, accentuated by strongly marked differences of pigmentation and mould of feature, as well as of habits and beliefs'.[61] The problem with blacks, wrote Bryant, was that they were 'only too easily distinguishable by virtue of their colour and social habits'. As with the anti-Common Market campaign, his presentation of the anti-immigration cause managed to do it more harm than good.

His next book *Protestant Island*, presented yet more rose-tinted history. Britain in 1699 'was a world of hedges, squires and parsons, of yeomen, cottages and ragged squatters, making their wares and pleasures after the manner of their forebears'. On he rhapsodized about how the Devon folk clotted their cream with sugar to crown their apple pies and, in the fields, 'milkmaids bore home their pails with music going before'.[62] There was little to choose between his dewy-eyed rural fantasies of the past and post-war Soviet propaganda films of beaming Ukrainian tractor-drivers.

The gap between Bryant's historical writing and romantic fiction narrowed yet further when he addressed the Foyle's literary lunch for Barbara Cartland's autobiography *I Seek the Miraculous*. After introducing the distinguished guests – Bishop Nerses of the Christian Church of Armenia, Margaret, Duchess of Argyll, Mr Horace Cutler of the Greater London Council, Miss Marjorie Proops, Mrs Sandra Harris, Mrs Mary Whitehouse and Mr Jimmy Young – he said that Barbara Cartland wrote 'like Evelyn Waugh, P.G. Wodehouse and Nancy Mitford, she never uses an unnecessary word. She says what she has to say.' Not content with that comparison with three of our greatest modern novelists, Bryant asserted that Florence Nightingale, Queen Mary and Cleopatra were great women and, 'by that definition, Barbara Cartland is a great woman'. If there were the slightest indication that Bryant was speaking tongue in cheek it would be unfair to quote him, but there is not.

At the lunch given for the publication of his book of essays and old *Illustrated London News* articles, *The Lion and the Unicorn*, in March 1970, he gave a bravura performance. He spoke with belaboured mock modesty about 'my own unimportant life', telling his audience that he had discovered a theme running through his life and work: 'I think it comes down to this – that I believe in England.' He went on to quote such homilies from his own book as 'the span of a man's life is a very short time in the history of a nation'.

In the summer of 1980, having divorced his second wife, Bryant proposed to Laura, dowager Duchess of Marlborough. In 1939 he had divorced his first wife after fifteen years of marriage, partly because she had no interest in climbing the social ladder with him.[63] His marriage to Anne Brooke, the daughter of the White Rajah of Sarawak, in February 1941 constituted a social upgrading. 'He was a philanderer, a womanizer,' remembers Rowse. 'He may have had a bit of a complex. Ultimately Anne wasn't very happy. She got madly jealous.'[64] None of this would be worth recording if it did not show Bryant's hypocrisy. In an article in *The Times* he had criticized Samuel Pepys's adultery – 'a horrible word, but one which Pepys by no stretch of charity could escape'.[65] Addressing the Foyle's lunch for the Duchess of Marlborough's autobiography, *Laughter from a Cloud*, Bryant compared her writing to that of Samuel Johnson, calling the book 'an immensely spirited book – and hers has been an immensely spirited life – so unlike my own'. Although his proposal of marriage was accepted at the time, nothing eventually came of it.

On his eightieth birthday, Bryant's publishers and Times Newspapers gave the dinner at the Vintners Hall in his honour. He sat next to Harold Macmillan, who had either forgotten *Unfinished Victory*, or had long since forgiven. One historian who attended the dinner remembered thinking how 'the old toady had found the right historical boots to lick in the end'. A journalist asked Hugh Trevor-Roper to say something about Bryant for his paper. 'Do you think he is a great historian?' he enquired. 'He is no Thucydides,' answered Trevor-Roper, tactfully, before slipping away. In the event the reply was considered too arcane to publish.

In April 1984 Harold Wilson wrote to Mrs Thatcher proposing Bryant, 'a great patriot' and 'our greatest historian', for the Order of Merit. Thatcher agreed with his sentiments, but had to point out that the OM was in the personal gift of the sovereign.[66] Baldwin, Chamberlain, Churchill, Attlee, Macmillan, Wilson, Callaghan and Thatcher had all, therefore, at some time or another paid their tributes to Bryant. Bryant died in 1985 and received fulsome obituaries in the newspapers. Not one mentioned his pre-war and wartime political views, or *Unfinished Victory*. A particularly warm tribute appeared in *Action*, the fascist newspaper, which praised him as having been 'passionate in his patriotism'. The former Blackshirt editor remembered how Bryant 'was regarded by a good many of Mosley's supporters in the post-war years as having had some sympathy with some aspects of the Mosley story, and again with some affection'.[67]

In June 1981, during one of his last addresses to a Foyle's lunch, Bryant said something about the writing of history which might serve as his epitaph:

> In the long run, the judgment of books would settle everything. We shall have Mr Hitler weighed accurately; you shall know the truth about Goering and Goebbels ... or our children will. Books are a refuge and a reservoir of power. The mills of books grind slowly but they grind exceeding small.

Archives

The unpublished papers and diaries of the individuals mentioned in the text can be found in the following archives

Vyvyan Adams (British Library of Political & Economic Science)
Leo Amery (private possession of Lord Amery)
Ralph Assheton (private possession of Lord Clitheroe)
Lady Astor (Reading University)
Clement Attlee (Bodleian Library)
Stanley Baldwin (Cambridge University Library)
Rear-Admiral Tufton Beamish (Churchill College, Cambridge)
Christopher Beaumont (private possession)
Lord Beaverbrook (House of Lords Records Office)
Robert Bernays (private possession of Mr Robert Bernays)
2nd Earl of Birkenhead (private possession of Lady Juliet Townsend)
Maitre Suzanne Blum (private possession)
Robert Bower (Churchill College, Cambridge)
Brendan Bracken (Churchill College, Cambridge)
Sir Arthur Bryant (Liddell Hart School of War Studies, University of London, and Imperial War Museum)
Patrick Buchan-Hepburn (Churchill College, Cambridge)
Sir Roy Bucher (National Army Museum)
Lawrence Burgis (Churchill College, Cambridge)
R.A. Butler (Trinity College, Cambridge)
Sir Alexander Cadogan (Churchill College, Cambridge)
Victor Cazalet (private possession of Sir Edward Cazalet)
Lord Cecil of Chelwood (British Library)
Lord Cherwell (Nuffield College, Oxford)
Neville Chamberlain (Birmingham University)
General Sir Philip Christison (Churchill College, Cambridge)

Winston Churchill (Churchill College, Cambridge)
Conservative and Unionist Party (Bodleian Library)
William Craven-Ellis (private possession of Mrs Doris Campbell)
Harry Crookshank (Bodleian Library)
Admiral Sir Andrew Cunningham (British Library)
Sir Charles Cunningham (India Office Library and Records)
Lionel Curtis (Bodleian Library)
Lord and Lady Davidson (House of Lords Records Office)
Geoffrey Dawson (Bodleian Library)
Somerset de Chair (private possession)
Sir Richard Denman (Bodleian Library)
Piers Dixon (private possession)
Henry Drummond Woolf (Leeds University)
Thomas Dugdale (private possession of Lord Crathorne)
Anthony Duff Cooper (Churchill College, Cambridge, and private possession of
    Lord Norwich)
Anthony Eden (Birmingham University)
Paul Einzig (Churchill College, Cambridge)
A.C. Graham (British Library of Political and Economic Science)
Lord Halifax (Borthwick Institute, York)
Lord Hankey (Churchill College, Cambridge)
Patrick Hannon (House of Lords Records Office)
Oliver Harvey (British Library)
Sir George Harvie-Watt (Churchill College, Cambridge)
Cuthbert Headlam (Durham County Records Office)
Viscount Hinchingbrooke (private collection of Mr John Montagu)
Samuel Hoare (Cambridge University Library)
Austin Hopkinson (private possession of Mr Anyas Hopkinson)
Leslie Hore-Belisha (Churchill College, Cambridge)
Florence Horsbrugh (Churchill College, Cambridge)
John Hughes-Hallett (Churchill College, Cambridge)
Thomas Inskip (Churchill College, Cambridge)
Lord Ismay (Liddell Hart School of War Studies, University of London, and
    India Office Library and Records)
Sir Evan Jenkins (India Office Library and Records)
Roger Keyes (Churchill College, Cambridge)
Alan Lennox-Boyd (Bodleian Library)
Professor Lindemann (Nuffield College, Oxford)
Sir David Llewellyn (private possession of Rhidian Llewellyn)
David Lloyd George (House of Lords Records Office)
Sir Hugh Lucas-Tooth (private possession of Sir John Lucas-Tooth)
Oliver Lyttelton (Churchill College, Cambridge)
William Mabane (West Yorkshire Archive Centre, Leeds)
Malcolm MacDonald (Durham University)
Sir Ernest Makins (private possession of Lord Sherfield)
David Margesson (Churchill College, Cambridge)
David Maxwell Fyfe (Churchill College, Cambridge)

Lady Alexandra Metcalfe (private possession)
John Moore-Brabazon (RAF Museum, Hendon)
Walter Monckton (Bodleian Library and private possession of Lord Monckton)
Henry Morris-Jones (Clwyd Records Office)
Lord and Lady Mountbatten (Southampton University and India Office Library and Records)
Sir Francis Mudie (India Office Library and Records)
Lord Munster (private possession of Mr John Birkbeck)
Gilbert Murray (Bodleian Library)
Harold Nicolson (Balliol College, Oxford)
1922 Committee (Bodleian Library)
Henry Page Croft (Churchill College, Cambridge)
Kenneth Pickthorn (private possession of Sir Charles Pickthorn)
Henry Pownall (Liddell Hart School of War Studies, University of London)
Leslie Pym (private possession of Lord Pym)
Sir Edward Ruggles-Brice (private possession of Sir John Ruggles-Brice)
Marquess of Salisbury (private possession of Lord Salisbury)
Lord Sanderson (House of Lords Records Office)
Lord Sankey (Bodleian Library)
Sir Reginald Savory (National Army Museum)
Sir George Schuster (Bodleian Library)
J.A. Scott (India Office Library and Records)
Sir John Simon (Bodleian Library)
Lord Slim (Churchill College, Cambridge)
Admiral Sir James Somerville (Churchill College, Cambridge)
Sir Ronald Storrs (Pembroke College, Cambridge)
Rear-Admiral Sueter (RAF Museum, Hendon)
Lord Swinton (Churchill College, Cambridge)
Edward Talbot (Borthwick Institute, York)
Lord Thorneycroft (private possession)
Euan Wallace (Bodleian Library)
Charles Waterhouse (private possession of Major Hugo Waterhouse)
A.A. Williams (India Office Library and Records)
Henry Willink (Churchill College, Cambridge)
Lord Wolmer (Bodleian Library)
Christopher York (private possession)

Notes

PRO refers to the Public Record Office, London

1: The House of Windsor and the Politics of Appeasement

1 Introduction to the Templewood Papers
2 Lord Templewood, *Nine Troubled Years* (1954), pp. 159–60
3 Kenneth Rose, *King George V* (1983), p. 387
4 Kenneth Young (ed.), *The Diaries of Sir Robert Bruce Lockhart*, vol. 1 (1973), 13 July 1933
5 Bruce Lockhart Papers, 13 July 1933
6 PRO FO 954/6/206
7 *Ibid.*
8 John Vincent (ed.), *The Crawford Papers* (1984), 15 November 1923
9 *Ibid.*
10 Robert Rhodes James, *Bob Boothby* (1991), p. 94
11 Nicolson Diary, 21 March 1949
12 John P. Mackintosh, *The British Cabinet* (1977), p. 423
13 Charlotte Mosley (ed.), *The Letters of Nancy Mitford* (1993), p. 291
14 Private Information
15 Nicolson Diary, 23 March 1954
16 *Ibid.*, 6 November 1953
17 *Ibid.*, 10 December 1936
18 Robert Rhodes James (ed.), *Chips: The Diaries of Sir Henry Channon* (1967), 23 November 1936
19 Cazalet Papers, 26 October 1937
20 Frances Donaldson, *A Twentieth-Century Life* (1992), p. 219
21 John Grigg in *The Times*, 11 November 1989
22 *Ibid.*
23 Cazalet Papers, 27 June 1937
24 'Documents on German Foreign Policy' (HMSO), series C, vol. 6, no. 202
25 Sarah Bradford, *George VI* (1989), p. 262
26 Chamberlain Papers, NC18/1/940
27 Rhodes James (ed.), *op. cit.*, 7 May 1937
28 Nicolson Diary, 12 February 1949
29 Rose, *op. cit.*, pp. 211–15
30 Martin Gilbert, *Exile and Return* (1978), p. 233
31 Trefor Evans (ed.), *The Killearn Diaries* (1972), 22 October 1937
32 Templewood, *op. cit.*, p. 224
33 Sir John Colville, *The Fringes of Power: Downing Street Diaries 1939–55* (1985), 7 August 1940
34 Robert Blake and W. Roger Louis (eds), *Churchill* (1993), pp. 188–90
35 Rose, *op. cit.*, p. 189
36 Young (ed.), *op. cit.*, 29 April 1955

37 Duff Hart-Davis (ed.), *End of an Era* (1936), 9 March 1916 and 12 March 1916

38 PRO FO 954/10/162, 9 June 1937

39 *Ibid.*, 954/6/388, 15 November 1937

40 Bradford, *op. cit.*, pp. 263-5

41 Lord Avon, *Facing the Dictators* (1962), p. 601

42 Private Information

43 Noble Frankland, *Witness of a Century* (1993), p. 383

44 PRO FO 954/10/276-8

45 'Documents on German Foreign Policy', series D, vol. 2, no. 315

46 *Ibid.*, p. 913

47 David Dilks (ed.), *The Diaries of Sir Alexander Cadogan 1938-45* (1971), p. 138

48 Halifax Papers, A2.278.26.2

49 Bernays Papers, 29 April 1938

50 Donald Cameron Watt, *How War Came* (1989), p. 138

51 Templewood Papers, RF3, 18 June 1938

52 R.A.C. Parker, *Chamberlain and Appeasement* (1993), p. 158

53 Duff Cooper Diary, 28 September 1938

54 James Pope-Hennessy, *Queen Mary* (1959), p. 591

55 John Grigg in *The Times*, 11 November 1989

56 John Wheeler-Bennett, *King George VI* (1958), p. 355

57 Harvey Diary, 14 July 1943

58 Wheeler-Bennett, *op. cit.*, p. 358

59 J.W. Pickersgill, *The Mackenzie King Record*, vol. 1 (1960), p. 255

60 Denis Judd, *King George VI* (1982), p. 166

61 David Duff, *George and Elizabeth* (1983), p. 156

62 Chamberlain Papers, NC 18/1/1108, 23 July 1939

63 Sir John Wheeler-Bennett, *Knaves, Fools and Heroes* (1974), p. 178

64 Evans (ed.), *op. cit.*, 29 August 1939

65 Philip Ziegler, *King Edward VIII* (1990), p. 407

66 Dilks (ed.), *op. cit.*, 9 September 1939

67 Wheeler-Bennett, *King George VI*, pp. 419-20

68 Halifax Papers, A4.410.4.10

69 Chamberlain Papers, NC 18/1/1/37

70 A.J.P. Taylor (ed.), *Off the Record* (1973), 20 January 1940

71 Vincent (ed.), *op. cit.*, 3 August 1939

72 Ziegler, *op. cit.*, p. 367

73 Brian Bond (ed.), *Chief of Staff: The Diaries of Lieutenant-General Sir Henry Pownall*, vol. 1 (1972), 12 June 1939

74 Colonel R. Macleod and Denis Kelly (eds.), *The Ironside Diaries 1937-40* (1962), 27 June 1939

75 Templewood Papers, XIII 2

76 Munster Papers, 22 November 1939

77 *Ibid.*

78 Macleod and Kelly (eds), *op. cit.*, 2 December 1939

79 Chamberlain Papers, NC 2/24A

80 Laurence Thomson, *1940* (1966), p. 23

81 Bond (ed.), *op. cit.*, 8 December 1939

82 Munster Papers, 14 December 1939

83 *Ibid.*

84 Chamberlain Papers, NC 18/1/1/37; Graeme Sligo, 'Hore-Belisha at the War Office' (Royal Military College of Australia BA, 1982), p. 106

85 Munster Papers, 10 February 1940

86 Wheeler-Bennett, *King George VI*, p. 433

87 Crookshank Diary, 7 January 1940

88 R.J. Minney (ed.) *The Private Papers of Hore-Belisha* (1960), 9 January 1940

89 *Ibid.*

90 Rhodes James (ed.), *op. cit.*, 17 January 1940

91 Munster Papers

92 Charles Stuart (ed.), *The Reith Diaries* (1975), 4 March 1940

93 Halifax Diary, 20 March 1940

94 Halifax Papers, A4.410.4.10

95 Royal Archives, G VI 069/04, 12 April 1940, and 069/05, 15 April 1940

96 Crookshank Diary, 10 May 1940

97 Wheeler-Bennett, *King George VI*, p. 439

98 *Ibid.*, pp. 439-40

99 *Ibid.*, p. 443

100 *Ibid.*, p. 444

101 Kenneth Rose, *Kings, Queens and Courtiers* (1985), p. 168

102 Lord Birkenhead interview with Sir Alan Lascelles

103 Nicolson Diary, 6 April 1955

104 Colville, *op. cit.*, 10 May 1940
105 Chamberlain Papers, NC 18/1/1157, 17 May 1940
106 Templewood Papers, RF 1–3
107 Martin Gilbert, *Winston S. Churchill, vol. 6: Their Finest Hour 1939–41* (1983), pp. 543–4
108 Crookshank Diary, 7 June 1940
109 Colville, *op. cit.*, 1 June 1940
110 Davidson Papers, Box 275
111 Headlam Diary, 24 May 1940
112 Blake and Louis (eds), *op. cit.*, p. 195
113 Dixon Papers, 15 July 1944
114 Roger Keyes, *Outrageous Fortune* (1984), pp. 308–10
115 *Ibid.*, p. 396
116 Wheeler-Bennett, *King George VI*, p. 463
117 Charles de Gaulle, *The Call to Honour* (1955), p. 107
118 *History Today*, December 1993, p. 14
119 Halifax Diary, 5 June 1940
120 *Ibid.*, 18 June 1940
121 Ben Pimlott (ed.), *The Second World War Diary of Hugh Dalton 1940–45* (1986), 31 May 1940
122 Wallace Diary, 16 September 1940
123 Lady Astor Papers, 13 August 1940
124 Michael Bloch, *Operation Willi* (1984), p. 41
125 Colville, *op. cit.*, 29 June 1940
126 'Documents on German Foreign Policy', series D, vol. 10 (B15/B002582–3)
127 Templewood Papers, XIII 16
128 Martin Gilbert, *Winston S. Churchill, vol. 5: Prophet of Truth 1922–39* (1976), p. 614
129 Private Information
130 Young (ed.), *op. cit.*, 4 July 1940
131 John Charmley, *Lord Lloyd* (1987), p. 218
132 Private Information
133 Halifax Papers, A2.278.26.4, 14 April 1941
134 Cazalet Papers, 17 July 1941
135 Roy Jenkins, *Truman* (1986), p. 72
136 Young (ed.), *op. cit.*, 28 March 1944; Jenkins, *ibid.* p. 72
137 John Barnes and David Nicholson (eds), *The Empire at Bay: The Leo Amery Diaries 1929–55* (1988), 9 July 1941

138 Nicolson Diary, 12 September 1940
139 Philip Ziegler, *Crown and People* (1978), p. 72
140 Theo Aaronson, *The Royal Family at War* (1993), p. 46
141 *Ibid.*, p. 49
142 Jeffrey Richards and D. Sheridan, *Mass-Observation at the Movies* (1987), p. 213
143 *Ibid.*, p. 398
144 Malcolm MacDonald, *People and Places* (1960), p. 160
145 Cazalet Papers, 20 August 1940
146 Dalton Diary, 19 December 1944
147 Talbot Papers, 16 November 1940
148 Nicolson Diary, 20 November 1940
149 Cazalet Papers, 3 June 1942
150 Nicolson Diary, 20 April 1954

2: Lord Mountbatten and the Perils of Adrenalin

1 Enoch Powell review of Philip Ziegler's *Mountbatten* on BBC Radio
2 Philip Ziegler, *Mountbatten* (1985), p. 21
3 Lord Zuckerman, *Six Men Out of the Ordinary* (1992), p. 167
4 Blum Papers
5 David Cannadine, *The Pleasures of the Past* (1992), p. 58
6 Private Information
7 *Spectator*, 3 August 1991
8 Kenneth Young (ed.), *The Diaries of Sir Robert Bruce Lockhart*, vol. 1 (1973), 7 October 1936
9 Michael Bloch, *The Secret File of the Duke of Windsor* (1988), p. 40
10 Interview: Captain Edward Dunsterville, 27 October 1992
11 Interview: Lady Mosley, 19 September 1992
12 Mountbatten Papers, K 10A, 3 June 1972
13 Robert Rhodes James (ed.), *Chips: The Diaries of Sir Henry Channon* (1967), 19 September 1944
14 Interview: Captain Edward Dunsterville, 27 October 1992
15 Interview: Leonard Groves, 22 September 1993
16 Richard Hough, *Bless Our Ship* (1991)
17 Captain Robert Whinney, *The U-Boat Peril* (1989), p. 201

18 Private Information
19 Ziegler, *op. cit.*, p. 132
20 Hough, *op. cit.*, p. 96
21 *Ibid.*, p. 101
22 Royal Archives, GVI 069/06
23 Trefor Evans (ed.), *The Killearn Diaries* (1972), 30 May 1941
24 Interview: Captain Philip Chubb, 21 January 1994
25 R.W. Thompson, *Churchill and Morton* (1976), 9 July 1960
26 *Spectator*, 12 December 1992
27 Zuckerman, *op. cit.*, p. 141
28 Interview: Sir Ian Jacob, 27 November 1992
29 Lord Lovat, *March Past* (1978), p. 252
30 Young (ed.), *op. cit.*, 29 August 1942
31 John Barnes and David Nicholson (eds), *The Empire at Bay: The Leo Amery Diaries 1929–55* (1988), 20 August 1942
32 Mountbatten Papers, K 25, 5 June 1972; Hugh G. Henry Jr, *A Reappraisal of the Dieppe Raid: Planning and Intelligence* (Diploma in Historical Studies Thesis, Cambridge, 1992), pp. 42–7
33 Mountbatten Papers, B 18
34 Nigel Hamilton, *Montgomery*, vol. 1 (1981), p. 517
35 Hughes-Hallett Papers
36 James Leasor, *Green Beach* (1982), p. 220
37 Mountbatten Papers, I 124
38 Hough, *op. cit.*, p. 175
39 Mountbatten Papers, C 180
40 Interview: Sir Ian Jacob, 27 November 1992
41 Nigel Hamilton, *Monty: Master of the Battlefield 1942–4*, vol. 2 (1983), p. 597
42 Correspondence with Sir David Fraser, 10 September 1991
43 *Sunday Times*, 17 March 1985
44 Cannadine, *op. cit.*, p. 64
45 Interview: Lord Amery, 14 October 1992
46 Cunningham Papers, MS 52571, 7 February 1944
47 Sir David Fraser, *Alanbrooke* (1983), p. 498
48 John Keegan (ed.), *Churchill's Generals* (1991), p. 220
49 Interview: General Sir Philip Christison, 10 June 1993
50 Mountbatten Papers, I 133, 14 November 1944
51 BBC video, *The Life and Times of Lord Mountbatten*, no. 8
52 Cannadine, *op. cit.*, p. 67; Tom Driberg, *Ruling Passions* (1977), p. 226
53 Mountbatten Papers, C 258, 11 May 1945
54 *Ibid.*, K 105; *The Times*, 2 January 1969
55 Dr Nicholas Owen (ed.), *Ending the Empire* (Contemporary Record, Winter 1992), p. 421
56 Lord Amery review of Philip Ziegler's *Mountbatten* in the *Financial Times*, 14 March 1985
57 Francis Williams, *A Prime Minister Remembers* (1961), p. 209
58 Larry Collins and Dominique Lapierre, *Mountbatten and the Partition of India*, vols 1 and 2 (New Delhi, 1982), p. 61
59 Private Information
60 Major-General Shahid Hamid, *Disastrous Twilight* (1986), 31 March 1947
61 Nicholas Mansergh (ed.), *The Transfer of Power 1942–7* (1970–83), (henceforth 'T o P'), vol. x, no. 64
62 Collins and Lapierre, *op. cit.*, p. 40
63 Ayesha Jalal, *Sole Spokesman* (1952), p. 256
64 *Ibid.*
65 William Shirer, *Gandhi* (1979), p. 9
66 Mountbatten Papers, C 40, 11 May 1944
67 India Office Library and Records (henceforth IOLR), F 200/200, 5 August 1947
68 *Ibid.*, F 200/203, 21 July 1947
69 Chaudri Mohammed Ali, *The Emergence of Pakistan* (1967), p. 125
70 IOLR, F 200/200, 23rd meeting, 26 April 1947
71 *Ibid.*, F200/161
72 Lord Ismay, *The Memoirs of Lord Ismay* (1960), p. 422
73 P. Hardy, *The Muslims of British India* (1972), p. 251
74 T o P, vol. XI, no. 39

75 Khalid Sayeed, *Pakistan: The Formative Phase* (1968), pp. 168–9
76 *Ibid.*
77 PRO PREM 8/541/x
78 R.J. Moore, *Making the New Commonwealth* (1989), p. 17
79 Hamid, *op. cit.*, 29 July 1947
80 Interview: Lord Thomas, 30 January 1994
81 Sir Penderel Moon, *Divide and Quit* (1961), p. 283
82 T o P, vol. x, no. 371
83 Sir Evan Jenkins, 'The Indus Rivers' (IOLR paper, 1948), p. 101 n. 71
84 Christopher Beaumont, 'The Truth of the Partition of the Punjab in August 1947' (privately distributed paper, 1989)
85 IOLR, F 180/79
86 Hamid, *op. cit.*, 9 August 1947
87 Ziegler, *op. cit.*, p. 421
88 *Daily Telegraph*, 28 February 1992
89 *Daily Telegraph*, 24 February 1992
90 Beaumont, *op. cit.*, p. 4
91 Alistair Lamb letter to the *Daily Telegraph*, February 1992
92 Interview: Christopher Beaumont, 15 May 1992
93 Latif Ahmed Sherwani, 'The Partition of India and Mountbatten' (The Council for Pakistan Studies, 1986)
94 Ismay Papers, III/7/13a, 12 February 1948; Interview: Christopher Beaumont, 29 January 1994
95 *Ibid.*, III/7/24a, 2 April 1948
96 *Ibid.*
97 Sir Penderel Moon correspondence with Beaumont, 17 January 1982
98 Hamid, *op. cit.*, p. 234
99 Dr Kanwar Sain, *Reminiscences of an Engineer* (New Delhi, 1978), pp. 117–24; Sir Penderel Moon correspondence with Beaumont, 5 January 1982
100 T o P, vol. XII, no. 405 n. 2
101 Hatfield Papers, K3
102 Charles Chenevix-Trench, *Viceroy's Agent* (1987), p. 347
103 C.H. Philips and M. Wainwright, *The Partition of India* (1970), pp. 531–4
104 *Ibid.*, p. 123
105 Ismay Papers, III/8/201
106 T o P, vol. XII, no. 335
107 Alistair Lamb, *Kashmir: A Disputed Legacy* (1991), pp. 103–22
108 T o P, vol. XI no. 229
109 E.W.R. Lumby, *The Transfer of Power in India* (1954), p. 232
110 Sir John Colville, *The Fringes of Power: Downing Street Diaries 1939–55* (1985), p. 641
111 Anthony Howard, *RAB: The Life of R.A. Butler* (1987) pp. 275–7
112 Janet Morgan, *Edwina Mountbatten* (1991), pp. 427–38
113 Hamid, *op. cit.*, p. 172
114 Morgan, *op. cit.*, p. 429; Ziegler, *op. cit.*, pp. 473–5
115 Woodrow Wyatt, *Confessions of an Optimist* (1985), p. 162
116 Aram Bakshian review of Janet Morgan's *Edwina Mountbatten* in the *American Spectator*, March 1992
117 Philip Ziegler review of *ibid.*, in the *Daily Telegraph*, 29 June 1991
118 Mountbatten Papers, E 30
119 Ismay Papers, III/8/22, 17 November 1947
120 Young (ed.), *op. cit.*, 26 August 1947
121 Ismay Papers, III/8, 10 August 1947
122 Savory Diary, 7 October 1947 and 8 October 1947
123 Dixon Papers, 17 December 1950
124 Savory Diary, 28 September 1947
125 Private Information
126 Philips and Wainwright, *op. cit.*, p. 121
127 Interview: Alan Campbell-Johnson, 10 August 1993
128 IOLR, F 200/203, 70th meeting, 12 August 1947
129 Gopal Khosla, *Stern Reckoning* (1949), p. 126
130 T o P, vols x, xi and xii *passim*
131 Indivar Kamtehar, *The End of the Colonial State in India 1942–7* (Cambridge PhD thesis, 1988)
132 Interview: Lieutenant-Colonel Patrick Massey, 27 February 1993
133 Collins and Lapierre, *op. cit.*, p. 74
134 IOLR, F 180/70
135 T o P, vol. x, no. 483
136 Savory Diary, 8 October 1947
137 Kamtehar, *op. cit.*, p. 146
138 M.A.K. Azad, *India Wins Freedom* (1960), pp. 170–1

139 Peter Townsend, *The Last Emperor* (1975), p. 227
140 Kamtehar, *op. cit.*, p. 148
141 Robin Jeffrey, *The Punjab Boundary Force and the Problems of Order August 1947* (*Modern Asian Studies*, 1974)
142 Hamid, *op. cit.*, 27 July 1947
143 Interview: Alan Campbell-Johnson, 10 August 1993
144 Hansard, 6 March 1947
145 Lord Brabourne in BBC video, *op. cit.*, no. 11
146 Interview: Alan Campbell-Johnson, 10 August 1993
147 T o P, vol. XII, no. 487
148 Hamid, *op. cit.*, September 1947; Savory Diary, 17 September 1947
149 PRO CAB 21/2602, 13 May 1947
150 *Ibid.*, 128/10, 23 May 1947
151 Savory Diary, 26 July 1947
152 Mohammed Ayub Khan, *Friends Not Masters* (1967), p. 70
153 Sir Francis Tuker, *While Memory Serves* (1949), p. 437
154 PRO CAB 128/10, 23 May 1947 and 20 September 1945; Moore, *op. cit.*, p. 43; PRO PREM 8/856
155 Collins and Lapierre, *op. cit.*, p. 26
156 Edward Behr, *Anyone Here Been Raped and Speaks English?* (1982), p. 66
157 Hamid, *op. cit.*, p. 234
158 *Ibid.*
159 Richard Hough, *Mountbatten: Hero of Our Time* (1980), p. 157
160 *The Times*, 2 January 1969
161 Tom Driberg, *The Best of Both Worlds* (1953), pp. 63–7
162 Lord Lambton, *The Mountbattens* (1989), pp. 42ff
163 IOLR, D 714/82
164 Khosla, *op. cit.*, pp. 89–215
165 Collins and Lapierre, *op. cit.*, p. 50
166 Private Information
167 Sir Penderel Moon, *Divide and Quit* (1982), p. 283
168 Mountbatten Papers, D 181
169 IOLR, F 200/85
170 Williams (ed.), *op. cit.*, p. 211
171 T o P, vol. x, no. 435
172 Ziegler, *op. cit.*, p. 439
173 Interview: Sir Algernon Rumbold, 28 February 1993

174 Savory Diary, 3 October 1947 and 20 November 1947
175 Ismay Papers, III/7
176 Louis Heren, *Memories of Times Past* (1988), p. 80, and *Hampstead and Highgate Express*, 29 March 1985
177 Brian Lapping, *End of Empire* (1989), pp. 135–6
178 *Ibid.*
179 IOLR, F 180/79
180 Interview: Anthony Montague Brown, 6 January 1993
181 Hansard, 28 October 1947
182 Interview: Lord Amery, 14 October 1992
183 Interview: Christopher Beaumont, 15 May 1992
184 S. Wolpert, *A New History of India* (1982), p. 348
185 Robert Rhodes James, *Anthony Eden* (1986), pp. 458 and 617
186 Zuckerman, *op. cit.*, p. 160
187 Denis Healey, *The Time of My Life* (1989), p. 258
188 *Encounter*, September 1981; Lord Zuckerman, *Men, Monkeys and Missiles* (1988), p. 466; Hugh Cudlipp, *Walking on the Water* (1976), p. 326
189 Zuckerman, *Six Men Out of the Ordinary*, p. 160
190 Ziegler, *op. cit.*, p. 300
191 *Sunday Times*, 17 March 1985
192 Private Information
193 *Ibid.*
194 BBC video, *op. cit.*, no. 12
195 Ziegler, *op. cit.*, p. 700

3: The Tories versus Churchill during the 'Finest Hour'

1 Sir David Hunt, *On the Spot* (1975), p. 54
2 Martin Gilbert, *Winston S. Churchill, vol. 5: Prophet of Truth 1922–39* (1976), p. 601
3 Private Information
4 Crathorne Papers
5 Private Information
6 Hatfield Papers, K3
7 Hansard, 8 May 1940
8 Crathorne Papers, 12 May 1940

9 *Ibid.*
10 Interview: Sir Charles Pickthorn, 15 June 1993
11 Butler Papers, G 14
12 Lennox-Boyd Papers, 10 May 1940
13 Simon Papers, Box 86
14 *Ibid.*
15 Chamberlain Papers, NC 7/11/33/35, 11 May 1940
16 Templewood Papers, XII 4
17 Hugh Dalton, *The Fateful Years* (1957), p. 388
18 Waterhouse Diary, 9 May 1940
19 de Chair Diary, 12 May 1940
20 Butler Papers, G 11
21 Waterhouse Diary, 11 May 1940
22 Sir Percy Harris, *Forty Years In and Out of Parliament* (1947), p. 152
23 Sir Patrick Donner, *Crusade* (1934), p. 80
24 D.C. Watt, *Personalities and Appeasement* (1991), p. 7
25 Hatfield Papers, K 3
26 *Ibid.*, A 1
27 Templewood Papers, XII 3
28 Sir John Colville, *The Fringes of Power: The Downing Street Diaries 1939–55* (1985), p. 131
29 Charles Lysaght, *Brendan Bracken* (1979), p. 176
30 Chamberlain Papers, NC 7/11/33/105
31 Norman Rose (ed.), *Baffy: The Diaries of Blanche Dugdale* (1973), p. 170
32 Halifax Diary, 13 May 1940
33 Lennox-Boyd Papers, 18 May 1940
34 Lysaght, *op. cit.,*, p. 126; Interview: Barbara Sendall, 9 February 1993
35 Nicolson Diary, 17 May 1940
36 Waterhouse Diary, 10 May 1940
37 Dawson Diary, 13 May 1940
38 Templewood Papers, XII 3
39 Private Information
40 Hatfield Papers, K 3
41 Chartwell Papers, 2/402
42 Colin Cross (ed.), *Life with Lloyd George: The Diary of A.J. Sylvester* (1975), 19 June 1940
43 *The Times*, 5 January 1966
44 Wallace Diary, 13 May 1940
45 *Ibid.*, 26 May 1940
46 Waterhouse Diary, 12 May 1940
47 de Chair Diary, 18 May 1940
48 Halifax Papers, 17 May 1940
49 Interview: Sir Charles Pickthorn 22 June 1993
50 Harris, *op. cit.*, p. 151
51 Sir Henry Morris-Jones, *Doctor in the Whips Room* (1955), p. 115
52 Wolmer Papers, 23 May 1940
53 Crathorne Papers, 24 May 1940
54 Kevin Jefferys, *The Churchill Coalition and Wartime Politics* (1970), p. 42
55 Sanderson Papers, Box 6
56 Wallace Diary, 5 June 1940
57 Chamberlain Papers, NC 18/1/1159
58 Cecil King, *With Malice Toward None* (1970), p. 48
59 King Diary, 7 June 1940
60 Waterhouse Diary, 6 June 1940
61 *Ibid.*
62 Cazalet Papers, 11 June 1940
63 Crathorne Papers, 18 June 1940
64 Cazalet Papers
65 Headlam Diary, 18 June 1940
66 Charles Eade (ed.), *Secret Session Speeches* (1946), p. 16
67 Waterhouse Diary, 19 June 1940
68 *Ibid.*, 25 June 1940
69 Templewood Papers, XIII 17
70 Rose (ed.), *op. cit.*, p. 173
71 Paul Einzig, *In the Centre of Things* (1960), p. 209
72 *Ibid.*, p. 210
73 Einzig Papers
74 Einzig, *op. cit.*, p. 221
75 Winston S. Churchill, *The Second World War, vol. 2: Their Finest Hour* (1949), p. 211
76 Jefferys, *op. cit.*, p. 46
77 Crookshank Diary, 4 July 1940
78 Chamberlain Papers, NC 7/11/33/92
79 Templewood Papers, XIII 17
80 Lord Brabazon, *The Brabazon Story* (1956), pp. 206–7
81 Davidson Papers, Box 276
82 Robert Rhodes James, *Chips: The Diaries of Sir Henry Channon* (1967), p. 262
83 Butler Papers, E 3/8/114
84 Waterhouse Diary, 23 July 1940
85 A.J.P. Taylor (ed.), *Off the Record* (1973), p. 175
86 Chamberlain Papers, NC 7/11/33/60

87 Headlam Diary, 31 July 1940
88 Waterhouse Diary, 6 August 1940
89 Morris-Jones Diary, 8 August 1940
90 *Ibid.*
91 Templewood Papers, XIII 17
92 A.W.B. Simpson, *In the Highest Degree Odious* (1992), p. 185
93 Hansard, 15 August 1940
94 Waterhouse Diary, 16 August 1940
95 Kenneth Young (ed.), *The Diaries of Sir Robert Bruce Lockhart*, vol. 2 (1980), 28 August 1940
96 de Chair Diary, 20 August 1940
97 Morris-Jones Diary, 5 September 1940
98 Crathorne Papers, 9 September 1940
99 Beamish Papers, 3/4
100 PRO PREM 4/22
101 *Ibid.*
102 Chamberlain Papers, NC 7/11/37/82
103 *Daily Mirror*, 28 September 1940
104 Emrys-Evans Papers, MS 58245
105 Wolmer Papers, 23 September 1940
106 Andrew Boyle, *Poor, Dear Brendan* (1974), p. 261
107 Chartwell Papers, 2/402
108 Headlam Diary, 4 October 1940
109 Chamberlain Papers, NC 7/11/33/85
110 Cross (ed.), *op. cit.*, 3 October 1940
111 Young (ed.), *op. cit.*, 6 September 1942
112 Rhodes James (ed.), *op. cit.*, 7 October 1940
113 Stuart Ball, 'The 1922 Committee', *Parliamentary History*, vol. 9 (1990), p. 150
114 Wallace Diary, 9 October 1940
115 Crookshank Diary, 9 October 1940
116 Nigel Fisher, *The Tory Leaders* (1977), p. 53
117 Sir George Harvie-Watt, *Most of My Life* (1980), p. 38
118 Crookshank and Wallace Diaries, 9 October 1940
119 Beamish Papers, 3/4
120 Crookshank Diary, 9 October 1940
121 Beamish Papers, 3/4
122 Interview: Sir Charles Pickthorn, 15 June 1993
123 1922 Committee minutes, 16 October 1940
124 Crathorne Papers, 18 October 1940
125 *Ibid.*, 27 October 1940
126 Chartwell Papers, 2/402
127 Beamish Papers, 3/4
128 Headlam Diary, 8 November 1940
129 Robert Rhodes James, *Bob Boothby: A Portrait* (1991), p. 275
130 Pym Diary, 8 November 1940
131 Woolton Diary, 22 October 1940 and 28 October 1940
132 Headlam Diary, 5 November 1940
133 Beaverbrook Papers, C 28
134 Correspondence with Lord Cudlipp, 1 November 1993
135 Craven-Ellis Papers and *Poole Herald*, 19 January 1939
136 Woolton Diary, 13 November 1940
137 Hansard, 12 November 1940; Adams Papers, Box 2
138 Beamish Papers, 3/4
139 Emrys-Evans Papers, *op. cit.*
140 Cazalet Papers, 27 October 1940
141 Lloyd George Papers, Box 5, folder 14
142 Headlam Diary, 28 November 1940
143 Crathorne Papers, 17 December 1940
144 Lord Birkenhead interview with Lord Stuart
145 Colville, *op. cit.*, 29 August 1940
146 Philip Goodhart, *The 1922 Committee* (1973), p. 102
147 1922 Committee minutes, 18 December 1940
148 Goodhart, *op. cit.*, p. 105
149 Harvey Papers, MS 58237
150 Margesson Papers, 1/4
151 Crathorne Papers, 16 January 1941 and 21 January 1941
152 Young (ed.), *op. cit.*, 29 December 1940
153 Ball, *op. cit.*, p. 150
154 Lord Findhorn, *Within the Fringe* (1967), p. 98
155 *Ibid.*, p. 91
156 *Ibid.*, p. 96
157 Robert E. Sherwood, *The White House Papers* (1948), p. 243
158 Morris-Jones Diary, 28 January 1941
159 W.J. Brown, *So Far* (1943), p. 222
160 Malcolm MacDonald Papers
161 Private Information
162 J.M. Lee, *The Churchill Coalition* (1980), p. 41
163 Waterhouse Diary, 6 February 1941
164 Lee, *op. cit.*, p. 121
165 Rhodes James (ed.), *op. cit.*, 15 April 1941

166 Beamish Papers, 3/4
167 *Ibid.*
168 Nicolson Diary, 7 May 1941
169 Templewood Papers, XIII 18
170 Sefton Delmer in *The Times Literary Supplement*, 9 November 1967
171 Headlam Diary, 19 May 1941
172 Makins Diary, 10 June 1941
173 Waterhouse Diary, 5 June 1941
174 Wolmer Papers, 18 June 1941
175 Chartwell Papers, 2/426
176 Davidson Papers, Box 283
177 Harvie-Watt, *op. cit.*, p. 2
178 Headlam Diary, 21 July 1941

4: Churchill, Race and the 'Magpie Society'

1 *Guardian*, 20 June 1992
2 Wilfrid Scawen Blunt, *My Diaries 1900–14* (1920), 20 October 1912
3 Martin Gilbert, *In Search of Churchill* (1994), p. 83
4 Ronald Hyam, *Elgin and Churchill at the Colonial Office* (1968), *passim*
5 Martin Gilbert, *Winston S. Churchill, vol. 5: Prophet of Truth 1922–39* (1976), p. 322 n. 1
6 R.W. Thompson (ed.), *Churchill and Morton* (1976), p. 64
7 *Ibid.*, p. 194; Robert Blake and W. Roger (eds), *Churchill* (1993), p. 147; Ronald Zweig, *Britain and Palestine during the Second World War* (1986), p. 174 n. 107; Christopher Thorne, *Allies of a Kind* (1978), pp. 57–7, 474
8 Lord Deedes, *Daily Telegraph*, 9 April 1994; Robert Harris, *Spectator*, 16 April 1994
9 W. Roger Louis, *In the Name of God, Go!* (1992), pp. 166
10 *Ibid.*, pp. 172–3
11 John Barnes and David Nicholson (eds), *The Empire at Bay: The Leo Amery Diaries 1929–55* (1988), 13 June 1944
12 David Dilks (ed.), *The Diaries of Sir Alexander Cadogan 1938–45*, (1971), 13 October 1942
13 R.A. Butler, *The Art of the Possible* (1971), p. 111
14 Thorne, *op. cit.*, pp. 277 and 730
15 Interview: Sir David Hunt, 21 December 1992, and letter, 17 April 1994
16 PRO PREM 11/91, 30 January 1952
17 Lord Moran, *Winston Churchill: The Struggle for Survival* (1966), 8 April 1955
18 *Ibid.*, 19 January 1952
19 Lennox-Boyd Papers
20 *The Times*, 2 January 1982
21 Dennis Kavanagh and Peter Morris, *Consensus Politics from Attlee to Thatcher* (1989), p. 11
22 PRO CO 1028/23
23 PRO CAB 28/10; Dixon Papers
24 Hansard, 19 November 1958
25 Zig Layton-Henry, *The Politics of Immigration* (1992); Panel of Immigration Statistics, *Immigration Statistics* (1985); David Butler, *British Political Facts* (1986), p. 328; Sheila Patterson, *Immigration and Race Relations* (1969), p. 3; E.J.B. Rose, *Colour and Citizenship* (1969)
26 Cabinet Minutes, 18 December 1952
27 *Ibid.*
28 Anthony Seldon, *Churchill's Indian Summer* (1981), pp. 90–1
29 Dixon Papers, 30 June 1967
30 Robert Carter, *The 1951–5 Conservative Government and the Racialisation of Black Immigration* (1987), p. 7
31 Private Information
32 Interview: Sir David Hunt, 21 December 1992
33 Cabinet Minutes, 3 February 1992
34 Hansard, 18 March 1954
35 *Daily Telegraph*, 11 August 1992
36 Ian Gilmour, *Inside Right* (1977), p. 134
37 *The Times*, 24 February 1972
38 Layton-Henry, *op. cit.*, p. 31
39 Interview: Sir David Hunt, 21 December 1992
40 PRO DO 35/5216
41 *Ibid.*
42 *Ibid.*; Dixon Papers, 30 June 1967
43 PRO CAB 127/77, 14 October 1954
44 PRO CAB 129/72, Memorandum 354, 22 November 1954
45 Seldon, *op. cit.*, p. 123
46 PRO CAB 127/77, 2 September 1955
47 PRO CAB 129/72, Memorandum 356, 23 November 1954
48 PRO CAB 129/77, 8 December 1954

49 PRO DO 35/5217, 19 November 1954
50 Gilmour, *op. cit.*, p. 134
51 Chandos Papers, 4/10
52 Seldon, *op. cit.*, pp. 126–7
53 Hansard, 11 June 1953
54 *Ibid.*, 18 February 1954
55 PRO DO 35/5216
56 Hansard, 16 December 1954
57 PRO DO 35/5216
58 Hansard, 29 June 1954
59 Anthony Howard (ed.), *The Crossman Diaries* (1975), 5 February 1965
60 Hansard, 5 November 1954
61 *Ibid.*
62 *Ibid.*, 16 December 1954
63 Private Information
64 *Ibid.*
65 Cabinet Minutes, 20 January 1955
66 *Spectator*, 4 February 1955
67 Cabinet Minutes, 31 May 1955
68 *Ibid.*, 17 February 1955
69 Carter, *op. cit.*, p. 14
70 *Spectator*, 4 March 1955
71 Sir David Hunt, *On the Spot* (1975), p. 53
72 Interview: Anthony Montague Browne, 6 January 1993
73 Hunt, *op. cit.*, p. 54
74 Gilmour, *op. cit.*, p. 133
75 Cabinet Minutes, 16 March 1955
76 *Ibid.*, 3 November 1955
77 Interview: Lord Hailsham, 27 November 1991
78 Hansard, 19 November 1958

5: Walter Monckton and the 'Retreat from Reality'

1 Lord Birkenhead interview with Lady Alexandra Metcalfe
2 Lord Birkenhead interview with Lord Long
3 Lord Birkenhead interview with Major Thornton
4 Interview: Sir Conrad Heron, 26 November 1992
5 Private Information
6 Lord Birkenhead interview with Lord Davidson
7 Dep Monckton Trustees 2, 16 March 1939
8 Halifax Diary, 16 August 1940
9 Dep Monckton Trustees 3, 17 March 1940
10 *Ibid.*, 25 September 1940
11 *Ibid.*, 2 November 1940
12 *Ibid.*, 12 November 1940
13 Lord Birkenhead, *Walter Monckton* (1969), p. 365
14 Dep Monckton Trustees 4, 20 June 1941
15 *Ibid.* 12, 12 January 1945
16 Ismay Papers, III/7/30A, 20 April 1948
17 R.A. Butler, *The Art of Memory* (1982), p. 131
18 Birkenhead, *op. cit.*, p. 325
19 Dep Monckton Box 49
20 Anthony Seldon, *Churchill's Indian Summer* (1981), p. 19
21 Dep Monckton Box 49
22 Hansard, 2 April 1946
23 Interview: Frank Johnson, 22 April 1994
24 Charles Lysaght, *Brendan Bracken* (1979), p. 287
25 Interview: Sir Conrad Heron, 26 November 1992
26 PRO LAB 34/55
27 PRO LAB 79/29
28 *Ibid.*
29 *History Today*, November 1993, p. 27
30 PRO LAB 34/15 and 16
31 Keith Middlemas, *Power, Competition and the State*, vol. 1 (1986), p. 221
32 Interview: Lord Orr-Ewing, 30 September 1992
33 Lord Birkenhead interview with Sir Robert Gould
34 Seldon, *op. cit.*, p. 202
35 Interview: Sir Conrad Heron, 26 November 1992
36 Seldon, *op. cit.*, p. 197
37 *Ibid.*, p. 203
38 *Ibid.*, p. 202
39 *Ibid.*, p. 206
40 John Lloyd, *Light and Liberty* (1990), p. 302
41 Henry Pelling, *The History of British Trade Unionism* (1992), p. 223
42 Butler, *op. cit.*, p. 136
43 Harold Watkinson, *Turning Points* (1986), p. 44

44 Sir James Goldsmith, *Counter-Culture*, vol. 2 (1988), p. 41
45 Interview: Lord Holderness, 16 November 1992
46 Seldon, *op. cit.*, p. 205
47 Conservative Party Archives, NUA 2/1 59
48 Interview: Lord Deedes, 9 September 1992
49 Conservative Research Department Archives, RGS-Gen., p. 570
50 Lord Birkenhead interview with Lord Stuart
51 Lord Birkenhead interview with Sir Wilfred Neden
52 Denis Barnes and Eileen Reid, *Governments and Trade Unions* (1980), p. 23
53 Butler, *op. cit.*, p. 137
54 Nigel Fisher, *Iain Macleod* (1973), p. 108
55 Seldon, *op. cit.*, p. 571
56 Samuel Brittan, *Steering the Economy* (1971), p. 193
57 Woolton Diary, 13 December 1954
58 Interview: Lord Aldington, 10 September 1992
59 Middlemas, *op. cit.*, p. 260
60 Hatfield Papers, file 208
61 Interview: Sir David Pitblado, 21 October 1992
62 Butler Papers, G46/8, 9 January 1955
63 Barnes and Reid, *op. cit.*, p. 24
64 Interview: Lord Orr-Ewing, 30 September 1992
65 Jack Jones, *Union Man* (1986), p. 135
66 Interview: Lord Tebbit, 1 April 1993
67 *Economist*, 15 January 1955
68 *New Statesman*, 8 January 1955
69 Frank Chapple, *Sparks Fly* (1984), p. 48
70 Martin Gilbert, *Winston S. Churchill*, vol. 8: *Never Despair 1945–65* (1988), p. 1143
71 Lord Birkenhead interview with Lord Chandos
72 Interview: Lord Tebbit, 1 April 1993
73 Butler Papers, H 2
74 Pelling, *op. cit.*, p. 230
75 Interview: David Astor, 10 November 1992
76 *The Times*, 5 November 1980
77 Monckton Papers
78 Private Information
79 Monckton Papers, 25 March 1959
80 *Ibid.*, 12 May 1959
81 *Ibid.*
82 Lord Birkenhead interview with Lord Chandos
83 Lord Birkenhead interview with Lord Home
84 PRO PREM 11/365
85 Dixon Papers, 21 January 1974

6: Patriotism: The Last Refuge of Sir Arthur Bryant

1 Private Information
2 Introduction to Bryant Papers
3 Arthur Bryant, *The Spirit of Conservatism* (1929), p. 170
4 Correspondence with Lord Dacre, 4 August 1993
5 Sir John Plumb, *The Making of a Historian* (1988), p. 276
6 *Ibid.*
7 Interview: A.L. Rowse, 7 February 1993
8 A.L. Rowse, *Friends and Contemporaries* (1989), p. 100
9 Arthur Bryant, *George V* (1936), p. 159
10 *The Times*, 4 May 1936
11 Arthur Bryant, *Stanley Baldwin* (1937), p. 191
12 Bryant Papers, C 46, 16 July 1937
13 Richard Griffiths, *Fellow Travellers of the Right* (1983), p. 43
14 Correspondence with John Warburton, 26 January 1994
15 Francis Yeats-Brown, *European Jungle* (1939), p. 316
16 Admiral Sir Barry Domvile, *By and Large* (1936), pp. 246–7
17 Bryant Papers, C 46
18 *Ibid*, 21 June 1937.
19 *Ibid.*, C 41, 9 September 1937
20 *Ibid.*, E 39, 29 July 1939
21 *Observer*, 13 June 1937
22 *Ibid.*, 5 September 1937
23 *Illustrated London News*, 15 August 1936
24 Arthur Bryant, *Humanity in Politics* (1934), p. 292
25 *The Ashridge Journal*, March 1938
26 Arthur Bryant, *The Saviour of the Navy* (1938), pp. 172–3

27 *Illustrated London News*, 10 September 1938
28 Bryant Papers, C 71, 28 September 1938
29 Bryant Papers, C 46
30 Drummond-Wolff Papers, MS 709/640
31 *The Times*, 3 April 1939
32 *Ibid.*, 30 June 1939
33 Bryant Papers, C 68, 3 July 1939
34 PRO PREM 1/333
35 *Ibid.*
36 *Ibid.*
37 David Irving, *The War Path* (1978), p. 229
38 Bryant Papers, C 46
39 *Ibid.*, E 48
40 *Ibid.*, C 69, 18 October 1939
41 *Ibid.*, 17 October 1939
42 *Ibid.*
43 *Illustrated London News*, 13 April 1940
44 Arthur Bryant, *Unfinished Victory* (1940), *passim*
45 *Ibid.*
46 *Ibid.*
47 *Ibid.*
48 *Ibid.*
49 Alistair Horne, *Harold Macmillan 1897–1956* (1988), p. 114
50 Correspondence with Lord Dacre, 7 August 1993
51 *Ibid.*
52 *Ibid.*, 4 August 1993
53 Interview: A.L. Rowse, 7 February 1993
54 Rowse, *op. cit.*, p. 98
55 *Illustrated London News*, 10 November 1951
56 Interview: A.L. Rowse, 7 February 1993
57 Lord Moran, *Winston Churchill: The Struggle for Survival* (1966), p. 715
58 Dixon Papers
59 *Illustrated London News*, 30 January 1965
60 Sir Arthur Bryant, *The Search for Justice* (1957), p. 266
61 *Illustrated London News*, 27 March 1963
62 Sir Arthur Bryant, *Protestant Island* (1967), p. 39
63 Interview: A.L. Rowse, 7 February 1993
64 *Ibid.*
65 Private Information; *The Times*, 26 June 1935
66 Philip Ziegler, *Wilson: The Authorised Life* (1993), p. 514
67 *Action*, February 1985; letter from John Warburton, 26 January 1994

Index